Life of Abraham Lincoln
by Frank Crosby

Life of Abraham Lincoln, Sixteenth President of the ...

Frank Crosby

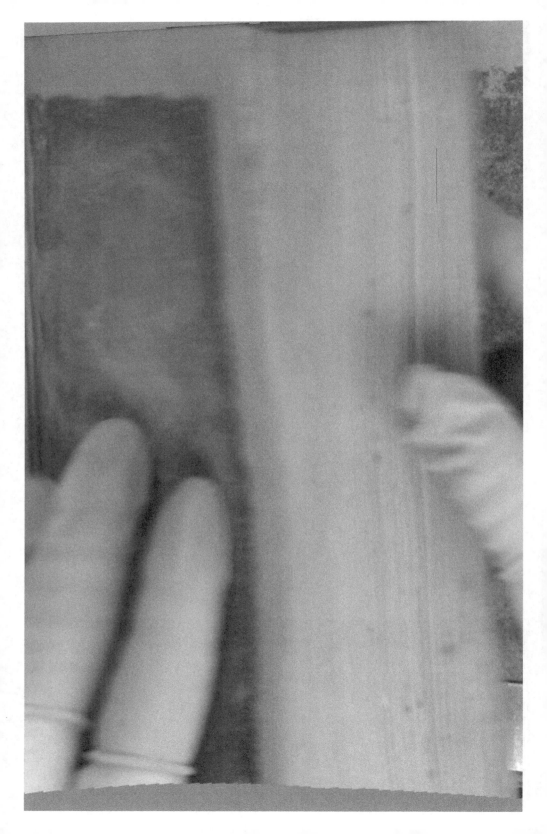

"If this country cannot be saved without giving up the principle of Liberty, I was about to say I would rather be assassinated on this spot than surrender it."

From Mr. Lincoln's Speech at Independence Hall, Philadelphia, February 21, 1861.

"I believe this Government cannot endure permanently half slave and half free."

Springfield, Illinois, June, 1858.

"I am exceedingly anxious that this Union, the Constitution, and the liberties of the people shall be perpetuated in accordance with the original idea for which the Revolution was made."

Trenton, New Jersey, February 21, 1861.

" Having thus chosen our course, without guile and with pure purpose, let us renew our trust in God, and go forward without fear and with manly hearts."

Message, July 5, 1861.

' In giving freedom to the slaves, we assure freedom to the free; honorable alike in what we give and what we preserve."

Message, December 1, 1862.

" I hope peace will come soon, and come to stay; and so come as to be worth the keeping in all future time."

Springfield Letter, August 26, 1863.

" The world will little note, nor long remember, what we say here; but it can never forget what the brave men, living and dead, did here."

Speech at Gettysburg, November 19, 1863.

"I shall not attempt to retract or modify the Emancipation Proclamation, nor shall I return to slavery any person who is free by the terms of that proclamation, or by any of the Acts of Congress."

Amnesty Proclamation, December 8, 1863.

"I claim not to have controlled events, but confess plainly that events have controlled me.

Letter to A. G. Hodges, April 4, 1864.

" With malice towards none, with charity for all, with firmness in the right, as God gives us to see the right, let us strive on to finish the work we are in."

Last Inaugural, March 4, 1865.

(1)

ABRAHAM LINCOLN

... OF THE ...

... PROCLAMATIONS AND
... ILLUSTRATING ...
... RATION.

BY FRANK CROSBY,
MEMBER OF THE PHILADELPHIA ...

"LET ALL THE ENDS THOU AIM'ST AT BE THY COUNTRY'S,
THY GOD'S AND TRUTH'S; THEN IF THOU FALL'ST
THOU FALL'ST A BLESSED MARTYR."

PHILADELPHIA:
PUBLISHED BY JOHN E. POTTER,
No. 617 SANSOM STREET.
1865.

238. 5 21.

A. Lincoln

LIFE OF ABRAHAM LINCOLN,

SIXTEENTH PRESIDENT OF THE UNITED STATES.

CONTAINING

HIS EARLY HISTORY AND POLITICAL CAREER; TOGETHER
WITH THE SPEECHES, MESSAGES, PROCLAMATIONS AND
OTHER OFFICIAL DOCUMENTS ILLUSTRATIVE OF
HIS EVENTFUL ADMINISTRATION.

BY FRANK CROSBY,
MEMBER OF THE PHILADELPHIA BAR.

"LET ALL THE ENDS THOU AIM'ST AT BE THY COUNTRY'S,
THY GOD'S AND TRUTH'S; THEN IF THOU FALL'ST
THOU FALL'ST A BLESSED MARTYR."

PHILADELPHIA:
PUBLISHED BY JOHN E. POTTER,
No. 617 SANSOM STREET.
1865.

PHILADELPHIA:
COLLINS, PRINTER, 705 JAYNE STREET.

DEDICATED

TO THE GOOD AND TRUE

OF THE NATION

REDEEMED—REGENERATED—DISENTHRALLED.

PREFACE.

An attempt has been made in the following pages to portray Abraham Lincoln, mainly in his relations to the country at large during his eventful administration.

With this view, it has not been deemed necessary to cumber the work with the minute details of his life prior to that time. This period has, therefore, been but glanced at, with a care to present enough to make a connected whole. His Congressional career, and his campaign with Senator Douglas are presented in outline, yet so, it is believed, that a clear idea of these incidents in his life can be obtained.

After the time of his election as President, however, a different course of treatment has been pursued. Thenceforward, to the close of his life, especial pains have been taken to present everything which should show him as he was—the Statesman persistent, resolute, free from boasting or ostentation, destitute of hate, never exultant, guarded in his prophecies, threatening none at home or abroad, indulging in no utopian dreams of a blissful future, moving quietly, calmly, conscientiously, irresistibly on to the end he saw with clearest vision.

Yet, even in what is presented as a complete record of his administration, too much must not be expected. It is impossible, for example, to thoroughly dissect the events of the great Rebellion in a work like the present. Nothing of the kind has been attempted. The prominent features only have been sketched; and that solely for the purpose of bringing into the distinct foreground him whose life is under consideration.

Various Speeches, Proclamations, and Letters, not vitally essential to the unity of the main body of the work, yet valuable as affording illustrations of the man—have been collected in the Appendix.

Imperfect as this portraiture must necessarily be, there is one conciliatory thought. The subject needs no embellishment. It furnishes its own setting. The acts of the man speak for themselves. Only such an arrangement is needed as shall show the bearing of each upon the other, the development of each, the processes of growth.

Those words of the lamented dead which nestle in our hearts so tenderly—they call for no explanation. Potent, searching, taking hold of our consciences, they will remain with us while reason lasts.

Nor will the people's interest be but for the moment. The baptism of blood to which the Nation has been called, cannot be forgotten for generations. And while memories of him abide, there will inevitably be associated with them the placid, quiet face, not devoid of mirth—its patient, anxious, yet withal hopeful expression—the sure, elastic step—the clearly cut, sharply defined speech of him, who, under Providence, was to lead us through the trial and anguish of those bitter days to the rest and refreshing of a peace, whose dawn only, alas! he was to see.

Though this work may not rise to the height required, it is hoped that it is not utterly unworthy of the subject. Such as it is —a labor of love—it is offered to those who loved and labored with the patriot and hero, with the earnest desire that it may not be regarded an unwarrantable intrusion upon ground on which any might hesitate to venture.   F. C.

Philadelphia, June, 1865.

CONTENTS.

CHAPTER VII.

PREPARING FOR WAR.

CHAPTER VIII.

THE FIRST SESSION OF CONGRESS.

CHAPTER IX.

CLOSE OF 1861.

CHAPTER X.

THE CONGRESS OF 1861-62.

CHAPTER XI.

THE SLAVERY QUESTION.

CHAPTER XII.

THE PENINSULAR CAMPAIGN.

CHAPTER XIII.

FREEDOM TO MILLIONS.

CHAPTER XIV.

LAST SESSION OF THE THIRTY-SEVENTH CONGRESS.

APPENDIX.

Mr. Lincoln's Speeches in Congress and Elsewhere, Proclamations, Letters, etc., not included in the Body of the Work.

LIFE OF ABRAHAM LINCOLN.

CHAPTER I.

BOYHOOD AND EARLY MANHOOD.

Preliminary—Birth of Abraham Lincoln—Removal from Kentucky—At Work—Self Education—Personal Characteristics—Another Removal—Trip to New Orleans—Becomes Clerk—Black Hawk War—Engages in Politics—Successive Elections to the Legislature—Anti-Slavery Protest—Commences Practice as a Lawyer—Traits of Character—Marriage—Return to Politics—Election to Congress.

THE leading incidents in the early life of the men who have most decidedly influenced the destinies of our republic, present a striking similarity. The details, indeed, differ; but the story, in outline, is the same—"the short and simple annals of the poor."

Of obscure parentage—accustomed to toil from their tender years—with few facilities for the education of the school— the most struggled on, independent, self-reliant, till by their own right hands they had hewed their way to the positions for which their individual talents and peculiarities stamped them as best fitted. Children of nature, rather than of art, they have ever in their later years—amid scenes and associations entirely dissimilar to those with which in youth and early manhood, they were familiar—retained somewhat indicative of their origin and training. In speech or in action —often in both—they have smacked of their native soil. If they have lacked the grace of the courtier, ample compensation has been afforded in the honesty of the man. If their

(13)

address was at times abrupt, it was at least frank and unmistakable. Both friend and foe knew exactly where to find them. Unskilled in the doublings of the mere politician or the trimmer, they have borne themselves straight forward to the points whither their judgment and conscience directed. Such men may have been deemed fit subjects for the jests and sneers of more cultivated Europeans, but they are none the less dear to us as Americans—will none the less take their place among those whose names the good, throughout the world, will not willingly let die.

Of this class, pre-eminently, was the statesman whose life and public services the following pages are to exhibit.

ABRAHAM LINCOLN, Sixteenth President of the United States, son of Thomas and Nancy Lincoln—the former a Kentuckian, the latter a Virginian—was born February 12th, 1809, near Hodgenville, the county-seat of what is now known as La Rue county, Kentucky. He had one sister, two years his senior, who died, married, in early womanhood; and his only brother, his junior by two years, died in childhood.

When nine years of age, he lost his mother, the family having, two years previously, removed to what was then the territory of Indiana, and settled in the southern part, near the Ohio river, about midway between Louisville and Evansville. The thirteen years which the lad spent here inured him to all the exposures and hardships of frontier life. An active assistant in farm duties, he neglected no opportunity of strengthening his mind, reading with avidity such instructive works as he could procure—on winter evenings, oftentimes, by the light of the blazing fire-place. As satisfaction for damage accidentally done to a borrowed copy of Weems' Life of Washington—the only one known to be in the neighborhood—he pulled fodder for two days for the owner.

At twenty years of age, he had reached the height of nearly six feet and four inches, with a comparatively slender yet uncommonly strong, muscular frame—a youthful giant among a race of giants.　Morally, he was proverbially honest, conscientious, and upright.

In 1830, his father again emigrated, halting for a year on the north fork of the Sangamon river, Illinois, but afterwards pushing on to Coles county, some seventy miles to the eastward, on the upper waters of the Kaskaskia and Embarrass, where his adventurous life ended in 1851, he being in his seventy-third year.　The first year in Illinois the son spent with the father; the next he aided in constructing a flat-boat, on which, with other hands, a successful trip to New Orleans and back was made.　This city—then the El Dorado of the Western frontiersman—had been visited by the young man, in the same capacity, when he was nineteen years of age.

Returning from this expedition, he acted for a year as clerk for his former employer, who was engaged in a store and flouring mill at New Salem, twenty miles below Springfield.　While thus occupied, tidings reached him of an Indian invasion on the western border of the State—since known as the Black Hawk war, from an old Sac chief of that name, who was the prominent mover in the matter.　In New Salem and vicinity, a company of volunteers was promptly raised, of which young Lincoln was elected captain—his first promotion.　The company, however, having disbanded, he again enlisted as a private, and during the three months' service of this, his first short military campaign, he faithfully discharged his duty to his country, persevering amid peculiar hardships and against the influences of older men around him.

With characteristic humor and sarcasm, while commenting, in a Congressional speech during the canvass of 1848, upon the efforts of General Cass's biographers to exalt their idol into a military hero, he thus alluded to this episode in his life :

"By the way, Mr. Speaker, did you know I am a military hero?　Yes, sir, in the days of the Black Hawk war, I fought, bled, and came away.　Speaking of General Cass's career, reminds me of my own.   I was not at Stillman's defeat, but I was about as near it as Cass to Hull's surrender; and like him, I saw the place very soon afterward.   It is quite certain I did not break my sword, for I had none to break; but I bent a musket pretty badly on one occasion.   If Cass broke his sword, the idea is, he broke it in desperation; I bent the musket by accident.   If General Cass went in advance of me in picking whortleberries, I guess I surpassed him in charges upon the wild onions.   If he saw any live, fighting Indians, it was more than I did, but I had a good many bloody struggles with the mosquitoes; and although I never fainted from loss of blood, I can truly say I was often very hungry.

" Mr. Speaker, if I should ever conclude to doff whatever our Democratic friends may suppose there is of black-cockade Federalism about me, and, thereupon, they should take me up as their candidate for the Presidency, I protest they shall not make fun of me as they have of General Cass, by attempting to write me into a military hero."

This bit of adventure over, Mr. Lincoln—who had determined to become a lawyer, in common with most energetic, enterprising young men of that period and section—embarked in politics, warmly espousing the cause of Henry Clay, in a State at that time decidedly opposed to his great leader, and received a gratifying evidence of his personal popularity where he was best known, in securing an almost unanimous vote in his own precinct in Sangamon county as a candidate for representative in the State Legislature, although a little later in the same canvass General Jackson, the Democratic candidate for the Presidency, led his competitor, Clay, one hundred and fifty-five votes.

While pursuing his law studies, he engaged in land surveying as a means of support.   In 1834, not yet having been admitted to the bar—a backwoodsman in manner, dress, and expression—tall, lank, and by no means prepossessing—he was first elected to the Legislature of his adopted State, being the youngest member, with a single exception. During this session he rarely took the floor to speak, content to play the part of an observer rather than of an actor. It was at this period that he became acquainted with Stephen A. Douglas, then a recent immigrant from Vermont, in connection with whom he was destined to figure so prominently before the country.

In 1836, he was elected for a second term. During this session, he put upon record, together with one of his col·· leagues, his views relative to slavery, in the following protest, bearing date March 3d, 1837 :—

" Resolutions upon the subject of domestic slavery having passed both branches of the General Assembly, at its present session, the undersigned hereby protest against the passage of the same.

" They believe that the institution of slavery is founded on both injustice and bad policy ; but that the promulgation of abolition doctrines tends rather to increase than abate its evils.

" They believe that the Congress of the United States has no power, under the Constitution, to interfere with the institution of slavery in the different States.

" They believe that the Congress of the United States has the power, under the Constitution, to abolish slavery in the District of Columbia ; but that the power ought not to be exercised, unless at the request of the people of said district."

In 1838 and 1840, he was again elected and received the vote of his party for the speakership. First elected at twenty-five, he had been continued so long as his inclination allowed, and until by his kind manners, his ability, and unquestioned integrity, he had won a position, when but a little past thirty, as the virtual leader of his party in Illinois. His reputation as a close and logical debater had been established ; his native talent as an orator had been developed ; his earnest zeal for his party had brought around him troops of friends ;

2

while his acknowledged goodness of heart had knit many to him, who, upon purely political grounds, would have held themselves aloof.

While a member of the Legislature, he had devoted himself, as best he could—considering the necessity he was under of eking out a support for himself, and the demands made upon his time by his political associates—to mastering his chosen profession, and in 1836 was admitted to practice. Securing at once a good amount of business, he began to rise as a most effective jury advocate, who could readily perceive, and promptly avail himself of, the turning points of a case. A certain quaint humor, withal, which he was wont to employ in illustration—combined with his sterling, practical sense, going straight to the core of things—stamped him as an original. Disdaining the tricks of the mere rhetorician, he spoke from the heart to the heart, and was universally regarded by those with whom he came in contact as every inch a man, in the best and broadest sense of that term. His thoughts, his manner, his address were eminently his own. Affecting none of the cant of the demagogue, the people trusted him, revered him as one of the best, if not the best, among them. Their sympathies were his—their weal his desire, their interests a common stock with his own.

Having permanently located himself at Springfield, the seat of Sangamon county—which ever after he called his home—he devoted himself to the practice of his profession, and on the 4th of November, 1842, married Mary Todd, daughter of the Hon. Robert S. Todd, of Lexington, Kentucky, a lady of accomplished manners and refined social tastes.

Although he had determined to retire from the political arena and taste the sweets which a life with one's own family can alone secure, his earnest wishes were at length overruled by the as earnest demands of that party with the success of which he firmly believed his country's best interests iden-

IN CONGRESS AND ON THE STUMP. 19

Elected to Congress.   A Whig throughout.   Mexican War.

tified, and in 1844 he thoroughly canvassed his State in behalf of Clay—afterward passing into Indiana, and daily addressing immense gatherings until the day of election. Over the defeat of the great Kentuckian he sorrowed as one almost without hope ; feeling it, indeed, far more keenly than his generous nature would have done, had it been a merely personal discomfiture.

Two years later, in 1846, Mr. Lincoln was persuaded to accept the Whig nomination for Congress in the Sangamon district, and was elected by an unprecedently large majority. Texas had meanwhile been annexed ; the Mexican war was in progress ; the Tariff of 1842 had been repealed.

With the opening of the Thirtieth Congress—December 6th, 1847—Mr. Lincoln took his seat in the lower house of Congress, Stephen A. Douglas also appearing for the first time as a member of the Senate.

CHAPTER II.

IN CONGRESS AND ON THE STUMP.

The Mexican War—Internal Improvements—Slavery in the District of Columbia—Public Lands — Retires to Private Life — Kansas-Nebraska Bill—Withdraws in favor of Senator Trumbull—Formation of Republican Party—Nominated for U. S. Senator—Opening Speech of Mr. Lincoln—Douglas Campaign—The Canvass—Tribute to the Declaration of Independence—Result of the Contest.

MR. LINCOLN was early recognized as one of the foremost of the Western men upon the floor of the House. His Congressional record is that of a Whig of those days. Believing that Mr. Polk's administration had mismanaged affairs with Mexico at the outset, he, in common with others of his party, was unwilling, while voting supplies and favoring suitable rewards for our gallant soldiers, to be forced into an unqualified indorsement of the war with that country from its beginning to its close.

20   LIFE OF ABRAHAM LINCOLN.

Resolutions of Inquiry.   Slavery in the District of Columbia.

Accordingly, December 22d, 1847, he introduced a series of resolutions of inquiry concerning the origin of the war, calling for definite official information, which were laid over under the rule, and never acted upon. Upon a test question on abandoning the war, without any material result accomplished, he voted with the minority in favor of laying that resolution upon the table.

In all questions bearing upon the matter of internal improvements, he took an active interest. He took manly ground in favor of the unrestricted right of petition, and favored a liberal policy toward the people in disposing of the public lands. He exerted himself during the canvass of 1848, to secure the election of General Taylor, delivering several effective campaign speeches in New England and the West.

At the second session of the Thirtieth Congress, he voted in favor of laying upon the table a resolution instructing the Committee on the District of Columbia to report a bill prohibiting the slave-trade in the District, and subsequently read a substitute which he favored. This substitute contained the form of a bill enacting that no person not already within the District, should be held in slavery therein, and providing for the gradual emancipation of the slaves already within the District, with compensation to the owners, if a majority of the legal voters of the District should assent to the act, at an election to be holden for the purpose. It made an exception of the right of citizens of the slave-holding States coming to the District on public business, to " be attended into and out of said District, and while there, by the necessary servants of themselves and their families."

In regard to the grant of public lands to the new States, to aid in the construction of railways and canals, he favored the interests of his own constituents, under such restrictions as the proper scope of these grants required.

Having declined to be a candidate for re-election, he retired once more to private life, resuming the professional practice which had been temporarily interrupted by his public duties, and taking no active part in politics through the period of General Taylor's administration, or in any of the exciting scenes of 1850.

The introduction of the Kansas-Nebraska bill by Stephen A. Douglas, in 1854, aroused him from his repose, and summoned him once more to battle for the right. In the canvass of that year, he was one of the most active leaders of the anti-Nebraska movement, addressing the people repeatedly from the stump, with all his characteristic earnestness and energy, and powerfully aided in effecting the remarkable political changes of that year in Illinois.

The Legislature that year having to choose a United States Senator, and for the first time in the history of the State, the election of one opposed to the Democratic party being within the reach of possibility, Mr. Lincoln, although the first choice of the great body of the opposition, with characteristic self-sacrificing disposition, appealed to his old Whig friends to go over in a solid body to Mr. Trumbull, a man of Democratic antecedents, who could command the full vote of the anti-Nebraska Democrats; and the latter was consequently elected. Mr. Lincoln was subsequently offered the nomination for Governor of Illinois, but declined the honor in favor of Col. William H. Bissell, who was elected by a decisive majority.

In the formation of the Republican party as such, Mr Lincoln bore an active and influential part, his name being presented, but ineffectually, at the first National Convention of that party, for Vice-President; laboring earnestly during the canvass of 1856, for the election of General Fremont, whose electoral ticket he headed.

After Mr. Douglas had taken ground against Mr. Buchanan's administration relative to the so-called Lecompton Constitution of Kansas, and had received the indorsement of the Democratic party of Illinois—his re-election as Senator depending upon the result of the State election in 1858— the Republican Convention of that year with shouts of applause, unanimously resolved that Abraham Lincoln was "the first and only choice of the Republicans of Illinois for the United States Senate, as the successor of Stephen A. Douglas." At the close of the proceedings, he delivered the following speech, which struck the key-note of his contest with Senator Douglas, one of the most exciting and remarkable ever witnessed in this country :

" GENTLEMEN OF THE CONVENTION :—If we could first know where we are, and whither we are tending, we could then better judge what to do, and how to do it. We are now far on into the fifth year, since a policy was initiated, with the avowed object, and confident promise of putting an end to slavery agitation. Under the operation of that policy, that agitation had not only not ceased, but has constantly augmented. In my opinion, it will not cease, until a crisis shall have been reached, and passed. 'A house divided against itself can not stand.' I believe this Government can not endure, permanently, half slave and half free. I do not expect the Union to be dissolved—I do not expect the house to fall—but I do expect it will cease to be divided. It will become all one thing, or all the other. Either the opponents of slavery will arrest the further spread of it, and place it where the public mind shall rest in the belief that it is in course of ultimate extinction, or its advocates will push it forward, till it shall become alike lawful in all the States, old as well as new—North as well as South.

" Have we no tendency to the latter condition ? Let any one who doubts, carefully contemplate that now almost complete legal combination—piece of machinery, so to speak— compounded of the Nebraska doctrine, and the Dred Scott decision. Let him consider not only what work the machinery is adapted to do, and how well adapted, but also let him study the history of its construction, and trace, if he can, or rather fail, if he can, to trace the evidences of design, and concert of action, among its chief master-workers from the beginning.

"But, so far, Congress only had acted; and an indorsement by the people, real or apparent, was indispensable, to save the point already gained, and give chance for more. The new year of 1854 found slavery excluded from more than half the States by State Constitutions, and from most of the national territory by Congressional prohibition. Four days later commenced the struggle, which ended in repealing that Congressional prohibition. This opened all the national territory to slavery, and was the first point gained.

"This necessity had not been overlooked, but had been provided for, as well as might be, in the notable argument of '*squatter sovereignty*,' otherwise called '*sacred right of self-government*,' which latter phrase, though expressive of the only rightful basis of any government, was so perverted in this attempted use of it as to amount to just this : that if any one man choose to enslave another, no third man shall be allowed to object. That argument was incorporated into the Nebraska Bill itself, in the language which follows : ' It being the true intent and meaning of this act not to legislate slavery into any Territory or State, nor exclude it therefrom; but to leave the people thereof perfectly free to form and regulate their domestic institutions in their own way, subject only to the Constitution of the United States.'

"Then opened the roar of loose declamation in favor of 'squatter sovereignty,' and 'sacred right of self-government.'

" ' But,' said opposition members, ' let us be more specific—let us *amend* the bill so as to expressly declare that the people of the territory *may* exclude slavery.' ' Not we,' said the friends of the measure ; and down they voted the amendment.

"While the Nebraska Bill was passing through Congress, a law case, involving the question of a negro's freedom, by reason of his owner having voluntarily taken him first into a free State and then a territory covered by the Congressional prohibition, and held him as a slave—for a long time in each— was passing through the U. S. Circuit Court for the District of Missouri; and both the Nebraska Bill and law suit were brought to a decision in the same month of May, 1854. The negro's name was 'Dred Scott,' which name now designates the decision finally made in the case.

"Before the then next Presidential election case, the law came to, and was argued in the Supreme Court of the United States; but the decision of it was deferred until *after* the election. Still, *before* the election, Senator Trumbull, on the floor of the Senate, requests the leading advocate of the Nebraska Bill to state *his opinion* whether a people of a territory can constitutionally exclude slavery from their limits; and the latter answers, 'That is a question for the Supreme Court.'

"The election came. Mr. Buchanan was elected, and the *indorsement*, such as it was, secured. That was the *second* point gained. The indorsement, however, fell short of a clear popular majority by nearly four hundred thousand votes, and so, perhaps, was not overwhelmingly reliable and satisfactory. The outgoing President in his last annual message, as impressively as possible echoed back upon the people the weight and authority of the indorsement.

"The Supreme Court met again; did not announce their decision, but ordered a re-argument. The Presidential inauguration came, and still no decision of the court; but the incoming President, in his Inaugural Address, fervently exhorted the people to abide by the forthcoming decision, *whatever it might be*. Then, in a few days came the decision.

"This was the third point gained.

"The reputed author of the Nebraska Bill finds an early occasion to make a speech at this capitol indorsing the Dred Scott decision, and vehemently denouncing all opposition to it. The new President, too, seizes the early occasion of the Silliman letter to indorse and strongly construe that decision, and to express his astonishment that any different view had ever been entertained. At length a squabble springs up between the President and the author of the Nebraska Bill on the mere question of fact, whether the Lecompton Constitution was or was not, in any just sense, made by the people of Kansas ; and, in that squabble, the latter declares that all he wants is a fair vote for the people, and that he cares not whether slavery be voted down or voted up. I do not understand his declaration that he cares not whether slavery be voted down or voted up, to be intended by him other than as an apt definition of the policy he would impress upon the public mind—the principle for which he declares he has suffered much, and is ready to suffer to the end.

"And well may he cling to that principle. If he has any parental feeling, well may he cling to it. That principle is the only shred left of his original Nebraska doctrine. Under the Dred Scott decision, 'squatter sovereignty' squatted out of existence, tumbled down like temporary scaffolding—like the mould at the foundry, served through one blast, and fell back into loose sand—helped to carry an election, and then was kicked to the winds. His late joint struggle with the Republicans, against the Lecompton Constitution, involves nothing of the original Nebraska doctrine. That struggle was made on a point—the right of a people to make their own Constitution—upon which he and the Republicans have never differed.

" The several points of the Dred Scott decision, in connection with Senator Douglas's ' care not' policy, constitute the piece of machinery in its present state of advancement. The working points of that machinery are :

" First, That no negro slave, imported as such from Africa, and no descendant of such, can ever be a citizen of any State, in the sense of that term as used in the Constitution of the United States.

"This point is made in order to deprive the negro, in every possible event, of the benefit of this provision of the United States Constitution, which declares that—'The citizens of each State shall be entitled to all the privileges and immunities of citizens in the several States.'

"Secondly, that 'subject to the Constitution of the United States,' neither Congress nor a Territorial Legislature can exclude slavery from any United States Territory.

"This point is made in order that individual men may fill up the Territories with slaves, without danger of losing them as property, and thus to enhance the chances of permanency to the institution through all the future.

"Thirdly, that whether the holding a negro in actual slavery in a free State makes him free, as against the holder, the United States courts will not decide, but will leave it to be decided by the courts of any slave State the negro may be forced into by the master.

"This point is made, not to be pressed immediately; but, if acquiesced in for a while, and apparently indorsed by the people at an election, then, to sustain the logical conclusion that what Dred Scott's master might lawfully do with Dred Scott, in the free State of Illinois, every other master may lawfully do with any other one, or one thousand slaves, in Illinois, or in any other free State.

"Auxiliary to all this, and working hand in hand with it, the Nebraska doctrine, or what is left of it, is to educate and mould public opinion, at least Northern public opinion, not to care whether slavery is voted down or voted up.

"This shows exactly where we now are, and partially also, whither we are tending.

"It will throw additional light on the latter, to go back and run the mind over the string of historical facts already stated. Several things will now appear less dark and mysterious than they did when they were transpiring. The people were to be left "perfectly free," "subject only to the Constitution." What the Constitution had to do with it, outsiders could not then see. Plainly enough now, it was an exactly fitted niche for the Dred Scott decision afterward to come in, and declare that perfect freedom of the people to be just no freedom at all.

"Why was the amendment expressly declaring the right of the people to exclude slavery, voted down? Plainly enough now, the adoption of it would have spoiled the niche for the Dred Scott decision.

"Why was the court decision held up? Why even a Senator's individual opinion withheld till after the Presidential election? Plainly enough now; the speaking out then would have damaged the "*perfectly free*" argument upon which the election was to be carried.

"Why the outgoing President's felicitation on the indorsement? Why the delay of a re-argument? Why the incoming President's advance exhortation in favor of the decision? These things look like the cautious patting and petting of a spirited horse preparatory to mounting him, when it is dreaded that he may give the rider a fall. And why the hasty after-indorsements of the decision, by the President and others?

"We cannot absolutely know that all these exact adaptations are the result of pre-concert. But when we see a lot of framed timbers, different portions of which we know have been gotten out, at different times and places, and by different workmen—Stephen, Franklin, Roger, and James, for instance—and when we see these timbers joined together, and see they exactly make the frame of a house or a mill, all the tenons and mortices exactly fitting, and all the lengths and proportions of the different pieces exactly adapted to their respective places, and not a piece too many or too few—not omitting even scaffolding—or, if a single piece be lacking, we can see the place in the frame exactly fitted and prepared to yet bring such piece in—in such a case, we find it impossible not to believe that Stephen and Franklin and Roger and James all understood one another from the beginning, and all worked upon a common plan or draft drawn up before the first blow was struck.

"It should not be overlooked that, by the Nebraska bill, the people of a State as well as Territory, were to be left *'perfectly free,' 'subject only to the Constitution.'* Why mention a State?   They were legislating for Territories, and not for or about States.   Certainly the people of a State are and ought to be subject to the Constitution of the United States; but why is mention of this lugged into this merely territorial law?   Why are the people of a Territory and the people of a State therein lumped together, and their relation to the Constitution therein treated as being precisely the same?

"While the opinion of the court, by Chief Justice Taney, in the Dred Scott case, and the separate opinions of all the concurring judges, expressly declare that the Constitution of the United States neither permits Congress nor a Territorial Legislature, to exclude slavery from any United States Territory, they all omit to declare whether or not the same Constitution permits a State, or the people of a State, to exclude it.   *Possibly,* this was a mere *omission;* but who can be quite sure, if McLean or Curtis had sought to get into the opinion a declaration of unlimited power in the people of a State to exclude slavery from their limits, just as Chase and Mace sought to get such declaration, in behalf of the people of a Territory, into the Nebraska bill—I ask, who can be quite sure that it would not have been voted down, in the one case as it had been in the other.

"The nearest approach to the point of declaring the power of a State over slavery, is made by Judge Nelson.   He approaches it more than once, using the precise idea, and almost the language, too, of the Nebraska Act. On one occasion his exact language is, 'except in cases where the power is restrained by the Constitution of the United States, the law of the State is supreme over the subject of slavery within its jurisdiction.'

" In what cases the power of the State is so restrained by the United States Constitution, is left an open question, precisely as the same question, as to the restraint on the power of the Territories was left open in the Nebraska Act. Put that and that together, and we have another nice little niche, which we may ere long, see filled with another Supreme Court decision, declaring that the Constitution of the United States does not permit a State to exclude slavery from its limits. And this may especially be expected if the doctrine of ' care not whether slavery be voted down or voted up,' shall gain upon the public mind sufficiently to give promise that such a decision can be maintained when made.

" Such a decision is all that slavery now lacks of being alike lawful in all the States. Welcome or unwelcome, such decision is probably coming, and will soon be upon us, unless the power of the present political dynasty shall be met and overthrown. We shall lie down pleasantly dreaming that the people of Missouri are on the verge of making their State free ; and we shall awake to the reality, instead, that the Supreme Court has made Illinois a slave State.

" To meet and overthrow the power of that dynasty, is the work now before all those who would prevent that consummation. That is what we have to do. But how can we best do it ?

" There are those who denounce us openly to their own friends, and yet whisper softly, that Senator Douglas is the *aptest* instrument there is, with which to effect that object. They do not tell us, nor has he told us, that he wishes any such object to be effected. They wish us to infer all, from the facts that he now has a little quarrel with the present head of the dynasty ; and that he has regularly voted. with us, on a single point, upon which he and we have never differed.

"They remind us that *he* is a very *great man*, and that the largest of us are very small ones. Let this be granted. But 'a *living dog* is better than a *dead lion.*' Judge Douglas, if not a *dead* lion for this work, is at least a *caged* and *toothless* one. How can he oppose the advances of slavery ? He don't care anything about it. His avowed mission is impressing the 'public heart' to care nothing about it.

"A leading Douglas Democrat newspaper thinks Douglas's superior talent will be needed to resist the revival of the African slave-trade. Does Douglas believe an effort to revive that trade is approaching ? He has not said so. Does he *really* think so ? But if it is, how can he resist it ? For years he has labored to prove it a *sacred right* of white men to take negro slaves into the new Territories. Can he possibly show that it is less a sacred right to buy them where they can be bought cheapest ? And, unquestionably they can be bought cheaper in Africa than in Virginia.

"He has done all in his power to reduce the whole question of slavery to one of a mere right of property ; and as such, how can he oppose the foreign slave-trade—how can he refuse that trade in that 'property' shall be 'perfectly free'—unless he does it as a *protection* to the home produc tion ? And as the home *producers* will probably not ask the protection, he will be wholly without a ground of opposition

"Senator Douglas holds, we know, that a man may rightfully be wiser to-day than he was yesterday — that he may rightfully change when he finds himself wrong. But can we for that reason run ahead and infer that he will make any particular change, of which he himself has given no intimation ? Can we safely base our action upon any such vague inferences ?

" Now, as ever, I wish not to misrepresent Judge Douglas's position, question his motives, or do aught that can be personally offensive to him. Whenever, *if ever*, he and we can come together on *principle*, so that our great cause may have assistance from his great ability, I hope to have interposed no adventitious obstacle.

" But clearly, he is not now with us—he does not pretend to be—he does not promise ever to be. Our cause, then, must be intrusted to, and conducted by its own undoubted friends—those whose hands are free, whose hearts are in the work—who do care for the result.

" Two years ago the Republicans of the nation mustered over thirteen hundred thousand strong. We did this under the single impulse of resistance to a common danger, with every external circumstance against us. Of strange, discordant, and even hostile elements, we gathered from the four winds, and formed and fought the battle through, under the constant hot fire of a disciplined, proud and pampered enemy. Did we brave all then to falter now ?—*now*—when that same enemy is wavering, dissevered and belligerent ?

" The result is not doubtful. We shall not fail—if we stand firm, we shall not fail. *Wise counsels* may *accelerate* or *mistakes delay* it, but, sooner or later, the victory is *sure* to come."

In this most vigorously prosecuted canvass Illinois was stumped throughout its length and breadth by both candidates and their respective advocates, and the struggle was watched with interest by the country at large. From county to county, from township to township, and village to village the two champions travelled, frequently in the same car or carriage, and in the presence of immense crowds of men, women, and children—for the wives and daughters of the hardy yeomanry were naturally interested—argued, face to face, the important points of their political belief, and contended nobly for the mastery.

In one of his speeches during this memorable campaign, Mr. Lincoln paid the following tribute to the Declaration of Independence :—

"These communities, (the thirteen colonies,) by their representatives in old Independence Hall, said to the world of men, 'we hold these truths to be self-evident, that all men are born equal; that they are endowed by their Creator with inalienable rights; that among these are life, liberty, and the pursuit of happiness.' This was their majestic interpretation of the economy of the universe. This was their lofty, and wise, and noble understanding of the justice of the Creator to His creatures. Yes, gentlemen, to all His creatures, to the whole great family of man. In their enlightened belief, nothing stamped with the Divine image and likeness was sent into the world to be trodden on, and degraded, and imbruted by its fellows. They grasped not only the race of men then living, but they reached forward and seized upon the furthest posterity. They created a beacon to guide their children and their children's children, and the countless myriads who should inhabit the earth in other ages. Wise statesmen as they were, they knew the tendency of prosperity to breed tyrants, and so they established these great self-evident truths that when, in the distant future, some man, some faction, some interest, should set up the doctrine that none but rich men, or none but white men, or none but Anglo-Saxon white men, were entitled to life, liberty, and the pursuit of happiness, their posterity might look up again to the Declaration of Independence, and take courage to renew the battle, which their fathers began, so that truth, and justice, and mercy, and all the humane and Christian virtues might not be extinguished from the land; so that no man would hereafter dare to limit and circumscribe the great principles on which the temple of liberty was being built.

"Now, my countrymen, if you have been taught doctrines conflicting with the great landmarks of the Declaration of

Independence; if you have listened to suggestions which would take away from its grandeur, and mutilate the fair symmetry of its proportions; if you have been inclined to believe that all men are not created equal in those inalienable rights enumerated by our chart of liberty, let me entreat you to come back—return to the fountain whose waters spring close by the blood of the Revolution.   Think nothing of me, take no thought for the political fate of any man whomsoever, but come back to the truths that are in the Declaration of Independence.

"You may do any thing with me you choose, if you will but heed these sacred principles.   You may not only defeat me for the Senate, but you may take me and put me to death. While pretending no indifference to earthly honors, I *do claim* to be actuated in this contest by something higher than an anxiety for office.   I charge you to drop every paltry and insignificant thought for any man's success.   It is nothing; I am nothing; Judge Douglas is nothing. *But do not destroy that immortal emblem of humanity—the Declaration of American Independence.*"

In the election which closed this contest, the Republican candidate received 126,084 votes; the Douglas Democrats, 121,940; and the Lecompton Democrats, 5,091.   Mr. Douglas was, however, re-elected to the Senate by the Legislature, in which, owing to the peculiar apportionment of the legislative districts his supporters had a majority of eight in joint ballot.

3

84 LIFE OF ABRAHAM LINCOLN.

The campaign of 1859.   His Cincinnati Speech.   Results of a Republican Triumph.

CHAPTER III.

BEFORE THE NATION.

Speeches in Ohio—Extract from his Cincinnati Speech—Visits the East—Celebrated
Speech at the Cooper Institute, New York—Interesting Incident.

THE issue of this contest with Douglas, seemingly a defeat, was destined in due time to prove a decisive triumph. Mr. Lincoln's reputation as a skillful debater and master of political fence was secure, and admitted throughout the land. During the year ensuing he again devoted himself almost exclusively to professional labors, delivering, however, in the campaign of 1859, at the earnest solicitation of the Republicans of Ohio, two most convincing speeches in that State, one at Columbus, and the other at Cincinnati.

In his speech in the latter city, alluding to the certainty of a speedy Republican triumph in the nation, Mr. Lincoln thus sketched what he regarded as the inevitable results of such a victory :

" I will tell you, so far as I am authorized to speak for the opposition, what we mean to do with you. We mean to treat you, as nearly as we possibly can, as Washington, Jefferson, and Madison treated you. We mean to leave you alone, and in no way interfere with your institution ; to abide by all and every compromise of the Constitution ; and, in a word, coming back to the original proposition to treat you, so far as degenerated men (if we have degenerated) may, imitating the example of those noble fathers, Washington, Jefferson, and Madison. We mean to remember that you are as good as we ; that there is no difference between us other than the difference of circumstances. We mean to recognize and bear in mind always that you have as good hearts in your bosoms as other people, or as we claim to have, and treat you accordingly. We mean to marry your girls when we have a chance—the white ones I mean—and I have the honor to inform you that I once did get a chance in that way.

"I have told you what we mean to do. I want to know, now, when that thing takes place, what you mean to do. I often hear it intimated that you mean to divide the Union whenever a Republican, or any thing like it, is elected President of the United States. [A voice, 'That is so.'] 'That is so,' one of them says. I wonder if he is a Kentuckian? [A voice, 'He is a Douglas man.'] Well, then, I want to know what you are going to do with your half of it? Are you going to split the Ohio down through, and push your half off a piece? Or are you going to keep it right alongside of us outrageous fellows? Or are you going to build up a wall some way between your country and ours, by which that movable property of yours can't come over here any more, and you lose it? Do you think you can better yourselves on that subject, by leaving us here under no obligation whatever to return those specimens of your movable property that come hither? You have divided the Union because we would not do right with you, as you think, upon that subject; when we cease to be under obligations to do any thing for you, how much better off do you think you will be? Will you make war upon us and kill us all? Why, gentlemen, I think you are as gallant and as brave men as live; that you can fight as bravely in a good cause, man for man, as any other people living; that you have shown yourselves capable of this upon various occasions; but, man for man, you are not better than we are, and there are not so many of you as there are of us. You will never make much of a hand at whipping us. If we were fewer in numbers than you, I think that you could whip us; if we were equal it would

36   LIFE OF ABRAHAM LINCOLN.

His Cincinnati Speech.   Visits the East.   Cooper Institute Speech.

likely be a drawn battle ; but being inferior in numbers, you will make nothing by attempting to master us.

" I say that we must not interfere with the institution of Slavery in the States where it exists, because the Constitution forbids it, and the general welfare does not require us to do so. We must not withhold an efficient fugitive slave law because the Constitution requires us, as I understand it, not to withhold such a law, but we must prevent the outspreading of the institution, because neither the constitution nor the general welfare requires us to extend it. We must prevent the revival of the African slave-trade and the enacting by Congress of a Territorial slave code. We must prevent each of these things being done by either Congresses or Courts. THE PEOPLE OF THESE UNITED STATES ARE THE RIGHTFUL MASTERS OF BOTH CONGRESSES AND COURTS, not to overthrow the Constitution, but to overthrow the men who pervert that Constitution."

In the spring of 1860, Mr. Lincoln yielded to the urgent calls which came to him from the East for his aid in the exciting canvasses then in progress in that section, and spoke at various places in Connecticut, New Hampshire, and Rhode Island, and also in New York city, and was everywhere warmly welcomed by immense audiences.

Without doubt, one of the greatest speeches of his life was that delivered by him in the Cooper Institute, in New York, on the 27th of February, 1860, in the presence of a crowded assembly which received him with the most enthusiastic demonstrations. We subjoin a full report of this masterly analysis of men and measures. After being introduced in highly complimentary terms by the venerable William Cullen Bryant, who presided on the occasion, he proceeded :

" MR. PRESIDENT AND FELLOW CITIZENS OF NEW YORK :— The facts with which I shall deal this evening are mainly old and familiar ; nor is there any thing new in the general use I shall make of them. If there shall be any novelty, it will be in the mode of presenting the facts, and the inferences and observations following that presentation.

"In his speech last autumn, at Columbus, Ohio, as reported in *The New York Times*, Senator Douglas said :

"'Our fathers, when they framed the Government under which we live, understood this question just as well, and even better than we do now.'

"I fully indorse this and I adopt it as a text for this discourse. I so adopt it because it furnishes a precise and agreed starting point for the discussion between Republicans and that wing of Democracy headed by Senator Douglas. It simply leaves the inquiry : 'What was the understanding those fathers had of the questions mentioned ?'

"What is the frame of Government under which we live ?

"The answer must be : 'The Constitution of the United States.' That Constitution consists of the original, framed in 1787 (and under which the present Government first went into operation), and twelve subsequently framed amendments, the first ten of which were framed in 1789.

"Who were our fathers that framed the Constitution ? I suppose the 'thirty-nine' who signed the original instrument may be fairly called our fathers who framed that part of the present Government. It is almost exactly true to say they framed it, and it is altogether true to say they fairly represented the opinion and sentiment of the whole nation at that time. Their names being familiar to nearly all, and accessible to quite all, need not now be repeated.

"I take these 'thirty-nine,' for the present, as being 'our fathers who framed the Government under which we live.'

"What is the question which, according to the text, those fathers understood just as well, and even better than we do now ?

"It is this : Does the proper division of local from federal authority, or any thing in the Constitution, forbid our Federal Government control as to slavery in our Federal Territories ?

"Upon this, Douglas holds the affirmative, and Republicans the negative. This affirmative and denial form an issue; and this issue—this question—is precisely what the text declares our fathers understood better than we.

"Let us now inquire whether the 'thirty-nine,' or any of them, ever acted upon this question; and if they did, how they acted upon it—how they expressed that better understanding.

"In 1784 — three years before the Constitution — the United States then owning the Northwestern Territory, and no other—the Congress of the Confederation had before them the question of prohibiting slavery in that Territory; and four of the 'thirty-nine' who afterward framed the Constitution were in that Congress, and voted on that question. Of these, Roger Sherman, Thomas Mifflin, and Hugh Williamson voted for the prohibition—thus showing that, in their understanding, no line dividing local from federal authority, nor any thing else, properly forbade the Federal Government to control as to slavery in federal territory. The other of the four—James McHenry—voted against the prohibition, showing that, for some cause, he thought it improper to vote for it.

"In 1787, still before the Constitution, but while the Convention was in session framing it, and while the Northwestern Territory still was the only territory owned by the United States—the same question of prohibiting slavery in the territory again came before the Congress of the Confederation; and three more of the 'thirty-nine' who afterward signed the Constitution, were in that Congress, and voted on the question. They were William Blount, William Few, and Abraham Baldwin; and they all voted for the prohibition—thus showing that, in their understanding, no line dividing local from federal authority, nor any thing else, properly forbids the Federal Government to control as to slavery in federal territory. This time the prohibition became a law, being part of what is now well known as the Ordinance of '87.

" The question of federal control of slavery in the territories, seems not to have been directly before the Convention which framed the original Constitution ; and hence it is not recorded that the 'thirty-nine' or any of them, while engaged on that instrument, expressed any opinion on that precise question.

" In 1789, by the First congress which sat under the Constitution, an act was passed to enforce the Ordinance of '87, including the prohibition of slavery in the North-western Territory. The bill for this act was reported by one of the 'thirty-nine,' Thomas Fitzsimmons, then a member of the House of Representatives from Pennsylvania. It went through all its stages without a word of opposition, and finally passed both branches without yeas and nays, which is equivalent to an unanimous passage. In this Congress there were sixteen of the 'thirty-nine' fathers who framed the original Constitution. They were John Langdon, Nicholas Gilman, Wm. S. Johnson, Roger Sherman, Robert Morris, Thos. Fitzsimmons, William Few, Abraham Baldwin, Rufus King, William Patterson, George Clymer, Richard Bassett, George Read, Pierce Butler, Daniel Carrol, James Madison.

" This shows that, in their understanding, no line dividing local from federal authority, nor any thing in the Constitution, properly forbade Congress to prohibit slavery in the federal territory ; else both their fidelity to correct principle, and their oath to support the Constitution, would have constrained them to oppose the prohibition.

"Again, George Washington, another of the 'thirty-nine,' was then President of the United States, and, as such, approved and signed the bill, thus completing its validity as a law, and thus showing that, in his understanding, no line dividing local from federal authority, nor any thing in the Constitution, forbade the Federal Government to control as to slavery in Federal territory.

"No great while after the adoption of the original Constitution, North Carolina ceded to the Federal Government the country now constituting the State of Tennessee; and a few years later Georgia ceded that which now constitutes the States of Mississippi and Alabama. In both deeds of cession it was made a condition by the ceding States that the Federal Government should not prohibit slavery in the ceded country. Besides this, slavery was then actually in the ceded country. Under these circumstances, Congress, on taking charge of these countries did not absolutely prohibit slavery within them. But they did interfere with it—take control of it— even there, to a certain extent. In 1798, Congress organized the Territory of Mississippi. In the act of organization they prohibited the bringing of slaves into the Territory, from any place without the United States, by fine and giving freedom to slaves so brought. This act passed both branches of Congress without yeas and nays. In that Congress were three of the 'thirty-nine' who framed the original Constitution. They were John Langdon, George Read, and Abraham Baldwin. They all, probably, voted for it. Certainly they would have placed their opposition to it upon record, if, in their understanding, any line dividing local from Federal authority, or any thing in the Constitution, properly forbade the Federal Government to control as to slavery in Federal territory.

"In 1803, the Federal Government purchased the Louisiana country. Our former territorial acquisitions came from certain of our own States; but this Louisiana country was acquired from a foreign nation. In 1804, Congress gave a territorial organization to that part of it which now constitutes the State of Louisiana. New Orleans, lying within that part, was an old and comparatively large city. There were other considerable towns and settlements, and slavery was extensively and thoroughly intermingled with the people. Congress did not, in the Territorial Act, prohibit slavery;

BEFORE THE NATION. **41**

His Speech at the Cooper Institute.   Slavery in Louisiana.   The Missouri Question.

but they did interfere with it—take control of it—in a more marked and extensive way than they did in the case of Mississippi. The substance of the provision therein made, in relation to slaves, was :

"*First.* That no slave should be imported into the territory from foreign parts.

"*Second.* That no slave should be carried into it who had been imported into the United States since the first day of May, 1798.

"*Third.* That no slave should be carried into it, except by the owner, and for his own use as a settler; the penalty in all the cases being a fine upon the violator of the law, and freedom to the slave.

" This act also was passed without yeas and nays. In the Congress which passed it, there were two of the 'thirty-nine.' They were Abraham Baldwin and Jonathan Dayton. As stated in the case of Mississippi, it is probable they both voted for it. They would not have allowed it to pass without recording their opposition to it, if, in their understanding, it violated either the line proper dividing local from Federal authority or any provision of the Constitution.

" In 1819–20, came and passed the Missouri question. Many votes were taken, by yeas and nays, in both branches of Congress, upon the various phases of the general question. Two of the 'thirty-nine'—Rufus King and Charles Pinckney— were members of that Congress. Mr. King steadily voted for slavery prohibition and against all compromises, while Mr. Pinckney as steadily voted against slavery prohibition and against all compromises. By this Mr. King showed that, in his understanding, no line dividing local from Federal authority, nor any thing in the Constitution, was violated by Congress prohibiting slavery in Federal territory ; while Mr. Pinckney, by his votes, showed that in his understanding there was some sufficient reason for opposing such prohibition in that case.

" The cases I have mentioned are the only acts of the 'thirty-nine,' or of any of them, upon the direct issue, which I have been able to discover.

" To enumerate the persons who thus acted, as being four in 1784, three in 1787, seventeen in 1789, three in 1798, two in 1804, and two in 1819–20—there would be thirty-one of them. But this would be counting John Langdon, Roger Sherman, William Few, Rufus King, and George Read, each twice, and Abraham Baldwin four times. The true number of those of the 'thirty-nine' whom I have shown to have acted upon the question, which, by the text they understood better than we, is twenty-three, leaving sixteen not shown to have acted upon it in any way.

" Here, then, we have twenty-three out of our 'thirty-nine' fathers who framed the government under which we live, who have, upon their official responsibility and their corporal oaths, acted upon the very question which the text affirms they 'understood just as well, and even better than we do now;' and twenty-one of them—a clear majority of the 'thirty-nine'—so acting upon it as to make them guilty of gross political impropriety, and wilful perjury, if, in their understanding, any proper division between local and Federal authority, or any thing in the Constitution they had made themselves, and sworn to support, forbade the Federal Government to control as to slavery in the Federal territories. Thus the twenty-one acted; and, as actions speak louder than words, so actions under such responsibility speak still louder.

" Two of the twenty-three voted against Congressional prohibition of slavery in the Federal Territories, in the instances in which they acted upon the question. But for what reasons they so voted is not known. They may have done so because they thought a proper division of local from Federal authority, or some provision or principle of the Constitution, stood in the way; or they may, without any such question, have voted against the prohibition, on what appeared to them to be sufficient grounds of expediency. No one who has sworn to support the Constitution, can conscientiously vote for what he understands to be an unconstitutional measure, however expedient he may think it; but one may and ought to vote against a measure which he deems constitutional, if, at the same time, he deems it inexpedient. It, therefore, would be unsafe to set down even the two who voted against the prohibition, as having done so because, in their understanding, any proper division of local from Federal authority, or any thing in the Constitution, forbade the Federal Government to control as to slavery in Federal Territory.

"The remaining sixteen of the 'thirty-nine,' so far as I have discovered, have left no record of their understanding upon the direct question of Federal control of slavery in the Federal Territories. But there is much reason to believe that their understanding upon that question would not have appeared different from that of their twenty-three compeers, had it been manifested at all.

" For the purpose of adhering rigidly to the text, I have purposely omitted whatever understanding may have been manifested, by any person, however distinguished, other than the 'thirty-nine' fathers who framed the original Constitution; and, for the same reason, I have also omitted whatever understanding may have been manifested by any of the 'thirty-nine' even, on any other phase of the general question of slavery. If we should look into their acts and declarations on those other phases, as the foreign slave-trade, and the morality and policy of slavery generally, it would appear to us that on the direct question of Federal control of slavery in Federal Territories, the sixteen, if they had acted at all, would probably have acted just as the twenty-three did. Among that sixteen were several of the most noted anti-slavery men of those times—as Dr. Franklin, Alexander

Hamilton, and Gouverneur Morris—while there was not one now known to have been otherwise, unless it may be John Rutledge, of South Carolina.

"The sum of the whole is, that of our 'thirty-nine' fathers who framed the original Constitution, twenty-one—a clear majority of the whole—certainly understood that no proper division of local from Federal authority nor any part of the Constitution, forbade the Federal Government to control slavery in the Federal Territories, while all the rest probably had the same understanding. Such, unquestionably, was the understanding of our fathers who framed the original Constitution; and the text affirms that they understood the question better than we.

"But, so far, I have been considering the understanding of the question manifested by the framers of the original Constitution. In and by the original instrument, a mode was provided for amending it; and, as I have already stated, the present frame of government under which we live consists of that original, and twelve amendatory articles framed and adopted since. Those who now insist that Federal control of slavery in Federal territories violates the Constitution, point us to the provisions which they suppose it thus violates; and, as I understand, they all fix upon provisions in these amendatory articles, and not in the original instrument. The Supreme Court in the Dred Scott case, plant themselves upon the fifth amendment, which provides that 'no person shall be deprived of property without due process of law;' while Senator Douglas and his peculiar adherents plant themselves upon the tenth commandment, providing that 'the powers not granted by the Constitution are reserved to the States respectively, and to the people.'

"Now, it so happens that these amendments were framed by the first Congress which sat under the Constitution—the identical Congress which passed the act already mentioned, enforcing the prohibition of slavery in the north-western territory.   Not only was it the same Congress, but they were the identical, same individual men who, at the same time within the session, had under consideration, and in progress toward maturity, these Constitutional amendments, and this act prohibiting slavery in all the territory the nation then owned.   The Constitutional amendments were introduced before, and passed after the act enforcing the Ordinance of '87 ; so that during the whole pendency of the act to enforce the Ordinance, the Constitutional amendments were also pending.

"That Congress, consisting in all of seventy-six members, including sixteen of the framers of the original Constitution, as before stated, were pre-eminently our fathers who framed that part of the government under which we live, which is now claimed as forbidding the Federal Government to control slavery in the Federal Territories.

"Is it not a little presumptuous in any one at this day, to affirm that the two things which that Congress deliberately framed, and carried to maturity at the same time, are absolutely inconsistent with each other ?   And does not such affirmation become impudently absurd when coupled with the other affirmation, from the same mouth, that those who did the two things alleged to be inconsistent, understood whether they were really inconsistent, better than we—better than he who affirms that they are inconsistent.

"It is surely safe to assume that the 'thirty-nine' framers of the original Constitution, and the seventy-six members of the Congress which framed the amendments thereto, taken together, do certainly include those who may be fairly called 'our fathers who framed the government under which we live.'   And so assuming, I defy any man to show that any one of them ever, in his whole life, declared that, in his understanding, any proper division of local from Federal authority, or any part of the Constitution, forbade the Federal government to control as to slavery in the Federal territories.   I go a step further. I defy any one to show that any living man in the whole world ever did, prior to the beginning of the present century (and I might almost say prior to the beginning of the last half of the present century), declare that, in his understanding, any proper division of local from Federal authority, or any part of the Constitution, forbade the Federal government to control as to slavery in the Federal territories. To those who now so declare, I give, not only 'our fathers who framed the government under which we live,' but with them all other living men within the century in which it was framed, among whom to search, and they shall not be able to find the evidence of a single man agreeing with them.

"Now, and here, let me guard a little against being misunderstood. I do not mean to say we are bound to follow implicitly in whatever our fathers did. To do so would be to discard all the lights of current experience—we reject all progress—all improvement. What I do say is, that if we would supplant the opinions and policy of our fathers in any case, we should do so upon evidence so conclusive, and argument so clear, that even their great authority, fairly considered and weighed, cannot stand; and most surely not in a case whereof we ourselves declare they understood the question better than we.

"If any man, at this day, sincerely believes that a proper division of local from Federal authority, or any part of the Constitution, forbids the Federal government to control as to slavery in the Federal territories, he is right to say so, and to enforce his position by all truthful evidence and fair argument which he can. But he has no right to mislead others, who have less access to history and less leisure to study it, into the false belief that 'our fathers, who framed the government under which we live,' were of the same opinion thus substituting falsehood and deception for truthful evidence and fair argument. If any man, at this day, sincerely believes 'our fathers, who framed the government under which wo live,' used and applied principles, in other cases, which ought to have led them to understand that a proper division of local from Federal authority, or some part of the Constitution, forbids the Federal government to control as to slavery in the Federal territories, he is right to say so. But he should, at the same time, brave the responsibility of declaring that, in his opinion, he understands their principles better than they did themselves; and especially should he not shirk that responsibility by asserting that they 'understood the question just as well, and even better than we do now.'

"But enough. Let all who believe that 'our fathers, who framed the government under which we live, understood this question just as well, and even better than we do now,' speak as they spoke, and act as they acted upon it. This is all Republicans ask, all Republicans desire, in relation to slavery. As those fathers marked it, so let it be again marked, as an evil not to be extended, but to be tolerated and protected only because of and so far as its actual presence among us makes that toleration and protection a necessity. Let all the guaranties those fathers gave it, be, not grudgingly, but fully and fairly maintained. For this Republicans contend, and with this, so far as I know or believe, they will be content.

"And now, if they would listen—as I suppose they will not—I would address a few words to the Southern people.

"I would say to them : You consider yourselves a reasonable and a just people; and I consider that, in the general qualities of reason and justice, you are not inferior to any other people. Still, when you speak of us Republicans, you do so only to denounce us as reptiles, or, at the best, as no better than outlaws. You will grant a hearing to pirates or murderers, but nothing like it to 'Black Republicans.' In all your contentions with one another, each of you deems an unconditional condemnation of 'Black Republicanism' as the first thing to be attended to. Indeed, such condemnation of

48　　LIFE OF ABRAHAM LINCOLN.

His Speech at the Cooper Institute.　　　　An Appeal to the South.

us seems to be an indispensable prerequisite—license, so to speak—among you to be admitted or permitted to speak at all.

"Now can you, or not, be prevailed upon to pause and to consider whether this is quite just to us, or even to yourselves?

"Bring forward your charges and specifications, and then be patient long enough to hear us deny or justify.

"You say we are sectional. We deny it. That makes an issue; and the burden of proof is upon you. You produce your proof; and what is it? Why, that our party has no existence in your section—gets no votes in your section. The fact is substantially true; but does it prove the issue? If it does, then, in case we should, without change of principle, begin to get votes in your section, we should thereby cease to be sectional. You cannot escape this conclusion; and yet, are you willing to abide by it? If you are, you will probably soon find that we have ceased to be sectional, for we shall get votes in your section this very year. You will then begin to discover, as the truth plainly is, that your proof does not touch the issue. The fact that we get no votes in your section is a fact of your making, and not of ours. And if there be fault in that fact, that fault is primarily yours, and remains so until you show that we repel you by some wrong principle or practice. If we do repel you by any wrong principle or practice, the fault is ours; but this brings us to where you ought to have started—to a discussion of the right or wrong of our principle. If our principle, put in practice, would wrong your section for the benefit of ours, or for any other object, then our principle, and we with it, are sectional, and are justly opposed and denounced as such. Meet us, then, on the question of whether our principle, put in practice, would wrong your section; and so meet it as if it were possible that something may be said on our side. Do you accept the challenge? No? Then you really believe that the principle which our fathers, who framed the government under which we live, thought so clearly right as to adopt it, and indorse it again and again upon their official oaths, is, in fact, so clearly wrong as to demand your condemnation without a moment's consideration.

"Some of you delight to flaunt in our faces the warning against sectional parties given by Washington in his Farewell Address.   Less than eight years before Washington gave that warning, he had, as President of the United States, approved and signed an act of Congress enforcing the prohibition of slavery in the Northwestern Territory, which act embodied the policy of the government upon that subject, up to and at the very moment he penned that warning; and about one year after he penned it he wrote Lafayette that he considered that prohibition a wise measure, expressing, in the same connection, his hope that we should some time have a confederacy of free States.

"Bearing this in mind, and seeing that sectionalism has since arisen upon this same subject, is that warning a weapon in your hands against us, or in our hands against you? Could Washington himself speak, would he cast the blame of that sectionalism upon us, who sustain his policy, or upon you, who repudiate it? We respect that warning of Washington, and we commend it to you, together with his example pointing to the right application of it.

"But you say you are conservative—eminently conservative—while we are revolutionary, destructive, or something of the sort.   What is conservatism? Is it not adherence to the old and tried against the new and untried? We stick to, contend for, the identical old policy on the point in controversy which was adopted by our fathers who framed the government under which we live; while you, with one accord, reject, and scout, and spit upon that old policy, and insist upon substituting something new.   True, you disagree among yourselves as to what that substitute shall be.   You

4

have considerable variety of new propositions and plans, but you are unanimous in rejecting and denouncing the old policy of the fathers.   Some of you are for reviving the foreign slave-trade; some for a Congressional Slave-Code for the Territories; some for Congress forbidding the Territories to prohibit slavery within their limits; some for maintaining slavery in the Territories through the Judiciary; some for the 'gur-reat pur-rinciple' that, 'if one man would enslave another, no third man should object,' fantastically called ' Popular Sovereignty;' but never a man among you in favor of Federal prohibition of slavery in Federal Territories, according to the practice of our fathers who framed the government under which we live.   Not one of all your various plans can show a precedent or an advocate in the century within which our government originated.   Consider, then, whether your claim of conservatism for yourselves, and your charge of destructivenesss against us, are based on the most clear and stable foundations.

"Again, you say we have made the slavery question more prominent than it formerly was.   We deny it.   We admit that it is more prominent, but we deny that we made it so.   It was not we, but you, who discarded the old policy of the fathers.   We resisted, and still resist, your innovation; and thence comes the greater prominence of the question.   Would you have that question reduced to its former proportions?   Go back to that old policy.   What has been will be again, under the same conditions.   If you would have the peace of the old times, re-adopt the precepts and policy of the old times.

" You charge that we stir up insurrections among your slaves.   We deny it.   And what is your proof?   Harper's Ferry!   John Brown!   John Brown was no Republican; and you have failed to implicate a single Republican in his Harper's Ferry enterprise.   If any member of our party is guilty in that matter, you know it, or you do not know it.

If you do know it, you are inexcusable to not designate the man, and prove the fact. If you do not know it, you are inexcusable to assert it, and especially to persist in the assertion after you have tried and failed to make the proof. You need not be told that persisting in a charge which one does not know to be true is simply malicious slander.

" Some of you admit that no Republican designedly aided or encouraged the Harper's Ferry affair; but still insist that our doctrines and declarations necessarily lead to such results. We do not believe it. We know we hold to no doctrine, and make no declarations which were not held to and made by our fathers who framed the government under which we live. You never deal fairly by us in relation to this affair. When it occurred, some important State elections were near at hand, and you were in evident glee with the belief that, by charging the blame upon us, you could get an advantage of us in those elections. The elections came, and your expectations were not quite fulfilled. Every Republican man knew that, as to himself, at least, your charge was a slander, and he was not much inclined by it to cast his vote in your favor. Republican doctrines and declarations are accompanied with a continual protest against any interference whatever with your slaves, or with you about your slaves. Surely, this does not encourage them to revolt. True, we do, in common with our fathers, who framed the government under which we live, declare our belief that slavery is wrong; but the slaves do not hear us declare even this. For any thing we say or do, the slaves would scarcely know there is a Republican party. I believe they would not, in fact, generally know it but for your misrepresentations of us in their hearing. In your political contest among yourselves, each faction charges the other with sympathy with Black Republicanism; and then, to give point to the charge, defines Black Republicanism to simply be insurrection, blood and thunder among the slaves.

" Slave insurrections are no more common now than they were before the Republican party was organized. What induced the Southampton insurrection, twenty-eight years ago, in which, at least, three times as many lives were lost as at Harper's Ferry ? You can scarcely stretch your very elastic fancy to the conclusion that Southampton was got up by Black Republicanism. In the present state of things in the United States, I do not think a general, or even a very extensive slave insurrection, is possible. The indispensable concert of action cannot be attained. The slaves have no means of rapid communication ; nor can incendiary free men, black or white, supply it. The explosive materials are everywhere in parcels ; but there neither are, nor can be supplied, the indispensable connecting trains.   -

" Much is said by southern people about the affection of slaves for their masters and mistresses ; and a part of it, at least, is true. A plot for an uprising could scarcely be devised and communicated to twenty individuals before some one of them, to save the life of a favorite master or mistress, would divulge it. This is the rule ; and the slave revolution in Hayti was not an exception to it, but a case occurring under peculiar circumstances. The gunpowder plot of British history, though not connected with the slaves, was more in point. In that case, only about twenty were admitted to the secret ; and yet one of them, in his anxiety to save a friend, betrayed the plot to that friend, and, by consequence, averted the calamity. Occasional poisoning from the kitchen, and open or stealthy assassinations in the field, and local revolts extending to a score or so, will continue to occur as the natural results of slavery ; but no general insurrection of slaves, as I think, can happen in this country for a long time. Whoever much fears, or much hopes, for such an event, will be alike disappointed.

" In the language of Mr. Jefferson, uttered many years ago, ' It is still in our power to direct the process of emancipation, and deportation, peaceably, and in such slow degrees, as that the evil will wear off insensibly; and their places be, *pari passu*, filled up by free white laborers. If, on the contrary, it is left to force itself on, human nature must shudder at the prospect held up.'

" Mr. Jefferson did not mean to say, nor do I, that the power of emancipation is in the Federal Government. He spoke of Virginia; and, as to the power of emancipation, I speak of the slaveholding States only.

" The Federal Government, however, as we insist, has the power of restraining the extension of the institution—the power to insure that a slave insurrection shall never occur on any American soil which is now free from slavery.

• " John Brown's effort was peculiar. It was not a slave insurrection. It was an attempt by white men to get up a revolt among slaves, in which the slaves refused to participate. In fact, it was so absurd that the slaves, with all their ignorance, saw plainly enough it could not succeed. That affair, in its philosophy, corresponds with the many attempts, related in history, at the assassination of kings and emperors. An enthusiast broods over the oppression of a people till he fancies himself commissioned by Heaven to liberate them. He ventures the attempt, which ends in little else than in his own execution. Orsini's attempt on Louis Napoleon, and John Brown's attempt at Harper's Ferry were, in their philosophy, precisely the same. The eagerness to cast blame on old England in the one case, and on New England in the other, does not disprove the sameness of the two things.

" And how much would it avail you, if you could, by the use of John Brown, Helper's book, and the like, break up the Republican organization? Human action can be modified to some extent, but human nature cannot be changed. There is a judgment and a feeling against slavery in this nation, which cast at least a million and a half of votes. You cannot destroy that judgment and feeling—that sentiment—by breaking up the political organization which rallies around it. You can scarcely scatter and disperse an army which has been formed into order in the face of your heaviest fire; but if you could, how much would you gain by forcing the sentiment which created it out of the peaceful channel of the ballot-box, into some other channel? What would that other channel probably be? Would the number of John Browns be lessened or enlarged by the operation?

" But you will break up the Union rather than submit to a denial of your Constitutional rights.

" That has a somewhat reckless sound; but it would be palliated, if not fully justified, were we proposing by the mere force of numbers, to deprive you of some right plainly written down in the Constitution. But we are proposing no such thing.

" When you make these declarations, you have a specific and well-understood allusion to an assumed Constitutional right of yours, to take slaves into the federal territories, and hold them there as property, but no such right is specifically written in the Constitution. That instrument is literally silent about any such right. We, on the contrary, deny that such a right has any existence in the Constitution, even by implication.

" Your purpose, then, plainly stated, is, that you will destroy the Government, unless you be allowed to construe and enforce the Constitution as you please, on all points in dispute between you and us. You will rule or ruin in all events.

" This, plainly stated, is your language to us. Perhaps you will say the Supreme Court has decided the disputed Constitutional question in your favor. Not quite so. But waiving the lawyer's distinction between dictum and decision, the Courts have decided the question for you in a sort of way. The Courts have substantially said, it is your Constitutional right to take slaves into the Federal Territories, and to hold them there as property.

" When I say the decision was made in a sort of way, I mean it was made in a divided Court by a bare majority of the Judges, and they not quite agreeing with one another in the reasons for making it; that it is so made as that its avowed supporters disagree with one another about its meaning, and that it was mainly based upon a mistaken statement of fact—the statement in the opinion that 'the right of property in a slave is distinctly and expressly affirmed in the Constitution.'

"An inspection of the Constitution will show that the right of property in a slave is not distinctly and expressly affirmed in it. Bear in mind the Judges do not pledge their judicial opinion that such right is impliedly affirmed in the Constitution; but they pledge their veracity that it is distinctly and expressly affirmed there—'distinctly' that is, not mingled with any thing else—'expressly' that is, in words meaning just that, without the aid of any inference, and susceptible of no other meaning.

" If they had only pledged their judicial opinion that such right is affirmed in the instrument by implication, it would be open to others to show that neither the word 'slave' nor 'slavery' is to be found in the Constitution, nor the word 'property' even, in any connection with language alluding to the things slave, or slavery, and that wherever in that instrument the slave is alluded to, he is called a 'person;' and wherever his master's legal right in relation to him is alluded to, it is spoken of as 'service or labor due,' as a 'debt' payable in service or labor. Also, it would be open to show, by contemporaneous history, that this mode of alluding to slaves and slavery, instead of speaking of them, was employed on purpose to exclude from the Constitution the idea that there could be property in man.

" To show all this is easy and certain.

" When this obvious mistake of the Judges shall be brought to their notice, is it not reasonable to expect that they will withdraw the mistaken statement, and reconsider the conclusion based upon it?

"And then it is to be remembered that 'our fathers, who framed the Government under which we live'—the men who made the Constitution—decided this same Constitutional question in our favor, long ago—decided it without a division among themselves, when making the decision; without division among themselves about the meaning of it after it was made, and so far as any evidence is left, without basing it upon any mistaken statement of facts.

"Under all these circumstances, do you really feel yourselves justified to break up this Government, unless such a court decision as yours is shall be at once submitted to, as a conclusive and final rule of political action.

"But you will not abide the election of a Republican President. In that supposed event, you say, you will destroy the Union; and then, you say, the great crime of having destroyed it will be upon us!

"That is cool. A highwayman holds a pistol to my ear, and mutters through his teeth, 'stand and deliver, or I shall kill you, and then you will be a murderer!'

"To be sure, what the robber demanded of me—my money—was my own; and I had a clear right to keep it; but it was no more my own than my vote is my own; and threat of death to me, to extort my money, and threat of destruction to the Union, to extort my vote, can scarcely be distinguished in principle.

"A few words now to Republicans. It is exceedingly desirable that all parts of this great Confederacy shall be at peace, and in harmony, one with another. Let us Republicans do our part to have it so. Even though much provoked, let us do nothing through passion and ill-temper. Even though the southern people will not so much as listen to us, let us calmly consider their demands, and yield to them if, in our deliberate view of our duty, we possibly can.

Judging by all they say and do, and by the subject and nature of their controversy with us, let us determine, if we can, what will satisfy them ?

" Will they be satisfied if the Territories be unconditionally surrendered to them ?   We know they will not.   In all their present complaints against us, the Territories are scarcely mentioned.   Invasions and insurrections are the rage now. Will it satisfy them if, in the future, we have nothing to do with invasions and insurrections ?   We know it will not. We so know because we know we never had any thing to do with invasions and insurrections ; and yet this total abstaining does not exempt us from the charge and the denunciation.

" The question recurs, what will satisfy them ?   Simply this : We must not only let them alone, but we must, somehow, convince them that we do let them alone.   This we know by experience, is no easy task.   We have been so trying to convince them from the very beginning of our organization, but with no success.   In all our platforms and speeches we have constantly protested our purpose to let them alone ; but this has had no tendency to convince them.   Alike unavailing to convince them is the fact that they have never detected a man of us in any attempt to disturb them.

" These natural, and apparently adequate means all failing, what will convince them ?   This, and this only : cease to call slavery *wrong*, and join them in calling it *right*.   And this must be done thoroughly—done in *acts* as well as in *words*. Silence will not be tolerated—we must place ourselves avowedly with them.   Douglas's new sedition law must be enacted and enforced, suppressing all declarations that slavery is wrong, whether made in politics, in presses, in pulpits, or in private.   We must arrest and return their fugitive slaves with greedy pleasure.   We must pull down our Free-State Constitutions.   The whole atmosphere must be disinfected from all taint of opposition to slavery, before they will cease to believe that all their troubles proceed from us.

"I am quite aware they do not state their case precisely in this way. Most of them would probably say to us, 'Let us alone, do nothing to us, and say what you please about slavery.' But we do let them alone—have never disturbed them—so that, after all, it is what we say which dissatisfies them. They will continue to accuse us of doing, until we cease saying.

"I am also aware they have not, as yet, in terms, demanded the overthrow of our Free-State Constitutions. Yet those Constitutions declare the wrong of slavery, with more solemn emphasis than do all other sayings against it; and when all these other sayings shall have been silenced, the overthrow of these Constitutions will be demanded, and nothing be left to resist the demand. It is nothing to the contrary, that they do not demand the whole of this just now. Demanding what they do, and for the reason they do, they can voluntarily stop nowhere short of this consummation. Holding, as they do, that slavery is morally right, and socially elevating, they cannot cease to demand a full national recognition of it, as a legal right and a social blessing.

" Nor can we justifiably withhold this, on any ground save our conviction that slavery is wrong. If slavery is right, all words, acts, laws, and constitutions against it, are themselves wrong, and should be silenced and swept away. If it is right, we cannot justly object to its nationality—its universality; if it is wrong, they cannot justly insist upon its extension—its enlargement. All they ask, we could readily grant, if we thought slavery right; all we ask, they could as readily grant, if they thought it wrong. Their thinking it right, and our thinking it wrong, is the precise fact upon which depends the whole controversy. Thinking it right, as they do, they are not to blame for desiring its full recognition, as being right; but, thinking it wrong, as we do, can we yield to them? Can we cast our votes with their view, and against our own? In view of our moral, social, and political responsibilities, can we do this?

" Wrong as we think slavery is, we can yet afford to let it alone where it is, because that much is due to the necessity arising from its actual presence in the nation ; but can we, while our votes will prevent it, allow it to spread into the National Territories, and to overrun us here in these Free States ?

" If our sense of duty forbids this, then let us stand by our duty, fearlessly and effectively.   Let us be diverted by none of those sophistical contrivances wherewith we are so industriously plied and belabored—contrivances such as groping for some middle ground between the right and the wrong, vain as the search for a man who should be neither a living man nor a dead man—such as a policy of ' dont care' on a question about which all true men do care—such as Union appeals beseeching true Union men to yield to Disunionists, reversing the Divine rule, and calling, not the sinners, but the righteous to repentance—such as invocations to Washington, imploring men to unsay what Washington said, and undo what Washington did.

" Neither let us be slandered from our duty by false accusations against us, not frightened from it by menaces of destruction to the Government, nor of dungeons to ourselves. Let us have faith that right makes might, and in that faith, let us, to the end, dare to do our duty as we understand it."

It was during this visit to New York that the following incident occurred, as related by a teacher in the Five-Points House of Industry, in that city :

" Our Sunday-school in the Five-Points was assembled, one Sabbath morning, a few months since, when I noticed a tall and remarkable-looking man enter the room and take a seat among us.   He listened with fixed attention to our exercises, and his countenance manifested such genuine interest that I approached him and suggested that he might be willing to say something to the children.   He accepted the invita-

60 LIFE OF ABRAHAM LINCOLN.

Visits a Sunday-school.　　　　Address.　　Republican National Convention.

tion with evident pleasure, and, coming forward, began a simple address, which at once fascinated every little hearer, and hushed the room into silence. His language was strikingly beautiful, and his tones musical with intensest feeling. The little faces around would droop into sad conviction as he uttered sentences of warning, and would brighten into sunshine as he spoke cheerful words of promise. Once or twice he attempted to close his remarks, but the imperative shout of ' Go on !' ' Oh, do go on !' would compel him to resume. As I looked upon the gaunt and sinewy frame of the stranger, and marked his powerful head and determined features, now touched into softness by the impressions of the moment, I felt an irrepressible curiosity to learn something more about him, and when he was quietly leaving the room I begged to know his name. He courteously replied, ' It is Abra'm Lincoln, from Illinois !''

CHAPTER IV.

NOMINATED AND ELECTED PRESIDENT.

The Republican National Convention—Democratic Convention—Constitutional Union Convention—Ballotings at Chicago—The Result—Enthusiastic Reception—Visit to Springfield—Address and Letter of Acceptance—The Campaign—Result of the Election—South Carolina's Movements—Buchanan's pusillanimity—Secession of states—Confederate Constitution—Peace Convention—Constitutional Amendments—Terms of the Rebels.

ON the 16th of May, 1860, the Republican National Convention met at Chicago, to present candidates for the Presidency and Vice-Presidency. The Democratic Convention had previously adjourned, after a stormy session of some two weeks, at which it was apparent that, if Mr. Douglas's friends persisted in placing him in nomination, another candidate would be presented by the wing opposed to his peculiar views on the slavery question, and the great party would thus be disrupted.   Another convention, claiming to represent, in a peculiarly individual manner, the party in favor of the Constitution and the Union, had met at Baltimore and put in nomination John Bell, of Tennessee, and Edward Everett, of Massachusetts.

The aspect seemed favorable for the election of the Republican candidates, and that convention, on the morning of the 18th of May—one day having been spent in organizing and another in the adoption of a platform of principles—amid the intense excitement of the twelve thousand people inside of the " Wigwam" (as the building was styled in which the body was in session), voted to proceed at once to ballot for a candidate for President of the United States.

Seven names were formally presented in the following order : William H Seward, of New York ; Abraham Lincoln, of Illinois ; William L. Dayton, of New Jersey ; Simon Cameron, of Pennsylvania ; Salmon P. Chase, of Ohio ; Edward Bates, of Missouri ; and John McLean, of Ohio.

On the first ballot Mr. Seward received 173 votes, Mr. Lincoln 102, Mr. Cameron 50, Mr. Chase 49, Mr. Bates 48, Mr. Dayton 14, Mr. McLean 12, and there were 16 votes scattered among candidates not put in nomination.   For a choice, 233 votes were required.

On the second ballot (Mr. Cameron's name having been withdrawn) the vote for the several candidates was as follows : Mr. Seward 184, Mr. Lincoln 181, Mr. Chase 42, Mr. Bates 35, Mr. Dayton 10, Mr. McLean 8, scattering 4.

The third ballot was immediately taken, and, when the call of the roll was ended, the footings were as follows : For Mr. Lincoln 231, Mr. Seward 180, Mr. Chase 24, Mr. Bates, 22, all others 7.   Immediately before the result was announced, four Ohio delegates changed their votes to Mr. Lincoln, giving him a majority.

The scene which followed—the wild, almost delirious out

burst of applause within and without the building, the congratulations, the hand-shakings, the various manifestations of joy, continued with scarcely any interruption for some three-quarters of an hour—was probably never before witnessed in a popular assembly.

The nomination having been made unanimous, the ticket was completed by the selection of Senator Hannibal Hamlin, of Maine, as Vice-President.

The country then felt that the right man had for once been put in the right place.   As a man of the people, in cordial sympathy with the masses, Mr. Lincoln enjoyed the unhesitating confidence of the sincere friends of free labor, regardless of party distinctions.   His tried integrity and incorruptible honesty gave promise of a return to the better days of the republic.   Every man, laboring for the advancement of his fellow, knew that in him humanity, irrespective of race or condition, had a tried and trusty friend.

The committee, appointed to apprise him of his nomination, found him at his home, in Springfield, a frame two-storied house, apparently about thirty-five or forty feet square, standing at the corner of two streets.   After entering the parlor, which was very plainly furnished, though in good taste, a brief address was made by the chairman of the convention, upon the utterance of the first sentence of which a smile played round Mr. Lincoln's large, firm-set mouth, his eyes lit up, and his face conveyed to those who then for the first time met him, an impression of that sincere, loving nature which those who had known him long and well had learned in some measure to comprehend and revere.

. In response to this address, Mr. Lincoln said :

" MR. CHAIRMAN AND GENTLEMEN OF THE COMMITTEE : I tender to you, and through you to the Republican National Convention, and all the people represented in it, my profoundest thanks for the high honor done me, which you now formally announce. Deeply, and even painfully sensible of the great responsibility which is inseparable from this high honor—a responsibility which I could almost wish had fallen upon some one of the far more eminent men and experienced statesmen whose distinguished names were before the Convention, I shall, by your leave, consider more fully the resolutions of the Convention, denominated the platform, and without unnecessary and unreasonable delay, respond to you, Mr. Chairman, in writing, not doubting that the platform will be found satisfactory, and the nomination gratefully accepted. And now I will not longer defer the pleasure of taking you, and each of you, by the hand."

In reply to the formal letter of the President of the Convention, apprising him of the nomination, Mr. Lincoln addressed the following :

"*Springfield, Illinois*, May 23d, 1860.

"HON. GEORGE ASHMAN, *President of the Republican National Convention.*

"SIR : I accept the nomination tendered me by the Convention over which you presided, and of which I am formally apprised in the letter of yourself and others, acting as a Committee of the Convention for that purpose.

"The declaration of principles and sentiments, which accompanies your letter, meets my approval; and it shall be my care not to violate, or disregard it, in any part.

"Imploring the assistance of Divine Providence, and with due regard to the views and feelings of all who were represented in the Convention; to the rights of all the States and Territories, and people of the nation; to the inviolability of the Constitution, and the perpetual union, harmony and prosperity of all, I am most happy to co-operate for the practical success of the principles declared by the Convention,

"Your obliged friend and fellow-citizen,

"ABRAHAM LINCOLN."

64   LIFE OF ABRAHAM LINCOLN.

Elected President.   The Electoral Vote.   The coming Storm.

The breach in the Democratic party, threatened at Charleston, was subsequently effected by the nomination of Stephen A. Douglas and Herschel V. Johnson, of Georgia, by one wing, and of John C. Breckinridge, of Kentucky, and Joseph Lane, of Oregon, by the other.

Although the election of Mr. Lincoln was, under the circumstances, almost a foregone conclusion, yet the canvass which ensued was acrimonious and vindictive in the extreme, the choicest selections from the rank Billingsgate vocabularies being lavished on the head of Mr. Linclon and his supporters.

On the 6th of November, 1860, Mr. Lincoln received 1,866,452 votes, securing the electoral votes of the States of Maine, New Hampshire, Vermont, Massachusetts, Rhode Island, Connecticut, New York, Pennsylvania, Ohio, Indiana, Illinois, Michigan, Iowa, Wisconsin, Minnesota, California, Oregon, and four votes of New Jersey, 180 in all; Douglas, 1,375,157 votes, and the electoral votes of Missouri, and three of New Jersey, 12 in all; Breckenridge, 847,953, and the votes of Maryland, Delaware, North Carolina, South Carolina, Georgia, Florida, Alabama, Louisiana, Mississippi, Arkansas, and Texas, 72 in all; and Bell, 590,631, and the votes of Virginia, Kentucky, and Tennessee, 39 in all.

And now was to be tested whether words were to ripen into deeds—whether threats would be reduced to practice— whether, indeed, there were madness enough in any State or States to attempt the life of the republic. Unfortunately, a short space of time elapsed before all doubts were at an end. Men were to be found—not confined to a single State, but representatives of nearly, if not quite all—not to be counted by scores or hundreds even, but by thousands, and soon by tens of thousands—ready to lay their unhallowed hands upon the Union, the ark of our nation's glory and strength.

To South Carolina belongs the bold, bad eminence of taking the initiation in this conspiracy against the interests of humanity. While this State—doomed forever after to an ignominy from which centuries of unquestioned loyalty cannot free her—was taking the requisite steps toward secession, the then President, James Buchanan, with a pusillanimity— to use no stronger term—which modern history certainly has never paralleled, in his annual message, after having urged the unconstitutionality of the proceeding, gave explicit notification that he had no constitutional power to prevent the proposed measures being hastened to successful completion. Neither, though appealed to, at a still earlier day, by the veteran chief of the army, to occupy and hold the United States on the Southern coast, could he find any warrant for protecting and defending the national property.

Surely nothing more could the conspirators have desired. On the 20th of December, 1860, South Carolina claims to secede — Government forts and arsenals are seized, and placed under the protection of the flag of the State. Georgia's Governor lays hand on the United States forts on the coast of that State, on the 3d of January, 1861 ; as did the Executive of Alabama on the following day.

Events of a startling nature follow in rapid succession. On the 9th of January, hostile shots are fired upon a vessel bringing tardy reinforcements to Fort Sumter, and Mississippi assumes to put herself out of the Union.   Alabama, Florida, and Georgia are not laggard ; nor are Texas and Louisiana found wanting.   Cabinet officers from the slave States either resigned, after having aided the fell work to their utmost, or remained only to hasten its consummation.   A new constitution, "temporary" in its nature, was declared by delegates from the seven States then in rebellion, and a President and Vice-President appointed.

Meanwhile a convention, composed of delegates from most of the Free States, and from all the border Slave States, was striving, at Washington, to heal existing difficulties by compromise.   Of its members some were acting in good faith, others were using it as a breakwater for the States already

5

in overt rebellion.   A series of resolutions, however, aiming at peace on the basis of a preserved Union was agreed to by a majority, and the body adjourned on the 1st of March.

On the 11th of February, moreover, the National House of Representatives unanimously adopted a resolution—shortly afterward concurred in by the Senate—providing for an amendment to the Constitution, forever prohibiting any Congressional legislation interfering with slavery in any State. Some there were, too, who were willing to concede almost every thing and surrender the long mooted question of slavery in the territories by the adoption of the so-called Crittenden resolutions, which were killed in cold blood by Southern Senators.

But no concession, short of actual national degradation, would satisfy the recusants.   Jefferson Davis, the head of the " Confederacy," on placing himself at the head of the rebellion, at Montgomery, Alabama, February 18th, modestly defined the position of himself and his co-conspirators thus :

" If a just perception of neutral interest shall permit us peaceably to pursue our separate political career, my most earnest desire will have been fulfilled.   But if this be denied us, and the integrity of our territory and jurisdiction be assailed, it will but remain for us with firm resolve to appeal to arms, and invoke the blessing of Providence on a just cause."

This was at once clinched by a recommendation that " a well-instructed, disciplined army, more numerous than would usually be required, on a peace establishment," should be at once organized and put in training for the emergency.

CHAPTER V.

TO WASHINGTON.

The Departure—Farewell Remarks—Speech at Toledo—At Indianapolis—At Cincinnati—At Columbus—At Steubenville—At Pittsburgh—At Cleveland—At Buffalo—At Albany—At Poughkeepsie—At New York—At Trenton—At Philadelphia—At "Independence Hall"—Flag-raising—Speech at Harrisburg—Secret Departure for Washington—Comments.

THUS matters stood—the air filled with mutterings of an approaching storm—the most filled with a certain undefinable anxiety—the hearts of many failing them through fear—when, on the morning of the 11th of February, 1861, the President elect with his family, bade adieu to that prairie home which, alas! he was never again to see.

The large throng which had assembled at the railway station on the occasion of his departure, he addressed in words replete with the pathos of every true manly nature:

"MY FRIENDS:—No one, not in my position, can appreciate the sadness I feel at this parting. To this people I owe all that I am. Here I have lived more than a quarter of a century; here my children were born, and here one of them lies buried. I know not how soon I shall see you again. A duty devolves upon me which is, perhaps, greater than that which has devolved upon any other man since the days of Washington. He never could have succeeded except for the aid of Divine Providence, upon which he at all times relied. I feel that I cannot succeed without the same Divine aid which sustained him; and in the same Almighty being I place my reliance for support, and I hope you, my friends, will all pray that I may receive that Divine assistance, without which I can not succeed, but with which success is certain. Again, I bid you all an affectionate farewell."

Along the route, multitudes gathered at the stations to greet him. At Toledo, Ohio, in reply to repeated calls, he appeared on the platform of the car and said:

"I am leaving you on an errand of national importance, attended, as you are aware, with considerable difficulties. Let us believe, as some poet has expressed it, 'Behind the cloud the sun is shining still.' I bid you an affectionate farewell."

At Indianapolis, on the evening of the same day, in reply to an official address of welcome, he gave the first direct public intimation of his views concerning the absorbing topics of the day, in which homely sense and cheerful pleasantry were blended with a skill beyond the power of mere art:

"FELLOW CITIZENS OF THE STATE OF INDIANA:—I am here to thank you for this magnificent welcome, and still more for the very generous support given by your State to that political cause, which, I think, is the true and just cause of the whole country, and the whole world. Solomon says, 'there is a time to keep silence;' and when men wrangle by the mouth, with no certainty that they mean the same thing while using the same words, it perhaps were as well if they would keep silence.

"The words 'coercion' and 'invasion' are much used in these days, and often with some temper and hot blood. Let us make sure, if we can, that we do not misunderstand the meaning of those who use them. Let us get the exact definitions of these words, not from dictionaries, but from the men themselves, who certainly deprecate the things they would represent by the use of the words.

"What, then, is coercion? What is invasion? Would the marching of an army into South Carolina, without the consent of her people, and with hostile intent toward them, be invasion? I certainly think it would, and it would be coercion also, if the South Carolinians were forced to submit. But if the United States should merely hold and retake its own forts and other property, and collect the duties on foreign importations, or even withhold the mails from places where they were habitually violated, would any or all of these things be invasion or coercion? Do our professed lovers of the Union, who spitefully resolve that they will resist coercion and invasion, understand that such things as these, on the part of the United States, would be coercion or invasion of a State? If so, their idea of means to preserve the object of their great affection would seem to be exceedingly thin and airy. If sick, the little pills of the homeopathist would be much too large for it to swallow. In their view, the Union, as a family relation, would seem to be no regular marriage, but rather a sort of 'free-love' arrangement, to be maintained on passional attraction.

"By the way, in what consists the special sacredness of a State? I speak not of the position assigned to a State in the Union by the Constitution, for that is a bond we all recognize. That position, however, a State cannot carry out of the Union with it. I speak of that assumed primary right of a State to rule all which is less than itself, and to ruin all which is larger than itself. If a State and a County, in a given case, should be equal in number of inhabitants, in what, as a matter of principle, is the State better than the County? Would an exchange of name be an exchange of rights? Upon what principle, upon what rightful principle, may a State, being no more than one-fiftieth part of the nation in soil and population, break up the nation, and then coerce a proportionably large sub-division of itself in the most arbitrary way? What mysterious right to play tyrant is conferred on a district or country with its people, by merely calling it a State? Fellow citizens, I am not asserting any thing. I am merely asking questions for you to consider. And now allow me to bid you farewell."

Proceeding to Cincinnati, he received a most enthusiastic

70   LIFE OF ABRAHAM LINCOLN.

To Washington.   Speech at Cincinnatti.   The Republican Policy.

welcome. Having been addressed by the mayor of the city, and escorted by a civic and military procession to the Burnet House, he addressed the assemblage in these words :

"FELLOW-CITIZENS : I have spoken but once before this in Cincinnati. That was a year previous to the late Presidential election. On that occasion in a playful manner, but with sincere words, I addressed much of what I said to the Kentuckians. I gave my opinion that we, as Republicans, would ultimately beat them as Democrats, but that they could postpone the result longer by nominating Senator Douglas for the Presidency than they could in any other way. They did not, in any true sense of the word, nominate Mr. Douglas, and the result has come certainly as soon as ever I expected.

"I also told them how I expected they would be treated after they should have been beaten, and now wish to call their attention to what I then said :

"'When we do, as we say we will, beat you, you perhaps want to know what we will do with you. I will tell you— as far as I am authorized to speak for the opposition—what we mean to do with you. We mean to treat you as near as we possibly can, as Washington, Jefferson, and Madison treated you. We mean to leave you alone, and in no way to interfere with your institutions; to abide by all and every compromise of the Constitution. In a word, coming back to the original proposition, to treat you, as far as degenerate men—if we have degenerated—may, according to the example of those noble fathers, Washington, Jefferson, and Madison. We mean to remember that you are as good as we ; that there is no difference between us other than the difference of circumstances. We mean to recognize and bear in mind always that you have as good hearts in your bosoms as other people, or as we claim to have, and to treat you accordingly.'

"Fellow-citizens of Kentucky, friends, brethren : May I call you such ? In my new position I see no occasion and feel no inclination to retract a word of this. If it shall not be made good be assured that the fault shall not be mine."

On the next morning he left Cincinnati, and arrived at Columbus, where he was received with every demonstration of enthusiasm. He visited the Governor in the Executive Chamber, and was subsequently introduced to the members of the Legislature in joint session, when he was formally welcomed by the Lieutenant-Governor, to whom Mr. Lincoln responded in these words :

"It is true, as has been said by the President of the Senate, that very great responsibility rests upon me in the position to which the votes of the American people have called me I am deeply sensible of that weighty responsibility. I cannot but know, what you all know, that without a name—perhaps without a reason why I should have a name—there has fallen upon me a task such as did not rest upon the Father of his Country. And so feeling, I cannot but turn and look for the support without which it will be impossible for me to perform that great task. I turn, then, and look to the American people, and to that God who has never forsaken them.

"Allusion has been made to the interest felt in relation to the policy of the new Administration. In this, I have received from some a degree of credit for having kept silence, from others some depreciation. I still think I was right. In the varying and repeatedly shifting scenes of the present, without a precedent which could enable me to judge for the past, it has seemed fitting, that before speaking upon the difficulties of the country I should have gained a view of the whole field. To be sure, after all, I would be at liberty to modify and change the course of policy as future events might make a change necessary.

"I have not maintained silence from any want of real anxicty. It is a good thing that there is no more than anxiety, for there is nothing going wrong. It is a consoling circumstance that when we look out there is nothing that really hurts anybody. We entertain different views upon political questions, but nobody is suffering any thing. This is a most consoling circumstance, and from it I judge that all we want is time and patience, and a reliance on that God who has never forsaken this people."

On the 14th of February, Mr. Lincoln proceeded to Pittsburgh. At Steubenville, on the route, in reply to an address, he said :

"I fear the great confidence placed in my ability is unfounded. Indeed, I am sure it is. Encompassed by vast difficulties, as I am, nothing shall be wanted on my part, if sustained by the American people and God. I believe the devotion to the Constitution is equally great on both sides of the river. It is only the different understanding of that instrument that causes difficulties. The only dispute is 'What are their rights?' If the majority should not rule who should be the judge? Where is such a judge to be found? We should all be bound by the majority of the American people —if not, then the minority must control. Would that be right? Would it be just or generous? Assuredly not." He reiterated, the majority should rule. If he adopted a wrong policy, then the opportunity to condemn him would occur in four years' time. "Then I can be turned out and a better man with better views put in my place."

The next morning he left for Cleveland, but before his departure he made an address to the people of Pittsburgh, in which he said :

"In every short address I have made to the people, and in every crowd through which I have passed of late, some allusion has been made to the present distracted condition of the country. It is naturally expected that I should say something upon this subject, but to touch upon it at all would involve an elaborate discussion of a great many questions and circumstances, would require more time than I can at present command, and would perhaps unnecessarily commit me upon matters which have not yet fully developed themselves.

" The condition of the country, fellow-citizens, is an extraordinary one, and fills the mind of every patriot with anxiety and solicitude.   My intention is to give this subject all the consideration which I possibly can before I speak fully and definitely in regard to it, so that, when I do speak, I may be as nearly right as possible.   And when I do speak, fellow-citizens, I hope to say nothing in opposition to the spirit of the Constitution, contrary to the integrity of the Union, or which will in any way prove inimical to the liberties of the people or to the peace of the whole country. And, furthermore, when the time arrives for me to speak on this great subject, I hope to say nothing which will disappoint the reasonable expectations of any man, or disappoint the people generally throughout the country, especially if their expectations have been based upon any thing which I may have heretofore said.

" Notwithstanding the troubles across the river [the speaker, smiling, pointed southwardly to the Monongahela river], there is really no crisis springing from any thing in the Government itself.   In plain words, there is really no crisis except an artificial one.   What is there now to warrant the condition of affairs presented by our friends ' over the river ?'   Take even their own view of the questions involved, and there is nothing to justify the course which they are pursuing.   I repeat it, then, there is no crisis, except such a one as may be gotten up at any time by turbulent men, aided by designing politicians.   My advice, then, under such circumstances, is to keep cool.   If the great American people will only keep their temper on both sides of the line, the trouble will come to an end, and the question which now distracts the country will be settled just as surely as all other difficulties of like character which have originated in this government have been adjusted.   Let the people on both

74   LIFE OF ABRAHAM LINCOLN.

To Washington.   Speech at Pittsburgh.   Speech at Cleveland.

sides keep their self-possession, and just as other clouds have cleared away in due time, so will this, and this great nation shall continue to prosper as heretofore."

He then referred to the subject of the tariff, and said:

"According to my political education, I am inclined to believe that the people in the various portions of the country should have their own views carried out through their representatives in Congress. That consideration of the tariff bill should not be postponed until the next session of the National Legislature. No subject should engage your representatives more closely than that of the tariff. If I have any recommendation to make, it will be that every man who is called upon to serve the people, in a representative capacity, should study the whole subject thoroughly, as I intend to do myself, looking to all the varied interests of the common country, so that, when the time for action arrives, adequate protection shall be extended to the coal and iron of Pennsylvania, and the corn of Illinois. Permit me to express the hope that this important subject may receive such consideration at the hands of your representatives that the interests of no part of the country may be overlooked, but that all sections may share in the common benefits of a just and equitable tariff."

Mr. Lincoln, upon his arrival in Cleveland, adverted to the same subject in the following terms:

"It is with you, the people, to advance the great cause of the Union and the Constitution, and not with any one man. It rests with you alone. This fact is strongly impressed on my mind at present. In a community like this, whose appearance testifies to their intelligence, I am convinced that the cause of liberty and the Union can never be in danger. Frequent allusion is made to the excitement at present existing in national politics. I think there is no occasion for any excitement. The crisis, as it is called, is altogether an artificial crisis. In all parts of the nation, there are differences of opinion in politics. There are differences of opinion even here. You did not all vote for the person who now addresses you. And how is it with those who are not here? Have they not all their rights as they ever had? Do they not have their fugitive slaves returned now as ever? Have they not the same Constitution that they have lived under for seventy odd years? Have they not a position as citizens of this common country, and have we any power to change that position? What, then, is the matter with them? Why all this excitement? Why all these complaints? As I said before, this crisis is all artificial. It has no foundation in fact. It was 'argued up,' as the saying is, and cannot be argued down. Let it alone, and it will go down itself."

On Saturday he proceeded to Buffalo, where he arrived at evening, and was met by an immense concourse of citizens, headed by Ex-President Fillmore.

Arriving at the hotel, Mr. Lincoln was welcomed in a brief speech by the acting chief magistrate, to which he made a brief reply, as follows:

" MR. MAYOR AND FELLOW CITIZENS:—I am here to thank you briefly for this grand reception given to me not personally, but as the representative of our great and beloved country. Your worthy Mayor has been pleased to mention in his address to me, the fortunate and agreeable journey which I have had from home—only it is rather a circuitous route to the Federal Capitol. I am very happy that he was enabled, in truth, to congratulate myself and company on that fact. It is true, we have had nothing thus far to mar the pleasure of the trip. We have not been met alone by those who assisted in giving the election to me; I say not alone, but by the whole population of the country through which we have passed. This is as it should be. Had the election fallen to any other of the distinguished candidates instead of myself, under the peculiar circumstances, to say the least, it would have been proper for all citizens to have greeted him as you now greet me. It is an evidence of the devotion of the whole people to the Constitution, the Union, and the perpetuity of the liberties of this country. I am unwilling, on any occasion, that I should be so meanly thought of as to have it supposed for a moment that these demonstrations are tendered to me personally. They are tendered to the country, to the institutions of the country, and to the perpetuity of the liberties of the country for which these institutions were made and created. Your worthy mayor has thought fit to express the hope that I may be able to relieve the country from the present, or, I should say, the threatened difficulties. I am sure I bring a heart true to the work. For the ability to perform it, I trust in that Supreme Being who has never forsaken this favored land, through the instrumentality of this great and intelligent people. Without that assistance I should surely fail; with it I cannot fail. When we speak of the threatened difficulties to the country, it is natural that it should be expected that something should be said by myself with regard to particular measures. Upon more mature reflection, however, I think,—and others will agree with me—that, when it is considered that these difficulties are without precedent, and never have been acted upon by any individual situated as I am, it is most proper that I should wait and see the developments, and get all the light possible, so that, when I do speak authoritatively, I may be as near right as possible. When I shall speak authoritatively, I hope to say nothing inconsistent with the Constitution, the Union, the rights of all the States, of each State, and of each section of the country, and not to disappoint the reasonable expectations of those who have confided to me their votes. In this connection, allow me to say that you, as a portion of the great American people, need only to maintain your composure, stand up to your sober convictions of right, to your obligations to the Constitution, and act in accordance with those sober convictions, and the clouds which now arise in the horizon will be dispelled, and we shall have a bright and glorious future ; and, when this generation shall have passed away, tens of thousands shall inhabit this country where only thousands inhabit it now. I do not propose to address you at length. I have no voice for it. Allow me again to thank you for this magnificent reception, and bid you farewell."

Mr. Lincoln then proceeded from Buffalo to Albany. Here he was met by the Mayor, the City Councils, and the Legislative Committees, and was conducted to the Capitol, where he was welcomed by Governor Morgan, and responded briefly, as follows :

"GOVERNOR MORGAN :—I was pleased to receive an invitation to visit the capital of the great Empire State of this nation, while on my way to the Federal capital. I now thank you, and you, the people of the capital of the State of New York, for this most hearty and magnificent welcome. If I am not at fault, the great Empire State at this time contains a larger population than did the whole of the United States of America at the time they achieved their national independence ; and I was proud to be invited to visit its capital, to meet its citizens as I now have the honor to do. I am notified by your governor that this reception is tendered by citizens without distinction of party. Because of this, I accept it the more gladly. In this country, and in any country where freedom of thought is tolerated, citizens attach themselves to political parties. It is but an ordinary degree of charity to attriute this act to the supposition that, in thus attaching themselves to the various parties, each man, in his own judgment, supposes he thereby best advances the interests of the whole country. And when an election is passed, it is altogether befitting a free people that, until the next election, they should be one people. The reception you have extended me to-day is not given to me personally. It should not be so, but as the representative, for the time being, of the majority of the nation

78   LIFE OF ABRAHAM LINCOLN.

To Washington.   Speech at Albany.   Addresses the Legislature.

If the election had fallen to any of the more distinguished citizens, who received the support of the people, this same honor should have greeted him that greets me this day, in testimony of the unanimous devotion of the whole people to the Constitution, the Union, and to the perpetual liberties of succeeding generations in this country. I have neither the voice nor the strength to address you at any greater length. I beg you will, therefore, accept my most grateful thanks for this manifest devotion—not to me but to the institutions of this great and glorious country."

He was then conducted to the Legislative halls, where, in reply to an address of welcome, he again adverted to the troubles of the country in the following terms:

" MR. PRESIDENT AND GENTLEMEN OF THE LEGISLATURE OF THE STATE OF NEW YORK :—It is with feelings of great diffidence, and, I may say, feelings even of awe, perhaps greater than I have recently experienced, that I meet you here in this place. The history of this great State, the renown of its great men, who have stood in this chamber, and have spoken their thoughts, all crowd around my fancy, and incline me to shrink from an attempt to address you. Yet I have some confidence given me by the generous manner in which you have invited me, and the still more generous manner in which you have received me. You have invited me and received me without distinction of party. I could not for a moment suppose that this has been done in any considerable degree with any reference to my personal self. It is very much more grateful to me that this reception and the invitation preceding it were given to me as the representative of a free people, than it could possibly have been were they but the evidence of devotion to me or to any one man. It is true that, while I hold myself, without mock-modesty, the humblest of all the individuals who have ever been elected President of the United States, I yet have a more difficult task to perform than any one of them has ever encountered. You have here generously tendered me the support, the united support, of the great Empire State. For this, in behalf of the nation—in behalf of the President and of the future of the nation—in behalf of the cause of civil liberty in all time to come—I most gratefully thank you. I do not propose now to enter upon any expressions as to the particular line of policy to be adopted with reference to the difficulties that stand before us in the opening of the incoming administration. I deem that it is just to the country, to myself, to you, that I should see every thing, hear every thing, and have every light that can possibly be brought within my reach to aid me before I shall speak officially, in order that, when I do speak, I may have the best possible means of taking correct and true grounds. For this reason, I do not now announce any thing in the way of policy for the new Administration. When the time comes, according to the custom of the Government, I shall speak, and speak as well as I am able for the good of the present and of the future of this country—for the good of the North and of the South—for the good of one and of the other, and of all sections of it. In the meantime, if we have patience, if we maintain our equanimity, though some may allow themselves to run off in a burst of passion, I still have confidence that the Almighty Ruler of the Universe, through the instrumentality of this great and intelligent people, can and will bring us through this difficulty, as he has heretofore brought us through all preceding difficulties of the country. Relying upon this, and again thanking you, as I forever shall, in my heart, for this generous reception you have given me, I bid you farewell."

At Albany, he was met by a delegation from the city authorities of New York, and on the 19th started for that city. At Poughkeepsie, he was welcomed by the Mayor of the city. Mr. Lincoln, in reply, said:

"I am grateful for this cordial welcome, and I am gratified that this immense multitude has come together, not to meet the individual man, but the man who, for the time being, will humbly but earnestly represent the majesty of the nation. These receptions have been given me at other places, and, as here, by men of different parties, and not by one party alone. It shows an earnest effort on the part of all to save, not the country, for the country can save itself, but to save the institutions of the country—those institutious under which, for at least three-quarters of a century, we have become the greatest, the most intelligent, and the happiest people in the world. These manifestations show that we all make common cause for these objects ; that if some of us are successful in an election, and others are beaten, those who are beaten are not in favor of sinking the ship in consequence of defeat, but are earnest in their purpose to sail it safely through the voyage in hand, and, in so far as they may think there has been any mistake in the election, satisfying themselves to take their chance of setting the matter right the next time. That course is entirely right. I am not sure—I do not pretend to be sure—that in the election of the individual who has been elected this term, the wisest choice has been made. I fear it has not. In the purposes and in the principles that have been sustained, I have been the instrument selected to carry forward the affairs of this Government. I can rely upon you, and upon the people of the country ; and with their sustaining hand, I think that even I shall not fail in carrying the Ship of State through the storm."

The reception of President Lincoln in New York City was a most imposing demonstration. Places of business were generally closed, and hundreds of thousands were in the streets. On the next day, he was welcomed to the city by Mayor Wood, and replied as follows :

" MR. MAYOR : It is with feelings of deep gratitude that I make my acknowledgments for the reception given me in the great commercial city of New York. I cannot but remember that this is done by a people who do not, by a majority, agree with me in political sentiment. It is the more grateful, because in this I see that, for the great principles of our Government, the people are almost unanimous. In regard to the difficulties that confront us at this time, and of which your Honor has thought fit to speak so becomingly and so justly, as I suppose, I can only say that I agree in the sentiments expressed. In my devotion to the Union, I hope I am behind no man in the nation. In the wisdom with which to conduct the affairs tending to the preservation of the Union, I fear that too great confidence may have been reposed in me ; but I am sure I bring a heart devoted to the work. There is nothing that could ever bring me to willingly consent to the destruction of this Union, under which not only the great commercial city of New York, but the whole country, acquired its greatness, except it be the purpose for which the Union itself was formed. I understand the ship to be made for the carrying and the preservation of the cargo, and so long as the ship can be saved with the cargo, it should never be abandoned, unless it fails the possibility of its preservation, and shall cease to exist, except at the risk of throwing overboard both freight and passengers. So long, then, as it is possible that the prosperity and the liberties of the people be preserved in this Union, it shall be my purpose at all times to use all my powers to aid in its perpetuation. Again thanking you for the reception given me, allow me to come to a close."

On the next day he left for Philadelphia. At Trenton he remained a few hours, and visited both Houses of the Legislature. On being received in the Senate, he thus addressed that body :

"MR. PRESIDENT AND GENTLEMEN OF THE SENATE OF THE STATE OF NEW JERSEY:—I am very grateful to you for the honorable reception of which I have been the object. I cannot but remember the place that New Jersey holds in our early his-

6

tory. In the early Revolutionary struggle, few of the States among the old Thirteen had more of the battle-fields of the country within its limits than old New Jersey. May I be pardoned, if, upon this occasion, I mention that away back in my childhood, the earliest days of my being able to read, I got hold of a small book, such a one as few of the younger members have ever seen, 'Weems' Life of Washington.' I remember all the accounts there given of the battle-fields and struggles for the liberties of the country, and none fixed themselves upon my imagination so deeply as the struggle here at Trenton, New Jersey. The crossing of the river—the contest with the Hessians—the great hardships endured at that time—all fixed themselves on my memory more than any single revolutionary event; and you all know, for you have all been boys, how these early impressions last longer than any others. I recollect thinking then, boy even though I was, that there must have been something more than common that those men struggled for. I am exceedingly anxious that that thing which they struggled for—that something even more than National Independence—that something that held out a great promise to all the people of the world to all time to come—I am exceedingly anxious that this Union, the Constitution, and the liberties of the people, shall be perpetuated in accordance with the original idea for which that struggle was made, and I shall be most happy indeed, if I shall be an humble instrument in the hands of the Almighty, and of this, His almost chosen people, for perpetuating the object of that great struggle. You give me this reception, as I understand, without distinction of party. I learn that this body is composed of a majority of gentlemen who, in the exercise of their best judgment in the choice of a Chief Magistrate, did not think I was the man. I understand, nevertheless, that they came forward here to greet me as the Constitutional President of the United States—as citizens of the United States, to meet the man who, for the time being, is the representative man of the nation, united by a purpose to perpetuate the Union and liberties of the people. As such, I accept this reception more gratefully than I could do did I believe it was tendered to me as an individual."

He then passed into the Chamber of the Assembly, and upon being introduced by the Speaker, addressed that body as follows :

" MR. SPEAKER AND GENTLEMEN :—I have just enjoyed the honor of a reception by the other branch of this Legislature, and I return to you and them my thanks for the reception which the people of New Jersey have given, through their chosen representatives, to me, as the representative, for the time being, of the majesty of the people of the United States. I appropriate to myself very little of the demonstrations of respect with which I have been greeted. I think little should be given to any man, but that it should be a manifestation of adherence to the Union and the Constitution. I understand myself to be received here by the representatives of the people of New Jersey, a majority of whom differ in opinion from those with whom I have acted. This manifestation is therefore to be regarded by me as expressing their devotion to the Union, the Constitution, and the liberties of the people. You, Mr. Speaker, have well said, that this is the time when the bravest and wisest look with doubt and awe upon the aspect presented by our national affairs. Under these circumstances, you will readily see why I should not speak in detail of the course I shall deem it best to pursue. It is proper that I should avail myself of all the information and all the time at my command, in order that when the time arrives in which I must speak officially, I shall be able to take the ground which I deem the best and safest, and from which I may have no occasion to swerve. I shall endeavor to take the ground I deem most just to the North, the East, the West, the South, and the whole country

I take it, I hope, in good temper—certainly with no malice towards any section.   I shall do all that may be in my power to promote a peaceful settlement of all our difficulties.   The man does not live who is more devoted to peace than I am—none who would do more to preserve it.   But it may be necessary to put the foot down firmly.   And if I do my duty, and do right, you will sustain me, will you not ?   Received, as I am, by the members of a Legislature, the majority of whom do not agree with me in political sentiments, I trust that I may have their assistance in piloting the Ship of State through this voyage, surrounded by perils as it is ; for if it should suffer shipwreck now, there will be no pilot ever needed for another voyage."

On his arrival in Philadelphia, he was received with great enthusiasm, and to an address from the Mayor Mr. Lincoln replied :

"MR. MAYOR AND FELLOW-CITIZENS OF PHILADELPHIA :— I appear before you to make no lengthy speech but to thank you for this reception.   The reception you have given me to-night is not to me, the man, the individual, but to the man who temporarily represents, or should represent, the majesty of the nation.   It is true, as your worthy Mayor has said, that there is anxiety among the citizens of the United States at this time.   I deem it a happy circumstance that this dissatisfied portion of our fellow-citizens do not point us to any thing in which they are being injured, or are about to be injured ; for which reason I have felt all the while justified in concluding that the crisis, the panic, the anxiety of the country at this time, is artificial.   If there be those who differ with me upon this subject, they have not pointed out the substantial difficulty that exists.   I do not mean to say that an artificial panic may not do considerable harm ; that it has done such I do not deny.   The hope that has been expressed by your Mayor, that I may be able to restore peace, harmony, and prosperity to the country, is most worthy of him ; and

TO WASHINGTON. 85

Speech in Philadelphia.   Visits Independence Hall.   ·   The National Flag

happy indeed will I be if I shall be able to verify and fulfil that hope. I promise you, in all sincerity, that I bring to the work a sincere heart. Whether I will bring a head equal to that heart, will be for future times to determine. It were useless for me to speak of details or plans now; I shall speak officially next Monday week, if ever. If I should not speak then, it were useless for me to do so now. If I do speak then, it is useless for me to do so now. When I do speak, I shall take such grounds as I deem best calculated to restore peace, harmony, and prosperity to the country, and tend to the perpetuity of the nation, and the liberty of these States and these people. Your worthy Mayor has expressed the wish, in which I join with him, that if it were convenient for me to remain with your city long enough to consult your merchants and manufacturers; or, as it were, to listen to those breathings rising within the consecrated walls wherein the Constitution of the United States, and, I will add, the Declaration of Independence, were originally framed and adopted. I assure you and your Mayor, that I had hoped on this occasion, and upon all occasions during my life, that I shall do nothing inconsistent with the teachings of these holy and most sacred walls. I never asked any thing that does not breathe from those walls. All my political warfare has been in favor of the teachings that come forth from these sacred walls. May my right hand forget its cunning, and my tongue cleave to the roof of my mouth, if ever I prove false to those teachings. Fellow-citizens, now allow me to bid you good-night."

On the next morning Mr. Lincoln visited the old "Independence Hall," for the purpose of raising the national flag over it. Here he was received with a warm welcome, and made the following address:

"I am filled with deep emotion at finding myself standing here, in this place, where were collected the wisdom, the patriotism, the devotion to principle, from which sprang the

86   LIFE OF ABRAHAM LINCOLN.

At Independence Hall.   Solemn Memories.   The Declaration of Independence.

institutions under which we live. You have kindly suggested to me that in my hands is the task of restoring peace to the present distracted condition of the country. I can say in return, sir, that all the political sentiments I entertain have been drawn, so far as I have been able to draw them, from the sentiments which originated and were given to the world from this hall. I have never had a feeling politically that did not spring from the sentiments embodied in the Declaration of Independence. I have often pondered over the dangers which were incurred by the men who assembled here, and framed and adopted that Declaration of Independence. I have pondered over the toils that were endured by the officers and soldiers of the army who achieved that independence. I have often inquired of myself what great principle or idea it was that kept this Confederacy so long together. It was not the mere matter of the separation of the colonies from the mother-land, but that sentiment in the Declaration of Independence which gave liberty, not alone to the people of this country, but, I hope, to the world for all future time. It was that which gave promise that in due time the weight would be lifted from the shoulders of all men. This is a sentiment embodied in the Declaration of Independence. Now, my friends, can this country be saved upon this basis? If it can, I will consider myself one of the happiest men in the world if I can help to save it. If it cannot be saved upon that principle, it will be truly awful. But if this country cannot be saved without giving up that principle, I was about to say I would rather be assassinated on this spot than surrender it. Now, in my view of the present aspect of affairs, there need be no bloodshed or war. There is no necessity for it. I am not in favor of such a course, and I may say, in advance, that there will be no blood shed unless it be forced upon the government, and then it will be compelled to act in self-defence.

"My friends, this is wholly an unexpected speech, and I

did not expect to be called upon to say a word when I came here. I supposed it was merely to do something towards raising the flag. I may, therefore, have said something indiscreet. I have said nothing but what I am willing to live by, and, if it be the pleasure of Almighty God, to die by."

The party then proceeded to a platform erected in front of the State House, when the President-elect was invited to raise the flag. Mr. Lincoln responded in a brief speech, stating his cheerful compliance with the request, and alluded to the original flag of thirteen stars, saying that the number had increased as time rolled on, and we now became a happy and a powerful people, each star adding to its prosperity. "The future," he added, "is in the hands of the people. It is on such an occasion as this that we can reason together, reaffirm our devotion to the country and the principles of the Declaration of Independence. Let us make up our mind, that when we do put a new star upon our banner, it shall be a fixed one, never to be dimmed by the horrors of war, but brightened by the contentment and prosperity of peace. Let us go on to extend the area of our usefulness, add star upon star, until their light shall shine upon five hundred millions of a free and happy people."

The President-elect then raised the flag to the top of the staff.

At half-past 9 o'clock the party left for Harrisburg. Both Houses of the Legislature were visited by Mr. Lincoln, and to an address of welcome he thus replied:

"I appear before you only for a very few brief remarks, in response to what has been said to me. I thank you most sincerely for this reception, and the generous words in which support has been promised me upon this occasion. I thank your great commonwealth for the overwhelming support it recently gave, not to me personally, but the cause, which I think a just one, in the late election. Allusion has been made to the fact—the interesting fact, perhaps we should say

—that I, for the first time, appear at the Capital of the great Commonwealth of Pennsylvania upon the birthday of the Father of his Country, in connection with that beloved anniversary connected with the history of this country. I have already gone through one exceedingly interesting scene this morning in the ceremonies at Philadelphia. Under the high conduct of gentlemen there, I was, for the first time, allowed the privilege of standing in Old Independence Hall, to have a few words addressed to me there, and opening up to me an opportunity of expressing, with much regret, that I had not more time to express something of my own feelings, excited by the occasion, somewhat to harmonize and give shape to the feelings that had been really the feelings of my whole life. Besides this, our friends there had provided a magnificent flag of the country. They had arranged it so that I was given the honor of raising it to the head of its staff. And when it went up I was pleased that it went to its place by the strength of my own feeble arm; when, according to the arrangement, the cord was pulled, and it flaunted gloriously to the wind without an accident, in the bright glowing sunshine of the morning, I could not help hoping that there was in the entire success of that beautiful ceremony at least something of an omen of what is to come. Nor could I help feeling then, as I often have felt, in the whole of that proceeding, I was a very humble instrument. I had not provided the flag; I had not made the arrangements for elevating it to its place. I had applied but a very small portion of my feeble strength in raising it. In the whole transaction I was in the hands of the people who had arranged it; and if I can have the same generous coöperation of the people of the nation, I think the flag of our country may yet be kept flaunting gloriously. I recur for a moment but to repeat some words uttered at the hotel in regard to what has been said about the military support which the General Government may expect from the Commonwealth of Pennsylvania in a proper emergency.   To guard against any possible mistake do I recur to this.   It is not with any pleasure that I contemplate the possibility that a necessity may arise in this country for the use of the military arm.   While I am exceedingly gratified to see the manifestation upon your streets of your military force here, and exceedingly gratified at your promise here to use that force upon a proper emergency— while I make these acknowledgements, I desire to repeat, in order to preclude any possible misconstruction, that I do most sincerely hope that we shall have no use for them ; that it will never become their duty to shed blood, and most especially never to shed fraternal blood.   I promise that, so far as I have wisdom to direct, if so painful a result shall in any wise be brought about, it shall be through no fault of mine.   Allusion has also been made by one of your honored speakers to some remark recently made by myself at Pittsburg, in regard to what is supposed to be the especial interest of this great Commonwealth of Pennsylvania.   I now wish only to say, in regard to that matter, that the few remarks which I uttered on that occasion were rather carefully worded.   I took pains that they should be so.   I have seen no occasion since to add to them or subtract from them. I leave them precisely as they stand, adding only now, that I am pleased to have an expression from you, gentlemen of Pennsylvania, significant that they are satisfactory to you. And now, gentlemen of the General Assembly of the Commonwealth of Pennsylvania, allow me to return you again my most sincere thanks."

Arrangements had been made for his departure from Harrisburg on the following morning ; but the timely discovery of a plot to assassinate him on his way through Baltimore—a plot in which several of the leading citizens of that place were believed to be interested, although the work was to be done by other hands—caused a change in the schedule, and on the evening of the day on which he had been received by the Legislature, he left on a special train for Philadelphia, and thence proceeded in the sleeping-car attached to the regular midnight train to Washington, where he arrived at an early hour on the morning of the 23d.

As an evidence how little the extent to which unscrupulous men were prepared to go, was understood at this time, it may be remarked that not a few made themselves very merry over this midnight ride—a leading pictorial even indulging itself in an attempt at a humorous illustration of it, an act which, viewed in the light of a startling event but little more than four years later, in which a native of the same city was directly concerned, would hardly have been repeated.

CHAPTER VI.

THE NEW ADMINISTRATION.

Speeches at Washington — The Inaugural Address — Its Effect—The Cabinet—Commissioners from Montgomery—Extract from A. H. Stephens's speech—Virginia Commissioners—Fall of Fort Sumter.

A FEW days after his arrival in Washington, the President elect was waited upon by the Mayor and other municipal authorities, welcoming him the city, to whom he made the following reply :

" Mr. MAYOR : I thank you, and through you the municipal authorities of this city who accompany you, for this welcome. And as it is the first time in my life since the present phase of politics has presented itself in this country, that I have said anything publicly within a region of country where the institution of slavery exists, I will take this occasion to say that I think very much of the ill feeling which has existed, and still exists, between the people in the sections from whence I came and the people here, is dependent upon a misunderstanding of one another. I therefore avail myself of this opportunity to assure you, Mr. Mayor, and all the gentlemen present, that I have not now, and never have had, any other than as kindly feelings towards you as towards the people of my own section. I have not now, nor never have had, any disposition to treat you in any respect otherwise than as my own neighbors. I have not now any purpose to withhold from you any of the benefits of the Constitution, under any circumstances, that I would not feel myself constrained to withhold from my neighbors; and I hope, in a word, that when we shall become better acquainted, and I say it with great confidence, we shall like each other the more. I thank you for the kindness of this reception."

On the following evening, at the close of a serenade tendered him by the Republican Association, he thus addressed the crowd:

"MY FRIENDS: I suppose that I may take this as a compliment paid to me, and as such please accept my thanks for it. I have reached this city of Washington under circumstances considerably differing from those under which any other man has ever reached it. I am here for the purpose of taking an official position amongst the people, almost all of whom were politically opposed to me, and are yet opposed to me as I suppose. I propose no lengthy address to you. I only propose to say, as I did on yesterday, when your worthy Mayor and Board of Aldermen called upon me, that I thought much of the ill feeling that has existed between you and the people of your surroundings and that people from amongst whom I came, has depended, and now depends, upon a misunderstanding.

"I hope that, if things shall go on as prosperously as I believe we all desire they may, I may have it in my power to remove something of this misunderstanding, that I may be enabled to convince you, and the people of your section of the country, that we regard you as in all things our equals, and in all things entitled to the same respect and the same treat-

ment that we claim for ourselves ; that we are in nowise disposed, if it were in our power, to oppress you, to deprive
you of any of your rights under the Constitution of the
United States, or even narrowly to split hairs with you in
regard to those rights, but are determined to give you, as far
as lies in our hands, all your rights under the Constitution—
not grudgingly, but fully and fairly. I hope that, by thus
dealing with you, we will become better acquainted, and be
better friends. And now, my friends, with these few remarks, and again returning my thanks for this compliment,
and expressing my desire to hear a little more of your good
music, I bid you good-night."

Never, in the history of the country, has the inaugural
address of any President been so anxiously awaited as was
that of Mr. Lincoln. The most of his countrymen, even in
States whose loyalty to the Government was beyond suspicion, were certain to be disappointed, whatever that inaugural might prove to be. An impression prevailed, for which
no good grounds could be shown, that somehow, in some in-
explicable way, this particular address would operate as a
panacea to heal the nation's malady. One class, who knew
not the man, hoped, almost against hope, that such concessions would be made to the rebels as would bridge over existing difficulties, and restore the good old times when men
could vend their goods and principles—or what served them
in lieu thereof—without being annoyed by war or rumor of
war. Another would be satisfied with nothing short of the
most positive and unqualified denunciations of the rebels,
coupled with the details in advance of dealing with them.
Still another were simply curious in the premises to know
what could be said. Whisperings, too, that the address would
be prevented by violence, and hints of assassination were
heard here and there.

All necessary precautions, however, having been taken to
guard against the latter contingencies, Mr. Lincoln appeared

at the east front of the capitol, and received, at the hour appointed, the oath of office from Chief Justice Taney.   Then followed, in a clear, steady tone of voice, in the presence of more than ten thousand of his fellow-citizens, the address :

"FELLOW-CITIZENS OF THE UNITED STATES :—In compliance with a custom as old as the Government itself, I appear before you to address you briefly, and to take, in your presence, the oath prescribed by the Constitution of the United States to be taken by the President before he enters on the execution of his office.

"I do not consider it necessary, at present, for me to discuss those matters of administration about which there is no special anxiety or excitement.   Apprehension seems to exist among the people of the Southern States, that, by the accession of a Republican Administration, their property and their peace and personal security are to be endangered.   There has never been any reasonable cause for such apprehension. Indeed, the most ample evidence to the contrary has all the while existed, and been open to their inspection.   It is found in nearly all the published speeches of him who now addresses you.   I do but quote from one of those speeches, when I declare that 'I have no purpose, directly or indirectly, to interfere with the institution of slavery in the States where it exists.'   I believe I have no lawful right to do so ; and I have no inclination to do so.   Those who nominated and elected me, did so with the full knowledge that I had made this, and made many similar declarations, and had never recanted them.   And, more than this, they placed in the platform, for my acceptance, and as a law to themselves and to me, the clear and emphatic resolution which I now read :

" 'Resolved, That the maintenance inviolate of the rights of the States, and especially the right of each State to order and control its own domestic institutions according to its own judgment exclusively, is essential to that balance of power on which the perfection and endurance of our political fabric depend ; and we denounce the lawless invasion, by armed force, of the soil of any State or Territory, no matter under what pretext, as among the gravest of crimes.'

"I now reiterate these sentiments ; and in doing so I only press upon the public attention the most conclusive evidence of which the case is susceptible, that the property, peace and security of no section are to be in anywise endangered by the now incoming administration.

"I add, too, that all the protection which, consistently with the Constitution and the laws, can be given, will be cheerfully given to all the States when lawfully demanded, for whatever cause, as cheerfully to one section as to another.

"There is much controversy about the delivering up of fugitives from service or labor. The clause I now read is as plainly written in the Constitution as any other of its provisions :

"'No person held to service or labor in one State under the laws thereof, escaping into another, shall, in consequence of any law or regulation therein, be discharged from such service or labor, but shall be delivered up on claim of the party to whom such service or labor may be due.'

"It is scarcely questioned that this provision was intended by those who made it for the reclaiming of what we call fugitive slaves ; and the intention of the lawgiver is the law.

"All members of Congress swear their support to the whole Constitution—to this provision as well as any other. To the proposition, then, that slaves whose cases come within the terms of this clause 'shall be delivered up,' their oaths are unanimous. Now, if they would make the effort in good temper, could they not, with nearly equal unanimity, frame and pass a law by means of which to keep good that unanimous oath ?

"There is some difference of opinion whether this clause should be enforced by National or by State authority ; but surely that difference is not a very material one. If the slave is to be surrendered, it can be of but little consequence to him or to others by which authority it is done ; and should any one, in any case, be content that this oath shall go unkept on a merely unsubstantial controversy as to how it shall be kept ?

" Again, in any law upon this subject, ought not all the safeguards of liberty known in civilized and humane jurisprudence to be introduced, so that a free man be not, in any case, surrendered as a slave ?   And might it not be well at the same time to provide by law for the enforcement of that clause in the Constitution which guarantees that ' the citizens of each State shall be entitled to all the privileges and immunities of citizens in the several States ? '

" I take the official oath to-day with no mental reservations, and with no purpose to construe the Constitution or laws by any hypercritical rules ; and while I do not choose now to specify particular acts of Congress as proper to be enforced, I do suggest that it will be much safer for all, both in official and private stations, to conform to and abide by all those acts which stand unrepealed, than to violate any of them, trusting to find impunity in having them held to be unconstitutional.

" It is seventy-two years since the first inauguration of a President under our National Constitution. During that period, fifteen different and very distinguished citizens have in succession administered the executive branch of the Government. They have conducted it through many perils, and generally with great success. Yet, with all this scope for precedent, I now enter upon the same task, for the brief constitutional term of four years, under great and peculiar difficulties.

" A disruption of the Federal Union, heretofore only menaced, is now formidably attempted. I hold that in the contemplation of universal law and of the Constitution, the Union of these States is perpetual. Perpetuity is implied, if not expressed, in the fundamental law of all national governments.

It is safe to assert that no government proper ever had a provision in its organic law for its own termination. Continue to execute all the express provisions of our National Constitution, and the Union will endure forever, it being impossible to destroy it, except by some action not provided for in the instrument itself.

"Again, if the United States be not a government proper, but an association of States in the nature of a contract merely, can it, as a contract, be peaceably unmade by less than all the parties who made it? One party to a contract may violate it—break it, so to speak; but does it not require all to lawfully rescind it? Descending from these general principles, we find the proposition that in legal contemplation the Union is perpetual, confirmed by the history of the Union itself.

"The Union is much older than the Constitution. It was formed, in fact, by the Articles of Association in 1774. It was matured and continued in the Declaration of Independence in 1776. It was further matured, and the faith of all the then thirteen States expressly plighted and engaged that it should be perpetual, by the Articles of the Confederation, in 1778; and, finally, in 1787, one of the declared objects for ordaining and establishing the Constitution was to form a more perfect Union. But if the destruction of the Union by one or by a part only of the States be lawfully possible, the Union is less than before, the Constitution having lost the vital element of perpetuity.

"It follows from these views that no State, upon its own mere motion, can lawfully get out of the Union; that resolves and ordinances to that effect, are legally void; and that acts of violence within any State or States against the authority of the United States, are insurrectionary or revolutionary, according to circumstances.

"I therefore consider that, in view of the Constitution and the laws, the Union is unbroken, and, to the extent of my ability, I shall take care, as the Constitution itself expressly enjoins upon me, that the laws of the Union shall be faithfully executed in all the States. Doing this, which I deem to be only a simple duty on my part, I shall perfectly perform it, so far as is practicable, unless my rightful masters, the American people, shall withold the requisition, or in some authoritative manner direct the contrary.

" I trust this will not be regarded as a menace, but only as the declared purpose of the Union that it will constitutionally defend and maintain itself.

" In doing this there need be no bloodshed or violence, and there shall be none unless it is forced upon the National authority.

" The power confided to me *will be used to hold, occupy, and possess the property and places belonging to the Government,* and collect the duties and imposts; but beyond what may be necessary for these objects there will be no invasion, no using of force against or among the people anywhere.

" Where hostility to the United States shall be so great and so universal as to prevent competent resident citizens from holding Federal offices, there will be no attempt to force obnoxious strangers among the people that object. While the strict legal right may exist of the Government to enforce the exercise of these offices, the attempt to do so would be so irritating, and so nearly impracticable withal, that I deem it best to forego, for the time, the uses of such offices.

" The mails, unless repelled, will continue to be furnished in all parts of the Union.

" So far as possible, the people everywhere shall have that sense of perfect security which is most favorable to calm thought and reflection.

" The course here indicated will be followed, unless current events and experience shall show a modification or change to be proper ; and in every case and exigency my best discretion will be exercised according to the circumstances actually existing, and with a view and hope of a peaceful solution of the

7

National troubles, and the restoration of fraternal sympathies and affections.

"That there are persons, in one section or another, who seek to destroy the Union at all events, and are glad of any pretext to do it, I will neither affirm nor deny. But if there be such, I need address no word to them.

"To those, however, who really love the Union, may I not speak, before entering upon so grave a matter as the destruction of our National fabric, with all its benefits, its memories, and its hopes? Would it not be well to ascertain why we do it? Will you hazard so desperate a step, while any portion of the ills you fly from have no real existence? Will you, while the certain ills you fly to are greater than all the real ones you fly from? Will you risk the commission of so fearful a mistake? All profess to be content in the Union if all constitutional rights can be maintained. Is it true, then, that any right, plainly written in the Constitution, has been denied? I think not. Happily the human mind is so constituted, that no party can reach to the audacity of doing this.

"Think, if you can, of a single instance in which a plainly-written provision of the Constitution has ever been denied. If, by the mere force of numbers, a majority should deprive a minority of any clearly-written constitutional right, it might, in a moral point of view, justify revolution; it certainly would, if such right were a vital one. But such is not our case.

"All the vital rights of minorities and of individuals are so plainly assured to them by affirmations and negations, guaranties and prohibitions in the Constitution, that controversies never arise concerning them. But no organic law can ever be framed with a provision specifically applicable to every question which may occur in practical administration. No foresight can anticipate, nor any document of reasonable length contain, express provisions for all possible questions. Shall fugitives from labor be surrendered by National or by

State authorities?   The Constitution does not expressly say. Must Congress protect slavery in the Territories?   The Constitution does not expressly say.   From questions of this class, spring all our constitutional controversies, and we divide upon them into majorities and minorities.

" If the minority will not acquiesce, the majority must, or the Government must cease.   There is no alternative for continuing the Government but acquiescence on the one side or the other.   If a minority in such a case will secede rather than acquiesce, they make a precedent which, in turn, will ruin and divide them, for a minority of their own will secede from them whenever a majority refuses to be controlled by such a minority.   For instance, why not any portion of a new Confederacy, a year or two hence, arbitrarily secede again, precisely as portions of the present Union now claim to secede from it?   All who cherish disunion sentiments are now being educated to the exact temper of doing this.   Is there such perfect identity of interests among the States to compose a new Union as to produce harmony only, and prevent renewed secession?   Plainly, the central idea of secession is the essence of anarchy.

"A majority held in restraint by constitutional check and limitation, and always changing easily with deliberate changes of popular opinions and sentiments, is the only true sovereign of a free people.   Whoever rejects it, does, of necessity, fly to anarchy or to despotism.   Unanimity is impossible; the rule of a majority, as a permanent arrangement, is wholly inadmissible.   So that, rejecting the majority principle, anarchy or despotism, in some form, is all that is left.

" I do not forget the position assumed by some that constitutional questions are to be decided by the Supreme Court, nor do I deny that such decisions must be binding in any case upon the parties to a suit, as to the object of that suit, while they are also entitled to a very high respect and consideration in all parallel cases by all other departments of the

Government; and while it is obviously possible that such decision may be erroneous in any given case, still the evil effect following it, being limited to that particular case, with the chance that it may be overruled and never become a precedent for other cases, can better be borne than could the evils of a different practice.

"At the same time the candid citizen must confess that if the policy of the Government upon the vital question affecting the whole people is to be irrevocably fixed by the decisions of the Supreme Court, the instant they are made, as in ordinary litigation between parties in personal actions, the people will have ceased to be their own masters, unless having to that extent practically resigned their Government into the hands of that eminent tribunal.

" Nor is there in this view any assault upon the Court or the Judges.   It is a duty from which they may not shrink, to decide cases properly brought before them ; and it is no fault of theirs if others seek to turn their decisions to political purposes.   One section of our country believes slavery is right and ought to be extended, while the other believes it is wrong and ought not to be extended ; and this is the only substantial dispute ; and the fugitive slave clause of the Constitution, and the law for the suppression of the foreign slave-trade, are each as well enforced, perhaps, as any law can ever be in a community where the moral sense of the people imperfectly supports the law itself.   The great body of the people abide by the dry legal obligation in both cases, and a few break over in each.   This, I think, can not be perfectly cured, and it would be worse in both cases after the separation of the sections than before.   The foreign slave-trade, now imperfectly suppressed, would be ultimately revived, without restriction, in one section ; while fugitive slaves, now only partially surrendered, would not be surrendered at all by the other.

" Physically speaking we can not separate ; we can not

remove our respective sections from each other, nor build an impassable wall between them. A husband and wife may be divorced, and go out of the presence and beyond the reach of each other, but the different parts of our country can not do this. They can not but remain face to face; and intercourse, either amicable or hostile, must continue between them. Is it possible, then, to make that intercourse more advantageous or more satisfactory after separation than before? Can aliens make treaties easier than friends can make laws? Can treaties be more faithfully enforced between aliens than laws can among friends? Suppose you go to war, you can not fight always; and when, after much loss on both sides, and no gain on either, you cease fighting, the identical questions as to terms of intercourse are again upon you.

" This country, with its institutions, belongs to the people who inhabit it. Whenever they shall grow weary of the existing government, they can exercise their constitutional right of amending, or their revolutionary right to dismember or overthrow it. · I can not be ignorant of the fact that many worthy and patriotic citizens are desirous of having the National Constitution amended. While I make no recommendation of amendment, I fully recognize the full authority of the people over the whole subject, to be exercised in either of the modes prescribed in the instrument itself, and I should, under existing circumstances, favor rather than oppose, a fair opportunity being afforded the people to act upon it.

" I will venture to add, that to me the Convention mode seems preferable, in that it allows amendments to originate with the people themselves, instead of only permitting them to take or reject propositions originated by others not especially chosen for the purpose, and which might not be precisely such as they would wish either to accept or refuse. I understand that a proposed amendment to the Constitution (which amendment, however, I have not seen) has passed Congress, to the effect that the Federal Government shall never interfere with the domestic institutions of States, including that of persons held to service.   To avoid misconstruction of what I have said, I depart from my purpose not to speak of particular amendments, so far as to say that, holding such a provision to now be implied constitutional law, I have no objection to its being made express and irrevocable.

"The Chief Magistrate derives all his authority from the people, and they have conferred none upon him to fix the terms for the separation of the States.   The people themselves, also, can do this if they choose, but the Executive, as such, has nothing to do with it.   His duty is to administer the present government as it came to his hands, and to transmit it unimpaired by him to his successor.   Why should there not be a patient confidence in the ultimate justice of the people?   Is there any better or equal hope in the world?   In our present differences is either party without faith of being in the right?   If the Almighty Ruler of nations, with his eternal truth and justice, be on your side of the North, or on yours of the South, that truth and that justice will surely prevail by the judgment of this great tribunal, the American people.   By the frame of the government under which we live, this same people have wisely given their public servants but little power for mischief, and have with equal wisdom provided for the return of that little to their own hands at very short intervals.   While the people retain their virtue and vigilance, no administration, by any extreme wickedness or folly, can very seriously injure the government in the short space of four years.

"My countrymen, one and all, think calmly and well upon this whole subject.   Nothing valuable can be lost by taking time.

"If there be an object to hurry any of you, in hot haste, to a step which you would never take deliberately, that object will be frustrated by taking time : but no good object can be frustrated by it.

"Such of you as are now dissatisfied, still have the old Constitution unimpaired, and on the sensitive point, the laws of your own framing under it; while the new administration will have no immediate power, if it would, to change either.

"If it were admitted that you who are dissatisfied hold the right side in the dispute, there is still no single reason for precipitate action. Intelligence, patriotism, Christianity, and a firm reliance on Him who has never yet forsaken this favored land, are still competent to adjust, in the best way, all our present difficulties.

"In your hands, my dissatisfied fellow-countrymen, and not in mine, is the momentous issue of civil war. The Government will not assail you.

"You can have no conflict without being yourselves the aggressors. You have no oath registered in Heaven to destroy the Government; while I shall have the most solemn one to 'preserve, protect, and defend' it.

"I am loath to close. We are not enemies, but friends We must not be enemies. Though passion may have strained, it must not break our bonds of affection.

"The mystic cords of memory, stretching from every battlefield and patriot grave to every living heart and hearthstone all over this broad land, will yet swell the chorus of the Union, when again touched, as surely they will be, by the better angels of our nature."

One point was established, at least, by this inaugural, whatever uncertainties might cluster about it—we had, at last, a Government. No Buchanan ruled the hour. Loyal men of every shade breathed more freely. At the same time, the whole drift was toward securing, if possible, an honorable reconciliation. If, after this lucid, temperate statement of the plans and purposes of the new Administration, the blow must fall, which all wished to avoid, it was encouraging to feel—as every one who heard Mr. Lincoln on that eventful day must have felt—that a man was at the helm who had firm faith that the organic law, so far from providing for the dissolution of the Union, had vitality and force within itself sufficient to defend the nation against dangers from within as well as from without.

The announcement of the President's cabinet, likewise—composed, as it was, of the ablest men in his own party, the majority of whom had been deemed worthy of presentation as candidates for the high office which he held—imparted confidence to all who wished well to the country. The able pen of the Secretary of State was at once called into requisition to communicate, through the newly appointed ministers abroad, the true state of affairs to the European powers. As speedily as possible the Departments were purged of disloyal officials, although the deceptions and subterfuges which constituted a goodly portion of the stock in trade of the rebellion rendered this a work of more time than was satisfactory to many.

The Davis dynasty, at Montgomery, having, on the 9th of March, passed an act to organize a Confederate army, two persons—one from Alabama and the other from Georgia—announced themselves, three days later, as "Confederate Commissioners," accredited for the purpose of negotiating a treaty. The President declined to recognize these "Commissioners," who were referred to a copy of his inaugural enclosed for a full statement of his views.

On the 21st of March, Alexander H. Stephens, of Georgia, Vice-President of the Montgomery traitors, up to that time regarded as one of the most moderate—as he certainly was one of the ablest—of the conspirators, in a speech at Savannah, silenced all questionings as to the intent of himself and co-workers.

He said on that occasion :

" The new Constitution (that adopted at Montgomery) has put at rest forever all the agitating questions relating to our peculiar institutions—African slavery as it exists among us —the proper status of the negro in our form of civilization. This was the immediate cause of the late rupture and present revolution.   Jefferson, in his forecast, had anticipated this as the rock upon which the old Union would split.   He was right. What was conjecture with him, is now a realized fact. But whether he fully comprehended the great truth upon which that rock stood and stands, may be doubted.   The prevailing ideas, entertained by him and most of the leading statesmen, at the time of the formation of the old Constitution, were, that the enslavement of the African was in violation of the laws of nature ; that it was wrong in principle, socially, morally, and politically.   It was an evil they knew not well how to deal with ; but the general opinion of the men of that day was, that, somehow or other, in the order of Providence, the institution would be evanescent and pass away.   *   *   *   *   *   *   *

" Our new Government is founded upon exactly the opposite ideas.   Its foundations are laid, its corner-stone rests upon the great truth that the negro is not equal to the white man ; that slavery, subordination to the superior race, is his natural and normal condition.   This, our new Government, is the first in the history of the world based upon this great physical, philosophical, and moral truth. *   *   *   *   It is upon this, as I have stated, our social fabric is firmly planted ; and I can not permit myself to doubt the ultimate success of a full recognition of this principle throughout the civilized and enlightened world.   *   *   *   *   This stone, which was rejected by the first builders, ' is become the chief stone of the corner' in our new edifice."

On the 13th of April, the President was waited upon by a committee from a Convention of the State of Virginia, which Convention was discussing the question whether to go with the States already in rebellion, or to remain in the Union, for the sake of furthering the ends of the rebels. The object of the visit, and its result, may be determined from Mr. Lincoln's response :

" GENTLEMEN :—As a committee of the Virginia Convention, now in session, you present me a preamble and resolution, in these words :

" 'WHEREAS, In the opinion of this Convention, the uncertainty which prevails in the public mind as to the policy which the Federal Executive intends to pursue towards the seceded States is extremely injurious to the industrial and commercial interests of the country, tends to keep up an excitement which is unfavorable to the adjustment of the pending difficulties, and threatens a disturbance of the public peace ; therefore,

" *Resolved*, That a committee of three delegates be appointed to wait on the President of the United States, present to him this preamble, and respectfully ask him to communicate to this Convention the policy which the Federal Executive intends to pursue in regard to the Confederate States.'

" In answer, I have to say, that having, at the beginning of my official term, expressed my intended policy as plainly as I was able, it is with deep regret and mortification I now learn there is great and injurious uncertainty in the public mind as to what that policy is, and what course I intend to pursue. Not having as yet seen occasion to change, it is now my purpose to pursue the course marked out in the inaugural address. I commend a careful consideration of the whole document as the best expression I can give to my purposes. As I then and therein said, I now repeat, 'The power confided in me, will be used to hold, occupy, and possess property and places belonging to the Government, and to collect the duties and imposts ; but beyond what is necessary for these objects, there will be no invasion, no using of force against or among the people anywhere.' By the words 'property and places belonging to the Government,' I chiefly allude to the military posts and property which were in possession of the government when it came into my hands. But if, as now appears to be true, in pursuit of a purpose to drive the United States authority from these places, an unprovoked assault has been made upon Fort Sumter, I shall hold myself at liberty to repossess it, if I can, like places which had been seized before the Government was devolved upon me, and in any event I shall, to the best of my ability, repel force by force. In case it proves true that Fort Sumter has been assaulted, as is reported, I shall, perhaps, cause the United States mails to be withdrawn from all the States which claim to have seceded, believing that the commencement of actual war against the Government justifies and possibly demands it. I scarcely need to say that I consider the military forts and property, situated within the States which claim to have seceded, as yet belonging to the Government of the United States, as much as they did before the supposed secession. Whatever else I may do for the purpose, I shall not attempt to collect the duties and imposts by any armed invasion of any part of the country—not meaning by this, however, that I may not land a force deemed necessary to relieve a fort upon the border of the country. From the fact that I have quoted a part of the inaugural address, it must not be inferred that I repudiate any other part, the whole of which I reaffirm, except so far as what I now say of the mails may be regarded as a modification."

Fort Sumter fell on the day following the reception of these commissioners, after every effort, consistent with the means at the disposal of the government, had been made to prevent what then seemed a catastrophe. This action could bear but one interpretation. A reconciliation of difficulties was utterly impracticable. An appeal had been made to the sword.

The power and authority of the United States had been defied and insulted. No loyal man could now hesitate. If, however, there were any who, even then, clung to the fallacy that compromise could save us, Abraham Lincoln was not of the number.

CHAPTER VII.

PREPARING FOR WAR.

Effects of Sumter's Fall—President's Call for Troops—Response in the Loyal States—In the Border States—Baltimore Riot—Maryland's Position—President's Letter to Maryland Authorities—Blockade Proclamation—Additional Proclamation—Comments Abroad —Second Call for Troops—Special Order for Florida—Military Movements.

SUMTER fell, but the nation arose. With one mind the Free States determined that the rebellion must be put down. All were ablaze with patriotic fire. The traitors at heart, who lurked in the loyal States, found it a wise precaution to float with the current. The shrewder ones among them saw well how such a course would give them vantage-ground when the reaction, which they hoped, and for which in secret they labored, should come. But the great mass of the people would not have admitted the possibility of any reaction— action was to continue the order of the day until the business in hand was finished.

On the 15th of April, 1861, the President issued his first proclamation:

"WHEREAS, The laws of the United States have been for some time past, and now are opposed, and the execution thereof obstructed, in the States of South Carolina, Georgia, Alabama, Florida, Mississippi, Louisiana, and Texas, by combinations too powerful to be suppressed by the ordinary course of judicial proceedings, or by the powers vested in the marshals by law ; now, therefore, I, ABRAHAM LINCOLN,

President of the United States, in virtue of the power in me vested by the Constitution and the laws, have thought fit to call forth, and hereby do call forth, the militia of the several States of the Union to the aggregate number of seventy-five thousand, in order to suppress said combinations and to cause the laws to be duly executed.

"The details for this object will be immediately communicated to the State authorities through the War Department. I appeal to all loyal citizens to favor, facilitate, and aid this effort to maintain the honor, the integrity, and existence of our national Union, and the perpetuity of popular government, and to redress wrongs already long enough endured. I deem it proper to say that the first service assigned to the forces hereby called forth, will probably be to repossess the forts, places, and property which have been seized from the Union; and in every event the utmost care will be observed, consistently with the objects aforesaid, to avoid any devastation, any destruction of, or interference with property, or any disturbance of peaceful citizens of any part of the country; and I hereby command the persons composing the combinations aforesaid, to disperse and retire peaceably to their respective abodes, within twenty days from this date.

"Deeming that the present condition of public affairs presents an extraordinary occasion, I do hereby, in virtue of the power in me vested by the Constitution, convene both Houses of Congress. The Senators and Representatives are, therefore, summoned to assemble at their respective chambers at twelve o'clock, noon, on Thursday, the fourth day of July next, then and there to consider and determine such measures as, in their wisdom, the public safety and interest may seem to demand.

"In witness whereof, I have hereunto set my hand, and caused the seal of the United States to be affixed.

"Done at the City of Washington, this fifteenth day of April, in the year of our Lord, one thousand eight hundred

110   LIFE OF ABRAHAM LINCOLN.

Response to the Call.   Border Slave States.   First Blood Shed.

and sixty-one, and of the independence of the United States the eighty-fifth.

"By the President: ABRAHAM LINCOLN.

"WILLIAM H. SEWARD, Secretary of State."

In response to this proclamation enthusiastic public meetings were held throughout the loyal States; all party lines seemed obliterated; enlistments were almost universal; Washington, which was at one time in imminent danger, was soon considered amply defended. The majority entertained no doubt that with the force summoned the rebellion would be nipped in the bud; the more sagacious minority shook their heads, and wished that a million of men had been asked.

An excellent opportunity was afforded to the border slave States for pronouncing their election—whether to stand by the Government, or, practically, to furnish aid and comfort to the rebels. Magoffin, Governor of Kentucky, was soon heard from: "Kentucky will furnish no troops," said he, "for the wicked purpose of subduing her sister Southern States." Letcher, of Virginia: "The militia of Virginia will not be furnished to the powers at Washington for any such case or purpose as they have in view;" and on the 17th, the State was dragooned into passing, in secret, an ordinance of secession, and immediately commenced those warlike preparations, whose evil fruits she was destined so soon and in so much sorrow to reap. The Executives of Tennessee and North Carolina refused compliance; and those States, together with Arkansas, went over to the "Confederacy."

How was the call for troops received by the rebel conclave at Montgomery? They laughed.

The first blood shed in the war was in the streets of Baltimore, on the 19th of April. Massachusetts troops, passing through that city for the defence of the common capitol, were attacked by a mob, instigated and encouraged by men of property and social standing. The State hung trembling in the balancé between loyalty and treason. Had its geographical position been other than it was, it would have undeniably embraced the fortune of the South. Its Governor was, however, strongly inclined to support the Government, although the peculiar circumstances in which he was placed called for peculiar tact and dexterity in management. It was seriously proposed that no more troops should be sent through Baltimore.

The day following this attack, the President sent the following letter in reply to a communication broaching this modest proposition :

       " *Washington,* April 20th, 1861.

" GOVERNOR HICKS AND MAYOR BROWN :

" GENTLEMEN :—Your letter by Messrs. Bond, Dobbin, and Brune, is received. I tender you both my sincere thanks for your efforts to keep the peace in the trying situation in which you are placed. For the future, troops *must* be brought here, but I make no point of bringing them *through* Baltimore.

" Without any military knowledge myself, of course I must leave details to General Scott. He hastily said this morning in presence of those gentlemen, ' March them *around* Baltimore, and not through it.'   .

" I sincerely hope the General, on fuller reflection, will consider this practical and proper, and that you will not object to it. By this a collision of the people of Baltimore with the troops will be avoided, unless they go out of the way to seek it. I hope you will exert your influence to prevent this. Now and ever, I shall do all in my power for peace, consistently with the maintenance of government.

     " Your obedient servant,

       "A. LINCOLN."

To a delegation of rebel sympathizers from the same State, who demanded a cessation of hostilities until Congress should assemble, and accompanied their demand with the statement that seventy-five thousand Marylanders would dispute the passage of any more United States troops over the soil of that State, he quietly remarked that he presumed there was room enough in the State to bury that number, and declined to accede to their proposal. The Maryland imbroglio was, after no great time, adjusted, and ample precautions taken to guard against any future trouble in that quarter.

On the 19th of April, every port of the States in rebellion was declared blockaded by the following proclamation :

"WHEREAS, An insurrection against the Government of the United States has broken out in the States of South Carolina, Georgia, Alabama, Florida, Mississippi, Louisiana, and Texas, and the laws of the United States for the collection of the revenue can not be efficiently executed therein conformably to that provision of the Constitution which requires duties to be uniform throughout the United States :

"AND WHEREAS, A combination of persons, engaged in such insurrection, have threatened to grant pretended letters of marque to authorize the bearers thereof to commit assaults on the lives, vessels, and property of good citizens of the country lawfully engaged in commerce on the high seas, and in waters of the United States :

"AND WHEREAS, An Executive Proclamation has already been issued, requiring the persons engaged in these disorderly proceedings to desist therefrom, calling out a militia force for the purpose of repressing the same, and convening Congress in extraordinary session to deliberate and determine thereon :

"Now, therefore, I, Abraham Lincoln, President of the United States, with a view to the same purposes before mentioned, and to the protection of the public peace, and the lives and property of quiet and orderly citizens pursuing their lawful occupations, until Congress shall have assembled and deliberated on the said unlawful proceedings, or until the same shall have ceased, have further deemed it advisable to set on foot a blockade of the ports within the States aforesaid, in pursuance of the laws of the United States, and of the laws of nations in such cases provided. For this purpose a competent force will be posted so as to prevent entrance and exit of vessels from the ports aforesaid. If, therefore, with a view to violate such blockade, a vessel shall approach, or shall attempt to leave any of the said ports, she will be duly warned by the commander of one of the blockading vessels, who will indorse on her register the fact and date of such warning; and if the same vessel shall again attempt to enter or leave the blockaded port, she will be captured and sent to the nearest convenient port, for such proceedings against her and her cargo as prize, as may be deemed advisable.

" And I hereby proclaim and declare, that if any person, under the pretended authority of said States, or under any other pretence, shall molest a vessel of the United States, or the persons or cargo on board of her, such person will be held amenable to the laws of the United States for the prevention and punishment of piracy.

" By the President :   ABRAHAM LINCOLN.

" WILLIAM H. SEWARD, Secretary of State."

On the 27th of April, the following additional proclamation was issued :

" WHEREAS, For the reasons assigned in my proclamation of the 19th instant, a blockade of the ports of the States of South Carolina, Georgia, Florida, Alabama, Louisiana, Mississippi, and Texas was ordered to be established ; AND WHEREAS, since that date public property of the United States has been seized, the collection of the revenue obstructed, and duly commissioned officers of the United States, while engaged in executing the orders of their superiors, have been arrested and held in custody as prisoners, or have been impeded in the discharge of their official duties, without due legal process, by persons claiming to act under authority of the States of Virginia and North Carolina, an efficient blockade of the ports of these States will therefore also be established.

"In witness whereof, I have hereunto set my hand, and caused the seal of the United States to be affixed.

"Done at the City of Washington, this 27th day of April, in the year of our Lord one thousand eight hundred and sixty-one, and of the independence of the United States the eighty-fifth.

"By the President:　　　　　　ABRAHAM LINCOLN.

"WILLIAM H. SEWARD, Secretary of State."

This greatly affected the commercial interests of the European powers, who made haste to announce that the blockade must be an effectual one, in order to be respected ; supposing, in common with the rebels, that they were demanding what would prove to be an impossibility.　To say that they erred decidedly in this opinion, is but stating a matter of general notoriety, and simply adds another to the list of serious mistakes made, during the progress of the war, by the two European nations most deeply interested in its issue.

It was soon perceived that more men would be needed in the field, Davis, in a message to his Congress, having proposed "to organize and hold in readiness for instant action, in view of the exigencies of the country, an army of six hundred thousand men."　On the 3d of May, accordingly, another call was made, in anticipation of its ratification at the extra session of Congress, which ratification took place, without opposition.

"WHEREAS, Existing exigencies demand immediate and adequate measures for the protection of the national Constitution and the preservation of the national Union by the suppression of the insurrectionary combinations now existing in several States for opposing the laws of the Union and obstructing the execution thereof, to which end a military force, in addition to that called forth by my Proclamation of the fifteenth day of April, in the present year, appears to be indispensably necessary, now, therefore, I, Abraham Lincoln, President of the United States, and Commander-in-chief of the Army and Navy thereof, and of the militia of the several States, when called into actual service, do hereby call into the service of the United States forty-two thousand and thirty-four volunteers, to serve for a period of three years, unless sooner discharged, and to be mustered into service as infantry and cavalry. The proportions of each arm, and the details of enrolment and organization will be made known through the Department of War; and I also direct that the regular army of the United States be increased by the addition of eight regiments of infantry, one regiment of cavalry, and one regiment of artillery, making altogether a maximum aggregate increase of twenty-two thousand seven hundred and fourteen officers and enlisted men, the details of which increase will also be made known through the Department of War; and I further direct the enlistment, for not less than one nor more than three years, of eighteen thousand seamen, in addition to the present force, for the naval service of the United States. The details of the enlistment and organization will be made known through the Department of the Navy. The call for volunteers, hereby made, and the direction of the increase of the regular army, and for the enlistment of seamen hereby given, together with the plan of organization adopted for the volunteers and for the regular forces hereby authorized, will be submitted to Congress as soon as assembled.

ꞏ "In the meantime, I earnestly invoke the coöperation of all good citizens in the measures hereby adopted for the effectual suppression of unlawful violence, for the impartial enforcement of constitutional laws, and for the speediest possible restoration of peace and order, and with those of happiness and prosperity throughout our country.

"In testimony whereof, I have hereunto set my hand, and caused the seal of the United States to be affixed.

"Done at the City of Washington, this third day of May, in the year of our Lord one thousand eight hundred and sixty-one, and of the Independence of the United States the eighty-fifth.

    "By the President: ABRAHAM LINCOLN.

"WILLIAM H. SEWARD, Secretary of State."

On the 10th of May, 1861, the following proclamation was promulgated:

"WHEREAS, An insurrection exists in the State of Florida, by which the lives, liberty, and property of loyal citizens of the United States are endangered.

"AND WHEREAS, It is deemed proper that all needful measures should be taken for the protection of such citizens and all officers of the United States in the discharge of their public duties in the State aforesaid.

"Now, therefore, be it known that I, Abraham Lincoln, President of the United States, do hereby direct the commander of the forces of the United States on the Florida coast to permit no person to exercise any office or authority upon the islands of Key West, the Tortugas, and Santa Rosa, which may be inconsistent with the laws and Constitution of the United States, authorizing him at the same time, if he shall find it necessary, to suspend there the writ of *habeas corpus*, and to remove from the vicinity of the United States fortresses all dangerous or suspected persons.

"In witness whereof, I have hereunto set my hand, and caused the seal of the United States to be affixed.

"Done at the City of Washington, this tenth day of May, in

the year of our Lord, one thousand eight hundred and sixty-one, and of the Independence of the United States the eighty-fifth.

"By the President :   ABRAHAM LINCOLN.
"WILLIAM H. SEWARD, Secretary of State."

Volunteers meanwhile presented themselves for the defence of the country in numbers greater than could be accepted, and the strife was who should secure the coveted distinction of a citizen soldier. An early movement upon the rebel army in Virginia was contemplated, and it was confidently anticipated that to advance was to put the enemies of the Government to flight.

CHAPTER VIII.

THE FIRST SESSION OF CONGRESS.

Opening of Congress—President's First Message—Its Nature—Action of Congress—Resolution Declaring the Object of the War—Bull Run—Its Effect.

THE first session of Congress during Mr. Lincoln's Administration commenced on the 4th of July, 1861, in pursuance of his call to that effect. The following message was transmitted from the Executive :

"FELLOW-CITIZENS OF THE SENATE AND. HOUSE OF REPRESENTATIVES :—Having been convened on an extraordinary occasion, as authorized by the Constitution, your attention is not called to any ordinary subject of legislation. At the beginning of the present Presidential term, four months ago, the functions of the Federal Government were found to be generally suspended within the several States of South Carolina, Georgia, Alabama, Mississippi, Louisiana and Florida, excepting only those of the Post-office Department.

" Within these States, all the Forts, Arsenals, Dock-Yards, Custom-Houses, and the like, including the movable and stationary property in and about them, had been seized, and were held in open hostility to this Government, excepting only Forts Pickens, Taylor and Jefferson, on and near the Florida coast, and Fort Sumter in Charleston harbor, South Carolina.   The forts thus seized had been put in improved condition, new ones had been built, and armed forces had been organized, and were organizing, all avowedly with the same hostile purpose.

" The forts remaining in possession of the Federal Government in and near these States were either besieged or menaced by warlike preparations, and especially- Fort Sumter was nearly surrounded by well-protected hostile batteries, with guns equal in quality to the best of its own, and outnumbering the latter as, perhaps, ten to one—a disproportionate share of the Federal muskets and rifles had somehow found their way into these States, and had been seized to be used against the Government.

"Accumulations of the public revenue lying within them had been seized for the same object.   The navy was scattered in distant seas, leaving but a very small part of it within the immediate reach of the Government.

" Officers of the Federal Army had resigned in great numbers, and of those resigning a large proportion had taken up arms against the Government.

" Simultaneously, and in connection with all this, the purpose to sever the Federal Union was openly avowed.   In accordance with this purpose an ordinance had been adopted in each of these States, declaring the States respectively to be separated from the National Union.   A formula for instituting a combined Government of those States had been promulgated, and this illegal organization, in the character of the ' Confederate States,' was already invoking recognition, aid and intervention from foreign powers.

"Finding this condition of things, and believing it to be an imperative duty upon the incoming Executive to prevent, if possible, the consummation of such attempt to destroy the Federal Union, a choice of means to that end became indispensable. This choice was made and was declared in the Inaugural Address.

"The policy chosen looked to the exhaustion of all peaceful measures before a resort to any stronger ones. It sought only to hold the public places and property not already wrested from the Government, and to collect the revenue, relying for the rest on time, discussion, and the ballot-box. It promised a continuance of the mails, at Government expense, to the very people who were resisting the Government, and it gave repeated pledges against any disturbances to any of the people, or any of their rights, of all that which a President might constitutionally and justifiably do in such a case; every thing was forborne, without which it was believed possible to keep the Government on foot.

"On the 5th of March, the present incumbent's first full day in office, a letter from Major Anderson, commanding at Fort Sumter, written on the 28th of February, and received at the War Department on the 4th of March, was by that Department placed in his hands. This letter expressed the professional opinion of the writer, that reinforcements could not be thrown into that fort within the time for its relief rendered necessary by the limited supply of provisions, and with a view of holding possession of the same, with a force less than twenty thousand good and well-disciplined men. This opinion was concurred in by all the officers of his command, and their memoranda on the subject were made inclosures of Major Anderson's letter. The whole was immediately laid before Lieutenant-General Scott, who at once concurred with Major Anderson in his opinion. On reflection, however, he took full time, consulting with other officers, both of the Army and Navy, and at the end of four days came reluctantly but decidedly to the same conclusion as before. He also stated at the same time that no such sufficient force was then at the control of the Government, or could be raised and brought to the ground, within the time when the provisions in the fort would be exhausted. In a purely military point of view, this reduced the duty of the Administration in the case to the mere matter of getting the garrison safely out of the fort.

" It was believed, however, that to so abandon that position, under the circumstances, would be utterly ruinous ; that the necessity under which it was to be done would not be fully understood ; that by many it would be construed as a part of a voluntary policy ; that at home it would discourage the friends of the Union, embolden its adversaries, and go far to insure to the latter a recognition abroad ; that, in fact, it would be our national destruction consummated. This could not be allowed. Starvation was not yet upon the garrison, and ere it would be reached, Fort Pickens might be reinforced. This last would be a clear indication of policy, and would better enable the country to accept the evacuation of Fort Sumter as a military necessity. An order was at once directed to be sent for the landing of the troops from the steamship Brooklyn into Fort Pickens. This order could not go by land, but must take the longer and slower route by sea. The first return news from the order was received just one week before the fall of Sumter. The news itself was that the officer commanding the Sabine, to which vessel the troops had been transferred from the Brooklyn, acting upon some *quasi* armistice of the late Administration, and of the existence of which the present Administration, up to the time the order was dispatched, had only too vague and uncertain rumors to fix attention, had refused to land the troops. To now reinforce Fort Pickens before a crisis would be reached at Fort Sumter, was impossible, rendered so by the near exhaustion of provisions at the latter named fort. In precaution against such a conjuncture the Government had a few days before commenced preparing an expedition, as well adapted as might be, to relieve Fort Sumter, which expedition was intended to be ultimately used or not, according to circumstances. The strongest anticipated case for using it was now presented, and it was resolved to send it forward as had been intended. In this contingency it was also resolved to notify the Governor of South Carolina that he might expect an attempt would be made to provision the fort, and that if the attempt should not be resisted there would be no attempt to throw in men, arms or ammunition, without further notice, or in case of an attack upon the fort. This notice was accordingly given, whereupon the fort was attacked and bombarded to its fall, without even awaiting the arrival of the provisioning expedition.

"It is thus seen that the assault upon and reduction of Fort Sumter, was in no sense, a matter of self-defense on the part of the assailants. They well knew that the garrison in the fort could by no possibility commit aggression upon them; they knew they were expressly notified that the giving of bread to the few brave and hungry men of the garrison was all which would, on that occasion, be attempted, unless themselves, by resisting so much, should provoke more. They knew that this Government desired to keep the garrison in the fort, not to assail them, but merely to maintain visible possession, and thus to preserve the Union from actual and immediate dissolution; trusting, as hereinbefore stated, to time, discussion, and the ballot-box for final adjustment, and they assailed and reduced the fort, for precisely the reverse object, to drive out the visible authority of the Federal Union, and thus force it to immediate dissolution; that this was their object the Executive well understood, having said to them in the Inaugural Address, 'You can have no conflict without being yourselves the aggressors.' He took pains not only to keep this declaration good, but also to keep the case so far from ingenious sophistry as that the world should not misunderstand it.   By the affair at Fort Sumter, with its surrounding circumstances, that point was reached.   Then and thereby the assailants of the Government began the conflict of arms—without a gun in sight, or in expectancy, to return their fire, save only the few in the fort sent to that harbor years before, for their own protection, and still ready to give that protection in whatever was lawful.   In this act, discarding all else, they have forced upon the country the distinct issue, immediate dissolution or blood, and this issue embraces more than the fate of these United States.   It presents to the whole family of man the question whether a Constitutional Republic or Democracy, a Government of the people, by the same people, can or can not maintain its territorial integrity against its own domestic foes.   It presents the question whether discontented individuals, too few in numbers to control the Administration according to the organic law in any case, can always, upon the pretenses made in this case, or any other pretenses, or arbitrarily without any pretense, break up their Government, and thus practically put an end to free government upon the earth.   It forces us to ask, 'Is there in all republics this inherent and fatal weakness?'   'Must a Government of necessity be too strong for the liberties of its own people, or too weak to maintain its own existence?'   So viewing the issue, no choice was left but to call out the war power of the Government, and so to resist the force employed for its destruction by force for its preservation.   The call was made, and the response of the country was most gratifying, surpassing, in unanimity and spirit, the most sanguine expectation.   Yet none of the States, commonly called Slave States, except Delaware, gave a regiment through the regular State organization.   A few regiments have been organized within some others of those States by individual enterprise, and received into the Government service.   Of course the seceded States, so called, and to

which Texas had been joined about the time of the inauguration, gave no troops to the cause of the Union. The Border
States, so called, were not uniform in their action, some of
them being almost for the Union, while in others, as in Virginia, North Carolina, Tennessee, and Arkansas, the Union
sentiment was nearly repressed and silenced. The course
taken in Virginia was the most remarkable, perhaps the most
important. A Convention, elected by the people of that
State to consider this very question of disrupting the Federal
Union, was in session at the capitol of Virginia when Fort
Sumter fell.

"To this body the people had chosen a large majority of
professed Union men. Almost immediately after the fall of
Sumter many members of that majority went over to the
original disunion minority, and with them adopted an ordinance for withdrawing the State from the Union. Whether
this change was wrought by their great approval of the
assault upon Sumter, or their great resentment at the Government's resistance to that assault, is not definitely known.
Although they submitted the ordinance for ratification to a
vote of the people, to be taken on a day then somewhat more
than a month distant, the Convention, and the Legislature.
which was also in session at the same time and place. with
leading men of the State, not members of either, immediately
commenced acting as if the State was already out of the
Union. They pushed military preparations vigorously forward all over the State. They seized the United States
Armory at Harper's Ferry, and the Navy Yard at Gosport,
near Norfolk. They received, perhaps invited into their
State, large bodies of troops, with their warlike appoint
ments, from the so-called seceded States.

"They formally entered into a treaty of temporary alliance
with the so-called Confederate States, and sent members to
their Congress at Montgomery, and finally they permitted
the insurrectionary Government to be transferred to their

capitol at Richmond. The people of Virginia have thus allowed this giant insurrection to make its nest within her borders, and this Government has no choice left but to deal with it where it finds it, and it has the less to regret as the oyal citizens have, in due form, claimed its protection. Those loyal citizens this Government is bound to recognize and protect as being in Virginia. In the Border States, so called, in fact the Middle States, there are those who favor a policy which they call armed neutrality, that is, an arming of those States to prevent the Union forces passing one way or the disunion forces the other, over their soil. This would be disunion completed. Figuratively speaking, it would be the building of an impassable wall along the line of separation, and yet not quite an impassable one, for under the guise of neutrality it would tie the hands of the Union men, and freely pass supplies from among them to the insurrectionists, which it could not do as an open enemy. At a stroke it would take all the trouble off the hands of secession, except only what proceeds from the external blockade. It would do for the disunionists that which of all things they most desire, feed them well, and give them disunion, without a struggle of their own. It recognizes no fidelity to the Constitution, no obligation to maintain the Union, and while very many who have favored it are doubtless loyal citizens, it is, nevertheless, very injurious in effect.

"Recurring to the action of the Government, it may be stated that at first a call was made for seventy-five thousand militia, and rapidly following this, a proclamation was issued for closing the ports of the insurrectionary districts by proceedings in the nature of a blockade. So far all was believed to be strictly legal.

"At this point the insurrectionists announced their purpose to enter upon the practice of privateering.

"Other calls were made for volunteers, to serve three years, unless sooner discharged, and also for large additions to the regular army and navy. These measures, whether strictly legal or not, were ventured upon under what appeared to be a popular demand and a public necessity, trusting then, as now, that Congress would ratify them.

"It is believed that nothing has been done beyond the constitutional competency of Congress. Soon after the first call for militia it was considered a duty to authorize the commanding general, in proper cases, according to his discretion, to suspend the privilege of the writ of habeas corpus; or, in other words, to arrest and detain, without resort to the ordinary processes and forms of law, such individuals as he might deem dangerous to the public safety. This authority has purposely been exercised, but very sparingly. Nevertheless, the legality and propriety of what has been done under it are questioned, and the attention of the country has been called to the proposition, that one who is sworn to take care that the laws be faithfully executed should not himself violate them. Of course some consideration was given to the questions of power and propriety before this matter was acted upon. The whole of the laws, which were required to be faithfully executed, were being resisted, and failing of execution in nearly one-third of the States. Must they be allowed to finally fail of execution, even had it been perfectly clear that, by use of the means necessary to their execution, some single law, made in such extreme tenderness of the citizen's liberty that practically it relieves more of the guilty than the innocent, should, to a very great extent, be violated? To state the question more directly, are all the laws but one to go unexecuted, and the Government itself to go to pieces, lest that one be violated? Even in such a case would not the official oath be broken, if the Government should be overthrown when it was believed that disregarding the single law would tend to preserve it?

"But it was not believed that this question was presented. It was not believed that any law was violated. The provision of the Constitution, that the privilege of the writ of habeas corpus shall not be suspended, unless when, in cases of rebellion or invasion, the public safety may require it, is equivalent to a provision that such privilege may be suspended when, in cases of rebellion or invasion, the public safety does require it. It was decided that we have a case of rebellion, and that the public safety does require the qualified suspension of the privilege of the writ, which was authorized to be made. Now, it is insisted that Congress, and not the Executive, is vested with this power. But the Constitution itself is silent as to which or who is to exercise the power; and as the provision was plainly made for a dangerous emergency, it cannot be believed that the framers of the instrument intended that in every case the danger should run its course until Congress could be called together, the very assembling of which might be prevented, as was intended in this case by the rebellion. No more extended argument is now afforded, as an opinion at some length will probably be presented by the Attorney-General. Whether there shall be any legislation on the subject, and if so, what, is subject entirely to the better judgment of Congress. The forbearance of this Government had been so extraordinary, and so long continued, as to lead some foreign nations to shape their action as if they supposed the early destruction of our National Union was probable. While this, on discovery, gave the Executive some concern, he is now happy to say that the sovereignty and rights of the United States are now everywhere practically respected by foreign powers, and a general sympathy with the country is manifested throughout the world.

"The reports of the Secretaries of the Treasury, War, and the Navy, will give the information, in detail, deemed necessary and convenient for your deliberation and action, while the Executive and all the Departments will stand ready to supply omissions or to communicate new facts considered important for you to know.

" It is now recommended that you give the legal means for making this contest a short and decisive one ; that you place at the control of the Government for the work, at least 400,000 men and $400,000,000 ; that number of men is about one-tenth of those of proper ages within the regions where apparently all are willing to engage, and the sum is less than a twenty-third part of the money value owned by the men who seem ready to devote the whole. A debt of $600,000,000 now is a less sum per head than was the debt of our Revolution when we came out of that struggle, and the money value in the country bears even a greater proportion to what it was then than does the population. Surely each man has as strong a motive now to preserve our liberties, as each had then to establish them.

"A right result at this time will be worth more to the world than ten times the men and ten times the money. The evidence reaching us from the country, leaves no doubt that the material for the work is abundant, and that it needs only the hand of legislation to give it legal sanction, and the hand of the Executive to give it practical shape and efficiency. One of the greatest perplexities of the Government is to avoid receiving troops faster than it can provide for them ; in a word, the people will save their Government if the Government will do its part only indifferently well. It might seem at first thought to be of little difference whether the present movement at the South be called secession or rebellion. The movers, however, well understand the difference. At the beginning they knew that they could never raise their treason to any respectable magnitude by any name which implies violation of law ; they knew their people possessed as much of moral sense, as much of devotion to law and order, and as much pride in its reverence for the history and government of their common country, as any other civilized and patriotic people.   They knew they could make no advancement directly in the teeth of these strong and noble sentiments.   Accordingly they commenced by an insidious debauching of the public mind; they invented an ingenious sophism, which, if conceded, was followed by perfectly logical steps through all the incidents of the complete destruction of the Union.   The sophism itself is that any State of the Union may, consistently with the nation's Constitution, and therefore lawfully and peacefully, withdraw from the Union without the consent of the Union or of any other State.

"The little disguise that the supposed right, is to be exercised only for just cause, themselves to be the sole judge of its justice, is too thin to merit any notice with rebellion. Thus sugar-coated, they have been drugging the public mind of their section for more than thirty years, and until at length they have brought many good men to a willingness to take up arms against the Government the day after some assemblage of men have enacted the farcical pretence of taking their State out of the Union, who could have been brought to no such thing the day before.   This sophism derives much, perhaps the whole of its currency, from the assumption that there is some omnipotent and sacred supremacy pertaining to a State, to each State of our Federal Union.   Our States have neither more nor less power than that reserved to them in the Union by the Constitution, no one of them ever having been a State out of the Union. The original ones passed into the Union before they cast off their British Colonial dependence, and the new ones came into the Union directly from a condition of dependence, excepting Texas, and even Texas, in its temporary independence, was never designated as a State.   The new ones only took the designation of States on coming into the Union, while that name was first adopted for the old ones in and by the Declaration of Independence.   Therein the United Colonies were declared to be *free* and *independent* States.   But even then the object plainly was not to declare their independence of one another of the Union, but directly the contrary, as their mutual pledge and their mutual action before, at the time, and afterward, abundantly show. The express plight of faith by each and all of the original thirteen States in the Articles of Confederation two years later that the Union shall be perpetual, is most conclusive. Having never been States either in substance or in name outside of the Union, whence this magical omnipotence of State rights, asserting a claim of power to lawfully destroy the Union itself? Much is said about the sovereignty of the States, but the word even is not in the National Constitution, nor, as is believed, in any of the State constitutions. What is sovereignty in the political sense of the word? Would it be far wrong to define it a political community without a political superior? Tested by this, no one of our States, except Texas, was a sovereignty, and even Texas gave up the character on coming into the Union, by which act she acknowledged the Constitution of the United States; and the laws and treaties of the United States, made in pursuance of States, have their status in the Union, made in pursuance of the Constitution, to be for her the supreme law. The States have their status in the Union, and they have no other legal status If they break from this, they can only do so against law and by revolution. The Union and not themselves, separately procured their independence and their liberty by conquest or purchase. The Union gave each of them whatever of independence and liberty it has. The Union is older than any of the States, and, in fact, it created them as States. Originally, some dependent Colonies made the Union, and in turn the Union threw off their old dependence for them, and made them States, such as they are. Not one of them ever had a State constitution independent of the Union. Of course it is not forgotten that all the new States formed their constitutions before they entered the Union; nevertheless,

9

dependent upon, and preparatory to coming into the Union. Unquestionably the States have the powers and rights reserved to them in and by the National Constitution.

"But among these surely are not included all conceivable powers, however mischievous or destructive,. but at most such only as were known in the world at the time as governmental powers, and certainly a power to destroy the Government itself had never been known as a governmental, as a merely administrative power. This relative matter of National power and State rights as a principle, is no other than the principle of generality and locality. Whatever concerns the whole should be conferred on the whole General Government, while whatever concerns only the State should be left exclusively to the State. This is all there is of original principle about it. Whether the National Constitution, in defining boundaries between the two, has applied the principle with exact accuracy, is not to be questioned. We are all bound by that defining without question. What is now combatted is the position that secession is consistent with the Constitution, is lawful and peaceful. It is not contended that there is any express law for it, and nothing should ever be implied as law which leads to unjust or absurd consequences. The nation purchased with money the countries out of which several of these States were formed. Is it just that they shall go off without leave and without refunding? The nation paid very large sums in the aggregate, I believe nearly a hundred millions, to relieve Florida of the aboriginal tribes. Is it just that she shall now be off without consent, or without any return? The nation is now in debt for money applied to the benefit of these so-called seceding States, in common with the rest. Is it just, either that creditors shall go unpaid, or the remaining States pay the whole? A part of the present National debt was contracted to pay the old debt of Texas. Is it just that she shall leave and pay no part of this herself? Again, if one State may secede, so may another, and when all shall have seceded none is left to pay the debts. Is this quite just to creditors ? Did we notify them of this sage view of ours when we borrowed their money ? If we now recognize this doctrine by allowing the seceders to go in peace, it is difficult to see what we can do if others choose to go, or to extort terms upon which they will promise to remain. The seceders insist that our Constitution admits of secession. They have assumed to make a National Constitution of their own, in which, of necessity, they have either discarded or retained the right of secession, as they insist exists in ours. If they have discarded it, they thereby admit that on principle it ought not to exist in ours ; if they have retained it, by their own construction of ours that shows that to be consistent, they must secede from one another whenever they shall find it the easiest way of settling their debts, or effecting any other selfish or unjust object. The principle itself is one of disintegration, and upon which no Government can possibly endure. If all the States save one should assert the power to drive that one out of the Union, it is presumed the whole class of seceder politicians would at once deny the power, and denounce the act as the greatest outrage upon State rights. But suppose that precisely the same act, instead of being called driving the one out, should be called the seceding of the others from that one, it would be exactly what the seceders claim to do, unless, indeed, they made the point that the one, because it is a minority, may rightfully do what the others, because they are a majority, may not rightfully do. These politicians are subtle, and profound in the rights of minorities. They are not partial to that power which made the Constitution, and speaks from the preamble, calling itself, ' We, the people.' It may be well questioned whether there is to-day a majority of the legally qualified voters of any State, except, perhaps, South Carolina, in favor of disunion. There is much reason to believe that the Union men are the majority in many, if not in every one of the so-called seceded States. The contrary has not been demonstrated in any one of them. It is ventured to affirm this, even of Virginia and Tennessee, for the result of an election held in military camps, where the bayonets are all on one side of the question voted upon, can scarcely be considered as demonstrating popular sentiment. At such an election all that large class who are at once for the Union and against coercion would be coerced to vote against the Union. It may be affirmed, without extravagance, that the free institutions we enjoy have developed the powers and improved the condition of our whole people beyond any example in the world. Of this we now have a striking and impressive illustration. So large an army as the Government has now on foot was never before known, without a soldier in it but who has taken his place there of his own free choice. But more than this, there are many single regiments whose members, one and another, possess full practical knowledge of all the arts, sciences, professions, and whatever else, whether useful or elegant, is known in the whole world, and there is scarcely one from which there could not be selected a President, a Cabinet, a Congress, and perhaps a Court, abundantly competent to administer the Government itself. Nor do I say this is not true also in the army of our late friends, now adversaries, in this contest. But it is so much better the reason why the Government which has conferred such benefits on both them and us should not be broken up. Whoever in any section proposes to abandon such a Government, would do well to consider in deference to what principle it is that he does it. What better he is likely to get in its stead, whether the substitute will give, or be intended to give so much of good to the people. There are some foreshadowings on this subject. Our adversaries have adopted some declarations of independence in which, unlike our good old one penned by Jefferson, they omit the words, 'all men are created equal.' Why? They have adopted a temporary National Constitution, in the preamble of which, unlike our good old one signed by Washington, they omit, ' We, the people,' and substitute, ' We, the deputies of the sovereign and independent States.' Why? Why this deliberate pressing out of view the rights of men and the authority of the people? This is essentially a people's contest. On the side of the Union it is a struggle for maintaining in the world that form and substance of Government whose leading object is to elevate the condition of men, to lift artificial weights from all shoulders, to clear the paths of laudable pursuit for all, to afford all an unfettered start and a fair chance in the race of life, yielding to partial and temporary departures from necessity. This is the leading object of the Government for whose existence we contend.

" I am most happy to believe that the plain people understand and appreciate this. It is worthy of note that while in this, the Government's hour of trial, large numbers of those in the army and navy who have been favored with the offices, have resigned and proved false to the hand which pampered them, not one common soldier or common sailor is known to have deserted his flag. Great honor is due to those officers who remained true despite the example of their treacherous associates, but the greatest honor and the most important fact of all, is the unanimous firmness of the common soldiers and common sailors. To the last man, so far as known, they have successfully resisted the traitorous efforts of those whose commands but an hour before they obeyed as absolute law. This is the patriotic instinct of plain people. They understand without an argument that the destroying the Government which was made by Washington means no good to them. Our popular Government has often been called an experiment. Two points in it our people have settled : the successful establishing and the successful administering of it. One still remains. Its successful maintenance against a formidable internal attempt to overthrow it. It is now for them to demonstrate to the world that those who can fairly carry an election, can also suppress a rebellion ; that ballots are the rightful and peaceful successors of bullets, and that when ballots have fairly and constitutionally decided, there can be no successful appeal except to ballots themselves at succeeding elections. Such will be a great lesson of peace, teaching men that what they cannot take by an election, neither can they take by a war, teaching all the folly of being the beginners of a war.

" Lest there should be some uneasiness in the minds of candid men as to what is to be the course of the Government toward the Southern States after the rebellion shall have been suppressed, the Executive deems it proper to say it will be his purpose then, as ever, to be guided by the Constitution and the laws, and that he probably will have no different understanding of the powers and duties of the Federal Government relatively to the rights of the United States and the people under the Constitution than that expressed in the Inaugural Address. He desires to preserve the Government that it may be administered for all, as it was administered by the men who made it. Loyal citizens everywhere have a right to claim this of their Government, and the Government has no right to withhold or neglect it. It is not perceived that in giving it there is any coercion, conquest or subjugation in any sense of these terms.

" The Constitution provided, and all the States have accepted the provision, ' that the United States shall guarantee to every State in this Union a Republican form of government,' but if a State may lawfully go out of the Union, having done so, it may also discard the Republican form of Government. So that to prevent its going out is an indispensable means to the end of maintaining the guaranty mentioned ; and when an end is lawful and obligatory, the indispensable means to it are also lawful and obligatory.

" It was with the deepest regret that the Executive found

the duty of employing the war power. In defence of the Government forced upon him, he could but perform this duty or surrender the existence of the Government. No compromise by public servants could in this case be a cure, not that compromises are not often proper, but that no popular government can long survive a marked precedent, that those who carry an election can only save the Government from immediate destruction by giving up the main point upon which the people gave the election. The people themselves and not their servants can safely reverse their own deliberate decisions.

"As a private citizen the Executive could not have consented that these institutions shall perish, much less could he, in betrayal of so vast and so sacred a trust as these free people had confided to him. He felt that he had no moral right to shrink, nor even to count the chances of his own life in what might follow.

" In full view of his great responsibility, he has so far done what he has deemed his duty. You will now, according to your own judgment, perform yours. He sincerely hopes that your views and your actions may so accord with his as to assure all faithful citizens who have been disturbed in their rights, of a certain and speedy restoration to them, under the Constitution and laws ; and having thus chosen our cause without guile, and with pure purpose, let us renew our trust in God, and go forward without fear and with manly hearts.

" July 4, 1861. ABRAHAM LINCOLN."

This document, it will be observed, sets forth in temperate language the facts bearing upon the rebellion in its then stage—facts so stated that the common people could readily comprehend the exact situation of affairs Such a message, always in place, was never more needed than at a juncture when—as seemed not altogether impossible to many—an appeal might yet have to be made again and again to the great mass of the people for men and money to maintain the unity of the nation. It may be safely asserted, that the messages of none of our Presidents have been so generally read and so thoroughly mastered by the average mind, as those of Mr. Lincoln, himself the tribune of the people.

Congress granted five hundred millions in money, and directed a call for five hundred thousand volunteers for the army; made provisions for a popular national loan; revised the tariff; passed a direct tax bill; adopted measures, moderate in their scope, for the confiscation of rebel property; legalized the official acts of the President during the emergency in which the country had been placed; and the House of Representatives, with but two dissentients, passed the following resolution:

"*Resolved, By the House of Representatives of the Congress of the United States,* That the present deplorable civil war has been forced upon the country by the disunionists of the Southern States, now in revolt against the Constitutional Government, and in arms around the capital; that in this national emergency Congress, banishing all feeling of mere passion or resentment, will recollect only its duty to the whole country; that this war is not waged on our part in any spirit of oppression, nor for any purpose of conquest or subjugation, nor purpose of authorizing or interfering with the rights or established institutions of the States, but to defend and maintain the supremacy of the Constitution, and to preserve the Union, with all the dignities, equality, and rights of the several States unimpaired, and that as soon as these objects are accomplished the war ought to cease."

On the 21st of July, the Army of the Union, under the direct command of General McDowell, and the general supervision of the veteran Scott—from whose onward movement against the rebels in Virginia so much had been expected—met with a serious reverse at Bull Run. They went forth, exulting in victory as certain; they came back a panic-stricken mob. For an instant, despondency took possession of every loyal heart; all manner of vague fears seized the people; Washington would be captured; the cause was lost.

It was but for an instant, however. The rebound came. Washington, which might easily have been captured and sacked, had the rebels known how to improve their success, was securely fortified and amply garrisoned. One did not then comprehend what now the most concede—that Bull Run was a necessary discipline—a school in which all learned somewhat—though, unfortunately, not all of us as much as we should. That came later.

CHAPTER IX.

CLOSE OF 1861.

Elation of the Rebels—Davis's boast—McClellan appointed Commander of Potomac Army—Proclamation of a National Fast—Intercourse with rebels forbidden—Fugitive slaves—Gen. Butler's views—Gen. MClellan's letter from Secretary Cameron—Act of August 6th.' 1861—Gen. Fremont's order—Letter of the President modifying the same—Instructions to Gen. Sherman—Ball's Bluff—Gen. Scott's retirement—Army of the Potomac.

The victory of the conspirators at Bull Run, as was to have been expected, elated them no little. Their President in his message was supercilious and confident. Lauding the prowess and determination of his confederates, he said:

" To speak of subjugating such a people, so united and determined, is to speak in a language incomprehensible to them : to resist attack on their rights or their liberties is with them an instinct. Whether this war shall last one, or three, or five years, is a problem they leave to be solved by the enemy alone. It will last till the enemy shall have withdrawn from their borders; till their political rights, their altars, and their homes are freed from invasion. Then, and then only, will they rest from this struggle to enjoy in peace, the blessings which, with the favor of Providence, they have secured by the aid of their own strong hearts and steady arms."

On the 25th, of July, a new commander was assigned to the Army of the Potomac, upon the warm recommendation of Gen. Scott; George B. McClellan, who had already become favorably known from his conducting a successful campaign in Western Virginia. With the extravagance so characteristic of the American people, this commander—whose laurels were yet to be won—was hailed as a young Napoleon, lauded to the skies, and failure under him regarded as an utter impossibility.

And the General betook himself to the organizing, disciplining, and supplying his army, to which large accessions were continually making from week to week.

On the 12th day of August was issued the following proclamation :

"WHEREAS, A joint committee of both Houses of Congress has waited on the President of the United States, and requested him to 'recommend a day of public humiliation, prayer, and fasting, to be observed by the people of the United States with religious solemnities, and the offering of fervent supplications to Almighty God for the safety and welfare of these States, His blessings on their arms, and a speedy restoration of peace.'

"AND WHEREAS, It is fit and becoming in all people, at all times, to acknowledge and revere the Supreme Government of God; to bow in humble submission to his chastisements; to confess and deplore their sins and transgressions, in the full conviction that the fear of the Lord is the beginning of wisdom, and to pray, with all fervency and contrition, for the pardon of their past offences, and for a blessing upon their present and prospective action.

"AND WHEREAS, When our own beloved country, once, by the blessing of God, united, prosperous, and happy, is now afflicted with faction and civil war, it is peculiarly fit for us to recognize the hand of God in this terrible visitation, and, in sorrowful remembrance of our own faults and crimes as a nation, and as individuals, to humble ourselves before Him, and to pray for His mercy—to pray that we may be spared further punishment, though most justly deserved; that our arms may be blessed and made effectual for the re-establishment of law, order, and peace throughout the wide extent of our country; and that the inestimable boon of civil and religious liberty, earned under His guidance and blessing by the labors and sufferings of our fathers, may be restored in all its original excellence;

" *Therefore, I,* Abraham Lincoln, President of the United States, do appoint the last Thursday in September next as a day of humiliation, prayer, and fasting for all the people of the nation. And I do earnestly recommend to all the people, and especially to all ministers and teachers of religion, of all denominations, and to all heads of families, to observe and keep that day, according to their several creeds and modes of worship, in all humility, and with all religious solemnity, to the end that the united prayer of the nation may ascend to the Throne of Grace, and bring down plentiful blessings upon our country.

" In testimony whereof, I have hereunto set my hand, and caused the seal of the United States to be affixed, this 12th day of August, A. D. 1861, and of the Independence of the United States of America the eighty-sixth.

" By the President; ABRAHAM LINCOLN.
" WILLIAM H. SEWARD, Secretary of State. "

And four days later the following:

"WHEREAS, On the 15th day of April, the President of the United States, in view of an insurrection against the laws, Constitution, and Government of the United States, which had broken out within the States of South Carolina, Georgia, Alabama, Florida, Mississippi, Louisiana, and Texas, and in pursuance of the provisions of an act entitled an act to provide for calling forth the militia to execute the laws of the Union, suppress insurrections and repel invasions, and to repeal the act now in force for that purpose, approved February 28th, 1795, did call forth the militia to suppress said insurrection and cause the laws of the Union to be duly executed—and the insurgents have failed to disperse by the time directed by the President; AND WHEREAS, such insurrection has since broken out and yet exists within the States of Virginia, North Carolina, Tennessee, and Arkansas; AND WHEREAS, the insurgents in all the said States claim to act under authority thereof, and such claim is not discarded or repudiated by the persons exercising the functions of government in such State or States, or in the part or parts thereof, in which such combinations exist, nor has such insurrection been suppressed by said States.

"Now, therefore, I, Abraham Lincoln, President of the United States, in pursuance of the Act of Congress approved July 13th, 1861, do hereby declare that the inhabitants of the said States of Georgia, South Carolina, Tennessee, Alabama, Louisiana, Texas, Arkansas, Mississippi, and Florida, except the inhabitants of that part of the State of Virginia lying west of the Allegheny Mountains, and of such other parts of that State and the other States hereinbefore named as may maintain a loyal adhesion to the Union and the Constitution, or may be, from time to time occupied and controlled by the forces of the United States engaged in the dispersion of said insurgents, are in a state of insurrection against the United States, and that all commercial intercourse between the same and the inhabitants thereof, with the exception aforesaid, and the citizens of other States and other parts of the United States, is unlawful, and will remain unlawful until such insurrection shall cease or has been suppressed; that all goods and chattels, wares and merchandise, coming from any of the said States, with the exceptions aforesaid, into other parts of the United States, without the special license and permission of the President, through the Secretary of the Treasury, or proceeding to any of the said States, with the exception aforesaid, by land or water, together with the vessel or vehicle conveying the same, or conveying persons to and from the said States, with the said exceptions, will be forfeited to the United States; and that, from and after fifteen days from the issuing of this proclamation, all ships and vessels belonging, in whole or in part, to any citizen or inhabitant of any of the said States, with the said exceptions, found at sea in any part of the United States, will be forfeited to the United States; and I hereby enjoin upon all District Attorneys, Marshals, and officers of the revenue of the military and naval forces of the United States, to be vigilant in the execution of the said act, and in the enforcement of the penalties and forfeitures imposed or declared by it, leaving any party who may think himself aggrieved thereby, to his application to the Secretary of the Treasury for the remission of any penalty or forfeiture, which the said Secretary is authorized by law to grant, if in his judgment, the special circumstances of any case shall require such a remission.

"In witness whereof, I have hereunto set my hand, and caused the seal of the United States to be affixed.

"Done in the City of Washington, this, the 16th day of August, in the year of our Lord one thousand eight hundred and sixty-one, and of the Independence of the United States of America the eighty-sixth.

"By the President: ABRAHAM LINCOLN.

"WILLIAM H. SEWARD, Secretary of State."

The question as to the disposition to be made of the slaves of rebel masters presented itself early in the contest, and it was at once perceived that its settlement would be attended with no little embarrassment.

As early as May 27th, 1861, General Butler, in command at Fortress Monroe, had informed the War Department as to his views relative to the fugitive slaves—that they were to be regarded as "contraband of war"—and Secretary Cameron, under date of May 30th, had instructed that commander neither to permit any interference by persons under his command with the relations of persons held to service under the laws of any State; nor, on the other hand, while such States remained in rebellion, to surrender such persons to their alleged masters, but to employ them in such service as would be most advantageous, keeping an account of the value of their labor and the expenses of their support—the question of their final disposition to be reserved for future determination.

At about the same time, General McClellan, advancing into Western Virginia to the aid of the loyal men of that section, used this language in his address to the people:

"Notwithstanding all that has been said by the traitors to induce you to believe that our advent among you will be signalized by interference with your slaves, understand one thing clearly—not only will we abstain from all such interference, but we will, on the contrary, with an iron hand, crush any attempt at insurrection on their part."

On the 8th of August, Secretary Cameron, in reply to a second letter from General Butler upon the same subject, said:

"GENERAL :—The important question of the proper disposition to be made of fugitives from service in the States in insurrection against the Federal Government, to which you have again directed my attention, in your letter of July 20th, has received my most attentive consideration. It is the desire of the President that all existing rights in all the States be fully respected and maintained. The war now prosecuted on the part of the Federal Government is a war for the Union.

for the preservation of all the Constitutional rights of the States and the citizens of the States in the Union ; hence no question can arise as to fugitives from service within the States and Territories in which the authority of the Union is fully acknowledged. The ordinary forms of judicial proceedings must be respected by the military and civil authorities alike for the enforcement of legal forms. But in the States wholly or in part under insurrectionary control, where the laws of the United States are·so far opposed and resisted that they can not be effectually enforced, it is obvious that the rights dependent upon the execution of these laws must temporarily fail, and it is equally obvious that the rights dependent on the laws of the States within which military operations are conducted must necessarily be subordinate to the military exigencies created by the insurrection, if not wholly forfeited by the treasonable conduct of the parties claiming them. To this the general rule of the right to service forms an exception. The act of Congress approved August 6, 1861, declares that if persons held to service shall be employed in hostility to the United States, the right to their services shall be discharged therefrom. It follows of necessity that no claim can be recognized by the military authority of the Union to the services of such persons when fugitives.

"A more difficult question is presented in respect to persons escaping from the service of loyal ·masters. It is quite apparent that the laws of the State under which only the service of such fugitives can be claimed must needs be wholly or almost wholly superseded, as to the remedies, by the insurrection and the military measures necessitated by it; and it is equally apparent that the substitution of military for judicial measures for the enforcement of such claims must be attended by great inconvenience, embarrassments and injuries. Under these circumstances, it seems quite clear that the substantial rights of loyal masters are still best protected by receiving such fugitives, as well as fugitives from disloyal masters, into the service of the United States, and employing them under such organizations and in such occupations as circumstances may suggest or require.   Of course a record should be kept showing the names and descriptions of the fugitives, the names and characters, as loyal or disloyal, of their masters, and such facts as may be necessary to a correct understanding of the circumstances of each case.

" After tranquility shall have been restored upon the return of peace, Congress will doubtless properly provide for all the persons thus received into the service of the Union, and for a just compensation to loyal masters.   In this way only, it would seem, can the duty and safety of the Government and just rights of all be fully reconciled and harmonized.   You will, therefore, consider yourself instructed to govern your future action in respect to fugitives from service by the premises herein stated, and will report from time to time, and at least twice in each month, your action in the premises to this Department   You will, however, neither authorize nor permit any interference by the troops under your command with the servants of peaceable citizens in a house or field, nor will you in any manner encourage such citizens to leave the lawful service of their masters, nor will you, except in cases where the public good may seem to require it, prevent the voluntary return of any fugitive to the service from which he may have escaped."

The Act of Congress to which allusion has already been made, as providing for the confiscation of the estates of persons in open rebellion against the Government, limited the penalty to property actually employed in the service of the rebellion, with the knowledge and consent of its owners; and, instead of emancipating slaves thus employed, left the disposition to be made of them to be determined by the United States Courts, or by subsequent legislation

General Fremont, in command of the Department of Missouri, in an order dated August 30th, declaring martial law established throughout that State, used the following language :

"Real and personal property of those who shall take up arms against the United States, or who shall be directly proven to have taken an active part with their enemies in the field, is declared confiscated to public use, and their slaves, if any they have, are hereby declared free men."

This order violated the above-named act, and could only be justified upon the ground of imperative military necessity Some correspondence which passed between the President and General Fremont upon this topic, resulted in the following official letter, dated Washington, D. C., Sept. 11, 1861 :

" MAJOR GENERAL JOHN C. FREMONT :—

"SIR,—Yours of the 8th, in answer to mine of the 2d inst., is just received. Assured that you, upon the ground, could better judge of the necessities of your position than I could at this distance, on seeing your proclamation of August 30, I perceived no general objection to it; the particular clause, however, in relation to the confiscation of property and the liberation of slaves, appeared to me to be objectionable in its non-conformity to the Act of Congress passed the 6th of last August, upon the same subjects, and hence I wrote you, expressing my wish that that clause should be modified accordingly. Your answer just received expresses the preference on your part that I should make an open order for the modification, which I very cheerfully do. It is, therefore, ordered that the said clause of the said proclamation be so modified, held and construed, as to conform with, and not to transcend the provisions on the same subject contained in the Act of Congress entitled 'An Act to confiscate property used for insurrectionary purposes,' approved

10

August 6, 1861, and that said Act be published at length with this order.

"Your obedient servant,

"A. LINCOLN."

In the instructions from the War Department to General Sherman, in command of the land forces destined to operate on the South Carolina coast, that commander was directed to govern himself relative to this class of persons, by the principles of the letters addressed to General Butler, exercising, however, his own discretion as to special cases. If particular circumstances seemed to require it, they were to be employed in any capacity, with such organization in squads, companies, or otherwise, as should be by him deemed most beneficial to the service. This, however, not to mean a general arming of them for military service. All loyal masters were to be assured that Congress would provide just compensation to them for any loss of the services of persons so employed.

This phase—varying and indefinite—at that time did that question present, which was at a later period to take, under the moulding hand of the President, body and form clearly defined and unmistakable.

The battle of Ball's Bluff—the first under the direction of the new commander on the Potomac—fought October 21st, was but Bull Run repeated; happily, however, on a somewhat smaller scale. A convenient scapegoat upon whom to throw the responsibility—General Stone—was found, and the indignation of the country was measurably, and for the time, appeased.

Directly after this affair, the veteran Scott having asked to be relieved from active service, his request was granted in the following highly complimentary order :

"*Executive Mansion, Washington*, Nov. 1, 1861.

"On the 1st day of November, A. D., 1861, upon his own application to the President of the United States, Brevet

Lieutenant-General Winfield Scott is ordered to be placed, and hereby is placed, upon the list of retired officers of the Army of the United States, without reduction in his current pay, subsistence, or allowances.

"The American people will hear with sadness and deep emotion that General Scott has withdrawn from the active control of the army, while the President and the unanimous Cabinet express their own and the nation's sympathy in his personal affliction, and their profound sense of the important public services rendered by him to his country during his long and brilliant career, among which will ever be gratefully distinguished his faithful devotion to the Constitution, the Union, and the flag, when assailed by a parricidal rebellion.

"ABRAHAM LINCOLN."

To General McClellan, now the ranking officer of the army, the duties of General-in-chief were assigned by the President.

The autumnal months passed away—gorgeous and golden —men thought them made for fighting, if fighting must be ; but no fighting for the Army of the Potomac—an occasional skirmish only—mainly reviews.

The winter months came—the dry season had passed. The Grand Army being now thoroughly organized, disci plined, and equipped went—to fight ?—no—into winter quarters.

And the people, patient ever and forgiving, when inclination impels, forgot Ball's Bluff—forgot what they had hoped for—trusted in the prudent caution of the general in command and waited for the springtide.

CHAPTER X.

THE CONGRESS OF 1861–2.

The Military Situation—Seizure of Mason and Slidell—Opposition to the Administration—
President's Message—Financial Legislation—Committee on the Conduct of the War—
Confiscation Bill.

AT the time of the re-assembling of Congress, December
2d, 1861, the military situation was by no means as promising
as the liberal expenditure of money and the earnest efforts of
the Administration toward a vigorous prosecution of the war
might have led the people to expect.   True, the National
Capitol had been protected, and Maryland, West Virginia,
Kentucky, and Missouri had not, as had been at various times
threatened, been brought in subjection to the rebels.   Nothing more, however—though this would have been judged no
little, had the people been less sanguine of great results immediately at hand—than this had been accomplished in the
East ; and in the West, large rebel forces threatened Kentucky
and Missouri, and the Mississippi river was in their possession from its mouth to within a short distance of the mouth
of the Ohio.

The seizure of the emissaries, Mason and Slidell likewise—
though afterwards disposed of by the Government in such a
way as to secure the acquiescence of the nation—taken in
connection with the position assumed by the British Government—in every way unpalatable to the mass of the people—
seemed likely to entangle us in foreign complications exceedingly undesirable at that juncture.   It was generally believed
that England and France, while neutral on the surface, were
in reality affording very material aid and comfort to the rebel
cause, our commercial interests being very seriously impaired

by the construction which those powers saw fit to place upon their duties as neutrals.

Efforts, moreover, were making to organize a formidable party in antagonism to the Administration, comprising the loose ends of every class of malcontents; those who had always opposed the war, though for a time cowed down by the outburst which followed the fall of Sumter; those who were satisfied that no more progress had been made; those who were inclined, constitutionally, to oppose any thing which any Administration, under any circumstances, might do; those who were beginning to tire of the war, and were ready to patch matters up in any way, so only that it should come to an end; and those who were on the alert for some chance whereby to make capital, political or pecuniary, for their own dear selves.

As a whole, affairs wore by no means a cheering aspect at the opening of this Session.

That the President was fully alive to the true state of the case, the views announced in the following message clearly show:

" FELLOW-CITIZENS OF THE SENATE AND HOUSE OF REPRE-SENTATIVES:—In the midst of unprecedented political troubles, we have cause of great gratitude to God for unusual good health and most abundant harvests.

" You will not be surprised to learn that, in the peculiar exigences of the times, our intercourse with foreign nations has been attended with profound solicitude, chiefly turning upon our own domestic affairs.

"A disloyal portion of the American people have, during the whole year, been engaged in an attempt to divide and destroy the Union. A nation which endures factious domestic division, is exposed to disrespect abroad; and one party, if not both, is sure, sooner or later, to invoke foreign intervention.

" Nations thus tempted to interfere, are not always able to

resist the counsels of seeming expediency and ungenerous ambition, although measures adopted under such influences seldom fail to be unfortunate and injurious to those adopting them.

"The disloyal citizens of the United States who have offered the ruin of our country, in return for the aid and comfort which they have invoked abroad, have received less patronage and encouragement than they probably expected. If it were just to suppose, as the insurgents have seemed to assume, that foreign nations, in this case, discarding all moral, social and treaty obligations, would act solely, and selfishly, for the most speedy restoration of commerce, including, especially, the acquisition of cotton, those nations appear, as yet, not to have seen their way to their objects more directly, or clearly, through the destruction than through the preservation of the Union. If we could dare to believe that foreign nations are actuated by no higher principle than this, I am quite sure a sound argument could be made to show them that they can reach their aim 'more readily and easily by aiding to crush this rebellion than by giving encouragement to it.

"The principal lever relied on by the insurgents for exciting foreign nations to hostility against us, as already intimated, is the embarrassment of commerce. Those nations, however, not improbably, saw from the first, that it was the Union which made, as well our foreign, as our domestic commerce. They can scarcely have failed to perceive that the effort for disunion produces the existing difficulty ; and that one strong nation promises more durable peace, and a more extensive, valuable and reliable commerce, than can the same nation broken into hostile fragments.

"It is not my purpose to review our discussions with foreign States ; because whatever might be their wishes or dispositions, the integrity of our country and the stability of our Government mainly depend, not upon them, but on the loyalty, virtue, patriotism and intelligence of the American people.   The correspondence itself, with the usual reservations, is herewith submitted.

"I venture to hope it will appear that we have practiced prudence and liberality toward foreign powers, averting causes of irritation, and with firmness maintaining our own rights and honor.

"Since, however, it is apparent that here, as in every other State, foreign dangers necessarily attend domestic difficulties, I recommend that adequate and ample measures be adopted for maintaining the public defences on every side.   While, under this general recommendation, provision for defending our sea-coast line readily occurs to the mind, I also, in the same connection, ask the attention of Congress to our great lakes and rivers.   It is believed that some fortifications and depots of arms and munitions, with harbor and navigation improvements, all at well-selected points upon these, would be of great importance to the National defence and preservation.   I ask attention to the views of the Secretary of War, expressed in his report, upon the same general subject.

"I deem it of importance that the loyal regions of East Tennessee and Western North Carolina should be connected with Kentucky, and other faithful parts of the Union, by railroad.   I therefore recommend, as a military measure, that Congress provide for the construction of such road as speedily as possible.   Kentucky, no doubt, will co-operate, and, through her Legislature, make the most judicious selection of a line.   The northern terminus must connect with some existing railroad; and whether the route shall be from Lexington or Nicholasville to the Cumberland Gap, or from Lebanon to the Tennessee line, in the direction of Knoxville, or on some still different line, can easily be determined. Kentucky and the General Government coöperating, the work can be completed in a very short time; and when done, it will be not only of vast present usefulness, but also a valuable permanent improvement, worth its cost in all the future.

"Some treaties, designed chiefly for the interests of commerce, and having no grave political importance, have been negotiated, and will be submitted to the Senate for their consideration.

"Although we have failed to induce some of the commercial powers to adopt a desirable amelioration of the rigor of maritime war, we have removed all obstructions from the way of this humane reform, except such as are merely of temporary and accidental occurrence.

"I invite your attention to the correspondence between Her Britannic Majesty's Minister, accredited to this Government, and the Secretary of State, relative to the detention of the British ship Perthshire, in June last, by the United States steamer Massachusetts, for a supposed breach of the blockade. As this detention was occasioned by an obvious misapprehension of the facts, and as justice requires that we should commit no belligerent act not founded in strict right, as sanctioned by public law, I recommend that an appropriation be made to satisfy the reasonable demand of the owners of the vessel for her detention.

"I repeat the recommendation of my predecessor, in his annual message to Congress in December last, in regard to the disposition of the surplus which will probably remain after satisfying the claims of the American citizens against China, pursuant to the awards of the commissioners under he act of the 3d of March, 1859. If, however, it should not be deemed advisable to carry that recommendation into effect, I would suggest that authority be given for investing the principal, over the proceeds of the surplus referred to, in good securities, with a view to the satisfaction of such other just claims of our citizens against China as are not unlikely to arise hereafter in the course of our extensive trade with that empire.

" By the act of the 5th of August last, Congress authorized the President to instruct the commanders of suitable vessels to defend themselves against and to capture pirates. This authority has been exercised in a single instance only. For the more effectual protection of our extensive and valuable commerce, in the Eastern seas especially, it seems to me that it would also be advisable to authorize the commanders of sailing vessels to recapture any prizes which pirates may make of United States vessels and their cargoes, and the consular courts, now established by law in Eastern countries, to adjudicate the cases, in the event that thisshould not be objected to by the local authorities.

" If any good reason exists why we should persevere longer in withholding our recognition of the independence and sovereignty of Hayti and Liberia, I am unable to discern it. Unwilling, however, to inaugurate a novel policy in regard to them without the approbation of Congress, I submit for your consideration the expediency of an appropriation for maintaining a charge d'affaires near each of those new States. It does not admit of doubt that important commercial advantages might be secured by favorable treaties with them.

" The operations of the treasury during the period which has elapsed since your adjournment, have been conducted with signal success. The patriotism of the people has placed at the disposal of the Government the large means demanded by the public exigencies. Much of the national loan has been taken by citizens of the industrial classes, whose confidence in their country's faith, and zeal for their country's deliverance from present peril, have induced them to contribute to the support of the Government the whole of their limited acquisitions. This fact imposes peculiar obligations to economy in disbursement, and energy in action.

" The revenue from all sources, including loans, for the financial year ending on the 30th of June, 1861, was eighty-six million eight hundred and thirty-five thousand nine hundred dollars and twenty-seven cents, and the expenditures for the same period, including payments on account of the public debt, were eighty-four million five hundred and seventy-eight thousand eight hundred and thirty-four dollars and forty-seven cents; leaving a balance in the treasury on the 1st of July of two million two hundred and fifty-seven thousand sixty-five dollars and eighty cents. For the first quarter of the financial year, ending on the 30th of September, 1861, the receipts from all sources, including the balance of the 1st of July, were one hundred and two million five hundred and thirty-two thousand five hundred and nine dollars and twenty-seven cents, and the expenses ninety-eight million two hundred and thirty-nine thousand seven hundred and thirty-three dollars and nine cents; leaving a balance on the 1st of October, 1861, of four million two hundred and ninety-two thousand seven hundred and seventy-six dollars and eighteen cents.

"Estimates for the remaining three-quarters of the year, and for the financial year 1863, together with his views of ways and means for meeting the demands contemplated by them, will be submitted to Congress by the Secretary of the Treasury. It is gratifying to know that the expenditures made necessary by the rebellion are not beyond the resources of the loyal people, and to believe that the same patriotism which has thus far sustained the Government will continue to sustain it till peace and Union shall again bless the land.

"I respectfully refer to the report of the Secretary of War for information respecting the numerical strength of the Army, and for recommendations having in view an increase of its efficiency and the well-being of the various branches of the service intrusted to his care. It is gratifying to know that the patriotism of the people has proved equal to the occasion, and that the number of troops tendered greatly exceeds the force which Congress authorized me to call into the field

"I refer with pleasure to those portions of his report which make allusion to the creditable degree of discipline already attained by our troops, and to the excellent sanitary condition of the entire army.

"The recommendation of the Secretary for an organization of the militia upon a uniform basis is a subject of vital importance to the future safety of the country, and is commended to the serious attention of Congress.

"The large addition to the regular army, in connection with the defection that has so considerably diminished the number of its officers, gives peculiar importance to his recommendation for increasing the corps of cadets to the greatest capacity of the Military Academy.

"By mere omission, I presume, Congress has failed to provide chaplains for hospitals occupied by volunteers. This subject was brought to my notice, and I was induced to draw up the form of a letter, one copy of which, properly addressed, has been delivered to each of the persons, and at the dates respectively named and stated, in a schedule, containing also the form of the letter, marked A, and herewith transmitted.

"These gentlemen, I understand, entered upon the duties designated, at the times respectively stated in the schedule, and have labored faithfully therein ever since. I therefore recommend that they be compensated at the same rate as chaplains in the army. I further suggest that general provision be made for chaplains to serve at hospitals, as well as with regiments.

"The report of the Secretary of the Navy presents in detail the operations of that branch of the service, the activity and energy which have characterized its administration, and the results of measures to increase its efficiency and power. Such have been the additions, by construction and purchase, that it may almost be said a navy has been created and brought into service since our difficulties commenced.

"Besides blockading our extensive coast, squadrons larger

than ever before assembled under our flag have been put afloat, and performed deeds which have increased our naval renown.

"I would invite special attention to the recommendation f the Secretary for a more perfect organization of the Navy by introducing additional grades in the service.

"The present organization is defective and unsatisfactory, and the suggestions submitted by the Department will, it is believed, if adopted, obviate the difficulties alluded to, promote harmony, and increase the efficiency of the Navy.

"There are three vacancies on the bench of the Supreme Court—two by the decease of Justices Daniel and McLean, and one by the resignation of Justice Campbell. I have so far forborne making nominations to fill these vacancies for reasons which I will now state. Two of the outgoing judges resided within the States now overrun by revolt; so that if successors were appointed in the same localities, they could not now serve upon their circuits; and many of the most competent men there probably would not take the personal hazard of accepting to serve, even here, upon the Supreme Bench. I have been unwilling to throw all the appointments northward, thus disabling myself from doing justice to the South on the return of peace; although I may remark that to transfer to the North one which has heretofore been in the South would not, with reference to territory and population, be unjust.

"During the long and brilliant judicial career of Judge McLean, his circuit grew into an empire—altogether too large for any one judge to give the courts therein more than a nominal attendance—rising in population from one million four hundred and seventy thousand and eighteen, in 1830, to six million one hundred and fifty-one thousand four hundred and five, in 1860.

"Besides this, the country generally has outgrown our present judicial system. If uniformity was at all intended, the system requires that all the States shall be accommodated with circuit courts, attended by supreme judges, while, in fact, Wisconsin, Minnesota, Iowa, Kansas, Florida, Texas, California, and Oregon, have never had any such courts. Nor can this well be remedied without a change in the system ; because the adding of judges to the Supreme Court, enough for the accommodation of all parts of the country, with circuit courts, would create a court altogether too numerous for a judicial body of any sort. And the evil, if it be one, will increase as new States come into the Union. Circuit courts are useful, or they are not useful ; if useful, no State should be denied them ; if not useful, no State should have them. Let them be provided for all, or abolished as to all.

" Three modifications occur to me, either of which, I think, would be an improvement upon our present system. Let the Supreme Court be of convenient number in every event. Then, first, let the whole country be divided into circuits of convenient size, the supreme judges to serve in a number of them corresponding to their own number, and independent circuit judges be provided for all the rest. Or, secondly, let the supreme judges be relieved from circuit duties, and circuit judges provided for all the circuits. Or, thirdly, dispense with circuit courts altogether, leaving the judicial functions wholly to the district courts, and an independent Supreme Court.

" I respectfully recommend to the consideration of Congress the present condition of the statute laws, with the hope that Congress will be able to find an easy remedy for many of th inconveniences and evils which constantly embarrass those engaged in the practical administration of them. Since the organization of the Government, Congress has enacted some five thousand acts and joint resolutions, which fill more than six thousand closely printed pages, and are scattered through many volumes. Many of these acts have been drawn in haste and without sufficient caution, so that their provisions are often obscure in themselves, or in conflict with each other, or at least so doubtful as to render it very difficut for even the best informed persons to ascertain precisely what the statute law really is.

"It seems to me very important that the statute laws should be made as plain and intelligible as possible, and be reduced to as small a compass as may consist with the fulness and precision of the will of the legislature and the perspicuity of its language. This well done, would, I think, greatly facilitate the labors of those whose duty it is to assist in the administration of the laws, and would be a lasting benefit to the people, by placing before them in a more accessible and intelligible form, the laws which so deeply concern their interests and their duties.

"I am informed by some whose opinions I respect, that all the acts of Congress now in force, and of a permanent and general nature, might be revised and re-written, so as to be embraced in one volume (or at most, two volumes) of ordinary and convenient size. And I respectfully recommend to Congress to consider the subject, and, if my suggestion be approved, to devise such plan as to their wisdom shall seem most proper for the attainment of the end proposed.

"One of the unavoidable consequences of the present insurrection, is the entire suppression, in many places, of all the ordinary means of administering civil justice by the officers and in the forms of existing law. This is the case, in whole or in part, in all insurgent States; and as our armies advance upon and take possession of parts of those States, the practical evil becomes more apparent. There are no courts nor officers to whom the citizens of other States may apply for the enforcement of their lawful claims against citizens of the insurgent States; and there is a vast amount of debt constituting such claims. Some have estimated it as high as two hundred million dollars, due in large part, from insurgents in open rebellion to loyal citizens, who are even now making great sacrifices in the discharge of their patriotic duty, to support the Government.

" Under these circumstances, I have been urgently solicited to establish by military power, courts to administer summary justice in such cases. I have thus far declined to do it, not because I had any doubt that the end proposed—the collection of the debts—was just and right in itself, but because I have been unwilling to go beyond the pressure of necessity in the unusual exercise of power. But the powers of Congress, I suppose, are equal to the anomalous occasion, and therefore I refer the whole matter to Congress, with the hope that a plan may be devised for the administration of justice in all such parts of the insurgent States and Territories as may be under the control of this Government, whether by a voluntary return to allegiance and order, or by the power of our arms. This, however, not to be a permanent institution, but a temporary substitute, and to cease as soon as the ordinary courts can be re-established in peace.

" It is important that some more convenient means should be provided, if possible, for the adjustment of claims against the Government, especially in view of their increased number by reason of the war. It is as much the duty of Government to render prompt justice against itself, in favor of citizens, as it is to administer the same between private individuals. The investigation and adjudication of claims, in their nature, belong to the judicial department ; besides, it is apparent that the attention of Congress will be more than usually engaged for some time to come with great national questions. It was intended, by the organization of the Court of Claims, mainly to remove this branch of business from the halls of Congress ; but while the court has proved to be an effective and valuable means of investigation, it in a great degree fails to effect the object of its creation for want of power to make its judgments final

" Fully aware of the delicacy, not to say the danger, of the subject, I commend to your careful consideration whether this power of making judgments final may not properly be given to the court, reserving the right of appeal on questions of law to the Supreme Court, with such other provisions as experience may have shown to be necessary.

" I ask attention to the report of the Postmaster General, the following being a summary statement of the condition of the department :

" The revenue from all sources during the fiscal year ending June 30th, 1861, including the annual permanent appropriation of seven hundred thousand dollars for the transportation of ' free mail matter,' was nine million forty-nine thousand two hundred and ninety-six dollars and forty cents, being about two per cent. less than the revenue for 1860.

" The expenditures were thirteen million six hundred and six thousand seven hundred and fifty-nine dollars and eleven cents, showing a decrease of more than eight per cent. as compared with those of the previous year, and leaving an excess of expenditure over the revenue for the last fiscal year of four million five hundred and fifty-seven thousand four hundred and sixty-two dollars and seventy-one cents.

" The gross revenue for the year ending June 30th, 1863, is estimated at an increase of four per cent. on that of 1861, making eight million six hundred and eighty-three thousand dollars, to which should be added the earnings of the department in carrying free matter, viz : seven hundred thousand dollars, making nine million three hundred and eighty-three thousand dollars.

" The total expenditures for 1863 are estimated at twelve million five hundred and twenty-eight thousand dollars, leaving an estimated deficiency of three million one hundred and forty-five thousand dollars to be supplied from the treasury, in addition to the permanent appropriation.

" The present insurrection shows, I think, that the extension of this District across the Potomac river, at the time of establishing the capital here, was eminently wise, and consequently that the relinquishment of that portion of it which lies within the State of Virginia was unwise and dangerous. I submit for your consideration the expediency of regaining that part of the District, and the restoration of the original boundaries thereof, through negotiations with the state of Virginia.

" The report of the Secretary of the Interior, with the accompanying documents, exhibits the condition of the several branches of the public business pertaining to that department. The depressing influences of the insurrection have been specially felt in the operations of the Patent and General Land Offices. The cash receipts from the sales of public lands during the past year have exceeded the expenses of our land system only about two hundred thousand dollars. The sales have been entirely suspended in the Southern States, while the interruptions to the business of the country, and the diversions of large numbers of men from labor to military service, have obstructed settlements in the new States and Territories of the North-west.

" The receipts of the Patent Office have declined in nine months about one hundred thousand dollars, rendering a large reduction of the force employed necessary to make it self-sustaining.

" The demands upon the Pension Office will be largely increased by the insurrection. Numerous applications for pensions, based upon the casualties of the existing war, have already been made. There is reason to believe that many who are now upon the pension rolls, and in receipt of the bounty of the Government, are in the ranks of the insurgent army, or giving them aid and comfort. The Secretary of the Interior has directed a suspension of the payment of the pensions of such persons upon the proof of their disloyalty. I recommend that Congress authorize that officer to cause the names of such persons to be stricken from the pension rolls

11

" The relations of the Government with the Indian tribes have been greatly disturbed by the insurrection, especially in the Southern Superintendency and in that of New Mexico The Indian country south of Kansas is in the possession of insurgents from Texas and Arkansas. The agents of the United States appointed since the 4th of March for this superintendency have been unable to reach their posts, while the most of those who were in office before that time have espoused the insurrectionary cause, and assume to exercise the powers of agents by virtue of commissions from the insurrectionists. It has been stated in the public press that a portion of those Indians have been organized as a military force, and are attached to the army of the insurgents. Although the Government has no official information upon this subject, letters have been written to the Commissioner of Indian Affairs by several prominent chiefs, giving assurance of their loyalty to the United States, and expressing a wish for the presence of Federal troops to protect them. It is believed that upon the repossession of the country by the Federal forces the Indians will readily cease all hostile demonstrations, and resume their former relations to the Government.

" Agriculture, confessedly the largest interest of the nation, has not a department, nor a bureau, but a clerkship only, assigned to it in the Government. While it is fortunate that this great interest is so independent in its nature as to not have demanded and extorted more from the Government, I respectfully ask Congress to consider whether something more can not be given voluntarily with general advantage.

"Annual reports exhibiting the condition of our agriculture, commerce, and manufactures, would present a fund of information of great practical value to the country. While I make no suggestion as to details, I venture the opinion that an agricultural and statistical bureau might profitably be organized.

" The execution of the laws for the suppression of the

African slave-trade has been confided to the Department of the Interior. It is a subject of gratulation that the efforts which have been made for the suppression of this inhuman traffic have been recently attended with unusual success. Five vessels being fitted out for the slave-trade have been seized and condemned. Two mates of vessels engaged in the trade, and one person in equipping a vessel as a slaver, have been convicted and subjected to the penalty of fine and imprisonment, and one captain, taken with a cargo of Africans on board his vessel, has been convicted of the highest grade of offence under our laws, the punishment of which is death.

" The Territories of Colorado, Dakota, and Nevada, created by the last Congress, have been organized, and civil administration has been inaugurated therein under auspices especially gratifying, when it is considered that the leaven of treason was found existing in some of these new countries when the Federal officers arrived there.

" The abundant natural resources of these Territories, with the security and protection afforded by organized government, will doubtless invite to them a large immigration when peace shall restore the business of the country to its accustomed channels. I submit the resolutions of the Legislature of Colorado, which evidence the patriotic spirit of the people of the Territory. So far, the authority of the United States has been upheld in all the Territories, as it is hoped it will be in the future. I commend their interests and defence to the enlightened and generous care of Congress.

" I recommend to the favorable consideration of Congress the interests of the District of Columbia. The insurrection has been the cause of much suffering and sacrifice to its inhabitants, and as they have no representative in Congress, that body should not overlook their just claims upon the Government.

"At your late session a joint resolution was adopted authorizing the President to take measures for facilitating a proper representation of the industrial interests of the United States at the exhibition of the industry of all nations, to be holden in London in the year 1862. I regret to say I have been unable to give personal attention to this subject—a subject at once so interesting in itself, and so extensively and intimately connected with the material prosperity of the world. Through the Secretaries of State and of the Interior a plan, or system, has been devised, and partly matured, and which will be laid before you.

"Under and by virtue of the act of Congress entitled 'An act to confiscate property used for insurrectionary purposes,' approved August 6, 1861, the legal claims of certain persons to the labor and service of certain other persons have become forfeited; and numbers of the latter, thus liberated, are already dependent on the United States, and must be provided for in some way. Besides this, it is not impossible that some of the States will pass similar enactments for their own benefit respectively, and by operation of which persons of the same class will be thrown upon them for disposal. In such case I recommend that Congress provide for accepting such persons from such States according to some mode of valuation, in lieu, *pro tanto*, of direct taxes, or upon some other plan to be agreed on with such States, respectively; that such persons, on such acceptance by the General Government, be at once deemed free; and, that, in any event, steps be taken for colonizing both classes (or the one first mentioned, if the other shall not be brought into existence) at some place or places in a climate congenial to them. It might be well to consider, too, whether the free colored people already in the United States could not, so far as individuals may desire, be included in such colonization.

"To carry out the plan of colonization may involve the acquiring of territory, and also the appropriation of money beyond that to be expended in the territorial acquisition. Having practiced the acquisition of territory for nearly sixty

years, the question of constitutional power to do so is no
longer an open one with us. The power was questioned at
first by Mr. Jefferson, who, however, in the purchase of
Louisiana, yielded his scruples on the plea of great expediency. If it be said that the only legitimate object of acquiring territory is to furnish homes for white men, this
measure effects that object, for the emigration of colored men
leaves additional room for white men remaining or coming
here. Mr. Jefferson, however, placed the importance of pro-
curing Louisiana more on political and commercial grounds
than on providing room for population.

" On this whole proposition, including the appropriation of
money with the acquisition of territory, does not the expediency amount to absolute necessity—that without which the
Government itself cannot be perpetuated ?

" The war continues. In considering the policy to be
adopted for suppressing the insurrection, I have been anxious
and careful that the inevitable conflict for this purpose shall
not degenerate into a violent and remorseless revolutionary
struggle. I have, therefore, in every case thought it proper
to keep the integrity of the Union prominent as the primary
object of the contest on our part, leaving all questions which
are not of vital military importance to the more deliberate
action of the legislature.

" In the exercise of my best discretion, I have adhered to
the blockade of the ports held by the insurgents, instead of
putting in force, by proclamation, the law of Congress
enacted at the late session for closing those ports.

" So, also, obeying the dictates of prudence, as well as the
obligations of law, instead of transcending, I have adhered to
the act of Congress to confiscate property used for insurrectionary purposes. If a new law upon the same subject shall
be proposed, its propriety will be duly considered. The
Union must be preserved ; and hence all indispensable means
must be employed. We should not be in haste to determine

that radical and extreme measures, which may reach the loyal as well as the disloyal, are indispensable.

"The inaugural address at the beginning of the administration, and the message to Congress at the late special session, were both mainly devoted to the domestic controversy out of which the insurrection and consequent war have sprung. Nothing now occurs to add or subtract to or from the principles or general purposes stated and expressed in those documents.

"The last ray of hope for preserving the Union peaceably expired at the assault upon Fort Sumter; and a general review of what has occurred since may not be unprofitable. What was painfully uncertain then is much better defined and more distinct now; and the progress of events is plainly in the right direction. The insurgents confidently claimed a strong support from north of Mason and Dixon's line, and the friends of the Union were not free from apprehension on the point. This, however, was soon settled definitely, and on the right side. South of the line, noble little Delaware led off right from the first. Maryland was made to *seem* against the Union. Our soldiers were assaulted, bridges were burned, and railroads torn up within her limits, and we were many days, at one time, without the ability to bring a single regiment over her soil to the capital. Now her bridges and railroads are repaired and open to the Government; she already gives seven regiments to the cause of the Union and none to the enemy; and her people, at a regular election, have sustained the Union by a larger majority and a larger aggregate vote than they ever before gave to any candidate or any question. Kentucky, too, for some time in doubt, is now decidedly, and, I think, unchangeably, ranged on the side of the Union. Missouri is comparitively quiet, and I believe can not again be overrun by the insurrectionists. These three States of Maryland, Kentucky and Missouri, neither of which would promise a single soldier at first, have now an aggregate of not less than forty thousand in the field for the Union ; while of their citizens certainly not more than a third of that number, and they of doubtful whereabouts and doubtful existence, are in arms against it. After a somewhat bloody struggle of months, winter closes on the Union people of Western Virginia, leaving them masters of their own country.

"An insurgent force of about fifteen hundred, for months dominating the narrow peninsular region, constituting the counties of Accomac and Northampton, and known as the eastern shore of Virginia, together with some contiguous parts of Maryland, have laid down their arms ; and the people there have renewed their allegiance to, and accepted the protection of the old flag. This leaves no armed insurrectionist north of the Potomac or east of the Chesapeake.

"Also we have obtained a footing at each of the isolated points, on the southern coast, of Hatteras, Port Royal, Tybee Island, near Savannah, and Ship Island ; and we likewise have some general accounts of popular movements, in behalf of the Union, in North Carolina and Tennessee.

"These things demonstrate that the cause of the Union is advancing steadily and certainly southward.

"Since your last adjournment, Lieut.-Gen. Scott has retired from the head of the army. During his long life, the nation has not been unmindful of his merit ; yet, on calling to mind how faithfully, ably and brilliantly he has served the country, from a time far back in our history, when few of the now living had been born, and thenceforward continually, I can not but think we are still his debtors. I submit, therefore, for your consideration, what further mark of recognition is due to him, and to ourselves, as a grateful people.

"With the retirement of Gen. Scott came the Executive duty of appointing, in his stead, a General-in-chief of the army. It is a fortunate circumstance that neither in council nor country was there, so far as I know, any difference of opinion as to the proper person to be selected. The retiring chief repeatedly expressed his judgment in favor of Gen. McClellan for the position, and in this the nation seemed to give a unanimous concurrence. The designation of Gen. McClellan is, therefore, in considerable degree, the selection of the country as well as of the Executive; and hence there is better reason to hope there will be given him the confidence and cordial support thus, by fair implication, promised, and without which he can not, with so full efficiency, serve the country.

"It has been said that one bad General is better than two good ones; and the saying is true, if taken to mean no more than that an army is better directed by a single mind, though inferior, than by two superior ones at variance and cross-purposes with each other.

"And the same is true in all joint operations wherein those engaged *can* have none but a common end in view, and *can* differ only as to the choice of means. In a storm at sea, no one on board *can* wish the ship to sink, and yet, not unfrequently, all go down together because too many will direct and no single mind can be allowed to control.

"It continues to develop that the insurrection is largely, if not exclusively, a war upon the first principle of popular government—the rights of the people. Conclusive evidence of this is found in the most grave and maturely-considered public documents, as well as in the general tone of the insurgents. In those documents we find the abridgment of the existing right of suffrage and the denial to the people of all right to participate in the selection of public officers, except the legislative, boldly advocated, with labored arguments to prove that large control of the people in government is the source of all political evil. Monarchy itself is sometimes hinted at as a possible refuge from the power of the people.

"In my present position I could scarcely be justified were I to omit raising a warning voice against this approach of returning despotism.

" It is not needed nor fitting here that a general argument should be made in favor of popular institutions ; but there is one point, with its connections, not so hackneyed as most others, to which I ask a brief attention. It is the effort to place *capital* on an equal footing with, if not above *labor*, in the structure of government. It is assumed that labor is available only in connection with capital—that nobody labors unless somebody else, owning capital, somehow by the use of it induces him to labor. This assumed, it is next considered whether it is best that capital shall *hire* laborers, and thus induce them to work by their own consent, or *buy* them, and drive them to it without their consent. Having proceeded so far, it is naturally concluded that all laborers are either *hired* laborers, or what we call slaves. And further, it is assumed that whoever is once a hired laborer is fixed in that condition for life.

" Now, there is no such relation between capital and labor as assumed ; nor is there any such thing as a free man being fixed for life in the condition of a hired laborer. Both these assumptions are false, and all inferences from them are groundless.

" Labor is prior to and independent of capital. Capital is only the fruit of labor, and could never have existed if labor had not first existed. Labor is the superior of capital, and deserves much the higher consideration. Capital has its rights, which are as worthy of protection as any other rights. Nor is it denied that there is, and probably always will be, a relation between labor and capital producing mutual benefits. The error is in assuming that the whole labor of community exists within that relation. A few men own capital, and that few avoid labor themselves, and with their capital hire or buy another few to labor for them. A large majority belong to neither class—neither work for others nor have others working for them. In most of the Southern States a majority of the whole people, of all colors, are neither slaves nor masters. while in the Northern a large majority are neither hirers nor hired. Men, with their families—wives, sons, and daughters—work for themselves, on their farms, in their houses, and in their shops, taking the whole product to themselves, and asking no favors of capital, on the one hand, nor of hired laborers or slaves on the other. It is not forgotten that a considerable number of persons mingle their own labor with capital—that is, they labor with their own hands, and also buy or hire others to labor for them ; but this is only a mixed, and not a distinct class. No principle stated is disturbed by the existence of this mixed class.

" Again, as has already been said, there is not, of necessity, any such thing as the free hired laborer being fixed to that condition for life. Many independent men everywhere in these States, a few years back in their lives, were hired laborers. The prudent, penniless beginner in the world, labors for wages awhile, saves a surplus with which to buy tools or land for himself, then labors on his own account another while, and at length hires another new beginner to help him. This is the just, and generous, and prosperous system, which opens the way to all—gives hope to all, and consequent energy, and progress, and improvement of condition to all. No men living are more worthy to be trusted than those who toil up from poverty ; none less inclined to take or touch aught which they have not honestly earned. Let them beware of surrendering a political power which they already possess, and which, if surrendered, will surely be used to close the door of advancement against such as they, and to fix new disabilities and burdens upon them, till all of liberty shall be lost.

" From the first taking of our National Census to the last are seventy years; and we find our population at the end of the period eight times as great as it was at the beginning. The increase of those other things which men deem desirable has been even greater. We thus have at one view what the popular principle, applied to Government through the machinery of the States and the Union, has produced in a given time, and also what if firmly maintained, it promises for the future. There are already among us those who, if the Union be preserved, will live to see it contain two hundred and fifty millions. The struggle *of* to-day is not altogether *for* to-day ; it is for a vast future also. With a reliance on Providence all the more firm and earnest, let us proceed in the great task which events have devolved upon us.

"ABRAHAM LINCOLN.

" WASHINGTON, December 3, 1861. "

At this session, provision was made for the issue of legal tender notes, and an internal revenue bill was matured, for the purposing of increasing largely the receipts of the Treasury, affording a basis for the payment of interest on authorized loans, and insuring confidence in the National currency.

A Congressional committee on the conduct of the war was also appointed, the evidence obtained by which was submitted to the President for his consideration and eventually given to the public.

A confiscation bill was passed, with a special provision for conditional pardon and amnesty, limiting the forfeiture of real estate to the lifetime of its rebel owners.

CHAPTER XI.

THE SLAVERY QUESTION.

Situation of the President—His Policy—Gradual Emancipation Message—Abolition of Slavery in the District of Columbia—Repudiation of General Hunter's Emancipation Order—Conference with Congressmen from the Border Slave States—Address to the same—Military Order—Proclamation under the Confiscation Act.

WHAT was to be the final disposition of the question of slavery could not be thrust aside. The intimate connection of this institution with our military operations, was perpetually forcing it upon the attention of the nation. This subject had, since it had been rendered patent to all, that it was to be no holiday struggle in which we were engaged, but a life and death grapple with desperate and determined foes, been ever present to Mr. Lincoln's mind. His action was, however, to a certain extent, not suffered to be independent. Could he have boldly assumed the initiative, assured that the great mass of the people were at his back, he could have acted far otherwise than he was necessitated to act, considering the delicate nature of the question, the utter lack of precedents, the intertwining of interests, the dangers resulting from a single misstep, the divisions on this point, existing in the ranks even of his own political supporters, and the conflicting views held by men whose loyalty and devotion to the country were unimpeachable.

He chose not to go far ahead of popular indications; he deemed it the wiser statesmanship, in the existing state of affairs, to keep in the lead but a little, feeling, so to speak, his way along—making haste slowly. That this would dissatisfy many of his political friends he well knew; but he, upon mature deliberation, decided that it was for the interest of the country, and that to that consideration everything else must yield.

On the 6th of March, 1862, he sent to the Congress the following message concerning this question, the resolution embodied in which, was passed by both Houses:

"FELLOW-CITIZENS OF THE SENATE AND HOUSE OF REPRESENTATIVES:—I recommend the adoption of a joint resolution by your honorable bodies, which shall be substantially as follows:

"*Resolved*, That the United States ought to coöperate with any State which may adopt gradual abolishment of slavery, giving to such State pecuniary aid, to be used by such State in its discretion, to compensate for the inconveniences, public and private, produced by such change of system.

" If the proposition contained in the resolution does not meet the approval of Congress and the country, there is the end ; but if it does command such approval, I deem it of importance that the States and people immediately interested, should be at once distinctly notified of the fact, so that they may begin to consider whether to accept or reject it. The Federal Government would find its highest interest in such a measure as one of the most efficient means of self-preservation. The leaders of the existing insurrection entertain the hope that this Government will ultimately be forced to acknowledge the independence of some part of the disaffected region, and that all the slave States north of such part will then say, ' the Union for which we have struggled being already gone, we now choose to go with the southern section.' To deprive them of this hope substantially ends the rebellion, and the initiation of emancipation completely deprives them of it as to all the States initiating it. The point is not that *all* the States tolerating slavery would very soon, if at all, initiate emancipation, but that, while the offer is equally made to all, the more northern shall, by such initiation, make it certain to the more southern that in no event will the former ever join the latter in their proposed confederacy. I say ' initiation,' because in my judgment, gradual, and not sudden emancipation, is better for all. In the mere financial or pecuniary view, any member of Congress, with the census tables and treasury reports before him, can readily see for himself how very soon the current expenditures of this war would purchase, at fair valuation, all the slaves in any named State. Such a proposition on the part of the general Government sets up no claim of a right by Federal authority to interfere with slavery within State limits, referring, as it does, the absolute control of the subject in each case to the State and its people immediately interested. It is proposed as a matter of perfectly free choice with them.

" In the annual message last December, I thought fit to

say, 'the Union must be preserved; and hence all indispensable means must be employed.' I said this not hastily, but deliberately. War has been made, and continues to be an indispensable means to this end. A practical re-acknowedgment of the national authority would render the war unecessary, and it would at once cease. If, however, resistance continues, the war must also continue, and it is impossible to foresee all the incidents which may attend, and all the ruin which may follow it. Such as may seem indispensable, or may obviously promise great efficiency toward ending the struggle, must and will come.

" The proposition now made, though an offer only, I hope it may be esteemed no offence to ask whether the pecuniary consideration tendered would not be of more value to the States and private persons concerned, than are the institutions and property in it, in the present aspect of affairs.

" While it is true that the adoption of the proposed resolution would be merely initiatory, and not within itself a practical measure, it is recommended in the hope that it would soon lead to important practical results. In full view of my great responsibility to my God and to my country, I earnestly beg the attention of Congress and the people to the subject.

" March 6, 1862.   ABRAHAM LINCOLN."

A bill abolishing slavery in the District of Columbia having passed both Houses of Congress early in April, the President, in communicating his approval of the measure, judged it necessary to accompany the same with the following message :

" FELLOW-CITIZENS OF THE SENATE AND HOUSE OF REPRESENTATIVES :—The act entitled 'An act for the release of certain persons held to service or labor in the District of Columbia,' has this day been approved and signed.

" I have never doubted the constitutional authority of Con gress to abolish slavery in this District, and I have ever desired to see the National Capital freed from the institution in some satisfactory way. Hence there has never been, in my mind, any question upon the subject except the one of expediency, arising in view of all the circumstances. If there be matters within and about this act which might have taken a course or shape more satisfactory to my judgment, I do not attempt to specify them. I am gratified that the two principles of compensation and colonization are both recognized and practically applied in the act.

"In the matter of compensation it is provided that claims may be presented within ninety days from the passage of the act, ' but not thereafter,' and there is no saving for minors, *femes-covert*, insane or absent persons. I presume this is an omission by mere oversight, and I recommend that it be supplied by an amendatory or supplemental act.

"April 16, 1862.   ABRAHAM LINCOLN."

The President's repudiation, by the following proclamation, of an emancipation order of General Hunter, was conclusive evidence that he was determined to keep the control of this vexed question in his own hands, and to suffer no military commander to exercise jurisdiction over it:

"WHEREAS, There appears in the public prints what purports to be a proclamation of Major-General Hunter, in the words and figures following, to wit:

'HEAD-QUARTERS, DEPARTMENT OF THE SOUTH,
'Hilton Head, S. C., May 9th, 1862.

'GENERAL ORDERS No. 11.

'The three States of Georgia, Florida, and South Carolina, comprising the Military Department of the South, having deliberately declared themselves no longer under the protection of the United States of America, and having taken up arms against the said United States, it becomes a military necessity to declare them under martial law. This was accordingly done on the twenty-fifth day of April, 1862. Slavery and martial law in a free country are altogether incompatible. The persons in these three States, Georgia,

Florida, and South Carolina, heretofore held as slaves, are therefore declared forever free.

'DAVID HUNTER, *Major-General Commanding.*
' Official :
' ED. W SMITH, *Acting Assistant Adjutant General.*'

"AND WHEREAS, The same is producing some excitement and misunderstanding,

"*Therefore*, I, Abraham Lincoln, President of the United States, proclaim and declare that the government of the United States had no knowledge or belief of an intention, on the part of General Hunter, to issue such a proclamation, nor has it yet any authentic information that the document is genuine ; and further, that neither General Hunter nor any other commander or person has been authorized by the government of the United States to make proclamation declaring the slaves of any State free, and that the supposed proclamation now in question, whether genuine or false, is altogether void, so far as respects such declaration.

"I further make known, that whether it be competent for me as commander-in-chief of the army and navy to declare the slaves of any State or States free, and whether at any time, or in any case, it shall become a necessity indispensable to the maintenance of the Government to exercise such supposed power, are questions which, under my responsibility, I reserve to myself, and which I cannot feel justified in leaving to the decision of commanders in the field. These are totally different questions from those of police regulations in armies and camps.

"On the sixth day of March last, by a special message, I recommended to Congress the adoption of a joint resolution, to be substantially as follows :

"*Resolved*, That the United States ought to coöperate with any State which may adopt a gradual abolishment of slavery, giving to such State pecuniary aid, to be used by such State in its discretion, to compensate for the inconveniences, public and private, produced by such change of system.'

" The resolution, in the language above quoted, was adopted by large majorities in both branches of Congress, and now stands an authentic, definite and solemn proposal of the nation to the States and people most immediately interested in the subject matter. To the people of these States I now earnestly appeal. I do not argue ; I beseech you to make the argu ments for yourselves. You cannot, if you would, be blind to the signs of the times. I beg of you a calm and enlarged consideration of them, ranging, if it may be, far above personal and partisan politics. This proposal makes common cause for a common object, casting no reproaches upon any. It acts not the Pharisee. The change it contemplates would come gently as the dews of Heaven, not rending or wrecking any thing. Will you not embrace it ? So much good has not been done by one effort in all past time, as in the Providence of God it is now your high privilege to do. May the vast future not have to lament that you have neglected it.

" In witness whereof, I have hereunto set my hand, and caused the seal of the United States to be affixed.

" Done at the City of Washington, this nineteenth day of May, in the year of our Lord one thousand eight hundred and sixty-two, and of the Independence of the United States the eighty-sixth.

     " By the President :   ABRAHAM LINCOLN.

" WILLIAM H. SEWARD, Secretary of State."

A short time before the adjournment of Congress, while the country was in a state of great despondency, owing to the miscarriage of the Peninsular Campaign, the President, knowing that whatever measures events should point out as necessary to put down the rebellion must be adopted, and anticipating that a blow directed at the institution of slavery would, probably, at no distant period have to be dealt. invited the Senators and Representatives of the Border Slave States to a conference, for the purpose of preparing their

12

minds for the happening of such a contingency. On this occasion he read to them the following carefully prepared address, to which he received an approving response from but nine of the twenty-nine :

" GENTLEMEN :——After the adjournment of Congress, now near, I shall have no opportunity of seeing you for several months. Believing that you of the Border States hold more power for good than any other equal number of members, I feel it a duty which I can not justifiably waive to make this appeal to you.

" I intend no reproach or complaint when I assure you that, in my opinion, if you all had voted for the resolution in the gradual emancipation message of last March, the war would now be substantially ended. And the plan therein proposed is yet one of the most potent and swift means of ending it. Let the States which are in rebellion see definitely and certainly that in no event will the States you represent ever join their proposed Confederacy, and they can not much longer maintain the contest. But you can not divest them of their hope to ultimately have you with them so long as you show a determination to perpetuate the institution within your own States. Beat them at elections, as you have overwhelmingly done, and, nothing daunted, they still claim you as their own. You and I know what the lever of their power is. Break that lever before their faces, and they can shake you no more forever.

" Most of you have treated me with kindness and consideration, and I trust you will not now think I improperly touch what is exclusively your own, when, for the sake of the whole country, I ask, ' Can you, for your States, do better than to take the course I urge ?' Discarding *punctilio* and maxims adapted to more manageable times, and looking only to the unprecedentedly stern facts of our case, can you do better in any possible event ? You prefer that the constitutional relations of the States to the nation shall be practically restored without disturbance of the institution ; and, if this were done, my whole duty in this respect, under the Constitution and my oath of office, would be performed. But it is not done, and we are trying to accomplish it by war. The incidents of the war can not be avoided. If the war continues long, as it must if the object be not sooner attained, the institution in your States will be extinguished by mere friction and abrasion— by the mere incidents of the war. It will be gone, and you will have nothing valuable in lieu of it. Much of its value is gone already. How much better for you and for your people to take the step which at once shortens the war, and secures substantial compensation for that which is sure to be wholly lost in any other event ! How much better to thus save the money which else we sink forever in the war ! How much better to do it while we can, lest the war, ere long, render us pecuniarily unable to do it ! How much better for you, as seller, and the nation, as buyer, to sell out and buy out that without which the war could never have been, than to sink both the thing to be sold and the price of it, in cutting one another's throats !

"I do not speak of emancipation at once, but of a decision at once to emancipate gradually. Room in South America for colonization can be obtained cheaply and in abundance, and when numbers shall be large enough to be company and encouragement for one another, the freed people will not be so reluctant to go.

"I am pressed with a difficulty not yet mentioned—one which threatens division among those who, united, are none too strong. An instance of it is known to you. General Hunter is an honest man. He was, and I hope still is, my friend. I valued him none the less for his agreeing with me in the general wish that all men everywhere could be freed He proclaimed all men free within certain States, and I repudiated the proclamation. He expected more good and less harm from the measure than I could believe would follow.

Yet, in repudiating it, I gave dissatisfaction, if not offence, to many whose support the country can not afford to lose. And this is not the end of it. The pressure in this direction is still upon me, and is increasing. By conceding what I now ask you can relieve me, and, much more, can relieve the country in this important point.

"Upon these considerations, I have again begged your attention to the Message of March last. Before leaving the Capitol, consider and discuss it among yourselves. You are patriots and statesmen, and as such, I pray you consider this proposition, and, at the least, commend it to the consideration of your States and people. As you would perpetuate popular government for the best people in the world, I beseech you that you do in no wise omit this. Our common country is in great peril, demanding the loftiest views and boldest action to bring a speedy relief. Once relieved, its form of government saved to the world, its beloved history and cherished memories are vindicated, and its happy future fully assured and rendered inconceivably grand. To you, more than to any others, the privilege is given to assure that happiness, and swell that grandeur, and to link your own names therewith forever."

On the twenty-second of July, the following order was issued :

"WAR DEPARTMENT, *Washington*, July 22d, 1862.

"*First.* Ordered that military commanders within the States of Virginia, North Carolina, Georgia, Florida, Alabama, Mississippi, Louisiana, Texas, and Arkansas, in an ordinary manner seize and use any property, real or personal, which may be necessary or convenient for their several commands, for supplies, or for other military purposes ; and that while property may be destroyed for proper military objects, none shall be destroyed in wantonness or malice.

"*Second.* That military and naval commanders shall employ as laborers, within and from said States, so many persons of African descent as can be advantageously used for military or naval purposes, giving them reasonable wages for their labor.

"*Third*. That, as to both property, and persons of African descent, accounts shall be kept sufficiently accurate and in detail to show quantities and amounts, and from whom both property and such persons shall have come, as a basis upon which compensation can be made in proper cases; and the several departments of this government shall attend to and perform their appropriate parts toward the execution of these orders. "By order of the President.

"EDWIN M. STANTON, Secretary of War."

And on the twenty-fifth of July, by proclamation, the Predent warned all persons to cease participating in aiding, countenancing, or abetting the rebellion, and to return to their allegiance, under penalty of the forfeitures and seizures provided by an act "to suppress insurrections, to punish treason and rebellion, to seize and confiscate the property of rebels, and for other purposes," approved July 17th, 1862.

CHAPTER XII.

THE PENINSULAR CAMPAIGN.

President's War Order—Reason for the same—Results in West and South-west—Army of the Potomac—Presidential Orders—Letter to McClellan—Order for Army Corps—The Issue of the Campaign—Unfortunate Circumstances—President's Speech at Union Meeting—Comments—Operations in Virginia and Maryland—In the West and South-west.

EARLY in 1862 appeared the following:

"*Executive Mansion, Washington*, January 27th, 1862

[President's General War Order, No. 1.]

"ORDERED, That the 22d day of February, 1862, be the day for a general movement of the land and naval forces of the United States against the insurgent forces.

"That especially the Army at and about Fortress Monroe, the Army of the Potomac, the Army of Western Virginia, the Army near Mumfordsville, Kentucky, the Army and Flotilla at Cairo, and a Naval force in the Gulf of Mexico, be ready for a movement on that day.

"That all other forces, both land and naval, with their respective commanders, obey existing orders for the time, and be ready to obey additional orders when duly given.

"That the Heads of Departments, and especially the Secretaries of War and of the Navy, with all their subordinates, and the General-in-chief, with all other commanders and subordinates of land and naval forces, will severally be held to their strict and full responsibilities for the prompt execution of this order.

"ABRAHAM LINCOLN."

In thus resuming whatever of his constitutional duties as Commander-in-chief of the army and navy might have been temporarily devolved upon others, and directing immediate and energetic aggressive measures, the President only acted as the exponent of the popular feeling, which had become manifest, of dissatisfaction at the apparently inexcusable want of action in military affairs.

In the West and South-west followed the successful battle at Mill Spring, Kentucky ; the capture of Forts Henry and Donelson, compelling the evacuation of Nashville, and ridding Kentucky of any organized rebel force ; the hardly contested, but successful battle of Pea Ridge, Arkansas, relieving Missouri, in a great degree ; victory for our arms wrested from the jaws of defeat at Shiloh ; and the occupation of New Orleans, giving control of the Mouth of the Mississippi.

What at the East ?——Roanoke Island.

Touching the movements of the Army of the Potomac, to which the country looked so expectantly for grand results, efficiently officered, thoroughly disciplined, and splendidly equipped as it was known or supposed to be, the first difficulty was to fix upon a plan. For the purpose of leading the attention of its General to something like a definite decision however, the order of January 27th was succeeded by the following :

"*Executive Mansion, Washington,* January 31st, 1862.
" ORDERED, That all the disposable force of the Army of the Potomac, after providing safely for the defence of Washington, be formed into an expedition for the immediate object of seizing and occupying a point upon the railroad south-westward of what is known as Manassas Junction ; all details to be in the discretion of the Commander-in-chief, and the expedition to move before, or on the twenty-second day of February next.

"ABRAHAM LINCOLN."

General McClellan objecting to this movement and earnestly urging a plan of advance upon Richmond by the Lower Rappahannock with Urbana as a base, the President addressed him the following letter :

"*Executive Mansion, Washington,* February 3d, 1862.
"MY DEAR SIR :—You and I have distinct and different plans for a movement of the Army of the Potomac ; yours to be done by the Chesapeake, up the Rappahannock to Urbana, and across land to the terminus of the railroad on the York river ; mine to move directly to a point on the railroad southwest of Manassas.

" If you will give satisfactory answers to the following questions, I shall gladly yield my plan to yours :

" First. Does not your plan involve a greatly larger expenditure of *time* and *money* than mine ?

" Second, Wherein is a victory *more certain* by your plan than mine ?

" Third. Wherein is a victory *more valuable* by your plan than mine ?

" Fourth. In fact, would it not be *less* valuable in this;

that it would break no great line of the enemy's communications, while mine would?

"Fifth. In case of disaster, would not a retreat be more difficult by your plan than mine?

　　　　　　"Yours, truly,　　　　　　　A. LINCOLN.
"MAJOR-GENERAL MCCLELLAN."

Which plain, practical questions were never directly answered.

This army being without any organization into Army Corps, the President, on the 8th of March, as a movement was about to be made toward Manassas, issued a peremptory order to the Commanding General to attend forthwith to such organization, naming the Corps and their Commanders, according to seniority of rank.

On the same day, the President, who had, against his own judgment, yielded the plan for an advance upon Richmond which should at the same time cover Washington, wise through experience, issued the following:

"*Executive Mansion, Washington*, March 8th, 1862.

"ORDERED. That no change of the base of operations of the Army of the Potomac shall be made without leaving in and about Washington such a force as, in the opinion of the General-in-chief and the commanders of Army Corps, shall leave said city entirely secure.

"That no more than two Army Corps (about fifty thousand troops) of said Army of the Potomac shall be moved *en route* or a new base of operations until the navigation of the Potomac, from Washington to the Chesapeake Bay, shall be freed from the enemy's batteries, and other obstructions, or until the President shall hereafter give express permission.

"That any movement as aforesaid, *en route* for a new base of operations, which may be ordered by the General-in-chief, and which may be intended to move upon Chesapeake Bay, shall begin to move upon the bay as early as the 18th of

| Movement. | Peninsular Campaign. | Results. |

March, instant, and the General-in-chief shall be responsible that it moves as early as that day.

"ORDERED, That the Army and Navy coöperate in an immediate effort to. capture the enemy's batteries upon the Potomac between Washington and the Chesapeake Bay.

"ABRAHAM LINCOLN.

"L. THOMAS, Adjutant-General."

Finally—after delays manifold, correspondence voluminous, discussions heated, and patience nearly worn threadbare—commenced that military movement, which has passed into history as the American Peninsular Campaign ; by virtue of which, commencing about the middle of March, 1862, a large body of finely disciplined troops—their numbers varying, according to various accounts, from one hundred thousand nine hundred and seventy, to one hundred and twenty-one thousand five hundred men—left Alexandria for Richmond, *via* Yorktown, and succeeded, after sanguinary battles, swamp sickness, severe exposures, and terrible hardships, in returning (how many of them ?) to Alexandria *via* Harrison's Landing, by about the middle of August, 1862.

That campaign was the most disastrous drawback of the war, not merely in the loss of men, nor in the failure to reach the end aimed at, but mainly in its enervating effect upon the supporters of the Government. It was Bull Run over again, only immensely magnified, indefinitely prolonged. Fortune seemed determined never to favor our Eastern braves.

Into the details of that campaign it is needless to enter here. Every schoolboy knows them by heart, so far as they are spread upon the record. Equally idle is it to attempt a criticism upon the campaign in a military point of view. That has been already done to a nauseating extent ; yet will, doubtless, continue to be done while the reader lives.

No details, nor military criticism therefore here. But that President Lincoln may fairly be presented in his relations to this campaign, certain observations must be made.   And this is the place to make them.

Conceding to General McClellan all the ability, patriotism, and bravery which have been claimed for him by his warmest admirers, there still remain some unfortunate circumstances connected with him, by reason of which—even though he, personally, were responsible for no single one of them—not all the ability, patriotism, and bravery of a Napoleon, Tell, and Bayard combined, could have secured in his person what this country needed for the rooting out of the great rebellion.

It was unfortunate for him that, at the very outset—when so little was known of him, when he had done so little— sycophantic flatterers should have exalted him at once into a great military chieftain.   Peculiarly unfortunate was this, considering that the changeable American people were to pass upon him and his actions—that people, in their relations to their leading men, with their "Hosannas" to-day and their "Crucify him's" to-morrow.   The sequel of "going up like a rocket" is not generally supposed to be particularly agreeable.

It was unfortunate for him that the opinion obtained, in the minds of many, impartial and competent to judge, that, in his case, caution had passed the bounds of prudence and run mad.   There are emergencies when every thing must be risked that nothing be lost.

It was unfortunate for him that he was made the especial pet of those individuals who were most clamorous against an Administration which, whatever its short comings, every candid man knew was earnestly intent upon ending the war upon such a basis as could alone, in its judgment, secure permanent peace.   If a subordinate general could not agree with his superiors, or content himself with matters purely military, he should have declined to remain in the service.

It was unfortunate for him that his especial friends sought, in print, and public speech, and private conversation, to create the impression that the President did not desire that he should succeed, owing to a fear that he might prove a formidable competitor at the next Presidential election. Peculiarly unfortunate, when one remembers that this President had, at the outbreak of the war, put at the head of three important military departments three of the most decided of his political opponents—Patterson, Butler, and McClellan—that no man ever occupied the Presidential chair, unless it be its first occupant, who had less selfishness and more disinterestedness in his composition than President Lincoln.

It was unfortunate for him that such desperate efforts were made by his supporters to fasten the responsibility for admitted failures upon other parties. This began at Ball's Bluff, as has already been noted. The Secretary of War was dragged in, as well as the President, in connection with the Peninsular Campaign. As to this last, nothing more to the point can be adduced than the words of a man, whose honesty and truthfulness were known wherever he was known—Abraham Lincoln—in a characteristic speech made by him at a Union meeting in Washington, August 6th, 1862, when the issue of the campaign was certain :·

" FELLOW-CITIZENS :—I believe there is no precedent for my appearing before you on this occasion ; but it is also true that there is no precedent for your being here yourselves, and I offer, in justification of myself and of you, that, upon examination, I have found nothing in the Constitution against it. I, however, have an impression that there are younger gentlemen who will entertain you better, and better address your understanding than I will or could, and therefore I propose but to detain you a moment longer.

" I am very little inclined on any occasion to say any thing unless I hope to produce some good by it. The only thing I think of just now not likely to be better said by some one else is a matter in which we have heard some other persons blamed for what I did myself. There has been a very widespread attempt to have a quarrel between General McClellan and the Secretary of War. Now, I occupy a position that enables me to observe, that at least these two gentlemen are not nearly so deep in the quarrel as some pretending to be their friends. General McClellan's attitude is such that, in the very selfishness of his nature, he cannot but wish to be successful, and I hope he will—and the Secretary of War is in precisely the same situation. If the military commanders in the field cannot be successful, not only the Secretary of War, but myself, for the time being the master of them both, can not be but failures. I know that General McClellan wishes to be successful, and I know he does not wish it any more than the Secretary of War for him, and both of them together no more than I wish it. Sometimes we have a dispute about how many men General McClellan has had, and those who would disparage him say that he has had a very large number, and those who would disparage the Secretary of War insist that General McClellan has had a very small number. The basis for this is, there is always a wide difference, and on this occasion perhaps a wider one, between the grand total on McClellan's rolls and the men actually fit for duty; and those who would disparage him talk of the grand total on paper, and those who would disparage the Secretary of War talk of those at present fit for duty. General McClellan has sometimes asked for things that the Secretary of War did not give him. General McClellan is not to blame for asking what he wanted and needed, and the Secretary of War is not to blame for not giving when he had none to give. And I say here, as far as I know, the Secretary of War has withheld no one thing at any time in my power to give him. I have no accusation against him. I believe he is a brave and able man, and I stand here, as justice requires me to do, to take upon myself what has been charged on the Secretary of War, as withholding from him. I have talked longer than I expected to, and now I avail myself of my privilege of saying no more."

It was unfortunate for him that the precedents were so numerous in American history for making a successful military man President. This must have embarrassed him no little, and tempted him into much of that correspondence which otherwise he would have avoided. Had it not been for these fatal precedents, he, assuredly, would not have leisurely seated himself at Harrison's Landing to write to the President a lengthy homily on affairs of State at a moment when it was doubtful whether he would long have an army of which he could be General in command.

Finally, it was unfortunate for him that he had not, when learning to command, learned also to obey. This would have spared himself and the country and the cause several entirely superfluous inflictions.

Whoever would form a correct estimate of President Lincoln's connection with the Peninsular campaign and its commander, must bear these facts in mind. Aside from all considerations of a purely military nature, they are indispensable in reaching an unbiassed decision.

What dogged the heels of this unfortunate campaign must be briefly told. Vigorous orders from Pope, "headquarters in the saddle," turned into most melancholy bombast by his failure, occasioned either by want of brains or willful lack of coöperation; a rebel invasion of Maryland; the battle of South Mountain gained under McClellan; Antietam, not the victory it might have been, for which a ream of reasons were given; the withdrawal of the rebels; Government hard at work urging McClellan to follow; supersedure of the latter by the President, who survived his cabinet in clinging to him; appointment of Burnside, much against his wishes; another defeat at Fredericksburg; and the Army of the Potomac in winter-quarters again.

Such is the summary in the East for A. D. 1862.

In the West, the year closed with the opening of the battle of Murfreesboro, and Vicksburg still held out against all our attempts to take it.

CHAPTER XIII.

FREEDOM TO MILLIONS.

Tribune Editorial—Letter to Mr. Greeley—Announcement of the Emancipation Proclamation—Suspension of the *Habeas Corpus* in certain cases—Order for Observance of the Sabbath—The Emancipation Proclamation.

AN editorial article having appeared in the *New York Tribune*, in the month of August, 1862, in the form of a letter addressed to the President, severely criticising his action relative to the question of slavery—a letter written in ignorance of the fact that a definite policy had already been matured, which would be announced at a suitable moment—Mr. Lincoln responded as follows:

"*Executive Mansion*, Washington, Aug. 22, 1862.

HON. HORACE GREELEY—*Dear Sir:* I have just read yours of the 19th, addressed to myself through the *New York Tribune*. If there be in it any statements or assumptions of fact which I may know to be erroneous, I do not now and here controvert them. If there be in it any inference which I may believe to be falsely drawn, I do not now and here argue against them. If there be perceptible in it an impatient and dictatorial tone, I waive it in deference to an old friend, whose heart I have always supposed to be right.

"As to the policy I 'seem to be pursuing,' as you say, I have not meant to leave any one in doubt.

"I would save the Union. I would save it the shortest way under the Constitution. The sooner the National authority can be restored, the nearer the Union will be 'the Union as it was.' If there be those who would not save the Union unless they could at the same time *save* Slavery, I do not agree with them. If there be those who would not save the Union unless they could at the same time *destroy* Slavery, I do not agree with them. My paramount object in this struggle *is* to save the Union, and is *not* either to save or destroy Slavery. If I could save the Union without freeing *any* slave, I would do it; and if I could do it by freeing *all* the slaves, I would do it; and if I could do it by freeing some and leaving others alone, I would also do that. What I do about Slavery and the colored race, I do because I believe it helps to save this Union; and what I forbear, I forbear because I do *not* believe it would help to save the Union. I shall do *less* whenever I shall believe what I am doing hurts the cause, and I shall do *more* whenever I shall believe doing more will help the cause. I shall try to correct errors when shown to be errors; and I shall adopt new views so fast as they shall appear to be true views. I have here stated my purpose according to my view of *official* duty, and I intend no modification of my oft-expressed *personal* wish that all men, every where, could be free.

                     " Yours,   A. LINCOLN."

What that policy was, every manly heart learned with delight when the following Proclamation appeared, the most important state-paper ever penned by any American President :

"I, ABRAHAM LINCOLN, President of the United States of America, and Commander-in-chief of the Army and Navy thereof, do hereby proclaim and declare, that hereafter, as heretofore, the war will be prosecuted for the object of practically restoring the constitutional relation between the United States and the people thereof, in those States in which that relation is, or may be, suspended or disturbed; that it is my purpose, upon the next meeting of Congress, to again recommend the adoption of a practical measure tendering pecuniary aid to the free acceptance or rejection of all the Slave States, so-called, the people whereof may not then be in rebellion against the United States, and which States may then have voluntarily adopted, or thereafter may voluntarily adopt, the immediate or gradual abolishment of slavery within their respective limits, and that the effort to colonize persons of African descent, with their consent, upon the continent or elsewhere, with the previously obtained consent of the government existing there, will be continued ; that on the first day of January, in the year of our Lord one thousand eight hundred and sixty-three, all persons held as slaves within any State, or any designated part of a State, the people whereof shall then be in rebellion against the United States, SHALL BE THEN, THENCEFORWARD AND FOREVER, FREE, and the Executive Government of the United States, including the military and naval authority thereof, will recognize and maintain the freedom of such persons, and will do no act or acts to repress such persons, or any of them, in any efforts they may make for their actual freedom ; that the Executive will, on the first day of January aforesaid, by proclamation, designate the States, and parts of States, if any, in which the people thereof respectively shall be in rebellion against the United States ; and the fact that any State, or the people thereof, shall on that day be in good faith represented in the Congress of the United States by members chosen thereto, at elections wherein a majority of the qualified voters of such State shall have participated, shall, in the absence of strong countervailing testimony, be deemed conclusive evidence that such State and the people thereof have not been in rebellion against the United States.

" That attention is hereby called to an act of Congress, entitled, 'An act to make an additional article of war,' approved March 13, 1862, and which act is in the words and figures following :

" '*Be it enacted by the Senate and House of Representatives of the United States of America, in Congress assembled,* That hereafter the following shall be promulgated as an additional Article of War for the government of the Army of the United States, and shall be observed and obeyed as such.

" '*Article* —. All officers or persons of the military or

naval service of the United States, are prohibited from employing any of the forces under their respective commands for the purpose of returning fugitives from service or labor who may have escaped from any persons to whom such service or labor is claimed to be due ; and any officer who shall be found guilty by a court-martial of violating this article shall be dismissed from the service.

"'*Section* 2. And be it further enacted, That this act shall take effect from and after its passage.'

"Also to the ninth and tenth sections of an act entitled, 'An act to suppress insurrection, to punish treason and rebellion, to seize and confiscate property of rebels, and for other purposes,' approved July 17, 1862, and which sections are in the words and figures following :

"'*Section* 9. And be it further enacted, That all slaves of persons who shall hereafter be engaged in rebellion against the government of the United States, or who shall in any way give aid or comfort thereto, escaping from such persons and taking refuge within the lines of the army; and all slaves captured from such persons or deserted by them, and coming under the control of the government of the United States, and all slaves of such persons found on (or being within) any place occupied by rebel forces and afterwards occupied by the forces of the United States, shall be deemed captives of war, and shall be forever free of their servitude, and not again held as slaves.

"*Section* 10. And be it further enacted, That no slave escaping into any State, Territory, or the District of Columbia, from any of the States, shall be delivered up, or in any way impeded or hindered of his liberty, except for crime, or some offence against the laws, unless the person claiming said fugitive shall first make oath that the person to whom the labor or service of such fugitive is alleged to be due, is his lawful owner, and has not been in arms against the United States in the present rebellion, nor in any way given aid and

13

comfort thereto; and no person engaged in the military or naval service of the United States shall, under any pretence whatever, assume to decide on the validity of the claim of any person to the service or labor of any other person, or surrender up any such person to the claimant, on pain of being dismissed from the service.

"And I do hereby enjoin upon, and order all persons engaged in the military and naval service of the United States to observe, obey and enforce within their respective spheres of service, the act and sections above recited.

"And the executive will in due time recommend that all citizens of the United States who shall have remained loyal thereto throughout the rebellion, shall (upon the restoration of the constitutional relation between the United States and their respective States and people, if the relation shall have been suspended or disturbed) be compensated for all losses by acts of the United States, including the loss of slaves.

"In witness whereof, I have hereunto set my hand and caused the seal of the United States to be affixed.

"Done at the City of Washington, this twenty-second day of September, in the year of our Lord one thousand eight hundred and sixty-two, and of the Independence of the United States the eighty-seventh.

"By the President: ABRAHAM LINCOLN.
"WILLIAM H. SEWARD, Secretary of State."

This herald of freedom to millions was, of course, intensely disliked by those who omitted no opportunity to cavil at the Administration. As efforts were making—not entirely without success—to embarrass the Government in securing the necessary reinforcements for the army, and certain lewd fellows of the baser sort holding themselves in readiness to take advantage of the bitter prejudices existing in the minds of a portion of the people against the negroes among us, the following proclamation was issued two days later, that no one might plead ignorance of results, if such treasonable practices should be persisted in :

" WHEREAS, It has become necessary to call into service, not only volunteers, but also portions of the militia of the States by draft, in order to suppress the insurrection existing in the United States, and disloyal persons are not adequately restrained by the ordinary processes of law from hindering this measure, and from giving aid and comfort in various ways to the insurrection :

" Now, therefore, be it ordered :

" *First.* That during the existing insurrection, and as a necessary measure for suppressing the same, all rebels and insurgents, their aiders and abettors, within the United States, and all persons discouraging volunteer enlistments, resisting militia drafts, or guilty of any disloyal practice affording aid and comfort to the rebels against the authority of the United States, shall be subject to martial law, and liable to trial and punishment by courts-martial or military commission.

" *Third.* That the writ of *habeas corpus* is suspended in respect to all persons arrested, or who are now, or hereafter during the rebellion shall be imprisoned in any fort, camp, arsenal, military prison, or other place of confinement, by any military authority or by the sentence of any court-martial or military commission.

" In witness whereof, I have hereunto set my hand, and caused the seal of the United States to be affixed.

" Done at the City of Washington, this twenty-fourth day of September, in the year of our Lord, one thousand eight hundred and sixty-two, and of the Independence of the United States the eighty-seventh.

" By the President : ABRAHAM LINCOLN.

" WILLIAM H. SEWARD, Secretary of State. "

It would be paying but a poor compliment to the sagacity which prompted this proclamation, if one were not obliged to say that it was exceedingly distasteful to many. Truth, however, compels us to add that the evils aimed at ceased, to a very great extent, shortly after its appearance.

The following order, issued November 16th, 1862, is but one among the many evidences of that deep and earnest reverence for Christianity which formed a noticeable feature, not only in most of Mr. Lincoln's official papers, but also in the character of the man :

"The President, Commander-in-chief of the Army and Navy, desires and enjoins the orderly observance of the Sabbath, by the officers and men in the military and naval service. The importance, for man and beast, of the prescribed weekly rest, the sacred rights of Christian soldiers and sailors, a becoming deference to the best sentiment of a Christian people, and a due regard for the Divine will, demand that Sunday labor in the army and navy be reduced to the measure of strict necessity.

"The discipline and character of the National forces should not suffer, nor the cause they defend be imperiled, by the profanation of the day or name of the Most High. 'At this time of public distress,' adopting the words of Washington in 1776, 'men may find enough to do in the service of God and their country, without abandoning themselves to vice and immorality.' The first general order issued by the Father of his Country, after the Declaration of Independence, indicates the spirit in which our institutions were founded and should ever be defended : 'The General hopes and trusts that every officer and man will endeavor to live and act as becomes a Christian soldier defending the dearest rights and liberties of his country.'   ABRAHAM LINCOLN."

On the 1st day of January, 1863, appeared that proclamation which was to supplement that of September 22d, 1862, crowning with complete fullness that great work and giving it health and being :

"WHEREAS, On the twenty-second day of September, in the year of our Lord one thousand eight hundred and sixty-two, a proclamation was issued by the President of the United States, containing, among other things, the following, to wit:

"That on the first day of January, in the year of our Lord one thousand eight hundred and sixty-three, all persons held as slaves within any State, or any designated part of a State, the people whereof shall then be in rebellion against the United States, shall be thenceforward and forever free, and the Executive Government of the United States, including the military and naval authority thereof, will recognize and maintain the freedom of such persons, and will do no act or acts to repress such persons, or any of them, in any efforts they may make for their actual freedom.

"That the Executive will, on the first day of January aforesaid, by proclamation, designate the States and parts of States, if any, in which the people thereof respectively shall then be in rebellion against the United States, and the fact that any State, or the people thereof, shall on that day be in good faith represented in the Congress of the United States by members chosen thereto at elections wherein a majority of the qualified voters of such State shall have participated, shall, in the absence of strong countervailing testimony, be deemed conclusive evidence that such State and the people thereof are not then in rebellion against the United States.

"Now, therefore, I, Abraham Lincoln, President of the United States, by virtue of the power in me vested as Commander-in-chief of the Army and Navy of the United States, in time of actual armed rebellion against the authority and Government of the United States, and as a fit and necessary war measure for repressing said rebellion, do, on this first day of January, in the year of our Lord one thousand eight hundred and sixty-three, and in accordance with my purpose so to do, publicly proclaimed for the full period of one hundred days from the day of the first above-mentioned order, designate, as the States and parts of States wherein the people thereof respectively are this day in rebellion against the United States, the following, to wit: Arkansas, Texas, Louisiana, except the parishes of St. Bernard, Plaquemines, Jefferson, St. John, St. Charles, St. James, Ascension, Assumption, Terre Bonne, Lafourche, St. Mary, St. Martin, and Orleans, including the city of New Orleans, Mississippi, Alabama, Florida, Georgia, South Carolina, North Carolina, and Virginia, except the forty-eight counties designated as West Virginia, and also the counties of Berkeley, Accomac, Northampton, Elizabeth City, York, Princess Ann, and Norfolk, including the cities of Norfolk and Portsmouth, and which excepted parts are, for the present, left precisely as if this proclamation were not issued.

"And by virtue of the power and for the purpose aforesaid, I do order and declare that all persons held as slaves within said designated States and parts of States are, and henceforward shall be free; and that the Executive Government of the United States, including the military and naval authorities thereof, will recognize and maintain the freedom of said persons.

"And I hereby enjoin upon the people so declared to be free, to abstain from all violence, unless in necessary self-defence, and I recommend to them, that in all cases, when allowed, they labor faithfully for reasonable wages.

"And I further declare and make known that such persons of suitable condition will be received into the armed service of the United States to garrison forts, positions, stations, and other places, and to man vessels of all sorts in said service.

"And upon this, sincerely believed to be an act of justice, warranted by the Constitution, upon military necessity, I invoke the considerate judgment of mankind and the gracious favor of Almighty God.

"In witness whereof, I have hereunto set my hand and caused the seal of the United States to be affixed.

"Done at the city of Washington, this first day of January, in the year of our Lord one thousand eight hundred and sixty-three, and of the Independence of the United States the eighty-seventh.

"By the President: ABRAHAM LINCOLN.

"W. H. SEWARD, Secretary of State."

CHAPTER XIV.

LAST SESSION OF THE THIRTY-SEVENTH CONGRESS.

Situation of the Country—Opposition to the Administration—President's Message.

DARK days for the friends of freedom in this country were those at the close of 1862. Prior to the autumn of that year the elections had shown a popular indorsement of the acts of the Administration. Then came a change. The three leading States—New York, Ohio, and Pennsylvania—through manifestations and misrepresentations which it is unnecessary here to detail, had been induced to give majorities against the Government. Not the least singular of the many remarkable instances of inconsistency which our political annals afford, was furnished in the State first-named, which had actually elected a "Peace" man as its Governor, on the platform of "a more vigorous prosecution of the war."

The failure of the Peninsular Campaign was charged upon the President. The war, it was asserted, had been perverted from its original purpose. It was no longer waged to preserve the Union, but to free the slave; or, in the more elegant phraseology of the day, it had become "a nigger war." With the ignorant and unthinking such statements passed as truths.

The number of those who, never having invested any principle in the struggle, had become tired of the war, had largely
increased.   The expectation of a draft—or a "conscription,"
as it better suited the objects of the disaffected to term it—
which was passed at the next session of Congress, made the
lukewarm love of many to wax cold.

Newspapers and stump-speakers had the hardihood to
demand peace upon any terms.   It was even claimed that an
opposition majority had been secured in the lower House of
the next Congress.   Their representatives in the Congress of
1862 began to re-assume those airs of insolence and defiance
which they had previously found it convenient to lay aside
for the time.

Dark days, indeed, when the Thirty-seventh Congress
assembled for its last session, on the 1st of December, 1862.

Yet there was one who never faltered in purpose, however
discouraging the prospect; one, who, assured that he was
right, was determined to follow the right, wherever it might
lead him.   And, though his careworn expression and anxious
look told plainly how the fearful responsibilities of his office
weighed upon him, he had ever a cheerful word, a happy
illustration, a kindly smile, or a look of sympathy for those
with whom he came in contact.

The essential portions of his Annual Message on this occasion are given below :

" FELLOW-CITIZENS OF THE SENATE AND HOUSE OF REPRE-
SENTATIVES :—Since your last annual assembling, another
year of health and bountiful harvests has passed.   And,
while it has not pleased the Almighty to bless us with a
return of peace, we can but press on, guided by the best light
He gives us, trusting that, in His own good time and wise
way, all will yet be well.   .   .   .   .

" If the condition of our relations with other nations is less
gratifying than it has usually been at former periods, it is cer-

tainly more satisfactory than a nation so unhappily distracted as we are, might reasonably have apprehended. In the month of June last there were some grounds to expect that the maritime powers which, at the beginning of our domestic difficulties, so unwisely and unnecessarily, as we think, recognized the insurgents as a belligerent, would soon recede from that position, which has proved only less injurious to themselves than to our own country. But the temporary reverses which afterward befell the National arms, and which were exaggerated by our own disloyal citizens abroad, have hitherto delayed that act of simple justice.

"The civil war, which has so radically changed, for the moment, the occupations and habits of the American people, has necessarily disturbed the social condition, and affected very deeply the prosperity of the nations with which we have carried on a commerce that has been steadily increasing throughout a period of half a century. It has, at the same time, excited political ambitions and apprehensions which have produced a profound agitation throughout the civilized world. In this unusual agitation we have forborne from taking part in any controversy between foreign States, and between parties or factions in such States. We have attempted no propagandism, and acknowledged no revolution. But we have left to every nation the exclusive conduct and management of its own affairs. Our struggle has been, of course, contemplated by foreign nations with reference less to its own merits, than to its supposed, and often exaggerated, effects and consequences resulting to those nations themselves. Nevertheless, complaint on the part of this Government, even if it were just, would certainly be unwise.

"The treaty with Great Britain for the suppression of the slave-trade, has been put into operation, with a good prospect of complete success. It is an occasion of special pleasure to acknowledge that the execution of it, on the part of Her Majesty's Government, has been marked with a jealous respect for the authority of the United States, and the rights of their moral and loyal citizens. . . . .

"Applications have been made to me by many free Americans of African descent to favor their emigration, with a view to such colonization, as was contemplated in recent acts of Congress.   Other parties, at home and abroad—some from interested motives, others upon patriotic considerations, and still others influenced by philanthropic sentiments—have suggested similar measures; while, on the other hand, several of the Spanish-American republics have protested against the sending of such colonies to their respective territories. Under these circumstances I have declined to move any such colony to any State, without first obtaining the consent of its Government, with an agreement on its part to receive and protect such emigrants in all the rights of freemen; and I have, at the same time, offered to the several States situated within the tropics, or having colonies there, to negotiate with them, subject to the advice and consent of the Senate, to favor the voluntary emigration of persons of that class to their respective territories, upon conditions which shall be equal, just, and humane.   Liberia and Hayti are, as yet, the only countries to which colonists of African descent from here, could go with certainty of being received and adopted as citizens; and I regret to say such persons, contemplating colonization, do not seem so willing to migrate to those countries, as to some others, nor so willing as I think their interest demands.   I believe, however, opinion among them in this respect is improving; and that, ere long, there will be an augmented and considerable migration to both these countries, from the United States. . . . . .

"I have favored the project for connecting the United States with Europe by an Atlantic telegraph, and a similar project to extend the telegraph from San Francisco, to connect by a Pacific telegraph with the line which is being extended across the Russian Empire.

"The Territories of the United States, with unimportant exceptions, have remained undisturbed by the civil war; and they are exhibiting such evidence of prosperity as justifies an expectation that some of them will soon be in a condition to be organized as States, and be constitutionally admitted into the Federal Union.

"The immense mineral resources of some of those territories ought to be developed as rapidly as possible. Every step in that direction would have a tendency to improve the revenues of the Government, and diminish the burdens of the people. It is worthy of your serious consideration whether some extraordinary measures to promote that end can not be adopted. The means which suggests itself as most likely to be effective, is a scientific exploration of the mineral regions in those Territories, with a view to the publication of its results at home and in foreign countries—results which can not fail to be auspicious.

"The condition of the finances will claim your most diligent consideration. The vast expenditures incident to the military and naval operations required for the suppression of the rebellion, have hitherto been met with a promptitude and certainty unusual in similar circumstances; and the public credit has been fully maintained. The continuance of the war, however, and the increased disbursements made necessary by the augmented forces now in the field, demand your best reflections as to the best modes of providing the necessary revenue, without injury to business, and with the least possible burdens upon labor.

"The suspension of specie payments by the banks, soon after the commencement of your last session, made large issues of United States notes unavoidable. In no other way could the payment of the troops, and the satisfaction of other just demands, be so economically or so well provided for. The judicious legislation of Congress, securing the receivability of these notes for loans and internal duties, and making them a legal tender for other debts, has made them a universal currency; and has satisfied, partially at least, and for the time, the long felt want of an uniform circulating medium, saving thereby to the people immense sums in discounts and exchanges.

" A return to specie payments, however, at the earliest period compatible with due regard to all interests concerned, should ever be kept in view. Fluctuations in the value of currency are always injurious, and to reduce these fluctuations to the lowest possible point, will always be a leading purpose in wise legislation. Convertibility, prompt and certain convertibility into coin, is generally acknowledged to be the best and the surest safeguard against them; and it is extremely doubtful whether a circulation of United States notes, payable in coin, and sufficiently large for the wants of the people, can be permanently, usefully and safely maintained.

" Is there, then, any other mode in which the necessary provision for the public wants can be made, and the great advantages of a safe and uniform currency secured?

" I know of none which promises so certain results, and is, at the same time, so unobjectionable, as the organization of banking associations, under a general Act of Congress, well guarded in its provisions. To such associations the Government might furnish circulating notes, on the security of the United States bonds deposited in the treasury. These notes, prepared under the supervision of proper officers, being uniform in appearance and security, and convertible always into coin, would at once protect labor against the evils of a vicious currency, and facilitate commerce by cheap and safe exchanges.

" A moderate reservation from the interest on the bonds would compensate the United States for the preparation and distribution of the notes, and a general supervision of the system, and would lighten the burden of that part of the public debt employed as securities. The public credit, moreover, would be greatly improved, and the negotiation of new loans greatly facilitated by the steady market demand for Government bonds which the adoption of the proposed system would create.

"It is an additional recommendation of the measure of considerable weight, in my judgment, that it would reconcile as far as possible, all existing interests, by the opportunity offered to existing institutions to reörganize under the act, substituting only the secured uniform national circulation for the local and various circulation, secured and unsecured, now issued by them.

"The receipts into the treasury, from all sources, including loans, and balance from the preceding year, for the fiscal year ending on the 30th June, 1862, were $583,885,247 06, of which sum $49,056,397 62 were derived from customs; $1,795,331 73 from the direct tax; from public lands, $152,203 77; from miscellaneous sources, $931,787 64; from loans in all forms, $529,692,460 50. The remainder, $2,257,065 80, was the balance from last year.

"The disbursements during the same period were for Congressional, Executive, and Judicial purposes, $5,939,009 29; for foreign intercourse, $1,339,710 35; for miscellaneous expenses, including the mints, loans, post office deficiencies, collection of revenue, and other like charges, $14,129,771 50; for expenses under the Interior Department, $3,102,985 52; under the War Department, $394,368,407 36; under the Navy Department, $42,674,569 69; for interest on public debt, $13,190,324 45; and for payment of public debt, including reimbursement of temporary loan, and redemptions $96,096, 922 09; making an aggregate of $570,841,700 25, and leaving a balance in the treasury on the first day of July, 1862, of $13,043,546 81.

"It should be observed that the sum of $96,096,922 09, expended for reimbursements and redemption of public debt, being included also in the loans made, may be properly deducted, both from receipts and expenditures, leaving the actual receipts for the year, $487,788,324 97 ; and the expenditures, $474,744,778 16. . . . .

" On the 22d day of September last a proclamation was issued by the Executive, a copy of which is herewith submitted.

" In accordance with the purpose expressed in the second paragraph of that paper, I now respectfully call your attention to what may be called ' compensated emancipation.'

"A nation may be said to consist of its territory, its people and its laws. The territory is the only part which is of certain durability. ' One generation passeth away and another generation cometh, but the earth abideth forever.' It is of the first importance to duly consider, and estimate, this ever-enduring part. That portion of the earth's surface which is owned and inhabited by the people of the United States, is well adapted to be the home of one national family ; and it is not well adapted for two or more. Its vast extent, and its variety of climate and productions, are of advantage, in this age, for one people, whatever they might have been in former ages. Steam, telegraphs and intelligence have brought these to be an advantageous combination for one united people.

" In the inaugural address I briefly pointed out the total inadequacy of disunion, as a remedy for the differences between the people of the two sections. I did so in language which I can not improve, and which, therefore, I beg to repeat :

" ' One section of our country believes Slavery is *right*, and ought to be extended, while the other believes it is *wrong*, and ought not to be extended. This is the only substantial dispute. The fugitive slave clause of the Constitution, and the law for the suppression of the foreign slave-trade, are each as well enforced, perhaps, as any law can ever be in a community where the moral sense of the people imperfectly supports the law itself. The great body of the people abide by the dry legal obligation in both cases, and a few break over in each. This, I think, can not be perfectly cured; and it would be worse in both cases *after* the separation of the sections, than before. The foreign slave-trade, now imperfectly suppressed, would be ultimately revived without restriction in one section; while fugitive slaves, now only partially surrendered, would not be surrendered at all by the other.

" ' Physically speaking, we can not separate. We can not remove our respective sections from each other, nor build an impassable wall between them. A husband and wife may be divorced, and go out of the presence, and beyond the reach of each other; but the different parts of our country can not do this. They cannot but remain face to face; and intercourse, either amicable or hostile, must continue between them. Is it possible, then, to make that intercourse more advantageous, or more satisfactory, *after* separation than *before?* Can aliens make treaties easier than friends can make laws? Can treaties be more faithfully enforced between aliens, than laws can among friends? Suppose you go to war, you can not fight always; and when, after much loss on both sides, and no gain on either, you cease fighting, the identical old questions, as to terms of intercourse, are again upon you.

" ' There is no line, straight or crooked, suitable for a National boundary, upon which to divide. Trace through, from east to west, upon the line between the free and slave country, and we shall find a little more than one-third of its length are rivers, easy to be crossed, and populated, or soon to be populated, thickly, upon both sides; while nearly all its remaining length are merely surveyors' lines, over which people may walk back and forth without any consciousness of their presence. No part of this line can be made any more difficult to pass, by writing it down on paper, or parchment, as a national boundary. The fact of separation, if it comes, gives up, on the part of the seceding, the fugitive slave clause, along with all other constitutional obligations upon the section seceded from, while I should expect no treaty stipulation would ever be made to take its place.

"But there is another difficulty.　The great interior region, bounded east by the Alleghanies, north by the British Dominions, west by the Rocky Mountains, and south by the line along which the culture of corn and cotton meets, and which includes part of Virginia, part of Tennessee, all of Kentucky, Ohio, Indiana, Michigan, Wisconsin, Illinois, Missouri, Kansas, Iowa, Minnesota, and The territories of Dakota, Nebraska, and part of Colorado, already has above ten millions of people, and will have fifty million within fifty years, if not prevented by any political folly or mistake.　It contains more than one-third of the country owned by the United States—certainly more than one million of square miles.　Once half as populous as Massachusetts already is, it would have more than seventy-five millions of people.　A glance at the map shows that, territorially speaking, it is the great body of the Republic.　The other parts are but marginal borders to it; the magnificent region sloping west from the Rocky Mountains to the Pacific, being the deepest, and also the richest, in undeveloped resources.　In the production of provisions, grains, grasses, and all which proceed from them, this great interior region is naturally one of the most important in the world.　Ascertain from the statistics the small proportion of the region which has, as yet, been brought into cultivation, and also the large and rapidly increasing amount of its products, and we shall be overwhelmed with the magnitude of the prospect presented.　And yet this region has no sea-coast, touches no ocean any where.　As part of one nation, its people now find, and may forever find, their way to Europe by New York, to South America and Africa by New Orleans, and to Asia by San Francisco.　But separate our common country into two nations, as designed by the present rebellion, and every man of this great interior region is thereby cut off from some one or more of these outlets, not, perhaps, by a physical barrier, but by embarrassing and onerous trade regulations.

"And this is true, *wherever* a dividing or boundary line may be fixèd. Place it between the now free and slave country, or place it south of Kentucky, or north of Ohio, and still the truth remains, that none south of it can trade to any port or place north of it, and none north of it can trade to any port or place south of it, except upon terms dictated by a government foreign to them. These outlets, east, west, and south, are indispensable to the well-being of the people inhabiting, and to inhabit, this vast interior region. *Which* of the three may be the best, is no proper question. All are better than either; and all, of right, belong to that people, and to their successors forever. True to themselves, they will not ask *where* a line of separation shall be, but will vow, rather, that there shall be no such line. Nor are the marginal regions less interested in these communications to, and through them, to the great outside world. They, too, and each of them, must have access to this Egypt of the West, without paying toll at the crossing of any National boundary.

" Our National strife springs not from our permanent part; not from the land we inhabit; not from our National homestead. There is no possible severing of this, but would multiply, and not mitigate, evils among us. In all its adaptations and aptitudes, it demands union, and abhors separation. In fact, it would, ere long, force reunion, however much of blood and treasure the separation might have cost.

"Our strife pertains to ourselves—to the passing generations of men; and it can, without convulsion, be hushed forever with the passing of one generation.

"In this view, I recommend the adoption of the following resolution and articles amendatory to the Constitution of the United States:

14

"*Resolved by the Senate and House of Representatives of the United States of America in Congress assembled,* (two-thirds of both Houses concurring,) That the following articles be proposed to the Legislatures (or conventions) of the several States as amendments to the Constitution of the United States, all or any of which articles, when ratified by three-fourths of the said Legislatures (or conventions), to be valid as part or parts of the said Constitution, viz. :

"*Article* ——. Every State, wherein Slavery now exists, which shall abolish the same therein, at any time, or times, before the first day of January, in the year of our Lord one thousand and nine hundred, shall receive compensation from the United States as follows, to wit :

" The President of the United States shall deliver, to every such States, bonds of the United States, bearing interest at the rate of —— per cent. per annum, to an amount equal to the aggregate sum of   for each slave shown to have been therein, by the eighth census of the United States, said bonds to be delivered to such State by installments, or in one parcel, at the completion of the abolishment, accordingly as the same shall have been gradual, or at one time, within such State ; and interest shall begin to run upon any such bond, only from the proper time of its delivery as aforesaid. Any State, having received bonds as aforesaid, and afterward re-introducing or tolerating slavery therein, shall refund to the United States the bonds so received, or the value thereof, and all interest paid thereon.

"*Article* ——. All slaves who shall have enjoyed actual freedom by the chances of the war, at any time before the end of the rebellion, shall be forever free ; but all owners of such, who shall not have been disloyal, shall be compensated for them, at the same rates as is provided for States adopting abolishment of slavery, but in such way, that no slave shall be twice accounted for.

"*Article* ——. Congress may appropriate money, and otherwise provide for colonizing free colored persons, with their own consent, at any place or places without the United States.

"I beg indulgence to discuss these proposed articles at some length. Without slavery, the rebellion could never have existed; without slavery, it could not continue.

"Among the friends of the Union, there is great diversity of sentiment, and of policy, in regard to slavery, and the African race among us. Some would perpetuate slavery; some would abolish it suddenly, and without compensation; some would abolish it gradually, and with compensation; some would remove the freed people from us, and some would retain them with us; and there are yet other minor diversities. Because of these diversities, we waste much strength in struggles among ourselves. By mutual concession we should harmonize, and act together. This would be compromise; but it would be compromise among the friends, and not with the enemies of the Union. These articles are intended to embody a plan of such mutual concessions. If the plan shall be adopted, it is assumed that emancipation will follow, at least in several of the States.

"As to the first article, the main points are: first, the emancipation; secondly, the length of time for consummating it—thirty-seven years; and thirdly, the compensation.

"The emancipation will be unsatisfactory to the advocates of perpetual slavery; but the length of time should greatly mitigate their dissatisfaction. The time spares both races from the evils of sudden derangement—in fact, from the necessity of any derangement—while most of those whose habitual course of thought will be disturbed by the measure, will have passed away before its consummation. They will never see it. Another class will hail the prospect of emancipation, but will deprecate the length of time. They will feel that it gives too little to the now living slaves. But it really gives them much. It saves them from the vagrant destitution

which must largely attend immediate emancipation in localities where their numbers are very great ; and it gives the
inspiring assurance that their posterity shall be free forever.
The plan leaves to each State, choosing to act under it, to
abolish slavery now, or at the end of the century, or at any
intermediate time, or by degrees extending over the whole
or any part of the period ; and it obliges no two States to
proceed alike.   It also provides for compensation, and, generally, the mode of making it.   This, it would seem, must
further mitigate the dissatisfaction of those who favor perpetual slavery, and especially of those who are to receive the
compensation.   Doubtless, some of those who are to pay, and
not to receive, will object.   Yet the measure is both just and
economical.   In a certain sense, the liberation of slaves is the
destruction of property—property acquired by descent, or by
purchase, the same as any other property.   It is no less true
for having been often said, that the people of the South are
not more responsible for the original introduction of this
property, than are the people of the· North ; and when it is
remembered how unhesitatingly we all use cotton and sugar,
and share the profits of dealing in them, it may not be quite
safe to say, that the South has been more responsible than the
North for its continuance.   If, then, for a common object, this
property is to be sacrificed, is it not just that it be done at a
common charge ?

"And if, with less money, or money more easily paid, we
can preserve the benefits of the Union by this means, than we
can by the war alone, is it not also economical to do it ?   Let
us consider it then.   Let us ascertain the sum we have expended in the war since compensated emancipation was proposed last March, and consider whether, if that measure had
been promptly accepted, by even some of the slave States, the
same sum would not have done more to close the war, than
has been otherwise done.   If so, the measure would save
money, and, in that view, would be a prudent and economical

measure.   Certainly it is not so easy to pay *something* as it is to pay *nothing;* but it is easier to pay a *large* sum, than it is to pay a *larger* one.   And it is easier to pay any sum *when* we are able, than it is to pay it *before* we are able. The war requires large sums, and requires them at once. The aggregate sum necessary for compensated emancipation, of course, would be large.   But it would require no ready cash ; nor the bonds even, any faster than the emancipation progresses.   This might not, and probably would not, close before the end of the thirty-seven years.   At that time we shall probably have a hundred millions of people to share the burden, instead of thirty-one millions, as now.   And not only so, but the increase of our population may be expected to continue for a long time after that period, as rapidly as before ; because our territory will not have become full.   I do not state this inconsiderately.   At the same ratio of increase which we have maintained, on an average, from our first National census, in 1790, until that of 1860, we should, in 1900, have a population of one hundred and three million, two hundred and eight thousand, four hundred and fifteen.   And why may we not continue that ratio far beyond that period ? Our abundant room—our broad National homestead—is our ample resource.   Were our territory as limited as are the British Isles, very certainly our population could not expand as stated.   Instead of receiving the foreign born, as now, we should be compelled to send part of the native born away. But such is not our condition.   We have two millions nine hundred and sixty-three thousand square miles.   Europe has three millions and eight hundred thousand, with a population averaging seventy-three and one third persons to the square mile.   Why may not our country, at some time, average as many ?   Is it less fertile ?   Has it more waste surface, by mountains, rivers, lakes, deserts, or other causes ?   Is it inferior to Europe in any natural advantage ?   If, then, we are. at some time, to be as populous as Europe, how soon ?   As to when this *may* be, we can judge by the past and the present, as to when it *will* be, if ever, depends much on whether we maintain the Union. Several of our States are already above the average of Europe—seventy-three and a third to the square mile. Massachusetts has one hundred and fifty-seven; Rhode Island, one hundred and thirty-three; Connecticut, ninety-nine; New York and New Jersey, each, eighty. Also two other great States, Pennsylvania and Ohio, are not far below, the former having sixty-three and the latter fifty-nine. The States already above the European average, except New York, have increased in as rapid a ratio, since passing that point, as ever before; while no one of them is equal to some other parts of our country, in natural capacity for sustaining a dense population.

" Taking the nation in the aggregate, and we find its population and ratio of increase, for the several decennial periods, to be as follows :

1790...............	3,929,827	
1800...............	5,305,937	35.02 per cent. ratio of increase.
1810...............	7,239,814	36.45 " "
1820...............	9,638,131	33.13 " "
1830...............	12,866,020	33.49 " "
1840...............	17,069,453	32.67 " "
1850...............	23,191,876	35.87 " "
1860...............	31,443,790	35.58 " "

" This shows an average decennial increase of 34.60 per cent. in population through the seventy years from our first to our last census yet taken. It is seen that the ratio of increase, at one of these seven periods, is either two per. cent. below, or two per cent. above, the average, thus showing how inflexible, and, consequently, how reliable, the law of increase, in our case is. Assuming that it will continue, gives the following results :

1870..	42,423,341
1880..	56,967,216

1890..	76,677,872
1900..	103,208,415
1910..	138,918,526
1920..	186,984,335
1930..	251,680,914

"These figures show that our country *may* be as populous as Europe now is, at some point between 1920 and 1930 —say about 1925—our territory, at seventy-three and a third persons to the square mile, being the capacity to contain 217,186,000.

"And we *will* reach this, too, if we do not ourselves relinquish the chance, by the folly and evil of disunion, or by long and exhausting war, springing from the only great element of National discord among us. While it can not be foreseen exactly how much one huge example of secession, breeding lesser ones indefinitely, would retard population, civilization, and prosperity, no one can doubt that the extent of it would be very great and injurious.

"The proposed emancipation would shorten the war, perpetuate peace, insure this increase of population, and proportionately the wealth of the country. With these, we should pay all the emancipation would cost, together with our other debt, easier than we should pay our other debt, without it. If we had allowed our old National debt to run at six per cent. per annum, simple interest, from the end of our Revolutionary struggle until to-day, without paying any thing on either principal or interest, each man of us would owe less upon that debt now, than each man owed upon it then; and this because our increase of men, through the whole period, has been greater than six per cent.; has run faster than the interest upon the debt. Thus, time alone relieves a debtor nation, so long as its population increases faster than unpaid interest accumulates on its debt.

"This fact would be no excuse for delaying payment of what is justly due; but it shows the great importance of time in this connection—the great advantage of a policy by which we shall not have to pay until we number a hundred millions, what, by a different policy, we would have to pay now, when we number but thirty-one millions. In a word, it shows that a dollar will be much harder to pay for the war, than will be a dollar for emancipation on the proposed plan. And then the latter will cost no blood, no precious life. It will be a saving of both.

"As to the second article, I think it would be impracticable to return to bondage the class of persons therein contemplated. Some of them, doubtless, in the property sense, belong to loyal owners; and hence, provision is made in this article for compensating such.

"The third article relates to the future of the freed people. It does not oblige, but merely authorizes, Congress to aid in colonizing such as may consent. This ought not to be regarded as objectionable, on the one hand, or on the other, in so much as it comes to nothing, unless by the mutual consent of the people to be deported, and the American voters, through their representatives in Congress.

"I can not make it better known than it already is, that I strongly favor colonization. And yet I wish to say there is an objection urged against free colored persons remaining in the country, which is largely imaginary, if not sometimes malicious.

"It is insisted that their presence would injure, and displace white labor and white laborers. If there ever could be a proper time for mere catch arguments, that time surely is not now. In times like the present, men should utter nothing for which they would not willingly be responsible through time and in eternity. Is it true, then, that colored people can displace any more white labor by being free, than by remaining slaves? If they stay in their old places, they jostle no white laborers; if they leave their old places, they leave them open to white laborers. Logically, there is neither more nor less of it.   Emancipation, even without deportation, would, probably enhance the wages of white labor, and, very surely, would not reduce them.   Thus, the customary amount of labor would still have to be performed; the freed people would surely not do more than their old proportion of it, and very probably, for a time, would do less, leaving an increased part to white laborers, bringing their labor into greater demand, and, consequently, enhancing the wages of it.   With deportation, even to a limited extent, enhanced wages to white labor is mathematically certain.   Labor is like any other commodity in the market—increase the demand for it, and you increase the price of it.   Reduce the supply of black labor, by colonizing the black laborer out of the country, and, by precisely so much you increase the demand for, and wages of, white labor.

"But it is dreaded that the freed people will swarm forth, and cover the whole land.   Are they not already in the land?   Will liberation make them any more numerous?   Equally distributed among the whites of the whole country, and there would be but one colored to seven whites.   Could the one, in any way, greatly disturb the seven?   There are many communities now, having more than one free colored person to seven whites; and this without any apparent consciousness of evil from it.   The District of Columbia, and the States of Maryland and Delaware, are all in this condition.   The District has more than one free colored to six whites; and yet, in its frequent petitions to Congress, I believe it has never presented the presence of free colored persons as one of its grievances.   But why should emancipation South send the freed people North?   People, of any color, seldom run, unless there be something to run from.   *Heretofore*, colored people, to some extent, have fled North from bondage; and *now*, perhaps, from both bondage and destitution.   But if gradual emancipation and deportation be adopted, they will have neither to flee from.   Their old masters will give them wages, at least until new laborers can be procured; and the freed men, in turn, will gladly give their labor for the wages, till new homes can be found for them, in congenial climes, and with people of their own blood and race. This proposition can be trusted on the mutual interests involved. And, in any event, can not the North decide for itself, whether to receive them?

"Again, as practice proves more than theory, in any case, has there been any irruption of colored people northward, because of the abolishment of slavery in this District last spring?

"What I have said of the proportion of free colored persons to the whites, in the District, is from the census of 1860, having no reference to persons called contrabands, nor to those made free by the Act of Congress abolishing slavery here.

"The plan consisting of these articles is recommended, not but that a restoration of the National authority would be accepted without its adoption.

"Nor will the war, nor proceedings under the proclamation of September 22d, 1862, be stayed because of the *recommendation* of this plan. Its timely *adoption*, I doubt not, would bring restoration, and thereby stay both.

"And, notwithstanding this plan, the recommendation that Congress provide by law for compensating any State which may adopt emancipation, before this plan shall have been acted upon, is hereby earnestly renewed. Such would be only an advance part of the plan, and the same arguments apply to both.

"This plan is recommended as a means, not in exclusion of, but in addition to, all others for restoring and preserving the National authority throughout the Union. The subject is presented exclusively in its economical aspect. The plan would, I am confident, secure peace more speedily, and maintain it more permanently, than can be done by force alone;

while all it would cost, considering amounts, and manner of payment, and times of payment, would be easier paid than will be the additional cost of the war, if we rely solely upon force.   It is much—very much—that it would cost no blood at all.

" The plan is proposed as permanent constitutional law. It cannot become such without the concurrence of, first, two-thirds of Congress, and, afterward, three-fourths of the States. The requisite three-fourths of the States, will necessarily include seven of the slave States.   Their concurrence, if obtained, will give assurance of their severally adopting emancipation, at no very distant day, upon the new constitutional terms.   This assurance would end the struggle now, and save the Union forever.

" I do not forget the gravity which should characterize a paper addressed to the Congress of the nation, by the Chief Magistrate of the nation.   Nor do I forget that some of you are my seniors ; nor that many of you have more experience than I, in the conduct of public affairs.   Yet I trust that, in view of the great responsibility resting upon me, you will perceive no want of respect to yourselves, in any undue earnestness I may seem to display.

" Is it doubted, then, that the plan I propose, if adopted, would shorten the war, and thus lessen its expenditure of money and of blood ?   Is it doubted that it would restore the national authority and national prosperity, and perpetuate both indefinitely ?   Is it doubted that we here—Congress and Executive—can secure its adoption ?   Will not the good people respond to a united and earnest appeal from us ?   Can we, can they, by any other means, so certainly or so speedily assure these vital objects ?   We can succeed only by concert. It is not, ' Can *any* of us *imagine* better ?' but, ' Can we *all* do better ?   Object whatsoever is possible, still the question recurs, ' Can we do better ?'   The dogmas of the quiet past are inadequate to the stormy present.   The occasion is piled high with difficulty, and we must rise with the occasion. As our case is new, so we must think anew, and act anew. We must disinthrall ourselves, and then we shall save our country.

"Fellow-citizens, *we* can not escape history. We of this Congress and this Administration, will be remembered in spite of ourselves. No personal significance, or insignificance, can spare one or another of us. The fiery trial through which we pass, will light us down, in honor or dishonor, to the latest generation. We *say* we are for the Union. The world will not forget that we say this. We know how to save the Union. The world knows we do know how to save it. We—even *we here*—hold the power, and bear the responsibility. In *giving* freedom to the *slave*, we *assure* freedom to the *free*—honorable alike in what we give and what we preserve. We shall nobly save, or meanly lose, the last best hope of earth. Other means may succeed; this could not fail. The way is plain, peaceful, generous, just — a way which, if followed, the world will forever applaud, and God must forever bless.

Dec. 1, 1862.   "ABRAHAM LINCOLN."

CHAPTER XV.

THE TIDE TURNED.

Military Successes—Favorable Elections—Emancipation Policy—Letter to Manchester (England) Workingmen—Proclamation for a National Fast—Letter to Erastus Corning—Letter to a Committee on recalling Vallandigham.

IT had been decreed by a kind Providence that the year 1863 was to mark a turn in the almost unbroken line of reverses which the Union army had experienced for some time previous.

True, Hooker, who had superseded Burnside in command
of the Army of the Potomac, had been signally repulsed at
Chancellorsville; but this was more than compensated by the
decided victory achieved by the same troops, under Meade,
over the rebels at Gettysburg. Grant, by the capture of
Vicksburg, and the surrender of Port Hudson, which was the
inevitable result, had opened the Mississippi to the Gulf, and
completely severed the bastard confederacy. We moreover
secured East Tennessee, and by the victories of Lookout
Mountain and Missionary Ridge, and the repulse of a rebel
attempt to retake Knoxville, paved the way for an offensive
movement into the vitals of Georgia.

The sober, second thought of the people was manifest.
Vallandigham in Ohio, who for his treasonable practices had
been tried by Burnside's order, convicted, and ordered South
to his friends, but who had been suffered to return *via* Canada,
and was put forward as the exponent of "Democracy" in
Ohio, was shelved by some one hundred thousand majority.
Pennsylvania, likewise, more than redeemed herself. In fact
every loyal State—except New Jersey—showed decided
majorities for the Administration.

In this election, be it remembered, the emancipation policy
of the President had entered largely as an element of discussion; and the results were the more gratifying as it established conclusively, that however unfavorable early indications might have been, the great pulse of the people beat in
unison with freedom for man as man. If in a contest like
that in which the nation was then engaged, all merely merce-
nary considerations could be overlooked, deep-rooted prejudices mastered, and long withheld rights cheerfully granted,
there would be, indeed, strong grounds to hope for the
progress of our race.

At the beginning of the year, the President received a
gratifying evidence of the appreciation in which his efforts for
freedom were held, in a testimonial of sympathy and confi-

dence from the workingmen of Manchester, England; to which address he made the following reply:

"*Executive Mansion*, Washington, January 19, 1863.

"TO THE WORKINGMEN OF MANCHESTER:—I have the honor to acknowledge the receipt of the address and resolutions which you sent me on the eve of the new year.

"When I came, on the 4th of March, 1861, through a free and constitutional election, to preside in the Government of the United States, the country was found at the verge of civil war. Whatever might have been the cause, or whosesoever the fault, one duty, paramount to all others, was before me, namely, to maintain and preserve at once the Constitution and the integrity of the Federal Republic. A conscientious purpose to perform this duty is the key to all the measures of administration which have been, and to all which will hereafter be pursued. Under our frame of government and my official oath, I could not depart from this purpose if I would. It is not always in the power of governments to enlarge or restrict the scope of moral results which follow the policies that they may deem it necessary, for the public safety, from time to time to adopt.

"I have understood well that the duty of self-preservation rests solely with the American people. But I have, at the same time, been aware that the favor or disfavor of foreign nations might have a material influence in enlarging and prolonging the struggle with disloyal men in which the country is engaged. A fair examination of history has seemed to authorize a belief that the past action and influences of the United States were generally regarded as having been beneficial toward mankind. I have, therefore, reckoned upon the forbearance of nations. Circumstances—to some of which you kindly allude—induced me especially to expect that, if justice and good faith should be practised by the United States, they would encounter no hostile influence on the part of Great Britain. It is now a pleasant duty to acknowledge the demonstration you have given of your desire that a spirit of peace and amity toward this country may prevail in the councils of your Queen, who is respected and esteemed in your own country only more than she is by the kindred nation which has its home on this side of the Atlantic.

"I know, and deeply deplore, the sufferings which the workingmen at Manchester, and in all Europe, are called to endure in this crisis. It has been often and studiously represented that the attempt to overthrow this Government, which was built upon the foundation of human rights, and to substitute for it one which should rest exclusively on the basis of human slavery, was likely to obtain the favor of Europe. Through the action of our disloyal citizens, the workingmen of Europe have been subjected to severe trial, for the purpose of forcing their sanction to that attempt. Under these circumstances, I can not but regard your decisive utterances upon the question as an instance of sublime Christian heroism, which has not been surpassed in any age or in any country. It is indeed an energetic and reinspiring assurance of the inherent power of truth, and of the ultimate and universal triumph of justice, humanity and freedom. I do not doubt that the sentiments you have expressed will be sustained by your great nation; and, on the other hand, I have no hesitation in assuring you that they will excite admiration, esteem, and the most reciprocal feelings of friendship among the American people. I hail this interchange of sentiment, therefore, as an augury that, whatever else may happen, whatever misfortune may befall your country or my own, the peace and friendship which now exist between the two nations will be, as it shall be my desire to make them, perpetual.   ABRAHAM LINCOLN."

On the 30th of March the following proclamation was issued in pursuance of a request to that effect from the Senate:

"WHEREAS, The Senate of the United States, devoutly

recognizing the supreme authority and just government of
Almighty God in all the affairs of men and of nations, has by
a resolution requested the President to designate and set
apart a day for National prayer and humiliation;

"AND WHEREAS, It is the duty of nations, as well as of
men, to own their dependence upon the overruling power of
God, to confess their sins and transgressions in humble sorrow,
yet with assured hope that genuine repentance will lead to
mercy and pardon, and to recognize the sublime truth announced in the Holy Scriptures, and proven by all history,
that those nations only are blessed whose God is the Lord;

"And, insomuch as we know that, by his Divine law,
nations, like individuals, are subjected to punishments and
chastisements in this world, may we not justly fear that the
awful calamity of civil war, which now desolates the land,
may be but a punishment inflicted upon us for our presumptuous sins, to the needful end of our National reformation as a
whole people? We have been the recipients of the choicest
bounties of Heaven. We have been preserved, these many
years, in peace and prosperity. We have grown in numbers,
wealth and power, as no other nation has ever grown. But
we have forgotten God. We have forgotten the gracious
hand which preserved us in peace, and multiplied and en-
riched and strengthened us; and we have vainly imagined, in
the deceitfulness of our hearts, that all these blessings were
produced by some superior wisdom and virtue of our own.
Intoxicated with unbroken success, we have become too self-
sufficient to feel the necessity of redeeming and preserving
grace, too proud to pray to the God that made us!

"It behooves us, then, to humble ourselves before the
offended Power, to confess our National sins, and to pray for
clemency and forgiveness.

"Now, therefore, in compliance with the request, and fully
concurring in the views of the Senate, I do, by this my proclamation, designate and set apart Thursday, the thirteenth

day of April, 1863, as a day of National humiliation, fasting and prayer. And I do hereby request all the people to abstain on that day from their ordinary secular pursuits, and to unite, at their several places of public worship and their respective homes, in keeping the day holy to the Lord, and devoted to the humble discharge of the religious duties proper to that solemn occasion.

"All this being done in sincerity and truth, let us then rest humbly in the hope, authorized by the Divine teachings, that the united cry of the Nation will be heard on high, and answered with blessings, no less than the pardon of our National sins, and restoration of our now divided and suffering country to its former happy condition of unity and peace.

" In witness whereof, I have hereunto set my hand, and caused the seal of the United States to be affixed.

" Done at the City of Washington, on this thirtieth day of March, in the year of our Lord one thousand eight hundred and sixty-three, and of the Independence of the United States the eighty-seventh.

    "By the President: "ABRAHAM LINCOLN.

" WILLIAM H. SEWARD, Secretary of State."

The following letter, which belongs in this place, will explain itself:

    "*Executive Mansion*, Washington, June 13th, 1863.

" HON. ERASTUS CORNING and others—*Gentlemen :*—Your letter of May 19th, inclosing the resolutions of a public meeting held at Albany, New York, on the 16th of the same month, was received several days ago.

" The resolutions, as I understand them, are resolvable into two propositions—first, the expression of a purpose to sustain the cause of the Union, to secure peace through victory, and to support the Administration in every constitutional and lawful measure to suppress the rebellion ; and, secondly, a

15

declaration of censure upon the Administration for supposed unconstitutional action, such as the making of military arrests. And from the two propositions a third is deduced, which is, that the gentlemen composing the meeting are resolved on doing their part to maintain our common Government and country, despite the folly or wickedness, as they may conceive, of any Administration. This position is eminently patriotic, and as such I thank the meeting and congratulate the nation for it. My own purpose is the same; so that the meeting and myself have a common object, and can have no difference, except in the choice of means or measures for effecting that object.

"And here I ought to close this paper, and would close it, if there were no apprehension that more injurious consequences than any merely personal to myself might follow the censures systematically cast upon me for doing what, in my view of duty, I could not forbear. The resolutions promise to support me in every constitutional and lawful measure to suppress the rebellion, and I have not knowingly employed, nor shall knowingly employ, any other. But the meeting, by their resolutions, assert and argue that certain military arrests and proceedings following them, for which I am ultimately responsible, are unconstitutional. I think they are not. The resolutions quote from the Constitution the definition of treason, and also the limiting safeguards and guaranties therein provided for the citizen on trial for treason, and on his being held to answer for capital, or otherwise infamous crimes; and in criminal prosecutions, his right to a speedy and public trial by an impartial jury. They proceed to resolve, 'that these safeguards of the rights of the citizen against the pretensions of arbitrary power were intended more *especially* for his protection in times of civil commotion.'

"And, apparently to demonstrate the proposition, the resolutions proceed: 'They were secured substantially to the

English people *after* years of protracted civil war, and were adopted into our Constitution at the *close* of the Revolution.' Would not the demonstration have been better if it could have been truly said that these safeguards had been adopted and applied *during* the civil wars and *during* our Revolution, instead of *after* the one and at the *close* of the other? I, too, am devotedly for them *after* civil war, and *before* civil war, and at all times, 'except when, in cases of rebellion or invasion, the public safety may require' their suspension. The resolutions proceed to tell us that these safeguards 'have stood the test of seventy-six years of trial, under our republican system, under circumstances which show that, while they constitute the foundation of all free government, they are the elements of the enduring stability of the Republic.' No one denies that they have so stood the test up to the beginning of the present rebellion, if we except a certain occurrence at New Orleans; nor does any one question that they will stand the same test much longer after the rebellion closes. But these provisions of the Constitution have no application to the case we have in hand, because the arrests complained of were not made for treason—that is, not for *the* treason defined in the Constitution, and upon conviction of which the punishment is death—nor yet were they made to hold persons to answer for any capital or otherwise infamous crimes; nor were the proceedings following, in any constitutional or legal sense, 'criminal prosecutions.' The arrests were made on totally different grounds, and the proceedings following accorded with the grounds of the arrest. Let us consider the real case with which we are dealing, and apply to it the parts of the Constitution plainly made for such cases.

" Prior to my installation here, it had been inculcated that any State had a lawful right to secede from the National Union, and that it would be expedient to exercise the right whenever the devotees of the doctrine should fail to elect a

President to their own liking. I was elected contrary to their liking, and accordingly, so far as it was legally possible, they had taken seven States out of the Union, and had seized many of the United States forts, and had fired upon the United States flag, all before I was inaugurated, and, of course, before I had done any official act whatever. The rebellion thus began soon ran into the present civil war; and, in certain respects, it began on very unequal terms between the parties. The insurgents had been preparing for it for more than thirty years, while the Government had taken no steps to resist them. The former had carefully considered all the means which could be turned to their account. It undoubtedly was a well-pondered reliance with them that, in their own unrestricted efforts to destroy Union, Constitution, and law together, the Government would, in a great degree, be restrained by the same Constitution and law from arresting their progress. Their sympathizers pervaded all departments of the Government, and nearly all communities of the people. From this material, under cover of 'liberty of speech,' 'liberty of the press,' and '*habeas corpus*,' they hoped to keep on foot among us a most efficient corps of spies, informers, suppliers, and aiders and abettors of their cause in a thousand ways. They knew that in times such as they were inaugurating, by the Constitution itself, the '*habeas corpus*' might be suspended; but they also knew they had friends who would make a question as to *who* was to suspend it; meanwhile, their spies and others might remain at large to help on their cause. Or if, as has happened, the Executive should suspend the writ, without ruinous waste of time, instances of arresting innocent persons might occur, as are always likely to occur in such cases, and then a clamor could be raised in regard to this which might be, at least, of some service to the insurgent cause. It needed no very keen perception to discover this part of the enemy's programme, so soon as, by open hostilities, their machinery was put fairly in motion. Yet, thoroughly imbued with a reverence for the guaranteed rights of individuals, I was slow to adopt the strong measures which by degrees I have been forced to regard as being within the exceptions of the Constitution, and as indispensable to the public safety. Nothing is better known to history than that courts of justice are utterly incompetent to such cases. Civil courts are organized chiefly for trials of individuals, or, at most, a few individuals acting in concert, and this in quiet times, and on charges of crimes well defined in the law. Even in times of peace, bands of horsethieves and robbers frequently grow too numerous and powerful for the ordinary courts of justice. But what comparison, in numbers, have such bands ever borne to the insurgent sympathizers even in many of the loyal States? Again, a jury too frequently has at least one member more ready to hang the panel, than to hang the traitor. And yet, again he who dissuades one man from volunteering, or induces one soldier to desert, weakens the Union cause as much as he who kills a Union soldier in battle. Yet this dissuasion or inducement may be so conducted as to be no defined crime of which any civil court would take cognizance.

"Ours is a case of rebellion—so called by the resolution before me—in fact, a clear, flagrant, and gigantic case of rebellion; and the provision of the Constitution that 'the privilege of the writ of *habeas corpus* shall not be suspended unless when, in cases of rebellion or invasion, the public safety may require it,' is *the* provision which specially applies to our present case. This provision plainly attests the understanding of those who made the Constitution, that ordinary courts of justice are inadequate to 'cases of rebellion'—attests their purpose that, in such cases, men may be held in custody whom the courts, acting on ordinary rules, would discharge. *Habeas corpus* does not discharge men who are proved to be guilty of defined crime; and its suspension is allowed by the Constitution on purpose that men may be arrested and held who can not be proved to be guilty of defined crime, 'when, in cases of rebellion or invasion, the public safety may require it.' This is precisely our present case—a case of rebellion, wherein the public safety *does* require the suspension. Indeed, arrests by process of courts, and arrests in cases of rebellion, do not proceed altogether upon the same basis. The former is directed at the small percentage of ordinary and continuous perpetration of crime ; while the latter is directed at sudden and extensive uprisings against the Government, which at most will succeed or fail in no great length of time. In the latter case arrests are made, not so much for what has been done as for what probably would be done. The latter is more for the preventive and less for the vindictive than the former. In such cases the purposes of men are much more easily understood than in cases of ordinary crime. The man who stands by and says nothing when the peril of his Government is discussed, can not be misunderstood. If not hindered, he is sure to help the enemy ; much more, if he talks ambiguously—talks for his country with 'buts,' and 'ifs' and 'ands.' Of how little value the constitutional provisions I have quoted will be rendered, if arrests shall never be made until defined crimes shall have been committed, may be illustrated by a few notable examples. General John C. Breckinridge, General Robert E. Lee, General Joseph E. Johnston, General John B. Magruder, General William B. Preston, General Simon B. Buckner, and Commodore Franklin Buchanan, now occupying the very highest places in the rebel war service, were all within the power of the Government since the rebellion began, and were nearly as well known to be traitors then as now. Unquestionably, if we had seized and held them, the insurgent cause would be much weaker. But no one of them had then committed any crime defined by law. Every one of them, if arrested, would have been discharged on *habeas corpus*, were the writ allowed to operate. In view of these and similar cases, I think the time not unlikely to come when I shall be blamed for having made too few arrests rather than too many.

"By the third resolution, the meeting indicate their opinion that military arrests may be constitutional in localities where rebellion actually exists, but that such arrests are unconstitutional in localities where rebellion or insurrection does *not* actually exist. They insist that such arrests shall not be made 'outside of the lines of necessary military occupation and the scenes of insurrection.' Inasmuch, however, as the Constitution itself makes no such distinction, I am unable to believe that there *is* any such constitutional distinction. I concede that the class of arrests complained of can be constitutional only when, in cases of rebellion or invasion, the public safety may require them; and I insist that in such cases they are Constitutional *wherever* the public safety does require them; as well in places to which they may prevent the rebellion extending, as in those where it may be already prevailing; as well where they may restrain mischievous interference with the raising and supplying of armies to suppress the rebellion, as where the rebellion may actually be; as well where they may restrain the enticing men out of the army, as where they would prevent mutiny in the army; equally constitutional at all places where they will conduce to the public safety, as against the dangers of rebellion or invasion. Take the particular case mentioned by the meeting. It is asserted, in substance, that Mr. Vallandigham was, by a military commander, seized and tried 'for no other reason than words addressed to a public meeting, in criticism of the course of the Administration, and in condemnation of the military orders of the general.' Now, if there be no mistake about this; if this assertion is the truth and the whole truth; if there was no other reason for the arrest, then I concede that the arrest was wrong. But the arrest, as I understand, was made for a very different reason. Mr. Vallandigham avows his hostility to the war on the part of the Union; and his arrest was made because he was laboring, with some effect, to prevent the raising of troops ; to encourage desertion from the army, and to leave the rebellion without an adequate military force to suppress it.   He was not arrested because he was damaging the political prospects of the Administration, or the personal interests of the commanding general, but because he was damaging the army, upon the existence and vigor of which the life of the nation depends.   He was warring upon the military, and this gave the military constitutional jurisdiction to lay hands upon him.   If Mr. Vallandigham was not damaging the military power of the country, then this arrest was made on mistake of fact, which I would be glad to correct on reasonably satisfactory evidence.

" I understand the meeting whose resolutions I am considering to be in favor of suppressing the rebellion by military force—by armies.   Long experience has shown that armies cannot be maintained unless desertions shall be punished by the severe penalty of death.   The case requires, and the law and the Constitution sanction, this punishment.   Must I shoot a simple-minded soldier boy who deserts, while I must not touch a hair of a wily agitator who induces him to desert ?   This is none the less injurious when effected by getting a father, or brother, or friend, into a public meeting, and there working upon his feelings till he is persuaded to write the soldier boy that he is fighting in a bad cause, for a wicked Administration of a contemptible Government, too weak to arrest and punish him if he shall desert.   I think that in such a case to silence the agitator and save the boy is not only constitutional, but withal a great mercy.

" If I be wrong on this question of constitutional power, my error lies in believing that certain proceedings are constitutional when, in cases of rebellion or invasion, the public safety requires them, which would not be constitutional when, in the absence of rebellion or invasion, the public safety does *not* require them ; in other words, that the Constitution is not, in its application, in all respects the same—in cases of rebellion or invasion involving the public safety, as it is in time of profound peace and public security. The Constitution itself makes the distinction; and I can no more be persuaded that the Government can constitutionally take no strong measures in time of rebellion, because it can be shown that the same could not be lawfully taken in time of peace, than I can be persuaded that a particular drug is not good medicine for a sick man, because it can be shown not to be good food for a well one. Nor am I able to appreciate the danger apprehended by the meeting, that the American people will, by means of military arrests during the rebellion, lose the right of public discussion, the liberty of speech and the press, the law of evidence, trial by jury, and *habeas corpus*, throughout the indefinite peaceful future, which I trust lies before them, any more than I am able to believe that a man could contract so strong an appetite for emetics, during temporary illness, as to persist in feeding upon them during the remainder of his healthful life.

"In giving the resolutions that earnest consideration which you request of me, I can not overlook the fact that the meeting speak as 'Democrats.' Nor can I, with full respect for their known intelligence, and the fairly presumed deliberation with which they prepared their resolutions, be permitted to suppose that this occurred by accident, or in any way other than that they preferred to designate themselves 'Democrats' rather than 'American Citizens.' In this time of National peril, I would have preferred to meet you on a level one step higher than any party platform; because I am sure that, from such more elevated position, we could do better battle for the country we all love than we possibly can from those lower ones where, from the force of habit, the prejudices of the past, and selfish hopes of the future, we are sure to expend much of our ingenuity and strength in finding fault with and aiming blows at each other. But, since you have denied me this, I will yet be thankful for the country's sake, that not all Democrats have done so. He on whose discretionary judgment Mr. Vallandigham was arrested and tried is a Democrat, having no old party affinity with me; and the judge who rejected the constitutional view expressed in these resolutions, by refusing to discharge Mr. Vallandigham on *habeas corpus*, is a Democrat of better days than these, having received his judicial mantle at the hands of President Jackson. And still more, of all those Democrats who are nobly exposing their lives and shedding their blood on the battle-field, I have learned that many approve the course taken with Mr. Vallandigham, while I have not heard of a single one condemning it. I can not assert that there are none such.

"And the name of Jackson recalls an incident of pertinent history: After the battle of New Orleans, and while the fact that the treaty of peace had been concluded was well known in the city, but before official knowledge of it had arrived, Gen. Jackson still maintained martial or military law. Now that it could be said the war was over, the clamor against martial law, which had existed from the first, grew more furious. Among other things, a Mr. Louiallier published a denunciatory newspaper article. Gen. Jackson arrested him. A lawyer by the name of Morrel procured the United States Judge Hall to issue a writ of *habeas corpus* to relieve Mr. Louiallier. Gen. Jackson arrested both the lawyer and the Judge. A Mr. Hollander ventured to say of some part of the matter that 'it was a dirty trick.' Gen. Jackson arrested him. When the officer undertook to serve the writ of *habeas corpus*, Gen. Jackson took it from him, and sent him away with a copy. Holding the judge in custody a few days, the general sent him beyond the limits of his encampment, and set him at liberty, with an order to remain till the ratification of peace should be regularly announced, or until the British should have left the Southern coast. A day or two more elapsed, the ratification of a treaty of peace was regularly announced, and the judge and others were fully liberated. A few days more, and the judge called Gen. Jackson into court and fined him $1,000 for having arrested him and the others named. The general paid the fine, and there the matter rested for nearly thirty years, when Congress refunded principal and interest. The late Senator Douglas, then in the House of Representatives, took a leading part in the debates, in which the constitutional question was much discussed. I am not prepared to say whom the journals would show to have voted for the measure.

"It may be remarked : First, that we had the same Constitution then as now ; secondly, that we then had a case of invasion, and now we have a case of rebellion ; and, thirdly, that the permanent right of the people to public discussion, the liberty of speech and of the press, the trial by jury, the law of evidence, and the *habeas corpus*, suffered no detriment whatever by that conduct of Gen. Jackson, or its subsequent approval by the American Congress.

"And yet, let me say that, in my own discretion, I do not know whether I would have ordered the arrest of Mr. Vallandigham. While I can not shift the responsibility from myself, I hold that, as a general rule, the commander in the field is the better judge of the necessity in any particular case. Of course, I must practise a general directory and revisory power in the matter.

"One of the resolutions expresses the opinion of the meeting that arbitrary arrests will have the effect to divide and distract those who should be united in suppressing the rebellion, and I am specifically called on to discharge Mr. Vallandigham. I regard this as, at least, a fair appeal to me on the expediency of exercising a constitutional power which I think exists. In response to such appeal, I have to say, it gave me pain when I learned that Mr. Vallandigham had been arrested—that is, I was pained that there should have seemed to be a necessity for arresting him—and that it will afford me great pleasure to discharge him so soon as I can, by any means, believe the public safety will not suffer by it. I further say that, as the war progresses, it appears to me, opinion and action which were in great confusion at first, take shape and fall into more regular channels, so that the necessity for strong dealing with them gradually decreases. I have every reason to desire that it should cease altogether ; and far from the least is my regard for the opinions and wishes of those who, like the meeting at Albany, declare their purpose to sustain the Government in every constitutional and lawful measure to suppress the rebellion.   Still, I must continue to do so much as may seem to be required by the public safety.   A. LINCOLN."

Mr. Lincoln, having been waited upon by a Committee of Ohio " Democrats," who urged him to recall Vallandigham, whom they sought to exalt as a " martyr to popular rights," addressed the following reply, the quiet sarcasm of which is not the least of its many good points :

"Washington, June 29, 1863.

" GENTLEMEN :—The resolutions of the Ohio Democratic State Convention, which you present me, together with your introductory and closing remarks, being, in position and argument, mainly the same as the resolutions of the Democratic meeting at Albany, New York, I refer you to my response to the latter as meeting most of the points in the former.

"This response you evidently used in preparing your remarks, and I desire no more than that it be used with accuracy.   In a single reading of your remarks, I only discovered one inaccuracy in matter which I suppose you took from that paper.   It is where you say, ' The undersigned are unable to agree with you in the opinion you have expressed that the Constitution is different in time of insurrection or invasion from what it is in time of peace and public security.'

"A recurrence to the paper will show you that I have not expressed the opinion you suppose.   I expressed the opinion that the Constitution is different *in its application* in cases of rebellion or invasion involving the public safety, from what it is in times of profound peace and public security.   And this opinion I adhere to, simply because, by the Constitution itself, things may be done in the one case which may not be done in the other.

" I dislike to waste a word on a merely personal point, but I must respectfully assure you that you will find yourselves at fault should you ever seek for evidence to prove your assumption that I ' opposed, in discussions before the people, the policy of the Mexican War.'

" You say : ' Expunge from the Constitution this limitation upon the power of Congress to suspend the writ of *habeas corpus*, and yet the other guaranties of personal liberty would remain unchanged.' Doubtless, if this clause of the Constitution, improperly called, as I think, a limitation upon the power of Congress, were expunged, the other guaranties would remain the same ; but the question is, not how those guaranties would stand with that clause *out* of the Constitution, but how they stand with that clause remaining in it, in case of rebellion or invasion involving the public safety.   If the liberty could be indulged in expunging that clause, letter and spirit, I really think the constitutional argument would be with you.

"My general view on this question was stated in the Albany response, and hence I do not state it now.   I only add that, as seems to me, the benefit of the writ of *habeas corpus* is the great means through which the guaranties of personal liberty are conserved and made available in the last resort ; and corroborative of this view is the fact that Mr. Vallandigham, in the very case in question, under the advice of able lawyers, saw not where else to go but to the *habeas corpus*.   But by the Constitution the benefit of the writ of *habeas corpus* itself may be suspended, when, in case of rebellion or invasion, the public safety may require it.

" You ask, in substance, whether I really claim that I may override all the guaranteed rights of individuals, on the plea of conserving the public safety—when I may choose to say the public safety requires it.   This question, divested of the phraseology calculated to represent me as struggling for an arbitrary personal prerogative, is either simply a question *who* shall decide, or an affirmation that *nobody* shall decide, what the public safety does require in cases of rebellion or invasion.   The Constitution contemplates the question as likely to occur for decision, but it does not expressly declare who is to decide it.   By necessary implication, when rebellion or invasion comes, the decision is to be made from time to time; and I think the man whom, for the time, the people have, under the Constitution, made their Commander-in-chief of the Army and Navy, is the man who holds the power and bears the responsibility of making it.   If he uses the power justly, the same people will probably justify him; if he abuses it, he is in their hands, to be dealt with by all the modes they have reserved to themselves in the Constitution.

" The earnestness with which you insist that persons can only, in times of rebellion, be lawfully dealt with in accordance with the rules for criminal trials and punishments in times of peace, induces me to add a word to what I said on that point in the Albany response.   You claim that men may, if they choose, embarrass those whose duty it is to combat a giant rebellion, and then be dealt with only in turn as if there were no rebellion.   The Constitution itself rejects this view.   The military arrests and detentions which have been made, including those of Mr. Vallandigham, which are not different in principle from the other, have been for *prevention*, and not for *punishment*—as injunctions to stay injury, as proceedings to keep the peace—and hence, like proceedings in such cases and for like reasons, they have not been accompanied with indictments, or trial by juries, nor in a single case by any punishment whatever beyond what is purely incidental to the prevention. The original sentence of imprisonment in Mr. Vallandigham's case was to prevent injury to the military service only, and the modification of it was made as a less disagreeable mode to him of securing the same prevention.

" I am unable to perceive an insult to Ohio in the case of Mr. Vallandigham. Quite surely nothing of this sort was or is intended. I was wholly unaware that Mr. Vallandigham was, at the time of his arrest, a candidate for the Democratic nomination for Governor, until so informed by your reading to me the resolutions of the convention. I am grateful to the State of Ohio for many things, especially for the brave soldiers and officers she has given, in the present national trial, to the armies of the Union.

" You claim, as I understand, that, according to my own position in the Albany response, Mr. Vallandigham should be released ; and this because, as you claim, he has not damaged the military service by discouraging enlistments, encouraging desertions, or otherwise ; and that if he had, he should have been turned over to the civil authorities under the recent Act of Congress. I certainly do not *know* that Mr. Vallandigham has specifically and by direct language advised against enlistments and in favor of desertions and resistance to drafting. We all know that combinations, armed, in some instances, to resist the arrest of deserters, began several months ago ; that more recently the like has appeared in resistance to the enrollment preparatory to a draft; and that quite a number of assassinations have occurred from the same *animus.* These had to be met by military force, and this again has led to bloodshed and death. And now, under a sense of responsibility more weighty and enduring than any which is merely official, I solemnly declare my belief that this hindrance of the military, including maiming and murder, is due to the cause in which Mr. Vallandigham has been engaged, in a greater degree than to any other cause; and it is due to him personally in a greater degree than to any other one man.

"These things have been notorious, known to all, and of course known to Mr. Vallandigham. Perhaps I would not be wrong to say they originated with his especial friends and adherents. With perfect knowledge of them he has frequently, if not constantly, made speeches in Congress and before popular assemblies; and if it can be shown that, with these things staring him in the face, he has ever uttered a word of rebuke or counsel against them, it will be a fact greatly in his favor with me, and one of which, as yet, I am totally ignorant. When it is known that the whole burden of his speeches has been to stir up men against the prosecution of the war, and that in the midst of resistance to it he has not been known in any instance to counsel against such resistance, it is next to impossible to repel the inference that he has counselled directly in favor of it.

"With all this before their eyes, the convention you represent have nominated Mr. Vallandigham for Governor of Ohio, and both they and you have declared the purpose to sustain the National Union by all constitutional means; but, of course, they and you, in common, reserve to yourselves to decide what are constitutional means, and, unlike the Albany meeting, you omit to state or intimate that, in your opinion, an army is a constitutional means of saving the Union against a rebellion, or even to intimate that you are conscious of an existing rebellion being in progress with the avowed object of destroying that very Union. At the same time, your nominee for Governor, in whose behalf you appeal, is known to you, and to the world, to declare against the use of an army to suppress the rebellion. Your own attitude, therefore, encourages desertion, resistance to the draft, and the like, because it teaches those who incline to desert and to escape the draft, to believe it is your purpose to protect them, and to hope that you will become strong enough to do so.

"After a personal intercourse with you, gentlemen of the Committee, I can not say I think you desire this effect to follow your attitude; but I assure you that both friends and enemies of the Union look upon it in this light. It is a substantial hope, and by consequence, a real strength to the enemy. If it is a false hope, and one which you would willingly dispel, I will make the way exceedingly easy. I send you duplicates of this letter, in order that you, or a majority of you, may, if you choose, indorse your names upon one of them, and return it thus indorsed to me, with the understanding that those signing are thereby committed to the following propositions, and to nothing else:

"1. That there is now a rebellion in the United States, the object and tendency of which is to destroy the National Union; and that, in your opinion, an army and navy are constitutional means for suppressing that rebellion.

"2. That no one of you will do any thing which, in his own judgment, will tend to hinder the increase, or favor the decrease, or lessen the efficiency of the Army and Navy, while engaged in the effort to suppress that rebellion; and—

"3. That each of you will, in his sphere, do all he can to have the officers, soldiers, and seamen of the Army and Navy, while engaged in the effort to suppress the rebellion, paid, fed, clad, and otherwise well provided and supported.

"And with the further understanding that upon receiving the letter and names thus indorsed, I will cause them to be published, which publication shall be, within itself, a revocation of the order in relation to Mr. Vallandigham.

"It will not escape observation that I consent to the release of Mr. Vallandigham upon terms not embracing any pledge from him or from others as to what he will or will not do. I do this because he is not present to speak for himself,

16

or to authorize others to speak for him ; and hence I shall expect that on returning he would not put himself practically in antagonism with the position of his friends.   But I do it chiefly because I thereby prevail on other influential gentlemen of Ohio to so define their position as to be of immense value to the army—thus more than compensating for the consequences of any mistake in allowing Mr. Vallandigham to return, so that, on the whole, the public safety will not have suffered by it.   Still, in regard to Mr. Vallandigham and all others, I must hereafter, as heretofore, do so much as the public service may seem to require.

"I have the honor to be respectfully, yours, etc.,

"ABRAHAM LINCOLN."

CHAPTER XVI.

LETTERS AND SPEECHES.

Speech at Washington—Letter to General Grant—Thanksgiving Proclamation—Letter
    concerning the Emancipation Proclamation—Proclamation for Annual Thanksgiving—
    Dedicatory Speech at Gettysburg.

ON the evening of the 4th of July, 1863, having been serenaded by many of the citizens of Washington, jubilant over the defeat of the rebels at Gettysburg, the President acknowledged the compliment thus :

"FELLOW-CITIZENS :—I am very glad indeed to see you tonight, and yet I will not say I thank you for this call ; but I do most sincerely thank Almighty God for the occasion on which you have called.   How long ago is it—eighty odd years—since, on the 4th of July, for the first time in the history of the world, a nation, by its representatives, assembled and declared as a self-evident truth, 'that all men are created equal ?' That was the birthday of the United States of America. Since then, the 4th of July has had several very peculiar recognitions. The two men most distinguished in the framing and support of the Declaration, were Thomas Jefferson and John Adams—the one having penned it, and the other sustained it the most forcibly in debate—the only two, of the fifty-five who signed it, who were elected Presidents of the United States. Precisely fifty years after they put their hands to the paper, it pleased Almighty God to take both from this stage of action. This was indeed an extraordinary and remarkable event in our history. Another President, five years after, was called from this stage of existence on the same day and month of the year; and now, on this last 4th of July just passed, when we have a gigantic rebellion, at the bottom of which is an effort to overthrow the principle that all men were created equal, we have the surrender of a most powerful position and army on that very day. And not only so, but in a succession of battles in Pennsylvania, near to us, through three days, so rapidly fought that they might be called one great battle, on the 1st, 2d, and 3d of the month of July, and on the 4th the cohorts of those who opposed the declaration that all men are created equal, 'turned tail' and run. Gentlemen, this is a glorious theme, and the occasion for a speech; but I am not prepared to make one worthy of the occasion. I would like to speak in terms of praise due to the many brave officers and soldiers who have fought in the cause of the Union and liberties of their country from the beginning of the war. These are trying occasions, not only in success, but for the want of success. I dislike to mention the name of one single officer, lest I might do wrong to those I might forget. Recent events bring up glorious names, and particularly prominent ones; but these I will not mention. Having said this much, I will now take the music."

The following letter, addressed to General Grant after the capture of Vicksburg, gives an insight into the transparent candor and frankness of the President:

"*Executive Mansion*, Washington, July 13th, 1863.

"MAJOR-GENERAL U. S. GRANT—*My Dear General:* I do not remember that you and I ever met personally. I write this now as a grateful acknowlednement of the almost inestimable service you have done the country. I write to say a word further. When you first reached the vicinity of Vicksburg, I thought you should do what you finally did—march the troops across the neck, run the batteries with the transports, and thus go below; and I never had any faith, except a general hope that you knew better than I, that the Yazoo Pass expedition, and the like, could succeed. When you got below, and took Port Gibson, Grand Gulf, and vicinity, I thought you should go down the river and join General Banks, and when you turned northward, east of the Big Black, I feared it was a mistake. I now wish to make the personal acknowledgment, that you were right and I was wrong.   "Yours, truly,

                      "A. LINCOLN."

The following was issued in commemoration of the victories at Vicksburg, Port Hudson, and Gettysburg:

"BY THE PRESIDENT OF THE UNITED STATES OF AMERICA. —A PROCLAMATION.—It has pleased Almighty God to hearken to the supplications and prayers of an afflicted people, and to vouchsafe to the Army and Navy of the United States, on the land and on the sea, victories so signal and so effective as to furnish reasonable grounds for augmented confidence that the Union of these States will be maintained, their Constitution preserved, and their peace and prosperity permanently secured; but these victories have been accorded, not without sacrifice of life, limb, and liberty, incurred by brave, patriotic, and loyal citizens. Domestic affliction, in every part of the country, follows in the train of these fearful bereavements. It is meet and right to recognize and confess the presence of the Almighty Father, and the power of his hand equally in these triumphs and these sorrows.

" Now, therefore, be it known, that I do set apart Thursday, the 6th day of August next, to be observed as a day for National Thanksgiving, praise, and prayer ; and I invite the people of the United States to assemble on that occasion in their customary places of worship, and in the form approved by their own consciences, render the homage due to the Divine Majesty, for the wonderful things he has done in the Nation's behalf, and invoke the influence of his Holy Spirit, to subdue the anger which has produced, and so long sustained, a needless and cruel rebellion ; to change the hearts of the insurgents ; to guide the counsels of the Government with wisdom adequate to so great a National emergency, and to visit with tender care, and consolation, throughout the length and breadth of our land, all those who, through the vicissitudes of marches, voyages, battles, and sieges, have been brought to suffer in mind, body, or estate ; and finally, to lead the whole nation through paths of repentance and submission to the Divine will, back to the perfect enjoyment of union and fraternal peace.

" In witness whereof, I have hereunto set my hand, and caused the seal of the United States to be affixed.

" Done at the City of Washington, this fifteenth day of July, in the year of our Lord one thousand eight hundred and sixty three, and of the Independence of the United States of America the eighty-eighth.

" By the President :   ABRAHAM LINCOLN.

" WILLIAM H. SEWARD, Secretary of State."

The following letter, written in August, 1863, in answer to an invitation to attend a meeting of unconditional Union men held in Illinois, gives at length the President's views at that time on his Emancipation proclamation :

" EXECUTIVE MANSION, Washington, August 26th, 1863.

" MY DEAR SIR :—Your letter inviting me to attend a mass meeting of unconditional Union men, to be held at the capital of Illinois on the third day of September, has been received. It would be very agreeable to me thus to meet my old friends at my own home ; but I cannot just now be absent from this city so long as a visit there would require. The meeting is to be of all those who maintain unconditional devotion to the Union ; and I am sure that my old political friends will thank me for tendering, as I do, the nation's gratitude to those other noble men whom no partisan malice or partisan hope can make false to the nation's life. There are those who are dissatisfied with me. To such I would say :—You désire peace, and you blame me that we do not have it. But how can we attain it ? There are but three conceivable ways :— First, to suppress the rebellion by force of arms. This I am trying to do. Are you for it ? If you are, so far we are agreed. If you are not for it, a second way is to give up the Union. I am against this. If you are, you should say so, plainly. If you are not for force, nor yet for dissolution, there only remains some imaginable compromise. I do not believe that any compromise embracing the maintenance of the Union is now possible. All that I learn leads to a directly opposite belief. The strength of the rebellion is its military—its army. That army dominates all the country and all the people within its range. Any offer of any terms made by any man or men within that range in opposition to that army is simply nothing for the present, because such man or men have no power whatever to enforce their side of a com- promise, if one were made with them. To illustrate : Sup- pose refugees from the South and peace men of the North get together in convention, and frame and proclaim a com- promise embracing the restoration of the Union. In what way can that compromise be used to keep General Lee's army out of Pennsylvania ? General Meade's army can keep Lee's army out of Pennsylvania, and I think can ultimately drive it out of existence. But no paper compromise to which the controllers of General Lee's army are not agreed, can at all affect that army. In an effort at such compromise we would waste time which the enemy would improve to our disadvantage, and that would be all. A compromise, to be effective, must be made either with those who control the rebel army, or with the people, first liberated from the domination of that army by the success of our army. Now, allow me to assure you that no word or intimation from the rebel army, or from any of the men controlling it, in relation to any peace compromise, has ever come to my knowledge or belief. All charges and intimations to the contrary are deceptive and groundless. And I promise you that if any such propositions shall hereafter come, it shall not be rejected and kept secret from you. I freely acknowledge myself to be the servant of the people, according to the bond of service, the United States Constitution; and that, as such, I am responsible to them. But, to be plain. You are dissatisfied with me about the negro. Quite likely there is a difference of opinion between you and myself upon that subject. I certainly wish that all men could be free, while you, I suppose, do not. Yet I have neither adopted nor proposed any measure which is not consistent with even your view, provided you are for the Union. I suggested compensated emancipation, to which you replied that you wished not to be taxed to buy negroes. But I have not asked you to be taxed to buy negroes, except in such way as to save you from greater taxation, to save the Union exclusively by other means.

" You dislike the emancipation proclamation, and perhaps would have it retracted. You say it is unconstitutional. I think differently. I think that the Constitution invests its Commander-in-chief with the law of war in time of war. The most that can be said, if so much, is, that the slaves are property. Is there, has there ever been, any question that by the law of war, property, both of enemies and friends, may be taken when needed? And is it not needed whenever taking it helps us or hurts the enemy? Armies, the world over, destroy enemies' property when they cannot use it; and even destroy their own to keep it from the enemy. Civilized belligerents do all in their power to help themselves or hurt the enemy, except a few things regarded as barbarous or cruel. Among the exceptions are the massacre of vanquished foes and non-combatants, male and female. But the proclamation, as law, is valid or is not valid. If it is not valid it needs no restriction. If it is valid it cannot be retracted, any more than the dead can be brought to life. Some of you profess to think that its retraction would operate favorably for the Union. Why better after the retraction than before the issue? There was more than a year and a half of trial to suppress the rebellion before the proclamation was issued, the last one hundred days of which passed under an explicit notice, that it was coming unless averted by those in revolt returning to their allegiance. The war has certainly progressed as favorably for us since the issue of the proclamation as before. I know as fully as one can know the opinions of others, that some of the commanders of our armies in the field, who have given us our most important victories, believe the emancipation policy and the aid of colored troops constitute the heaviest blows yet dealt to the rebellion, and that at least one of those important successes could not have been achieved when it was but for the aid of black soldiers. Among the commanders holding these views are some who have never had any affinity with what is called abolitionism or with 'republican party politics,' but who hold them purely as military opinions. I submit their opinions as being entitled to some weight against the objections often urged that emancipation and arming the blacks are unwise as military measures, and were not adopted as such in good faith. You say that you will not fight to free negroes. Some of them seem to be willing to fight for you—but no matter. Fight you, then, exclusively to save the Union. I issued the proclamation on purpose to aid you in saving the Union.

Whenever you shall have conquered all resistance to the Union, if I shall urge you to continue fighting, it will be an apt time then for you to declare that you will not fight to free negroes.   I thought that in your struggle for the Union, to whatever extent the negroes should cease helping the enemy, to that extent it weakened the enemy in his resistance to you. Do you think differently ?   I thought that whatever negroes can be got to do as soldiers, leaves just so much less for white soldiers to do in saving the Union.   Does it appear otherwise to you ?   But negroes, like other people, act upon motives. Why should they do any thing for us if we will do nothing for them ?   If they stake their lives for us they must be prompted by the strongest motive, even the promise of freedom. And the promise being made, must be kept.   The signs look better.   The Father of Waters again goes unvexed to the sea.   Thanks to the great North-west for it.   Nor yet wholly to them.   Three hundred miles up they met New England, Empire, Keystone, and Jersey, hewing their way right and left.   The Sunny South, too, in more colors than one, also lent a hand.   On the spot, their part of the history was jotted down in black and white.   The joy was a great national one, and let none be banned who bore an honorable part in it ; and, while those who have cleared the great river may well be proud, even that is not all.   It is hard to say that any thing has been more bravely and better done than at Antietam, Murfreesboro', Gettysburg, and on many fields of less note.   Nor must Uncle Sam's web feet be forgotten. At all the waters' margins they have been present—not only on the deep sea, the broad bay, and the rapid river, but also up the narrow, muddy bayou ; and wherever the ground was a little damp they have been and made their tracks.   Thanks to all.   For the great Republic—for the principles by which it lives and keeps alive—for man's vast future—thanks to all. Peace does not appear so far distant as it did.   I hope it will come soon, and come to stay : and so come as to be worth the keeping in all future time. It will then have been proved that among freemen there can be no successful appeal from the ballot to the bullet, and that they who take such appeal are sure to lose their case and pay the cost. And then there will be some black men who can remember that, with silent tongue, and clenched teeth, and steady eye, and well poised bayonet, they have helped mankind on to this great consummation; while I fear that there will be some white men unable to forget that with malignant heart and deceitful speech they have striven to hinder it. Still let us not be over sanguine of a speedy final triumph. Let us be quite sober. Let us diligently apply the means, never doubting that a just God, in his own good time, will give us the rightful result.

     " Yours very truly,   ABRAHAM LINCOLN."

Desirous of inaugurating the custom of setting apart each year a common day throughout the land for thanksgiving and prayer, Mr. Lincoln issued the following :

"BY THE PRESIDENT OF THE UNITED STATES OF AMERICA.— A PROCLAMATION :—The year that is drawing towards its close has been filled with the blessings of fruitful fields and healthful skies. To these bounties, which are so constantly enjoyed that we are prone to forget the source from which they come, others have been added which are of so extraordinary a nature that they can not fail to even penetrate and soften the heart which is habitually insensible to the ever watchful providence of Almighty God. In the midst of a civil war of unequalled magnitude and severity, which has sometimes seemed to invite and provoke the aggressions of foreign States, peace has been preserved with all nations, order has been maintained, the laws have been respected and obeyed, and harmony has prevailed everywhere, except in the theatre of military conflict. While that theatre has been greatly contracted by the advancing armies and navies of the Union, the needful diversion of wealth and strength from the fields of peaceful industry to the national defence, has not arrested the plow, the shuttle, or the ship. The axe has enlarged the borders of our settlements, and the mines, as well of iron and coal as of the precious metals, have yielded even more abundantly than heretofore. Population has steadily increased, notwithstanding the waste that has been made in the camp, the siege, and the battle-field ; and the country, rejoicing in the consciousness of augmented strength and vigor, is permitted to expect a continuance of years, with a large increase of freedom. No human counsel hath devised, nor hath any mortal hand worked out these great things. They are the gracious gifts of the Most High God, who, while dealing with us in anger for our sins, hath nevertheless remembered mercy.

"It hath seemed to me fit and proper that they should be solemnly, devoutly, and gratefully acknowledged, as with one heart and voice, by the whole American people. I do, there-fore, invite my fellow-citizens in every part of the United States, and also those who are at sea, and those who are sojourning in foreign lands, to set apart and observe the last Thursday of November next as a day of thanksgiving and prayer to our beneficent Father, who dwelleth in the heavens. And I recommend to them that, while offering up the ascrip-tions justly due to him for such signal deliverances and bless-ings, they do also, with humble penitence for our National perverseness and disobedience, commend to his tender care all those who have become widows, orphans, mourners, or sufferers, in the lamentable civil strife in which we are unavoidably engaged, and fervently implore the interposition of the Almighty hand to heal the wounds of the nation, and to restore it, as soon as may be consistent with the Divine purposes, to the full enjoyment of peace, harmony, tranquillity, and union.

"In testimony whereof, I have hereunto set my hand, and caused the seal of the United States to be affixed.

"Done at the City of Washington, this, the third day of

October, in the year of our Lord one thousand eight hundred
and sixty-three, and of the Independence of the United States
the eighty-eighth.

"By the President: ABRAHAM LINCOLN.
"WILLIAM H. SEWARD, Secretary of State."

On the 19th of November, 1863, President Lincoln delivered
the following dedicatory address upon the occasion of conse-
crating a National Cemetery at Gettysburg, for the secure
rest of those brave men who yielded up their lives in behalf
of their country during the three days' battle at that place:

"Fourscore and seven years ago our fathers brought forth
upon this continent a new nation, conceived in Liberty, and
dedicated to the proposition that all men are created equal.
Now we are engaged in a great civil war, testing whether
that nation, or any nation so conceived and so dedicated, can
long endure. We are met on a great battle-field of that war.
We are met to dedicate a portion of it as the final resting-
place of those who here gave their lives that that nation
might live. It is altogether fitting and proper that we should
do this.

"But in a larger sense we can not dedicate, we can not
consecrate, we can not hallow this ground. The brave men,
living and dead, who struggled here, have consecrated it far
above our power to add or detract. The world will little
note, nor long remember what we say here, but it can never
forget what they did here. It is for us, the living, rather to
be dedicated here to the unfinished work that they have thus
far so nobly carried on. It is rather for us to be here dedicated to the great task remaining before us—that from these
honored dead we take increased devotion to the cause for
which they here gave the last full measure of devotion—that
we here highly resolve that the dead shall not have died in
vain, that the nation shall, under God, have a new birth of
freedom, and that the government of the people, by the
people, and for the people, shall not perish from the earth."

THE THIRTY-EIGHTH CONGRESS. 253

Organization of the House.   Different Opinions as to Reconstruction.

CHAPTER XVII.

THE THIRTY-EIGHTH CONGRESS.

Organization of the House—Different Opinions as to Reconstruction—Provisions for Pardon of Rebels—President's Proclamation of Pardon—Annual Message—Explanatory Proclamation.

UPON the assembling of the Thirty-eighth Congress, December 7th, 1863—that Congress, in the lower branch of which the Opposition had counted upon a majority—the supporters of the Government found no difficulty in electing their candidates for Speaker by a majority of twenty, nor a radical anti-slavery man as Chaplain, albeit against the latter was offered as candidate an Episcopalian Bishop, nameless here, who had had the effrontery since the outbreak of the war to appear before the public as a defender of the institution upon Christian principles.

With the success of our arms—movements toward an organization of the local governments in the States of Tennessee, Louisiana, and Arkansas being in progress—the difficult question as to the principles upon which such reorganization should be effected presented itself for settlement.

Some took the ground that, by virtue of their rebellion, the disloyal States had lapsed into mere territorial organizations, and should remain in that condition until again admitted into the Union.

Others contended that this would be, in effect, to recognize secession, and maintained that, whatever might have been the acts of the inhabitants of any State, the State as such still constituted an integral member of the Union, entitled to all privileges as such, whenever a sufficient number of loyal citizens chose to exercise the right of suffrage—the General

254   LIFE OF ABRAHAM LINCOLN.

Different Opinions as to Reconstruction.   Proclamation of Pardon.

Government seeing to it, as was its duty under the Constitution, that a republican form was guarantied. As to what number of loyal inhabitants should suffice, opinions differed.

Congress had provided, by an act approved July 17, 1862:

That the President is hereby authorized, at any time hereafter, by proclamation, to extend to persons who may have participated in the existing rebellion in any State or part thereof, pardon and amnesty, with such exceptions, and at such time, and on such conditions, as he may deem expedient for the public welfare.

In accordance with this authority, the following proclamation was issued by Mr. Lincoln, by which it appeared he held himself pledged, before the world and to the persons immediately affected by it, to make an adherence to the policy of emancipation, inaugurated by him, a condition precedent to any act of clemency to be exercised by himself:

" WHEREAS, In and by the Constitution of the United States, it is provided that the President 'shall have power to grant reprieves and pardons for offences against the United States, except in cases of impeachment;' and whereas, a rebellion now exists whereby the loyal State Governments of several States have for a long time been subverted, and many persons have committed and are now guilty of treason against the United States; and whereas, with reference to said rebellion and treason, laws have been enacted by Congress declaring forfeitures and confiscation of property and liberation of slaves, all upon terms and conditions therein stated; and also declaring that the President was thereby authorized at any time thereafter, by proclamation, to extend to persons who may have participated in the existing rebellion, in any State or part thereof, pardon and amnesty, with such exceptions and at such times and on such conditions as he may deem expedient for the public welfare; and whereas, the

Congressional declaration for limited and conditional pardon accords with well-established judicial exposition of the pardoning power ; and whereas, with reference to said rebellion, the President of the United States has issued several proclamations, with provisions in regard to the liberation of slaves; and whereas, it is now desired by some persons heretofore engaged in said rebellion, to resume their allegiance to the United States, and to reinaugurate loyal State Governments within and for their respective States ; therefore,

"I, Abraham Lincoln, President of the United States, do proclaim, declare, and make known to all persons who have, directly or by implication, participated in the existing rebellion, except as hereinafter excepted, that a full pardon is hereby granted to them and each of them, with restoration of all rights of property, except as to slaves, and in property cases where rights of third parties shall have intervened, and upon the condition that every such person shall take and subscribe an oath, and thenceforward keep and maintain said oath inviolate ; and which oath shall be registered for permanent preservation, and shall be of the tenor and effect following, to-wit :

" ' I, —— ——, do solemnly swear, in presence of Almighty God, that I will henceforth faithfully support, protect and defend the Constitution of the United States, and the Union of the States thereunder ; and that I will, in like manner, abide by and faithfully support all acts of Congress passed during the existing rebellion with reference to slaves, so long and so far as not repealed, modified, or held void by Congress, or by decision of the Supreme Court ; and that I will, in like manner, abide by and faithfully support all proclamations of the President made during the existing rebellion having reference to slaves, so long and so far as not modified or declared void by decision of the Supreme Court.   So help me God.'

"The persons excepted from the benefits of the foregoing

provisions are all who are, or shall have been, civil or diplomatic officers or agents of the so-called Confederate Government; all who have left judicial stations under the United States to aid the rebellion; all who are, or shall have been, military or naval officers of the said so-called Confederate Government, above the rank of colonel in the army, or of lieutenant in the navy; all who left seats in the United States Congress to aid the rebellion; all who resigned commissions in the Army or Navy of the United States, and afterward aided the rebellion; and all who have engaged in any way in treating colored persons, or white persons in charge of such, otherwise than lawfully as prisoners of war, and which persons may have been found in the United States service as soldiers, seamen, or in any other capacity.

"And I do further proclaim, declare, and make known, that whenever, in any of the States of Arkansas, Texas, Louisiana, Mississippi, Tennessee, Alabama, Georgia, Florida, South Carolina, and North Carolina, a number of persons, not less than one-tenth in number of the votes cast in such State at the Presidential election of the year of our Lord 1860, each having taken the oath aforesaid, and not having since violated it, and being a qualified voter by the election law of the State existing immediately before the so-called act of secession, and excluding all others, shall re-establish a State Government which shall be republican, and in nowise contravening said oath, such shall be recognized as the true Government of the State, and the State shall receive thereunder the benefits of the constitutional provision which declares that 'the United States shall guarantee to every State in this Union a republican form of government, and shall protect each of them against invasion; and on application of the Legislature, or the Executive, (when the Legislature cannot be convened,) against domestic violence.'

"And I do further proclaim, declare, and make known that any provision which may be adopted by such State Government in relation to the freed people of such State, which shall recognize and declare their permanent freedom, provide for their education, and which may yet be consistent, as a temporary arrangement, with their present condition as a laboring, landless, and homeless class, will not be objected to by the National Executive. And it is suggested as not improper, that, in constructing a loyal State Government in any State, the name of the State, the boundary, the subdivisions, the Constitution, and the general code of laws, as before the rebellion, be maintained, subject only to the modifications made necessary by the conditions hereinbefore stated, and such others, if any, not contravening said conditions, and which may be deemed expedient by those framing the new State Government.

" To avoid misunderstanding, it may be proper to say that this proclamation, so far as it relates to State Governments, has no reference to States wherein loyal State Governments have all the while been maintained. And for the same reason, it may be proper to further say that whether members sent to Congress from any State shall be admitted to seats constitutionally, rests exclusively with the respective Houses, and not to any extent with the Executive. And still further, that this proclamation is intended to present the people of the States wherein the National authority has been suspended, and loyal State Governments have been subverted, a mode in and by which the National authority and loyal State Governments may be re-established within said States, or in any of them ; and, while the mode presented is the best the Executive can suggest, with his present impressions, it must not be understood that no other possible mode would be acceptable.

" Given under my hand at the city of Washington, the eighth day of December, A. D. 1863, and of the Independence of the United States of America the eighty-eighth.

"ABRAHAM LINCOLN "

17

The Annual Message sent in to Congress on the 9th day of December, omitting matters of but temporary interest—is as follows:

"FELLOW-CITIZENS OF THE SENATE AND HOUSE OF REPRESENTATIVES:—Another year of health and sufficiently abundant harvests, has passed. For these, and especially for the improved condition of our National affairs, our renewed and profoundest gratitude to God is due.

"We remain in peace and friendship with foreign powers.

"The efforts of disloyal citizens of the United States to involve us in foreign wars, to aid an inexcusable insurrection, have been unavailing. Her Britannic Majesty's Government, as was justly expected, have exercised their authority to prevent the departure of new hostile expeditions from British ports. The Emperor of France has, by a like proceeding, promptly vindicated the neutrality which he proclaimed at the beginning of the contest. Questions of great intricacy and importance have arisen, out of the blockade and other belligerent operations, between the Government and several of the maritime powers, but they have been discussed, and, as far as was possible, accommodated in a spirit of frankness, justice, and mutual good will. It is especially gratifying that our prize courts, by the impartiality of their adjudications, have commanded the respect and confidence of maritime powers.

"The supplementary treaty between the United States and Great Britain for the suppression of the African slave trade, made on the 17th of February last, has been duly ratified, and carried into execution. It is believed that, so far as American ports and American citizens are concerned, that inhuman and odious traffic has been brought to an end. . . .

"Incidents occurring in the progress of our civil war have forced upon my attention the uncertain state of international questions touching the rights of foreigners in this country and of United States citizens abroad. In regard to some

Governments, these rights are at least partially defined by treaties. In no instance, however, is it expressly stipulated that, in the event of civil law, a foreigner residing in this country, within the lines of the insurgents, is to be exempted from the rule which classes him as a belligerent, in whose behalf the Government of his country can not expect any privileges or immunities distinct from that character. I regret to say, however, that such claims have been put forward, and, in some instances, in behalf of foreigners who have lived in the United States the greater part of their lives.

"There is reason to believe that many persons born in foreign countries, who have declared their intention to become citizens, or who have been fully naturalized, have evaded the military duty required of them by denying the fact, and thereby throwing upon the Government the burden of proof. It has been found difficult or impracticable to obtain this proof, from the want of guides to the proper sources of information. These might be supplied by requiring clerks of courts, where declarations of intention may be made or naturalizations effected, to send, periodically, lists of the names of the persons naturalized, or declaring their intention to become citizens, to the Secretary of the Interior, in whose Department those names might be arranged and printed for general information.

" There is also reason to believe that foreigners frequently become citizens of the United States for the sole purpose of evading duties imposed by the laws of their native countries, to which, on becoming naturalized here, they at once repair, and, though never returning to the United States, they still claim the interposition of this Government as citizens. Many altercations and great prejudices have heretofore arisen out of this abuse. It is, therefore, submitted to your serious consideration. It might be advisable to fix a limit, beyond which no citizen of the United States residing abroad may claim the interposition of his Government.

"The right of suffrage has often been assumed and exercised by aliens, under pretences of naturalization, which they have disavowed when drafted into the military service. I submit the expediency of such an amendment of the law as will make the fact of voting an estoppel against any plea of exemption from military service, or other civil obligation, on the ground of alienage. . . . . .

"The condition of the several organized Territories is generally satisfactory, although Indian disturbances in New Mexico have not been entirely suppressed. The mineral resources of Colorado, Nevada, Idaho, New Mexico, and Arizona, are proving far richer than has been heretofore understood. I lay before you a communication on this subject from the Governor of New Mexico. I again submit to your consideration the expediency of establishing a system for the encouragement of immigration. Although this source of national wealth and strength is again flowing with greater freedom than for several years before the insurrection occurred, there is still a great deficiency of laborers in every field of industry, especially in agriculture and in our mines, as well of iron and coal as of the precious metals. While the demand for labor is thus increased here, tens of thousands of persons, destitute of remunerative occupation, are thronging our foreign consulates, and offering to emigrate to the United States if essential, but very cheap, assistance can be afforded them. It is easy to see that, under the sharp discipline of civil war, the nation is beginning a new life. This noble effort demands the aid, and ought to receive the attention and support, of the Government.

"Injuries, unforeseen by the Government and unintended, may, in some cases, have been inflicted on the subjects or citizens of foreign countries, both at sea and on land, by persons in the service of the United States. As this Government expects redress from other powers when similar injuries are inflicted by persons in their service upon citizens of the United States, we must be prepared to do justice to foreigners. If the existing judicial tribunals are inadequate to this purpose, a special court may be authorized, with power to hear and decide such claims of the character referred to as may have arisen under treaties and the public law. Conventions for adjusting the claims by joint commission, have been proposed to some Governments, but no definite answer to the propositions has yet been received from any.

" In the course of the session, I shall probably have occasion to request you to provide indemnification to claimants where decrees of restitution have been rendered, and damages awarded by admiralty courts, and in other cases, where this Government may be acknowledged to be liable in principle, and where the amount of that liability has been ascertained by an informal arbitration.

" The proper officers of the Treasury have deemed themselves required, by the law of the United States upon the subject, to demand a tax upon the incomes of foreign consuls in this country. While such demand may not, in strictness, be in derogation of public law, or perhaps of any existing treaty between the United States and a foreign country, the expediency of so far modifying the act as to exempt from tax the income of such consuls as are not citizens of the United States, derived from the emoluments of their office, or from property not situated in the United States, is submitted to your serious consideration. I make this suggestion upon the ground that a comity which ought to be reciprocated exempts our consuls, in all other countries, from taxation to the extent thus indicated. The United States, I think, ought not to be exceptionally illiberal to international trade and commerce.

"The operations of the Treasury during the last year have been successfully conducted. The enactment by Congress of a National Banking Law has proved a valuable support of the public credit; and the general legislation in relation to loans has fully answered the expectations of its favorers. Some amendments may be required to perfect existing laws; but no change in their principles or general scope is believed to be needed.

"Since these measures have been in operation, all demands on the Treasury, including the pay of the Army and Navy, have been promptly met and fully satisfied. No considerable body of troops, it is believed, were ever more amply provided and more liberally and punctually paid; and it may be added that by no people were the burdens incident to a great war ever more cheerfully borne.

"The receipts during the year from all sources, including loans and the balance in the Treasury at its commencement, were $901,125,674 86, and the aggregate disbursements, $895,796,630 65, leaving a balance on the 1st of July, 1863, of $5,329,044 21. Of the receipts there were derived from customs, $69,059,642 40; from internal revenue, $37,640,787 95; from direct tax, $1,485,103 61; from lands, $167,617 17; from miscellaneous sources, $3,046,615 35; and from loans, $776,682,361 57; making the aggregate, $901,125,674 86. Of the disbursements, there were, for the civil service, $23,253,922 08; for pensions and Indians, $4,216,520 79; for interest on public debt, $24,729,846 51; for the War Department, $599,298,600 83; for the Navy Department, $63,211,105 27; for payment of funded and temporary debt, $181,086,635 07; making the aggregate, $895,796,630 65; and leaving the balance of $5,329,044 21. But the payment of funded and temporary debt, having been made from moneys borrowed during the year, must be regarded as merely nominal payments, and the moneys borrowed to make them as merely nominal receipts; and their amount, $181,086,635 07, should therefore be deducted both from receipts and disbursements. This being done, there remain as actual receipts, $720,039,039 79; and the actual disbursements, $714,709,995 58, leaving the balance as already stated.

"The actual receipts and disbursements for the first quarter, and the estimated receipts and disbursements for the remaining three quarters, of the current fiscal year 1864, will be shown in detail by the report of the. Secretary of the Treasury, to which I invite your attention. It is sufficient to say here that it is not believed that actual results will exhibit a state of the finances less favorable to the country than the estimates of that officer heretofore submitted; while it is confidently expected that at the close of the year both disbursements and debt will be found very considerably less than has been anticipated.

"The report of the Secretary of War is a document of great interest. It consists of—

"1. The military operations of the year, detailed in the report of the General-in-Chief.

"2. The organization of colored persons into the war service.

"3. The exchange of prisoners, fully set forth in the letter of General Hitchcock.

"4. The operations under the act for enrolling and calling out the National forces, detailed in the report of the Provost Marshal General.

"5. The organization of the Invalid Corps; and,

"6. The operation of the several departments of the Quartermaster General, Commissary General, Paymaster General, Chief of Engineers, Chief of Ordnance, and Surgeon General.

"It has appeared impossible to make a valuable summary of this report, except such as would be too extended for this place, and hence I content myself by asking your careful attention to the report itself.

" The duties devolving on the Naval branch of the service during the year, and throughout the whole of this unhappy contest, have been discharged with fidelity and eminent success. The extensive blockade has been constantly increasing in efficiency, and the Navy has expanded ; yet on so long a line it has so far been impossible to entirely suppress illicit trade. From returns received at the Navy Department, it appears that more than one thousand vessels have been captured since the blockade was instituted, and that the value of prizes already sent in for adjudication, amounts to over thirteen million dollars.

" The naval force of the United States consists, at this time, of five hundred and eighty-eight vessels, completed and in the course of completion, and of these seventy-five are iron-clad or armored steamers. The events of the war give an increased interest and importance to the Navy, which will probably extend beyond the war itself.

" The armored vessels in our Navy, completed and in service, or which are under contract and approaching completion, are believed to exceed in number those of any other Power. But while these may be relied upon for harbor defence and coast service, others, of greater strength and capacity, will be necessary for cruising purposes, and to maintain our rightful position on the ocean.

" The change that has taken place in naval vessels and naval warfare since the introduction of steam as a motive power for ships-of-war, demands either a corresponding change in some of our existing navy-yards, or the establishment of new ones, for the construction and necessary repairs of modern naval vessels. No inconsiderable embarrassment, delay, and public injury have been experienced from the want of such Governmental establishments. The necessity of such a navy-yard, so furnished, at some suitable place upon the

Atlantic seaboard, has, on repeated occasions, been brought to the attention of Congress by the Navy Department, and is again presented in the report of the Secretary which accompanies this communication. I think it my duty to invite your special attention to this subject, and also to that of establishing a yard and depot for naval purposes upon one of the Western rivers. A naval force has been created on those interior waters, and under many disadvantages, within little more than two years, exceeding in numbers the whole naval force of the country at the commencement of the present Administration. Satisfactory and important as have been the performances of the heroic men of the Navy at this interesting period, they are scarcely more wonderful than the success of our mechanics and artisans in the production of war vessels, which has created a new form of naval power.

"Our country has advantages superior to any other nation in our resources of iron and timber, with inexhaustible quantities of fuel in the immediate vicinity of both, and all available and in close proximity to navigable waters. Without the advantage of public works, the resources of the nation have been developed, and its power displayed, in the construction of a navy of such magnitude, which has, at the very period of its creation, rendered signal service to the Union.

"The increase of the number of seamen in the public service, from seven thousand five hundred men in the spring of 1861, to about thirty-four thousand at the present time, has been accomplished without special legislation or extraordinary bounties to promote that increase. It has been found, however, that the operation of the draft, with the high bounties paid for army recruits, is beginning to affect injuriously the naval service, and will, if not corrected, be likely to impair its efficiency, by detaching seamen from their proper vocation and inducing them to enter the army. I therefore respectfully suggest that Congress might aid both the army and naval services by a definite provision on this subject, which would at the same time be equitable to the communities more especially interested.

"I commend to your consideration the suggestions of the Secretary of the Navy in regard to the policy of fostering and training seamen, and also the education of officers and engineers for the naval service. The Naval Academy is rendering signal service in preparing midshipmen for the highly responsible duties which in after-life they will be required to perform. In order that the country should not be deprived of the proper quota of educated officers for which legal provision has been made at the Naval School, the vacancies caused by the neglect or omission to make nominations from the States in insurrection have been filled by the Secretary of the Navy. The school is now more full and complete than at any former period, and in every respect entitled to the favorable consideration of Congress.

"During the past fiscal year the financial condition of the Post Office Department has been one of increasing prosperity, and I am gratified in being able to state that the actual postal revenue has nearly equaled the entire expenditures; the latter amounting to $11,314,206 84, and the former to $11,163,789 59, leaving a deficiency of but $150,417 25. In 1860, the year immediately preceding the rebellion, the deficiency amounted to $5,656,705 49, the postal receipts of that year being $2,645,722 19 less than those of 1863. The decrease since 1860 in the annual amount of transportation has been only about twenty-five per cent., but the annual expenditure on account of the same has been reduced thirty-five per cent. It is manifest, therefore, that the Post Office Department may become self-sustaining in a few years, even with the restoration of the whole service.

"The quantity of land disposed of during the last and the first quarter of the present fiscal years was 3,841,549 acres, of which 161,911 acres were sold for cash, 1,456,514 acres were taken up under the homestead law, and the residue disposed of under laws granting lands for military bounties, for railroad and other purposes. It also appears that the sale of public lands is largely on the increase.

" It has long been a cherished opinion of some of our wisest statesmen that the people of the United States had a higher and more enduring interest in the early settlement and substantial cultivation of the public lands than in the amount of direct revenue to be derived from the sale of them. This opinion has had a controlling influence in shaping legislation upon the subject of our National domain. I may cite, as evidence of this, the liberal measures adopted in reference to actual settlers; the grants to the States of the overflowed lands within their limits; in order to their being reclaimed and rendered fit for cultivation; the grants to railway companies of alternate sections of land upon the contemplated lines of their roads, which, when completed, will so largely multiply the facilities for reaching our distant possessions. This policy has received its most signal and beneficent illustration in the recent enactment granting homesteads to actual settlers. Since the 1st day of January last, the before-mentioned quantity of 1,456,514 acres of land have been taken up under its provisions. This fact and the amount of sales furnish gratifying evidence of increasing settlement upon the public lands, notwithstanding the great struggle in which the energies of the Nation have been engaged, and which has required so large a withdrawal of our citizens from their accustomed pursuits.

" The measures provided at your last session for the removal of certain Indian tribes, have been carried into effect. Sundry treaties have been negotiated which will, in due time, be submitted for the constitutional action of the Senate. They contain stipulations for extinguishing the possessory rights of the Indians to large and valuable tracts of lands. It is hoped that the effect of these treaties will result in the establishment of permanent friendly relations with such of these tribes as have been brought into frequent and bloody collision with our outlying settlements and emigrants. Sound policy and our imperative duty to these wards of the Government demand our anxious and constant attention to their material well-being, to their progress in the arts of civilization, and above all, to that moral training which, under the blessing of Divine Providence, will confer upon them the elevated and sanctifying influences, the hopes and consolations of the Christian faith.

"When Congress assembled a year ago, the war had already lasted nearly twenty months; and there had been many conflicts on both land and sea, with varying results. The rebellion had been pressed back into reduced limits; yet the tone of public feeling and opinion, at home and abroad, was not satisfactory. With other signs, the popular elections, then just past, indicated uneasiness among ourselves, while, amid much that was cold and menacing, the kindest words coming from Europe were uttered in accents of pity that we were too blind to surrender a hopeless cause. Our commerce was suffering greatly by a few armed vessels built upon and furnished from foreign shores; and we were threatened with such additions from the same quarter as would sweep our trade from the sea and raise our blockade. We had failed to elicit from European Governments any thing hopeful upon this subject. The preliminary Emancipation Proclamation, issued in September, was running its assigned period to the beginning of the new year. A month later the final proclamation came, including the announcement that colored men of suitable condition would be received into the war service. The policy of emancipation, and of employing black soldiers, gave to the future a new aspect, about which hope, and fear, and doubt contended in uncertain conflict. According to our political system, as a matter of civil administration, the General Government had no lawful power to effect emancipation in any State ; and for a long time it had been hoped that the rebellion could be suppressed without resorting to it as a military measure.   It was all the while deemed possible that the necessity for it might come, and that, if it should, the crisis of the contest would then be presented.   It came, and as was anticipated, it was followed by dark and doubtful days.   Eleven months having now passed, we are permitted to take another review.   The rebel borders are pressed still further back, and by the complete opening of the Mississippi the country dominated by the rebellion is divided into distinct parts, with no practical communication between them.   Tennessee and Arkansas have been substantially cleared of insurgent control, and influential citizens in each, owners of slaves and advocates of slavery at the beginning of the rebellion, now declare openly for emancipation in their respective States.   Of those States not included in the Emancipation Proclamation, Maryland and Missouri, neither of which, three years ago, would tolerate any restraint upon the extension of slavery into new Territories, only dispute now as to the best mode of removing it within their own limits.

"Of those who were slaves at the beginning of the rebellion, full one hundred thousand are now in the United States military service, about one-half of which number actually bear arms in the ranks ; thus giving the double advantage of taking so much labor from the insurgent cause, and supplying the places which otherwise must be filled with so many white men.   So far as tested, it is difficult to say they are not as good soldiers as any.   No servile insurrection, or tendency to violence or cruelty, has marked the measures of emancipation and arming the blacks.   These measures have been much discussed in foreign countries, and contemporary with such discussion the tone of public sentiment there is much improved.   At home the same measures have been fully discussed, supported, criticised, and denounced, and the annual elections following are highly encouraging to those whose official duty it is to bear the country through this great trial. Thus we have the new reckoning. The crisis which threatened to divide the friends of the Union is past.

"Looking now to the present and future, and with reference to a resumption of the National authority within the States wherein that authority has been suspended, I have thought fit to issue a proclamation, a copy of which is herewith transmitted. On examination of this proclamation it will appear, as is believed, that nothing is attempted beyond what is amply justified by the Constitution. True, the form of an oath is given, but no man is coerced to take it. The man is only promised a pardon in case he voluntarily takes the oath. The Constitution authorizes the Executive to grant or withhold the pardon at his own absolute discretion; and this includes the power to grant on terms, as is fully established by judicial and other authorities.

"It is also proffered that if, in any of the. States named, a State Government shall be, in the mode prescribed, set up, such Government shall be recognized and guarantied by the United States, and that under it the State shall, on the constitutional conditions, be protected against invasion and domestic violence. The constitutional obligation of the United States to guarantee to every State in the Union a republican form of government, and to protect the State, in the cases stated, is explicit and full. But why tender the benefits of this provision only to a State Government set up in this particular way? This section of the Constitution contemplates a case wherein the element within a State favorable to republican government, in the Union, may be too feeble for an opposite and hostile element external to or even within the State; and such are precisely the cases with which we are now dealing.

"An attempt to guarantee and protect a revived State Government, constructed in whole, or in preponderating part, from the very element against whose hostility and violence it is to be protected, is simply absurd. There must be a test by which to separate the opposing element, so as to build only from the sound; and that test is a sufficiently liberal one, which accepts as sound whoever will make a sworn re-cantation of his former unsoundness.

"But if it be proper to require, as a test of admission to the political body, an oath of allegiance to the Constitution of the United States, and to the Union under it, why also to the laws and proclamations in regard to slavery? Those laws and proclamations were enacted and put forth for the purpose of aiding in the suppression of the rebellion. To give them their fullest effect, there had to be a pledge for their main-tenance. In my judgment they have aided, and will further aid, the cause for which they were intended. To now aban-don them would be not only to relinquish a lever of power, but would also be a cruel and an astounding breach of faith. I may add at this point that, while I remain in my present position, I shall not attempt to retract or modify the Eman-cipation Proclamation; nor shall I return to slavery any person who is free by the terms of that proclamation, or by any of the acts of Congress. For these and other reasons, it is thought best that support of these measures shall be included in the oath; and it is believed the Executive may lawfully claim it in return for pardon and restoration of for-feited rights, which he has clear constitutional power to withhold altogether, or grant upon the terms which he shall deem wisest for the public interest. It should be observed, lso, that this part of the oath is subject to the modifying and abrogating power of legislation and supreme judicial decision.

"The proposed acquiescence of the National Executive in any reasonable temporary State arrangement for the freed people, is made with the view of possibly modifying the con-fusion and destitution which must, at best, attend all classes by a total revolution of labor throughout whole States. It is hoped that the already deeply afflicted people in those States may be somewhat more ready to give up the cause of their affliction, if, to this extent, this vital matter be left to themselves; while no power of the National Executive to prevent an abuse, is abridged by the proposition.

"The suggestion in the proclamation as to maintaining the political framework of the States on what is called reconstruction, is made in the hope that it may do good without danger of harm. It will save labor, and avoid great confusion

"But why any proclamation now upon this subject? This question is beset with the conflicting views that the step might be delayed too long or be taken too soon. In some States the elements for resumption seem ready for action, but remain inactive, apparently for want of a rallying point—a plan of action. Why shall A adopt the plan of B, rather than B that of A? And if A and B should agree, how can they know but that the General Government here will reject their plan? By the proclamation a plan is presented which may be accepted by them as a rallying point, and which they are assured in advance will not be rejected here. This may bring them to act sooner than they otherwise would.

"The objection to a premature presentation of a plan by the National Executive consists in the danger of committals on points which could be more safely left to further developments. Care has been taken to so shape the document as to avoid embarrassment from this source. Saying that, on certain terms, certain classes will be pardoned, with rights restored, it is not said that other classes or other terms will never be included. Saying that reconstruction will be accepted, if presented in a specific way; it is not said it will never be accepted in any other way.

"The movements, by State action, for emancipation in several of the States, not included in the Emancipation Proclamation, are matters of profound congratulation. And while I do not repeat in detail what I have heretofore so earnestly urged upon this subject, my general views and feelings remain unchanged; and I trust that Congress will omit no fair opportunity of aiding these important steps to a great consummation.

"In the midst of other cares, however important, we must not lose sight of the fact that the war power is still our main reliance. To that power alone can we look, yet for a time, to give confidence to the people in the contested regions that the insurgent power will not again overrun them. Until that confidence shall be established, little can be done anywhere for what is called reconstruction. Hence our chiefest care must still be directed to the Army and Navy, who have thus far borne their harder part so nobly and well. And it may be esteemed fortunate that in giving the greatest efficiency to these indispensable arms, we do also honorably recognize the gallant men, from commander to sentinel, who compose them, and, to whom, more than to others, the world must stand indebted for the home of freedom disenthralled, regenerated, enlarged, and perpetuated.

Dec. 8, 1863.   "ABRAHAM LINCOLN."

On the twenty-sixth of March, 1864, the following proclamation, explanatory of the one issued on the eighth of December, 1863, was published:

"WHEREAS, It has become necessary to define the cases in which insurgent enemies are entitled to the benefits of the Proclamation of the President of the United States, which was made on the 8th day of December, 1863, and the manner in which they shall proceed to avail themselves of these benefits;

"AND WHEREAS, The objects of that proclamation were to suppress the insurrection and to restore the authority of the United States;

18

"AND WHEREAS, The amnesty therein proposed by the President was offered with reference to these objects alone;

"Now, therefore, I, Abraham Lincoln, President of the United States, do hereby proclaim and declare that the said proclamation does not apply to the cases of persons who, at the time when they seek to obtain the benefits thereof, by taking the oath thereby prescribed, are in military, naval or civil confinement or custody, or under bonds or on parole of the civil, military or naval authorities or agents of the United States, as prisoners of war, or persons detained for offences of any kind, either before or after conviction; and that on the contrary, it does apply only to those persons who, being at large and free from any arrest, confinement or duress, shall voluntarily come forward and take the said oath, with the purpose of restoring peace and establishing the national authority.

"Prisoners excluded from the amnesty offered in the said proclamation may apply to the President for clemency, like all other offenders, and their application will receive due consideration.

"I do further declare and proclaim that the oath prescribed in the aforesaid proclamation of the 8th of December, 1863, may be taken and subscribed to before any commanding officer, civil, military or naval, in the service of the United States, or any civil or military officer of a State or Territory not in insurrection, who, by the laws thereof, may be qualified for administering oaths.

"All officers who receive such oaths are hereby authorized to give certificates thereon to the persons respectively by whom they are made, and such officers are hereby required to transmit the original records of such oaths at as early a day as may be convenient to the Department of State, where they will be deposited and remain in the archives of the Government.

"The Secretary of State will keep a register thereof, and

will, on application, in proper cases, issue certificates of such records in the customary form of official certificates.

"In testimony whereof, I have hereunto set my hand and caused the seal of the United States to be affixed.

"Done at the city of Washington, this twenty-sixth day of March, in the year of our Lord one thousand eight hundred and sixty-four, and of the Independence of the United States the eighty-eighth.

"By the President: "ABRAHAM LINCOLN.

"W. H. SEWARD, Secretary of State."

CHAPTER XVIII.

PROGRESS.

President's Speech at Washington—Speech to a New York Committee—Speech in Baltimore—Letter to a Kentuckian—Employment of Colored Troops—Davis's Threat—General Order—President's Order on the Subject.

ON the night of the eighteenth of March, 1864, in response to a call from the multitude at a fair held in the Patent Office at Washington, in aid of an organization for the relief of Union soldiers everywhere, Mr. Lincoln spoke as follows :

"LADIES AND GENTLEMEN :—I appear, to say but a word. This extraordinary war in which we are engaged falls heavily upon all classes of people, but the most heavily upon the soldier. For it has been said, 'All that a man hath will he give for his life ;' and, while all contribute of their substance, the soldier puts his life at stake, and often yields it up in his country's cause. The highest merit, then, is due to the soldier.

"In this extraordinary war, extraordinary developments have manifested themselves, such as have not been seen in former wars ; and among these manifestations nothing has

276   LIFE OF ABRAHAM LINCOLN.

The Women of America.   Speech to the Workingmen.

been more remarkable than these fairs for the relief of suffering soldiers and their families.' And the chief agents in these fairs are the women of America. I am not accustomed to the use of the language of eulogy; I have never studied the art of paying compliments to women; but I must say, that, if all that has been said by orators and poets, since the creation of the world, in praise of women, were applied to the women of America, it would not do them justice for their conduct during this war. I will close by saying, God bless the women of America!"

Three days later, a committee appointed by the Workingmen's Democratic Republican Association of New York waited on the President, and presented him with an address informing him that he had been elected a member of that organization. After the chairman had stated the object of the visit, Mr. Lincoln made the following reply:

"GENTLEMEN OF THE COMMITTEE:—The honorary membership in your Association so generously tendered is gratefully accepted. You comprehend, as your address shows, that the existing rebellion means more and tends to more than the perpetuation of African slavery—that it is, in fact, a war upon the rights of all working people. Partly to show that the view has not escaped my attention, and partly that I cannot better express myself, I read a passage from the message to Congress in December, 1861:

"'It continues to develop that the insurrection is largely, if not exclusively, a war upon the first principle of popular government—the rights of the people. Conclusive evidence of this is found in the most grave and maturely considered public documents, as well as in the general tone of the insurgents. In those documents we find the abridgement of the existing right of suffrage, and the denial to the people of all right to participate in the selection of public officers, except the legislative body, boldly advocated with labored arguments, to prove that large control of the people in government is the source of all political evil. Monarchy is sometimes hinted at as a possible refuge from the power of the people. In my present position, I could scarcely be justified were I to omit raising my voice against this approach of returning despotism.

" 'It is not needed or fitting here that a general argument should be made in favor of popular institutions ; but there is one point, with its connections, not so hackneyed as most others, to which I ask a brief attention. It is the effort to place *capital* on an equal footing with, if not above, *labor* in the structure of the Government. It is assumed that labor is available only in connection with capital ; that nobody labors unless somebody else owning capital somehow, by use of it, induces him to labor.

" 'This assumed, it is next considered whether it is best that capital shall *hire* laborers, and thus induce them to work by their own consent, or *buy them* and drive them to it without their consent. Having proceeded so far, it is naturally concluded that all laborers are either hired laborers or what we call slaves. And, further, it is assumed that whoever is once a hired laborer is fixed in that condition for life. Now there is no such relation between capital and labor as assumed, nor is there any such thing as a free man being fixed for life in the condition of a hired laborer. Both of these assumptions are false, and all inferences from them are groundless.

" 'Labor is prior to and independent of capital. Capital is only the fruit of labor, and never could have existed if labor had not first existed. Labor is the support of capital, and deserves much the higher consideration. Capital has its rights, which are as worthy of protection as any other rights. Nor is it denied that there is, and probably always will be, a relation between labor and capital producing mutual benefits. The error is in assuming that the whole labor of a community exists within that relation.　A few men own capital, and that few avoid labor themselves, and with that capital hire or buy another few to labor for them.

"'A large majority belong to neither class—neither work for others nor have others working for them.　In most of the Southern States a majority of the whole people, of all colors, are neither slaves nor masters, while, in the Northern States, a large majority are neither hirers nor hired.　Men with their families—wives, sons, and daughters—work for themselves on their farms, in their houses, and in their shops, taking the whole product to themselves, and asking no favors of capital on the one hand nor of hired laborers or slaves on the other. It is not forgotten that a considerable number of persons mingle their own labor with capital—that is, they labor with their own hands and also buy or hire others to labor for them ; but this is only a mixed and not a distinct class.　No principle stated is disturbed by the existence of this mixed class.

"'Again.　As has already been said, there is not of necessity any such thing as the free hired laborer being fixed to that condition for life.　Many independent men everywhere in these States, a few years back in their lives, were hired laborers.　The prudent, penniless beginner in the world labors for wages awhile, saves a surplus with which to buy tools or lands for himself, then labors on his own account another while, and at length hires another new beginner to help him.　This is the just, and generous, and prosperous system which opens the way to all—gives hope to all, and consequent energy, and progress, and improvement to all.　No men living are more worthy to be trusted than those who toil up from poverty — none less inclined to take or touch aught which they have not honestly earned.　Let them beware of surrendering a political power which they already possess, and which, if surrendered, will surely be used to close the door of advancement against such as they, and to fix new disabilities and burdens upon them till all of liberty shall be lost.'

"The views then expressed remain unchanged—nor have I much to add. None are so deeply interested to resist the present rebellion as the working people. Let them beware of prejudices working disunion and hostility among themselves. The most notable feature of a disturbance in your city last summer, was the hanging of some working people by other working people. It should never be so. The strongest bond of human sympathy, outside of the family relation, should be one uniting all working people, of all nations, tongues, and kindreds. Nor should this lead to a war upon property or the owners of property. Property is the fruit of labor; property is desirable; is a positive good in the world. That some should be rich, shows that others may become rich, and hence is just encouragement to industry and enterprise. Let not him who is houseless pull down the house of another, but let him labor diligently and build one for himself; thus, by example, assuring that his own shall be safe from violence when built."

And in Baltimore — that Baltimore through which, in February, 1861, he had been compelled to pass by stealth, to avoid the assassin, on his way to his inauguration—on the 18th of April, 1864, the anniversary eve of that murder of loyal citizens armed in defence of their imperilled country— Mr. Lincoln spoke at a similar Fair, and spoke, too, of slavery, as of an institution practically annihilated in Maryland.

Truly some advance had been made during those three years, so pregnant with events!

"LADIES AND GENTLEMEN :—Calling it to mind that we are in Baltimore, we cannot fail to note that the world moves. Looking upon the many people I see assembled here to serve as they best may the soldiers of the Union, it occurs to me that three years ago those soldiers could not pass through Baltimore. I would say, blessings upon the men who have wrought these changes, and the ladies who have assisted them. This change which has taken place in Baltimore, is part only of a far wider change that is taking place all over the country.

"When the war commenced, three years ago, no one expected that it would last this long, and no one supposed that the institution of slavery would be materially affected by it. But here we are. The war is not yet ended, and slavery has been very materially affected or interfered with. So true is it that man proposes and God disposes.

"The world is in want of a good definition of the word liberty. We all declare ourselves to be for liberty, but we do not all mean the same thing. Some mean that a man can do as he pleases with himself and his property. With others, it means that some men can do as they please with other men and other men's labor. Each of these things are called liberty, although they are entirely different. To give an illustration: A shepherd drives the wolf from the throat of his sheep when attacked by him, and the sheep, of course, thanks the shepherd for the preservation of his life; but the wolf denounces him as despoiling the sheep of his liberty—especially if it be a black sheep.

"This same difference of opinion prevails among some of the people of the North. But the people of Maryland have recently been doing something to properly define the meaning of the word, and I thank them from the bottom of my heart for what they have done and are doing.

"It is not very becoming for a President to make a speech at great length, but there is a painful rumor afloat in the country, in reference to which a few words shall be said. It is reported that there has been a wanton massacre of some hundreds of colored soldiers at Fort Pillow, Tennessee, during a recent engagement there, and it is fit to explain.

some facts in relation to the affair. It is said by some persons that the Government is not, in this matter, doing its duty. At the commencement of the war, it was doubtful whether black men would be used as soldiers or not. The matter was examined into very carefully, and after mature deliberation, the whole matter resting as it were with himself, he, in his judgment, decided that they should.

"He was responsible for the act to the American people, to a Christian nation, to the future historian, and above all, to his God, to whom he would have, one day, to render an account of his stewardship. He would now say that in his opinion the black soldier should have the same protection as the white soldier, and he would have it. It was an error to say that the Government was not acting in the matter. The Government has no direct evidence to confirm the reports in existence relative to this massacre, but he himself believed the facts in relation to it to be as stated. When the Government does know the facts from official sources, and they prove to substantiate the reports, retribution will be surely given."

Mr. Lincoln's policy upon the question of slavery, is tersely presented in the following letter written by him to a Kentuckian, dated Executive Mansion, Washington, April 4, 1864.

"A. G. HODGES, ESQ., Frankfort, Ky. :

"MY DEAR SIR : — You ask me to put in writing the substance of what I verbally said the other day in your presence, to Governor Bramlette and Senator Dixon. It was about as follows :

"I am naturally anti-slavery. If slavery is not wrong, nothing is wrong. I can not remember when I did not so think and feel. And yet, I have never understood that the Presidency conferred upon me an unrestricted right to act officially upon this judgment and feeling. It was in the oath I took, that I would, to the best of my ability, preserve, pro-

tect and defend the Constitution of the United States. I
could not take the office without taking the oath. Nor was
it my view, that I might take an oath to get power, and
break the oath in using the power. I understood, too, that in
ordinary civil administration, this oath even forbade me to
practically indulge my primary, abstract judgment, on the
moral question of slavery. I had publicly declared this many
times, and in many ways. And I aver that, to this day, I
have done no official act in mere deference to my abstract
judgment and feeling on slavery.

"I did understand, however, that my oath to preserve the
Constitution to the best of my ability, imposed upon me the
duty of preserving, by every indispensable means, the Government—that Nation—of which that Constitution was the
organic law. Was it possible to lose the Nation, and yet
preserve the Constitution ?

"By general law, life and limb must be protected : yet often
a limb must be amputated to save a life ; but a life is never
wisely given to save a limb. I feel that measures, otherwise
unconstitutional, might become lawful, by becoming indispensable to the preservation of the Constitution, through the
preservation of the Nation. Right or wrong, I assumed this
ground and now avow it. I could not feel that to the best
of my ability I had even tried to preserve the Constitution, if
to save slavery or any minor matter, I should permit the
wreck of Government, Country and Constitution, all together
When early in the war, Gen. Fremont attempted military
emancipation, I forbade it, because I did not then think it an
indispensable necessity. When a little later, Gen. Cameron,
then Secretary of War, suggested the arming of the blacks, I
objected, because I did not yet think it an indispensable
necessity. When, still later, Gen. Hunter attempted military
emancipation, I again forbade it, because I did not yet think
the indispensable necessity had come.

"When, in March, and May, and July, 1862, I made

earnest and successive appeals to the Border States to favor compensated emancipation, I believed the indispensable necessity for military emancipation and arming the blacks would come, unless averted by that measure. They declined the proposition, and I was, in my best judgment, driven to the alternative of either surrendering the Union, and with it the Constitution, or of laying strong hand upon the colored element. I chose the latter. In choosing it, I hoped for greater gain than loss ; but of this I was not entirely confident. More than a year of trial now shows no loss by it, in our foreign relations ; none in our home popular sentiment ; none in our white military force—no loss by it anyhow or anywhere. On the contrary, it shows a gain of quite a hundred and thirty thousand soldiers, seamen, and laborers. These are palpable facts, about which, as facts, there can be no caviling. We have the men, and we could not have had them without the measure.

"And now, let any Union man who complains of the measure, test himself, by writing down in one line that he is for subduing the rebellion by force of arms, and in the next that he is for taking these one hundred and thirty thousand men from the Union side, and placing them where they would be, but for the measure he condemns. If he can not face his cause so stated, it is only because he can not face the truth.

" I add a word, which was not in the verbal conversation. In telling this tale, I attempt no compliment to my own sagacity. I claim not to have controlled events, but confess plainly that events have controlled me. Now, at the end of three years' struggle, the Nation's condition is not what either party or any man devised or expected. God alone can claim it. Whither it is tending, seems plain. If God now wills the removal of a great wrong, and wills also that we of the North, as well as you of the South, shall pay fairly for our complicity in that wrong, impartial history will find

therein new cause to attest and revere the justice and goodness
of God.   Yours truly,

                                             "A. LINCOLN."

The results of the employment of negro soldiers—a measure
which, at the time it was first announced, caused no little
commotion among the over-sensitive in the loyal States, and
was looked upon with disfavor by many white soldiers, as well
—as shown in the above letter, precluded further arguments
upon the question.

The Davis combination at Richmond, having announced
that none of the immunities recognized under the laws of war
would be granted to colored soldiers or their officers, General
Orders No. 100, under date of April 24, 1863, "previously
approved by the President," promulgating general instructions
for the government of our armies, was issued, containing
the following:

"The law of nations knows of no distinction of color; and
if an enemy of the United States should enslave and sell any
captured persons of their army, it would be a case for the
severest retaliation, if not redressed upon complaint. The
United States cannot retaliate by enslavement; therefore,
death must be the retaliation for this crime against the law
of nations.

"All troops of the enemy known or discovered to give no
quarter in general, or to any portion of the army, will receive
none."

The following order of the President, issued by him as
Commander-in-chief, and communicated to the entire army,
deals with this subject alone:

        "*Executive Mansion*, Washington, July 30, 1863.

"It is the duty of every Government to give protection to
its citizens, of whatever class, color or condition, and especially to those who are duly organized as soldiers in the
public service. The law of nations, and the usages and cus-

toms of war, as carried on by civilized powers, prohibit no distinction as to color in the treatment of prisoners of war as public enemies.   To sell or enslave any captured person, on account of his color, and for no offence against the laws of war, is a relapse into barbarism, and a crime against the civilization of the age.

"The Government of the United States will give the same protection to all its soldiers; and if the enemy shall sell or enslave any one because of his color, the offence shall be punished by retaliation upon the enemy's prisoners in our possession.

"It is therefore ordered, that for every soldier of the United States killed in violation of the laws of war, a rebel soldier shall be executed; and for every one enslaved by the enemy or sold into slavery, a rebel soldier shall be placed at hard labor on the public works, and continued at such labor until the one shall be released and receive the treatment due to a prisoner of war.   ABRAHAM LINCOLN."

CHAPTER XIX.

RENOMINATED.

Lieut. Gen. Grant—His Military Record—Continued Movements—Correspondence with the President—Across the Rapidan—Richmond Invested—President's Letter to a Grant Meeting—Meeting of Republican National Convention—The Platform—The Nomination —Mr. Lincoln's Reply to the Committee of Notification—Remarks to Union League Committee—Speech at a Serenade—Speech to Ohio Troops.

IN 1864, those grand military combinations were planned and had their commencement which were to give the quietus to that gigantic rebellion, which, as we had been gravely and repeatedly assured by patronizing foreigners and ill-wishers of the Republic here at home, could never be subdued—to which, they being judges, the United States would eventually be forced to succumb.

On the 2nd of March, the President approved a bill, passed by Congress on the 26th of February, reviving the grade of Lieutenant-General in the Army, to which position he at once nominated, and the Senate unanimously confirmed, Ulysses S. Grant, then Major-General.

Like the President, Gen. Grant sprang from "plain people;" arose from humble circumstances, and had none of those advantages of birth, or family connections, or large estate, which have so often furnished such material leverage for men who have attained distinction. Entering the army as Colonel of an Illinois regiment, on the point of being disbanded, which within a month he had made noticeable for its discipline and character, even when compared with those noteworthy regiments which Illinois has furnished; promoted to the grade of Brigadier-General; preventing, by the battle of Belmont— criticised at the time, but, like many other engagements, little understood—the reinforcement of the rebels in Southern Missouri by troops from Columbus; seizing, with a strong force, which he had quietly gathered near Smithland, almost at one fell swoop, Forts Henry and Donelson—a rebel army, with artillery, and material, being captured in each; starting the till then defiant rebels on a run from Kentucky and Tennessee, which did not end until they reached Corinth; next fighting the battle of Shiloh, a critical point of the war, with Sherman as Chief Lieutenant—Shiloh, of which he said, at the close of the first day's fight, when every thing seemed against us, "Tough work to-day, but we'll beat them to-morrow;" superseded by Buell, patiently sitting at the long, unprofitable siege of Corinth, until he was transferred to Vicksburg, which in due time greeted him with the surrender of another rebel army, reopening the Father of Waters to navigation; then Chattanooga, which he ordered Thomas to hold fast, and not to give up, if he starved—and it was not given up, and East Tennessee was freed from rebels; these had been the prominent points of Grant's military career during the rebellion up to the time when he was summoned to the command of all the armies then engaged in its suppression.

On the 9th of March, being upon official business at Washington, the General was invited to the White House, and addressed as follows by the President, who handed him his commission :

"GENERAL GRANT :—The expression of the nation's approbation of what you have already done, and its reliance on you for what remains to do in the existing great struggle, is now presented with this commission, constituting you Lieutenant-General of the Army of the United States.

"With this high honor devolves on you an additional responsibility. As the country herein trusts you, so, under God, it will sustain you. I scarcely need add, that with what I here speak for the country, goes my own hearty personal concurrence."

Sherman having been left in command in the south-west, with instructions to capture Atlanta, the vital point in Georgia, commenced that grand series of flanking movements, which, for a time, seemed to occasion intense satisfaction to the rebels, whose commander, Johnston, upon all occasions had Sherman exactly where he wished him ; while Grant— taciturn, cool, and collected, with no set speeches, no flourish of reviews—proceeded with the difficult task which he had taken in hand—the annihilation or capture of Lee's army, the mainstay of the rebels' military resources, and the occupation of Richmond.

On the 80th of April, the President addressed the following letter to the new Commander :

" LIEUTENANT-GENERAL GRANT :—Not expecting to see you before the spring campaign opens, I wish to express in this way my entire satisfaction with what you have done up to this time, so far as I understand it. The particulars of your plan I neither know, nor seek to know. You are vigilant

288   LIFE OF ABRAHAM LINCOLN.

President's Letter.   Grant's Reply.   Beginning Right

and self-reliant ; and pleased with this, I wish not to obtrude any restraints or constraints upon you. While I am very anxious that any great disaster or capture of our men in great numbers shall be avoided, I know that these points are less likely to escape your attention than they would be mine.

"If there be any thing wanting which is in my power to give, do not fail to let me know it. And now, with a brave army and a just cause, may God sustain you !

"Yours, very truly,   A. LINCOLN."

To which the General, from Culpepper Court House, Va., on the 1st of May, thus replied :

"TO THE PRESIDENT :—Your very kind letter is just received. The confidence you express for the future and satisfaction for the past, in my military administration, is acknowledged with pride. It shall be my earnest endeavor that you and the country shall not be disappointed.

"From my first entrance into the volunteer service of the country to the present day, I have never had cause of complaint, have never expressed or implied a complaint against the Administration, or the Secretary of War, for throwing any embarrassment in the way of my vigorously prosecuting what appeared to be my duty.

"Indeed, since the promotion which placed me in command of all the armies, and in view of the great responsibility and importance of success, I have been astonished at the readiness with which every thing asked for has been yielded, without even an explanation being asked. Should my success be less than I desire and expect, the least I can say is, the fault is not with you.

"Very truly, your obedient servant,

"U. S. GRANT, Lieutenant-General."

Beginning at the right end—profiting by the experience of others—wasting no time nor strength in mere display—

RENOMINATED. 289

Army of the Potomac Moves.   Rebels Outgeneralled.   Grant secures his Position

promptly breaking up, as an essential preliminary, the cliques and cabals which had so long hindered the usefulness of the Army of the Potomac—when the Lieutenant-General was at last ready, he moved across the Rapidan, was attacked impetuously by Lee with his whole army before he had fairly posted his own—"Any other man," said Mr. Lincoln, " would have been on this side of the Rapidan after the first three days' fighting"—still fought—moved by the left flank—fought on—prepared, after six days very heavy work, as he telegraphed the President, "to fight it out on that line, if it took all summer"—outgeneralled Lee at Spottsylvania Court House—secured his position—and held it till the contemplated movements in other quarters should place the prize he aimed at within his grasp.

Holding his ground, undeterred by an attempted diversion, in July, in the shape of a rebel raid toward Washington and an invasion of Maryland—a favorite summer pastime, in those days, for the Confederates—he bided his time, his teeth fixed, and the utmost efforts of his wily opponent could not induce him to relax that grim hold.   Richmond papers sneered and scolded and abused—proved that he ought to have acted entirely otherwise—asseverated. that he was no strategist, but simply a lucky blunderer, a butcher on a vast scale ; and rebel sympathizers in the North served up, in talk and print, approved re-hashes of the same staple, and were in the highest dudgeon that General McClellan was not recalled instanter to save the Capital at least, if not to take Richmond.   But Grant still held on—the teeth still set—and could not be moved.

While this campaign was progressing, the President addressed the following letter to the Committee of Arrangements of a mass meeting in New York, which had been called as a testimonial of confidence in General Grant, and of satisfaction that his efforts had been crowned with so large a measure of success :

19

290   LIFE OF ABRAHAM LINCOLN.

President's Letter.   Grant's Remarkable Campaign.   Republican National Convention.

"*Executive Mansion*, Washington, June 3d, 1864.

"GENTLEMEN :—Your letter inviting me to be present at a mass meeting of the loyal citizens to be held at New York on the 4th instant, for the purpose of expressing gratitude to Lieutenant-General Grant for his signal services, was received yesterday. It is impossible for me to attend. I approve, nevertheless, whatever may tend to strengthen and sustain General Grant and the noble armies now under his direction. My previous high estimate of General Grant has been maintained and heightened by what has occurred in the remarkable campaign he is now conducting ; while the magnitude and difficulty of the task before him do not prove less than I expected. He and his brave soldiers are now in the midst of their great trial, and I trust that at your meeting you will so shape your good words that they may turn to men and guns moving to his and their support.

"Yours truly,   A. LINCOLN."

On the 7th of June, the Republican National Convention met at Baltimore for the purpose of nominating candidates for the Presidency and Vice-Presidency.

For some time prior to the assembling of this body, the popular voice had pronounced decidedly in favor of the re-nomination of Mr. Lincoln. State Legislatures, mass meetings, State Conventions, the large majority of the loyal press demanded that the man, to whose election, constitutionally effected, the rebels had refused to submit and who, during three years of the most arduous labors, had evinced his patriotism, his ability, and his integrity, should have the satisfaction of seeing the work commenced by himself as President brought to a successful completion while an incumbent of the same high office.

A few, however, in the ranks of the loyal and patriotic, were not satisfied that the good work, whose consummation they so ardently and perhaps, impatiently, desired, had been pushed forward as vigorously and earnestly as it might have been under other auspices. A portion of these favored the postponement of the Convention till a later day, after the fourth of July ensuing, in the expectation that the country would be in a better condition to judge whether, indeed, Mr. Lincoln was the best man for the place. Another portion had already assembled at Chicago and put in nomination, upon a platform devoted mainly to criticisms of Mr. Lincoln's Administration without any practical or pertinent suggestion as to the points wherein improvement was to be made, General Fremont for the Presidency and General Cochrane as Vice-President. The former had therefore resigned his commission in the army, not having been in active service for some time, and accepted the nomination conditionally that the Baltimore Convention nominated no other candidate than Mr. Lincoln.

This opposition, however, was more apparent than real. The general feeling throughout the country was to support that man heartily who should secure the nomination of the Republican Convention, waiving all minor questions for the sake of the common weal.

On the second day, the convention adopted by acclamation the following platform :

"*Resolved*, That it is the highest duty of every American citizen to maintain against all their enemies the integrity of the Union and the paramount authority of the Constitution and laws of the United States; and that, laying aside all differences of political opinion, we pledge ourselves as Union men, animated by a common sentiment, and aiming at a common object, to do every thing in our power to aid the Government in quelling by force of arms the rebellion now raging against its authority, and in bringing to the punishment due to their crimes, the rebels and traitors arrayed against it.

"*Resolved*, That we approve the determination of the Government of the United States not to compromise with rebels, nor to offer any terms of peace except such as may be based upon an 'unconditional surrender' of their hostility and a return to their just allegiance to the Constitution and laws of the United States, and that we call upon the Government to maintain this position and to prosecute the war with the utmost possible vigor to the complete suppression of the rebellion, in full reliance upon the self-sacrifice, the patriotism, the heroic valor, and the undying devotion of the American people to their country and its free institutions.

"*Resolved*, That, as Slavery was the cause, and now constitutes the strength, of this rebellion, and as it must be always and everywhere hostile to the principles of republican government, justice and the national safety demand its utter and complete extirpation from the soil of the Republic; and that we uphold and maintain the acts and proclamations by which the Government, in its own defence, has aimed a death-blow at this gigantic evil. We are in favor, furthermore, of such an amendment to the Constitution, to be made by the people in conformity with its provisions, as shall terminate and forever prohibit the existence of Slavery within the limits of the jurisdiction of the United States.

"*Resolved*, That the thanks of the American people are due to the soldiers and sailors of the army and of the navy, who have perilled their lives in defence of their country, and in vindication of the honor of the flag; that the Nation owes to them some permanent recognition of their patriotism and their valor, and ample and permanent provision for those of their survivors who have received disabling and honorable wounds in the service of the country; and that the memories of those who have fallen in its defence shall be held in grateful and everlasting remembrance.

"*Resolved*, That we approve and applaud the practical wisdom, the unselfish patriotism, and unswerving fidelity to the Constitution and the principles of American liberty, with which Abraham Lincoln has discharged, under circumstances of unparalleled difficulty, the great duties and responsibilities of the presidential office; that we approve and indorse, as demanded by the emergency, and essential to the preservation of the Nation, and as within the Constitution, the measures and acts which he has adopted to defend the Nation against its open and secret foes; that we approve especially the Proclamation of Emancipation, and the employment as Union soldiers of men heretofore held in Slavery; and that we have full confidence in his determination to carry these and all other constitutional measures essential to the salvation of the country into full and complete effect.

"*Resolved*, That we deem it essential to the general welfare that harmony should prevail in the National councils, and we regard as worthy of public confidence and official trust those only who cordially indorse the principles contained in those resolutions, and which should characterize the administration of the Government.

"*Resolved*, That the Government owes to all men employed in its armies, without regard to distinction of color, the full protection of the laws of war; and that any violation of these laws or of the usages of civilized nations in the time of war by the Rebels now in arms, should be made the subject of full and prompt redress.

"*Resolved*, That the foreign immigration, which in the past has added so much to the wealth and development of resources and increase of power to this Nation, the asylum of the oppressed of all nations, should be fostered and encouraged by a liberal and just policy.

"*Resolved*, That we are in favor of the speedy construction of the railroad to the Pacific.

"*Resolved*, That the national faith pledged for the redemption of the public debt must be kept inviolate, and that for this purpose we recommend economy and rigid responsibility in the public expenditures, and a vigorous and just system of taxation; that it is the duty of every loyal State to sustain the credit and promote the use of the national currency.

"*Resolved*, That we approve the position taken by the Government that the people of the United States can never regard with indifference the attempt of any European power to overthrow by force, or to supplant by fraud the institutions of any republican government on the Western Continent; and that they will view with extreme jealousy, as menacing to the peace and independence of this our country the efforts of any such power to obtain new footholds for monarchical governments, sustained by a foreign military force in near proximity to the United States."

Upon the first ballot for a candidate for President, ABRAHAM LINCOLN received the vote of every State, except Missouri, whose delegates voted for Gen. Grant. The nomination having, on motion of a Missourian, been made unanimous, a scene of the wildest enthusiasm followed, the whole convention being on their feet shouting, and the band playing "Hail Columbia."

For Vice-President, the following names were presented: Andrew Johnson, of Tennessee; Hannibal Hamlin, of Maine; Gen. L. H. Rousseau, of Kentucky; and Daniel S. Dickinson, of New York.

As the vote proceeded, it was soon apparent that ANDREW JOHNSON was to be the nominee; and before the result was announced the various States whose delegations had been divided, commenced changing their votes, and went unanimously for Mr. Johnson, amid the greatest enthusiasm.

On the 9th of June, Mr. Lincoln was waited on by a committee of the convention, and notified of his nomination by the chairman, ex-Governor Dennison, of Ohio, who, in the course of his address, said:

"I need not say to you, sir, that the Convention, in thus

unanimously nominating you for re-election, but gave utterance to the almost universal voice of the loyal people of the country.   To doubt of your triumphant election would be little short of abandoning the hope of a final suppression of the rebellion and the restoration of the Government over the insurgent States.   Neither the Convention nor those represented by that body entertained any doubt as to the final result, under your administration, sustained by the loyal people, and by our noble army and gallant navy.   Neither did the Convention, nor do this Committee doubt the speedy suppression of this most wicked and unprovoked rebellion."

In reply the President said :

" MR. CHAIRMAN AND GENTLEMEN OF THE COMMITTEE :—I will neither conceal my gratification nor restrain the expression of my gratitude that the Union people, through their Convention, in the continued effort to save and advance the nation, have deemed me not unworthy to remain in my present position.   I know no reason to doubt that I shall accept the nomination tendered ; and yet, perhaps, I should not declare definitely before reading and considering what is called the platform.

" I will say now, however, that I approve the declaration in favor of so amending the Constitution as to prohibit slavery throughout the nation.   When the people in revolt, with the hundred days explicit notice that they could within those days resume their allegiance without the overthrow of their institutions, and that they could not resume it afterward, elected to stand out, such an amendment of the Constitution as is now proposed became a fitting and necessary conclusion to the final success of the Union cause.

" Such alone can meet and cover all cavils.   I now perceive its importance, and embrace it.   In the joint name of Liberty and Union let us labor to give it legal form and practical effect."

On the following day, in reply to a congratulatory address from a deputation of the National Union League, the President said :

"GENTLEMEN :—I can only say in response to the remarks of your Chairman, I suppose, that I am very grateful for the renewed confidence which has been accorded to me, both by the Convention and by the National League. I am not insensible at all to the personal compliment there is in this ; yet I do not allow myself to believe that any but a small portion of it is to be appropriated as a personal compliment to me.

"The Convention and the Nation, I am assured, are alike animated by a higher view of the interests of the country for the present and the great future, and that part I am entitled to appropriate as a compliment is only that which I may lay hold of, as being the opinion of the Convention and the League, that I am not entirely unworthy to be entrusted with the place I have occupied for the last three years.

" I have not permitted myself, gentlemen, to conclude that I am the best man in the country ; but I am reminded in this connection, of the story of an old Dutch farmer, who remarked to a companion once, that 'it was not best to swop horses when crossing streams.' "

Prolonged and tumultuous laughter followed this last characteristic remark, given with that telling force which only those who had the privilege of meeting Mr. Lincoln in his moments of relaxation and semi-*abandon* can appreciate.

Having been serenaded, on the 9th, by the delegation from Ohio, he addressed the assemblage as follows :

"GENTLEMEN :—I am very much obliged to you for this compliment. I have just been saying, and will repeat it, that the hardest of all speeches I have to answer is a serenade. I never knew what to say on such occasions.

" I suppose you have done me this kindness in connection with the action of the Baltimore Convention, which has recently taken place, and with which, of course, I am very well satisfied What we want still more than Baltimore Conventions or Presidential elections, is success under General Grant.

" I propose that you constantly bear in mind that the support you owe to the brave officers and soldiers in the field is of the very first importance, and we should therefore lend all our energies to that point.

" Now, without detaining you any longer, I propose that you help me to close up what I am now saying with three rousing cheers for General Grant and the officers and soldiers under his command."

And the cheers were given with a will, the President leading off and waving his hat with as much earnestness as the most enthusiastic individual present.

To a regiment of Ohio troops, one hundred days men, volunteers for the emergency then upon the country, who called, on the 11th, upon Mr. Lincoln, he spoke as follows:

" SOLDIERS :—I understand you have just come from Ohio —come to help us in this the nation's day of trial, and also of its hopes. I thank you for your promptness in responding to the call for troops. Your services were never needed more than now. I know not where you are going. You may stay here and take the places of those who will be sent to the front; or you may go there yourselves. Wherever you go, I know you will do your best. Again I thank you. Good-bye.

298   LIFE OF ABRAHAM LINCOLN.

Philadelphia Sanitary Fair.   President's Speech.   War Terrible.

CHAPTER XX

RECONSTRUCTION.

President's Speech at Philadelphia—Philadelphia Fair—Correspondence with Committee of National Convention—Proclamation of Martial Law in Kentucky—Question of Reconstruction—President's Proclamation on the subject—Congressional Plan.

ON the 16th of June, the President was present at a Fair held in Philadelphia in aid of that noble organization, the United States Sanitary Commission, which was productive of so much good during the war, placing as it did, the arrangements for the care and comfort of our brave boys on a basis which no nation—not France, not England, though experienced in war, and generally of admirable promptitude in availing themselves of all facilities to its successful prosecution—had ever before been able to secure.

On the occasion of this visit, Philadelphia witnessed one of her largest crowds. Not less than fifteen thousand people were straining to get a glimpse of their beloved President at one and the same moment.

After the customary hand-shaking, borne by the victim with contagious good humor, a collation was served, at the close of which, in acknowledgment of a toast to his health, drank with the heartiest sincerity by all present, the President said :

"I suppose that this toast is intended to open the way for me to say something. War at the best is terrible ; and this of ours in its magnitude and duration is one of the most terrible the world has ever known. It has deranged business totally in many places, and perhaps in all.

"It has destroyed property, destroyed life, and ruined homes. It has produced a national debt and a degree of taxation unprecedented in the history of this country. It has caused mourning among us until the heavens may almost be said to be hung in black. And yet it continues. It has had accompaniments not before known in the history of the world.

"I mean the Sanitary and Christian Commissions, with their labors for the relief of the soldiers, and the Volunteer Refreshment Saloon, understood better by those who hear me than by myself. These Fairs, too, first began at Chicago, then held in Boston, Cincinnati, and other cities.

"The motive and object which lies at the bottom of them is worthy of the most that we can do for the soldier who goes to fight the battles of his country. By the fair and tender hand of woman is much, very much, done for the soldier, continually reminding him of the care and thought of him at home. The knowledge that he is not forgotten is grateful to his heart.

"And the view of these institutions is worthy of thought. They are voluntary contributions, giving proof that the national resources are not at all exhausted, and that the national patriotism will sustain us through all. It is a pertinent question—when is this war to end ?

"I do not wish to name a day when it will end, lest the end should not come at the given time. We accepted this war, and did not begin it. We accepted it for an object, and when that object is accomplished, the war will end ; and I hope to God it will never end until that object is accomplished.

"We are going through with our task, so far as I am concerned, if it takes us three years longer. I have not been in the habit of making predictions, but I am almost tempted now to hazard one. I will. It is that Grant is this evening in a position, with Meade and Hancock of Pennsylvania, where he can never be dislodged by the enemy until Richmond is taken.

"If I shall discover that General Grant may be facilitated in the capture of Richmond by rapidly pouring to him a large number of armed men at the briefest notice, will you go? [Cries of 'Yes.'] Will you march on with him? [Cries of 'Yes, yes.']

"Then I shall call upon you when it is necessary."

The following correspondence passed between Mr. Lincoln and the Committee of the National Convention relative to his nomination:

"New York, June 14, 1864.

"HON. ABRAHAM LINCOLN:

"SIR:—The National Union Convention, which assembled in Baltimore on June 7, 1864, has instructed us to inform you that you were nominated with enthusiastic unanimity, for the Presidency of the United States for four years from the 4th of March next.

"The resolutions of the Convention, which we have already had the honor of placing in your hands, are a full and clear statement of the principles which inspired its action, and which, as we believe, the great body of Union men in the country heartily approve. Whether those resolutions express the national gratitude to our soldiers and sailors, or the national scorn of compromise with rebels, and consequent dishonor; or the patriotic duty of Union and success; whether they approve the Proclamation of Emancipation, the Constitutional amendment, the employment of former slaves as Union soldiers, or the solemn obligation of the Government promptly to redress the wrongs of every soldier of the Union, of whatever color or race; whether they declare the inviolability of the pledged faith of the nation, or offer the national hospitality to the oppressed of every land, or urge the union, by railroad, of the Atlantic and Pacific oceans; whether they recommend public economy and a vigorous taxation, or assert the fixed popular opposition to the establishment of avowed force of foreign monarchies in the immediate neighborhood of the United States, or declare that those only are worthy of official trust who approve unreservedly the views and policy indicated in the resolutions—they were equally hailed with the heartiness of profound conviction.

" Believing with you, sir, that this is the people's war for the maintenance of a government which you have justly described as ' of the people, by the people, for the people,' we are very sure that you will be glad to know, not only from the resolutions themselves, but from the singular harmony and enthusiasm with which they were adopted, how warm is the popular welcome of every measure in the prosecution of the war, which is as vigorous, unmistakable, and unfaltering as the National purpose itself. No right, for instance, is so precious and sacred to the American heart as that of personal liberty. Its violation is regarded with just, instant, and universal jealousy. Yet in this hour of peril every faithful citizen concedes that, for the sake of National existence and the common welfare, individual liberty may, as the Constitution provides in case of rebellion, be sometimes summarily constrained, asking only with painful anxiety that in every instance, and to the least detail, that absolutely necessary power shall not be hastily or unwisely exercised.

" We believe, sir, that the honest will of the Union men of the country was never more truly represented than in this Convention. Their purpose we believe to be the overthrow of armed rebels in the field, and the security of permanent peace and Union by liberty and justice under the Constitution. That these results are to be achieved amid cruel perplexities, they are fully aware. That they are to be reached only by cordial unanimity of counsel, is undeniable. That good men may sometimes differ as to the means and the time, they know. That in the conduct of all human affairs the highest duty is to determine, in the angry conflict of passion, how much good may be practically accomplished, is their sincere persuasion. They have watched your official course, therefore, with unflagging attention ; and amid the bitter taunts of eager friends and the fierce denunciations of enemies, now moving too fast for some, now too slowly for others, they have seen you throughout this tremendous contest patient, sagacious, faithful, just, leaning upon the heart of the great mass of the people, and satisfied to be moved by its mighty pulsation.

"It is for this reason that, long before the Convention met, the popular instincts had plainly indicated you as its candidate ; and the Convention, therefore, merely recorded the popular will. Your character and career proves your unswerving fidelity to the cardinal principles of American Liberty and of the American Constitution. In the name of that Liberty and Constitution, sir, we earnestly request your acceptance of this nomination ; reverently commending our beloved country, and you, its Chief Magistrate, with all its brave sons who, on sea and land, are faithfully defending the good old American cause of equal rights, to the blessings of Almighty God, we are, sir, very respectfully, your friends and fellow-citizens.

"WILLIAM DENNISON, *Ohio*, Chairman.
"And signed by the Committee."

"*Executive Mansion*, Washington, June 27th, 1863.

"Hon. WILLIAM DENNISON and others :

"A Committee of the National Union Convention :

"GENTLEMEN :—Your letter of the 14th inst, formally notifying me that I had been nominated by the Convention you represent for the Presidency of the United States for four years from the 4th of March next, has been received. The nomination is gratefully accepted, as the Resolutions of the Convention—called the Platform—are heartily approved.

"While the resolution in regard to the supplanting of Republican Government upon the Western Continent is fully concurred in, there might be misunderstanding were I not to say that the position of the Government in relation to the action of France in Mexico, as assumed through the State Department and endorsed by the Convention, among the measures and acts of the Executive, will be faithfully maintained so long as the state of facts shall leave that position pertinent and applicable.

"I am especially gratified that the soldiers and seamen were not forgotten by the Convention, as they forever must and will be remembered by the grateful country for whose salvation they devote their lives.

"Thanking you for the kind and complimentary terms in which you have communicated the nomination and other proceedings of the Convention, I subscribe myself,

"Your obedient servant,   ABRAHAM LINCOLN."

On the 5th of July, appeared the following proclamation, ordering martial law in Kentucky:

"WHEREAS, By a proclamation, which was issued on the 15th day of April, 1861, the President of the United States announced and declared that the laws of the United States had been for some time past, and then were, opposed and the execution thereof obstructed, in certain States therein mentioned, by combinations too powerful to be suppressed by the ordinary course of judicial proceedings, or by the power vested in the marshals by law; and,

"WHEREAS, Immediately after the issuing of the said proclamation, the land and naval force of the United States were put into activity to suppress the said insurrection and rebellion; and,

"WHEREAS, The Congress of the United States, by an act approved on the 3d day of March, 1863, did enact that during the said rebellion the President of the United States, whenever in his judgment the public safety may require it, is authorized to suspend the privilege of the writ of *habeas cor-*

pus in any case throughout the United States, or any part thereof; and,

"WHEREAS, The said insurrection and rebellion still continues, endangering the existence of the Constitution and Government of the United States; and,

"WHEREAS, The military forces of the United States are now actively engaged in suppressing the said insurrection and rebellion in various parts of the States where the said rebellion has been successful in obstructing the laws and public authorities, especially in the States of Virginia and Georgia; and,

"WHEREAS, On the 15th day of September last, the President of the United States duly issued his proclamation, wherein he declared that the privilege of the writ of *habeas corpus* should be suspended throughout the United States, in cases where, by the authority of the President of the United States, the military, naval, and civil officers of the United States, or any of them, hold persons under their command or in their custody either as prisoners of war, spies, or aiders or abettors of the enemy, or officers, soldiers, or seamen, enrolled, or drafted, or mustered, or enlisted in, or belonging to, the land or naval forces of the United States, or as deserters therefrom, or otherwise amenable to military law or the rules and articles of war, or the rules and regulations prescribed for the military or naval service by authority of the President of the United States, or for resisting a draft, or for any other offence against the military or naval service; and,

"WHEREAS, Many citizens of the State of Kentucky have joined the forces of the insurgents, have on several occasions entered the said State of Kentucky in large force, and not without aid and comfort furnished by disaffected and disloyal citizens of the United States residing therein, have not only greatly disturbed the public peace, but have overborne the civil authorities and made flagrant civil war, destroying property and life in various parts of the State; and,

"WHEREAS, It has been made known to the President of the United States by the officers commanding the National armies, that combinations have been formed in the said State of Kentucky, with a purpose of inciting the rebel forces to renew the said operations of civil war within the said State, and thereby to embarrass the United States armies now operating in the said States of Virginia and Georgia, and even to endanger their safety;

" Now, therefore, I, ABRAHAM LINCOLN, President of the United States, by virtue of the authority vested in me by the Constitution and laws, do hereby declare, that in my judgment the public safety especially requires that the suspension of the privilege of the writ of *habeas corpus*, so proclaimed in the said proclamation of the fifteenth of September, 1863, be made effectual, and be duly enforced in and throughout the said State of Kentucky, and that martial law be for the present ordered therein. I do therefore hereby require of the military officers in the said State that the privilege of the writ of *habeas corpus* be effectually suspended within the said State, according to the aforesaid proclamation, and that martial law be established therein, to take effect from the date of this proclamation, the said suspension and establishment of martial law to continue until this proclamation shall be revoked or modified, but not beyond the period when the said rebellion shall have been suppressed or come to an end. And I do hereby require and command as well military officers as all civil officers and authorities existing or found within the said State of Kentucky, to take notice of this proclamation and to give full effect to the same. The martial law herein proclaimed, and the things in that respect herein ordered, will not be deemed or taken to interfere with the holding of elections, or with the proceedings of the Constitutional Legislature of Kentucky, or with the administration of justice in the courts of law existing therein between citizens of the United States in suits or proceedings which do not affect the

20

military operations or the constituted authorities of the Government of the United States.

"In witness whereof, I have hereunto set my hand and caused the seal of the United States to be affixed.

"Done at the City of Washington, this fifth day of July, in the year of our Lord one thousand eight hundred and sixty-four, and of the Independence of the United States the eighty-eighth.

"By the President: ABRAHAM LINCOLN.
"WILLIAM H. SEWARD, Secretary of State."

The question as to what principles should be adopted in reconstructing the rebel States, as fast as the insurrection within their limits should be suppressed, had already, as remarked upon a former page, presented itself as one to be met and disposed of. Congress having, at almost the last moment of its session, passed a bill intended to meet this case, the President issued the following proclamation, on the 9th of July, practically approving the same and accepting its spirit, but making exception in the case of Louisiana and Arkansas, which States had been reorganized according to the spirit and intent of a previous proclamation, making the will of one-tenth of the voters of a State sufficient for its return to allegiance—the bill under notice requiring the votes of a majority:

"WHEREAS, At the last session, Congress passed a bill to guarantee to certain States whose Governments have been usurped or overthrown, a republican form of government, a copy of which is hereunto annexed; and,

"WHEREAS, The said bill was presented to the President of the United States for his approval, less than one hour before the *sine die* adjournment of said session, and was not signed by him; and,

"WHEREAS, The said bill contains, among other things, a plan for restoring the States in rebellion to the proper practical relation in the Union, which plan presents the sense of Congress upon that subject, and which plan it is now thought fit to lay before the people for their consideration:

"Now, therefore, I, ABRAHAM LINCOLN, President of the United States, do proclaim, declare, and make known, that, while I am, as I was in December last, when by proclamation I propounded a plan for restoration, unprepared, by a formal approval of this bill, to be inflexibly committed to any single plan of restoration, and while I am also unprepared to declare that the Free State Constitutions and Governments already adopted and installed in Arkansas and Louisiana shall be set aside and held for naught, thereby repelling and discouraging the loyal citizens who have set up the same, as to further effort, or to declare a constitutional competency in Congress to establish slavery in States, but am at the same time sincerely hoping and expecting that a constitutional amendment abolishing slavery throughout the nation may be adopted; nevertheless I am fully satisfied with the system of restoration contained in the bill as one very proper plan for the loyal people of any State choosing to adopt it, and that I am and at all times shall be prepared to give the Executive aid and assistance to any such people, so soon as the military resistance to the United States shall have been suppressed in any such State, and the people thereof shall have sufficiently returned to their obedience to the Constitution and the laws of the United States, in which cases military Governors will be appointed, with directions to proceed according to the bill.

"In testimony whereof, I have hereunto set my hand, and caused the seal of the United States to be affixed.

"Done at the City of Washington, this eighth day of July, in the year of our Lord one thousand eight hundred and sixty four, and of the Independence of the United States of America the eighty-ninth.

"By the President: ABRAHAM LINCOLN.
"WILLIAM H. SEWARD, Secretary of State."

The following is the bill, a copy of which was annexed to the proclamation :

"A BILL to guarantee to certain States whose Governments have been overthrown or usurped, a Republican form of Government.

"*Be it enacted by the Senate and House of Representatives of the United States of America, in Congress assembled*, That in the States declared in rebellion against the United States, the President shall, by and with the advice and consent of the Senate, appoint for each a Provisional Governor, whose pay and emoluments shall not exceed those of a Brigadier General of Volunteers, who shall be charged with the civil administration of such State, until a State Government therein shall be recognized as hereinafter provided.

"SECTION 2. *And be it further enacted*, That so soon as the military resistance to the United States shall have been suppressed in any such State, and the people thereof shall have sufficiently returned to their obedience to the Constitution and laws of the United States, the Provisional Governor shall direct the Marshal of the United States, as speedily as may be, to name a sufficient number of deputies, and to enroll all white male citizens of the United States, resident in the State, in their respective counties, and to require each one to take the oath to support the Constitution of the United States, and in his enrollment to designate those who take and those who refuse to take that oath, which rolls shall be forthwith returned to the Provisional Governor ; and if the persons taking that oath shall amount to a majority of the persons enrolled in the State, he shall, by proclamation, invite the loyal people of the State to elect delegates to a Convention, charged to declare the will of the people of the State, relative to the reëstablishment of a State Government subject to, and in conformity with the Constitution of the United States.

"SECTION 3. That the Convention shall consist of as many members as both Houses of the last Constitutional State Legislature, apportioned by the Provisional Governor among the counties, parishes, or districts of the State, in proportion to the white population returned as electors by the Marshal, in compliance with the provisions of this Act. The Provisional Governor shall, by proclamation, declare the number of delegates to be elected by each county, parish, or election district; name a day of election not less than thirty days thereafter; designate the place of voting in each county, parish, or election district, conforming as nearly as may be convenient, to the places used in the State elections next preceding the rebellion; appoint one or more Commissioners to hold the election at each place of voting, and provide an adequate force to keep the peace during the election.

"SECTION 4. That the delegates shall be elected by the loyal white male citizens of the United States, of the age of twenty-one years, and resident at the time in the county, parish, or election district in which they shall offer to vote, and enrolled as aforesaid, or absent in the military service of the United States, and who shall take and subscribe the oath of allegiance to the United States in the form contained in the Act of Congress of July 2, 1862; and all such citizens of the United States who are in the military service of the United States, shall vote at the head-quarters of their respective commands, under such regulations as may be prescribed by the Provisional Governor for the taking and return of their votes; but no person who has held or exercised any office, civil or military, State or Confederate, under the rebel usurpation, or who has voluntarily borne arms against the United States, shall vote or be eligible to be elected as delegate at such election.

"SECTION 5. That the said Commissioners, or either of them, shall hold the election in conformity with this Act, and so far as may be consistent therewith, shall proceed in the manner used in the State prior to the rebellion. The oath of allegiance shall be taken and subscribed on the poll-book in the form above described, but every person known by or proved to the Commissioners to have held or exercised any office, civil or military, State or Confederate, under the rebel usurpation, or to have voluntarily borne arms against the United States, shall be excluded, though he offer to take the oath; and in case any person who shall have borne arms against the United States shall offer to vote, he shall be deemed to have borne arms voluntarily, unless he shall prove the contrary by the testimony of a qualified voter. The poll-book, showing the name and oath of each voter, shall be returned to the Provisional Governor by the Commissioner of elections, or the one acting, and the Provisional Governor shall canvass such return, and declare the person having the highest number of votes elected.

" SECTION 6. That the Provisional Governor shall, by proclamation, convene the delegates elected as aforesaid, at the Capital of the State, on a day not more than three months after the election, fixing at least thirty days' notice of such day. In case the said Capital shall in his judgment be unfit, he shall in his proclamation appoint another place. He shall preside over the deliberations of the Convention, and administer to each delegate, before taking his seat in the Convention, the oath of allegiance to the United States in the form above prescribed.

" SECTION 7. That the Convention shall declare, on behalf of the people of the State, their submission to the Constitution and laws of the United States, and shall adopt the following provisions, hereby prescribed by the United States in the execution of the Constitutional duty to guarantee a republican form of government to every State, and incorporate them in the Constitution of the State; that is to say:

" *First.* No person who has held or exercised any office, civil or military, except offices merely ministerial, and military offices below the grade of Colonel, State or corporate, under the usurping power, shall vote for, or be a member of the Legislature, or Governor.

"*Second.* Involuntary servitude is forever prohibited, and the freedom of all persons is guaranteed in said State.

"*Third.* No debt, State or corporate, created by or under the sanction of the usurping power, shall be recognized or paid by the State.

"SECTION 8. That when the Convention shall have adopted these provisions, it shall proceed to reëstablish a republican form of Government, and ordain a Constitution containing these provisions, which, when adopted, the Convention shall, by ordinance, provide for submitting to the people of the State entitled to vote under this law, at an election to be held in the manner prescribed by the Act for the election of delegates, but at a time and place named by the Convention, at which Election the said Electors, and none others, shall vote directly for or against such Constitution and form of State government; and the returns of said election shall be made to the Provisional Governor, who shall canvass the same in the presence of the electors, and if a majority of the votes cast shall be for the Constitution and form of government, he shall certify the same, with a copy thereof, to the President of the United States, who, after obtaining the assent of Congress, shall, by proclamation, recognize the government so established, and none other, as the Constitutional Government of the State, and from the date of such recognition, and not before, Senators, and Representatives, and Electors for President and Vice-President may be elected in such State, according to the laws of the State and of the United States.

"SECTION 9. That if the Convention shall refuse to reëstablish the State Government on the conditions aforesaid, the Provisional Governor shall declare it dissolved; but it shall be the duty of the President, whenever he shall have reason to believe that a sufficient number of the people of the

State entitled to vote under this Act, in number not less than a majority of those enrolled, as aforesaid, are willing to reëstablish a State Government on the conditions aforesaid, to direct the Provisional Governor to order another election of delegates to a Convention for the purpose and in the manner prescribed in this Act, and to proceed in all respects as hereinbefore provided, either to dissolve the Convention, or to certify the State Government reëstablished by it to the President.

" SECTION 10.   That, until the United States shall have recognized a republican form of State Government, the Provisional Governor in each of said States shall see that this Act, and the laws of the United States, and other laws of the State in force when the State Government was overthrown by the rebellion, are faithfully executed within the State ; but no law or usage whereby any person was heretofore held in involuntary servitude shall be recognized or enforced by any Court or officer in such State, and the laws for the trial and punishment of white persons shall extend to all persons, and jurors shall have the qualifications of voters under this law for delegates to the Convention.   The President shall appoint such officers provided for by the laws of the State when its government was overthrown as he may find necessary to the civil administration of the State, all which officers shall be entitled to receive the fees and emoluments provided by the State laws for such officers.

" SECTION 11.   That, until the recognition of a State Government, as aforesaid, the Provisional Governor shall, under such regulations as he may prescribe, cause to be assessed, levied, and collected, for the year eighteen hundred and sixty-four, and every year thereafter, the taxes provided by the laws of such State to be levied during the fiscal year preceding the overthrow of the State Government thereof, in the manner prescribed by the laws of the State, as nearly as may be ; and the officers appointed, as aforesaid, are vested with all powers of levying and collecting such taxes, by distress or sale, as were vested in any officers or tribunal of the State Government aforesaid for those purposes. The proceeds of such taxes shall be accounted for to the Provisional Governor, and be by him applied to the expenses of the administration of the laws in such State, subject to the direction of the President, and the surplus shall be deposited in the Treasury of the United States, to the credit of such State, to be paid to the State upon an appropriation therefor, to be made when a republican form of government shall be recognized therein by the United States.

" SECTION 12. That all persons held to involuntary servitude or labor in the States aforesaid, are hereby emancipated and discharged therefrom, and they and their posterity shall be forever free. And if any such persons or their posterity shall be restrained of liberty, under pretence of any claim to such service or labor, the Courts of the United States shall, on *habeas corpus*, discharge them.

" SECTION 13. That if any person declared free by this Act, or any law of the United States, or any proclamation of the President, be restrained of liberty, with intent to be held in or reduced to involuntary servitude or labor, the person convicted before a Court of competent jurisdiction of such Act, shall be punished by fine of not less than one thousand five hundred dollars, and be imprisoned for not less than five or more than twenty years.

" SECTION 14. That every person who shall hereafter hold or exercise any office, civil or military, except offices merely ministerial, and military offices below the grade of Colonel, in the rebel service, State or Corporate, is hereby declared not to be a citizen of the United States."

314   LIFE OF ABRAHAM LINCOLN.

Proclamation for a Fast.   Humiliation and Prayer Recommended.

CHAPTER XXI.

PRESIDENTIAL CAMPAIGN OF 1864.

Proclamation for a Fast—Speech to Soldiers—Another Speech—"To Whom it may Concern"—Chicago Convention—Opposition Embarrassed—Resolution No. 2—McClellan's Acceptance—Capture of the Mobile Forts and Atlanta—Proclamation for Thanksgiving Remarks on Employment of Negro Soldiers—Address to Loyal Marylanders.

On the 7th of July the following proclamation for a National Fast appeared :

" WHEREAS, The Senate and House of Representatives, at their last session, adopted a concurrent resolution which was approved on the third day of July instant, and which was in the words following :

" ' That the President of the United States is requested to appoint a day of humiliation and prayer by the people of the United States; that he request his constitutional advisers at the head of the Executive Departments to unite with him, as Chief Magistrate of the Nation, at the city of Washington, and the members of Congress, and all magistrates, all civil, military and naval officers, all soldiers, sailors, and marines, with all loyal and law-abiding people, to convene at their usual places of worship, or wherever they may be, to confess and to repent of their manifold sins ; to implore the compassion and forgiveness of the Almighty, that, if consistent with His will, the existing rebellion may be speedily suppressed, and the supremacy of the Constitution and laws of the United States may be established throughout all the States ; to implore Him, as the Supreme Ruler of all the world, not to destroy us as a people, nor suffer us to be destroyed by the hostility or connivance of other nations, or by obstinate adhesion to our own counsels, which may be in conflict with His eternal purposes, and to implore him to enlighten the mind of the Nation to know and to do his will, humbly believing that it is not in accord ever with his will that our place should be maintained as a wicked people among the family of nations; to implore him to grant to our armed defenders and the masses of the people that courage, power of resistance, and endurance necessary to secure that result; to implore him in his infinite goodness to soften the hearts, enlighten the minds, and quicken the consciences of those in rebellion, that they may lay down their arms and speedily return to their allegiance to the United States, that they may not be utterly destroyed, that the effusion of blood may be stayed, and that unity and fraternity may be restored, and peace established throughout all our borders.'

"Now, therefore, I, Abraham Lincoln, President of the United States, cordially concurring with the Congress of the United States in the penitential and pious sentiments expressed in the aforesaid resolution, and heartily approving of the devotional design and purpose thereof, do hereby appoint the first Thursday of August next, to be observed by the people of the United States as a day of National humiliation and prayer.

"I do hereby further invite and request the heads of the Executive Department of this Government, together with all legislators, all Judges and magistrates, and all other persons exercising authority in the land, whether civil, military, or naval, and all soldiers, seamen and marines in the National service, and all other loyal and law-abiding people of the United States, to assemble in their professed places of public worship on that day, and there to render to the Almighty and merciful Ruler of the universe such homage and such confessions, and to offer him such supplications, as the Congress of the United States have in their aforesaid resolution so solemnly, so earnestly, and so reverently recommended.

"In testimony whereof, I have hereunto set my hand, and caused the seal of the United States to be affixed.

"Done at the City of Washington, this, the seventh day of July, in the year of our Lord one thousand eight hundred and sixty-four, and of the Independence of the United States the eighty-ninth.

"By the President:　　　ABRAHAM LINCOLN.

"WILLIAM H. SEWARD, Secretary of State."

To some Ohio volunteers, about to return home at the expiration of their term of service, who had called upon the President to pay him their respects, he spoke, on the 18th of August, thus:

"SOLDIERS: You are about to return to your homes and your friends, after having, as I learn, performed in camp a comparatively short term of duty in this great contest. I am greatly obliged to you and to all who have come forward at the call of their country.

"I wish it might be more generally and universally understood what the country is now engaged in. We have, as all will agree, a free Government, where every man has a right to be equal with every other man. In this great struggle, this form of government and every form of human rights is endangered if our enemies succeed. There is more involved in this contest than is realized by every one. There is involved in this struggle the question whether your children and my children shall enjoy the privileges we have enjoyed. I say this, in order to impress upon you, if you are not already so impressed, that no small matter should divert us from our great purpose.

"There may be some inequalities in the practical working of our system. It is fair that each man shall pay taxes in exact proportion for the value of his property; but if we should wait, before collecting a tax, to adjust the taxes upon each man in exact proportion to every other man, we should never collect any tax at all. There may be mistakes made somewhere ; things may be done wrong, which the officers of Government do all they can to prevent mistakes.

"But I beg of you, as citizens of this great Republic, not to let your minds be carried off from the great work we have before us.   This struggle is too large for you to be diverted from it by any small matter.   When you return to your homes, rise up to the height of a generation of men, worthy of a free government, and we will carry out the great work we have commenced.   I return you my sincere thanks, soldiers, for the honor you have done me this afternoon."

And again, on the 22d of August, under similar circumstances :

" SOLDIERS :—I suppose you are going home to see your families and friends.   For the services you have done in this great struggle in which we are engaged, I present you sincere thanks for myself and the country.

" I almost always feel inclined, when I say any thing to soldiers, to impress upon them, in a few brief remarks, the importance of success in this contest.   It is not merely for to-day, but for all time to come, that we should perpetuate for our children's children that great and free Government which we have enjoyed all our lives.   I beg you to remember this, not merely for my sake, but for yours.   I happen temporarily to occupy this big White House.   I am a living witness that any one of your children may look to come here as my father's child has.

" It is in order that each one of you may have, through this free Government which we have enjoyed, an open field and a fair chance for your industry, enterprise, and intelligence ; that you may all have equal privileges in the race of life, with all its desirable human aspirations ; it is for this that the struggle should be maintained, that we may not lose our birthrights—not only for one, but for two or three years.

The nation is worth fighting for, to secure such an unquestionable jewel."

During the excitement accompanying the rebel attempts upon the National Capitol, during the month of July, heretofore noticed, representations were made to the President that certain individuals, professing to represent the rebel leaders, were in Canada, anxious to enter into negotiations, with a view to the restoration of peace.

In response to this suggestion, Mr. Lincoln issued the following paper, which was very unsatisfactory to those who affected to believe that peace could be secured upon any basis short of the recognition of the Southern Confederacy, unless the rebels in arms were thoroughly defeated, dated, Executive Mansion, Washington, July 18, 1864.

"To whom it may concern.—Any proposition which embraces the restoration of peace, the integrity of the Union, and the abandonment of slavery, and which comes by and with authority that can control the armies now at war against the United States, will be received and considered by the Executive Government of the United States, and will be met by liberal terms on other substantial and collateral points, and the bearers thereof shall have safe conduct both ways.

"Abraham Lincoln."

This ended that attempt to divide the supporters of the Administration.

On the 29th of August, 1864, assembled at Chicago the National Convention of the Democratic party. This had been preceded by a "Mass Peace Convention," at Syracuse, on the 18th of August, at which it had been resolved, among other things, that it was the duty of the Chicago Convention to give expression to a beneficent sentiment of peace and to declare as the purpose of the Democratic party, if it should recover power, to cause the desolating war to cease by the calling of a National Convention, in which all the States should be represented in their sovereign capacity; and that, to that end, an immediate armistice should be declared of sufficient duration to give the States and the people ample time and opportunity to deliberate upon and finally conclude a form of Union.

There were two factions represented at Chicago: one, unqualifiedly in favor of peace at any price, upon any terms, with any concessions; the other, disposed to take every possible advantage of the mistakes of the Administration, but not possessed of effrontery sufficient to pronounce boldly for a cessation of hostilities in any and every event.

Thus embarrassed, what was left of the still great Democratic party—that party which had swayed the country for so many years, and whose disruption in 1860 was the immediate occasion of the war that ensued—determined to do what it never before, in all its history, had ventured upon. It essayed to ride, at one and the same time, two horses going in diametrically opposite directions.

To conciliate whatever feeling in favor of a prosecution of the war there might be in their ranks, without at the same time going too far in that direction, and to secure as many soldiers' votes as possible, they put in nomination for the Presidency, Gen. McClellan. To neutralize this apparent tendency toward war, they associated the General with George H. Pendleton, of Ohio, as a candidate for the Vice-Presidency—a man, who, during his entire Congressional career as member of the National House of Representatives, had avowed himself and voted as a Peace-at-any-price individual, from the very outset.

The bane and antidote having thus been blended, as only political chemists would have attempted, the candidates were placed upon a platform, the second resolution of which was as follows:

"*Resolved*, That this Convention does explicitly declare, as the sense of the American people, that, after four years of failure to restore the Union by the experiment of war, during which, under the pretence of a military necessity or war power higher than the Constitution, the Constitution itself has been disregarded in every part, and public liberty and private right alike trodden down, and the material prosperity of the country essentially impaired, justice, humanity, liberty, and the public welfare demand that immediate efforts be made for a cessation of hostilities, with a view to an ultimate Convention of all the States, or other peaceable means, to the end that at the earliest practicable moment peace may be restored on the basis of the Federal Union of the States."

This accomplished, the Convention adjourned, having provided for its indefinite existence by empowering its chairman to reconvene it, whenever, in his judgment, it should be thought necessary.

McClellan accepted the nomination, happy to know that when it was made, the record of his public life was kept in view.   In his letter of acceptance, he talked all around the peace proposition, ignored the idea of a cessation of hostilities, and went for the whole Union.   The document, though sufficiently general and indefinite to answer the purpose, failed to satisfy the ultra-peace men of his party.

Thus, in the midst of a civil war, unparalleled in the world's history, the extraordinary spectacle was presented of a great people entering with earnestness upon a political campaign, one of whose issues—indeed, the main one—was as to the continuance of that war, with all its hardships and burdens.

Just after the adjournment of the Chicago Convention, Sherman's occupation of Atlanta and the capture of the forts in the harbor of Mobile, were announced, seeming to intimate that the war had not been, up to that time, wholly a failure. The thanks of the Nation were tendered by the President to the officers and men connected with these operations, national salutes ordered, and the following proclamation issued, dated September 3d, 1864.

" The signal success that Divine Providence has recently vouchsafed to the operations of the United States fleet and army in the harbor of Mobile, and the reduction of Fort Powell, Fort Gaines, and Fort Morgan, and the glorious achievements of the army under Major-General Sherman, in the State of Georgia, resulting in the capture of the city of Atlanta, call for devout acknowledgment of the Supreme Being in whose hands are the destinies of nations.

" It is therefore requested that on next Sunday, in all places of worship in the United States, thanksgiving be offered to Him for His mercy in preserving our national existence against the insurgent rebels who have been waging a cruel war against the Government of the United States for its overthrow, and also that prayer be made for Divine protection to our brave soldiers and their leaders in the field, who have so often and so gallantly perilled their lives in battling with the enemy, and for blessing and comfort from the Father of Mercies to the sick, wounded, and prisoners, and to the orphans and widows of those who have fallen in the service of their country, and that He will continue to uphold the Government of the United States against all the efforts of public enemies and secret foes.

"ABRAHAM LINCOLN."

Mr. Lincoln's views relative to the employment of negroes as soldiers were again and fully expressed about this time in a conversation with leading gentlemen from the West. On that occasion he said :

" The slightest knowledge of arithmetic will prove to any man that the rebel armies cannot be destroyed by Democratic strategy. It would sacrifice all the white men of the North to do it. There are now in the service of the United States

21

nearly two hundred thousand able-bodied colored men, most of them under arms, defending and acquiring Union territory. The Democratic strategy demands that these forces be disbanded, and that the masters be conciliated by restoring them to slavery. The black men, who now assist Union prisoners to escape, are to be converted into our enemies, in the vain hope of gaining the good-will of their masters. We shall have to fight two nations instead of one.

"You can not conciliate the South, if you guarantee to them ultimate success; and the experience of the present war proves their success is inevitable, if you fling the compulsory labor of millions of black men into their side of the scale. Will you give our enemies such military advantages as insure success, and then depend upon coaxing, flattery, and concession to get them back into the Union? Abandon all the forts now garrisoned by black men, take two hundred thousand men from our side and put them in the battle-field or corn-field against us, and we would be compelled to abandon the war in three weeks.

"We have to hold territory in inclement and sickly places; where are the Democrats to do this? It was a free fight; and the field was open to the War Democrats to put down this rebellion by fighting against both master and slave, long before the present policy was inaugurated.

"There have been men base enough to propose to me to return to slavery our black warriors of Port Hudson and Olustee, and thus win the respect of the masters they fought. Should I do so, I should deserve to be damned in time and eternity. Come what will, I will keep my faith with friend and foe. My enemies pretend I am now carrying on this war for the sole purpose of abolition. So long as I am President, it shall be carried on for the sole purpose of restoring the Union. But no human power can subdue this rebellion without the use of the Emancipation policy, and every other policy calculated to weaken the moral and physical forces of the rebellion.

"Freedom has given us two hundred thousand men raised on Southern soil. It will give us more yet. Just so much it has subtracted from the enemy; and, instead of checking the South, there are now evidences of a fraternal feeling growing up between our men and the rank and file of the rebel soldiers. Let my enemies prove to the country that the destruction of slavery is not necessary to the restoration of the Union. I will abide the issue."

On the 19th of October, the President having been serenaded by the loyal Marylanders of the District of Columbia, said:

"I am notified that this is a compliment paid me by the loyal Marylanders resident in this district. I infer that the adoption of the new Constitution for the State furnishes the occasion, and that in your view the extirpation of slavery constitutes the chief merit of the new Constitution.

"Most heartily do I congratulate you, and Maryland, and the Nation, and the world upon the event. I regret that it did not occur two years sooner, which, I am sure, would have saved to the nation more money than would have met all the private loss incident to the measure; but it has come at last, and I sincerely hope its friends may fully realize all their anticipations of good from it, and that its opponents may, by its effects, be agreeably and profitably disappointed.

"A word upon another subject: Something said by the Secretary of State, in his recent speech at Auburn, has been construed by some into a threat that, if I shall be beaten at the election, I will between then and the end of my constitutional term do what I may be able to ruin the Government. Others regard the fact that the Chicago Convention adjourned, not *sine die*, but to meet again, if called to do so by a particular individual, as the ultimatum of a purpose that, if the nominee shall be elected, he will at once seize control of the Government.

"I hope the good people will permit themselves to suffer no uneasiness on either point. I am struggling to maintain the Government, not to overthrow it. I therefore say that, if I shall live, I shall remain President until the fourth of March. And whoever shall be constitutionally elected, therefore, in November, shall be duly installed as President on the fourth of March; and that, in the interval, I shall do my utmost that whoever is to hold the helm for the next voyage, shall start with the best possible chance to save the ship.

"This is due to our people, both on principle and under the Constitution. Their will, constitutionally expressed, is the ultimate law for all. If they should deliberately resolve to have immediate peace, even at the loss of their country and their liberties, I know not the power or the right to resist them. It is their own business, and they must do as they please with their own.

"I believe, however, that they are all resolved to preserve their country and their liberty; and in this, in office or out of it, I am resolved to stand by them. I may add, that in this purpose—to save the country and its liberties—no class of people seem so nearly unanimous as the soldiers in the field and the seamen afloat. Do they not have the hardest of it? Who shall quail, when they do not? God bless the soldiers and seamen and all their brave commanders!"

CHAPTER XXII.

RE-ELECTED.

Presidential Campaign of 1864—Fremont's Withdrawal—Wade and Davis —Peace and War Democrats—Rebel Sympathizers—October Election—Result of Presidential Election—Speech to Pennsylvanians—Speech at a Serenade—Letter to a Soldier's Mother—Opening of Congress—Last Annual Message.

THE Presidential campaign of 1864, was, in several of its aspects, an anomaly. The amount of low blackguard and slang dealt out against the Administration, was perhaps to have been expected in a land where personal abuse seems to have become regarded as so vital an accompaniment of a National Election, that its absence in any exciting canvass would give rise to grave fears that positive Constitutional requirements had been disregarded.

Though freedom, in such instances, far too often is wrested into the vilest abuse, it was in truth passing strange that an Administration should be so violently assailed by its opponents as despotic and tyrannical, when the very fact that such strictures and comments were passed upon it, without let or hindrance, by word of mouth and on the printed page, afforded a proof that the despotism, if such there were, was either too mild or too weak to enforce even a decent treatment of itself and its acts. It is safe to say, that, within the limits of that section with which we were under any circumstances to establish harmonious and peaceful relations, according to the requirements of the opposition, not one speech in a hundred, not one editorial in a thousand, would have been permitted under precisely similar circumstances.

General Fremont withdrew his name shortly after the Chicago nominations, that he might not distract and divide the friends of the Union. In his letter of withdrawal he said :

"The policy of the Democratic party signifies either separation, or reëstablishment, with slavery. The Chicago platform is simply separation. General McClellan's letter of acceptance, is reestablishment with slavery. . . . . . The Republican candidate, on the contrary, is pledged to the reëstablishment of Union without slavery."

Senator Wade and Henry Winter Davis, who had joined in a manifesto to the people, bitterly denunciatory of the President's course in issuing his reconstruction proclamation, entered manfully into the canvass in behalf of the Baltimore nominees. The ranks of the supporters of the Government closed steadily up, and pressed on to a success, of which they could not, with their faith in manhood and republican principles, suffer themselves to doubt.

The Opposition were not entirely in accord. It was a delicate position in which the full-blooded Peace Democrat found himself, obliged as he was to endorse a man whose only claim for the nomination was the reputation which he had made as a prominent General engaged in prosecuting an "unnatural, unholy war." Nor did it afford much alleviation to his distress to remember that this candidate had been loudly assailed in the Convention as the first mover in the matter of arbitrary arrests, against which a sturdy outcry had long been raised by himself and friends. It was unpleasant, moreover, not to be able to forget that the same candidate had been the first to suggest a draft—or "conscription," as your true peace man would call it : that measure so full of horrors, against which unconstitutional act such an amount of indignation had been expended.

Nor was the situation of the War Democrat, if he were indeed honestly and sincerely such, much better. He could not shut his eyes to the fact, that his candidate's military record, whatever else it might have established, did not evince very remarkable vigor and celerity in his movements, as compared with other Generals then and since prominently before the public. Even had he blundered energetically, in that there would have been some consolation. The thought, not unpleasant to the Pendletonian, of the possibility of the General's death during his term of office, stirred up certain other thoughts which he would rather have avoided.

However, it must be said, that, taken as a whole, the Opposition came up to the work more vigorously than might have been supposed, and carried on their campaign in as blustering and defiant a style as if victory were sure to perch upon their banners. There was the usual amount of cheap enthusiasm, valiant betting, and an unusual amount, many thought, of cheating—at least, the results of investigations at Baltimore and Washington, conducted by a military tribunal, to a casual observer appeared to squint in that direction.

Richmond papers were, for a marvel, quite unanimous in the desire that Mr. Lincoln should not be reëlected. The rebel Vice-President declared that the Chicago movement was "the only ray of light which had come from the North during the war." European sympathizers with the rebellion, likewise, were opposed to Mr. Lincoln's reëlection, and their organs on the Continent and in the provinces did their best to abuse him shockingly.

The State elections in Ohio, Pennsylvania, and Indiana, occurring in October, created much consternation in the opposition ranks—that in the latter State particularly, which had been set down positively as upon their side, but insisted, upon that occasion, in common with the first two in pronouncing unequivocally in favor of the Administration candidates.

The result could no longer be doubtful. Yet the most of the supporters of McClellan kept up their talk, whatever their thoughts may have been.

No opportunity for talk, even, was afforded when the results of the election of November 8th became known.

Abraham Lincoln and Andrew Johnson—whom an opposition journal, with rarest refinement and graceful courtesy, concentrating all its malignity into the intensest sentence possible, had characterized as "a rail-splitting buffoon and a boorish tailor, both from the backwoods, both growing up in uncouth ignorance"—these men of the people carried every loyal State, except Kentucky, New Jersey, and Delaware, the vote of soldiers in service having been almost universally given to them.

Of the four million, thirty-four thousand, seven hundred and eighty-nine votes cast, Mr. Lincoln received, according to official returns, two million, two hundred and twenty-three thousand, and thirty-five ; a majority on the aggregate popular vote, of four hundred and eleven thousand, two hundred and eighty-one.

The President elect by a plurality in 1860, he was reëlected in 1864 by a majority decisive and unmistakable.

Having been serenaded early in the morning following his reëlection, by Pennsylvanians then in Washington, he thus gave utterance to his feelings :

"FRIENDS AND FELLOW-CITIZENS :—Even before I had been informed by you that this compliment was paid me by loyal citizens of Pennsylvania friendly to me, I had inferred that you were of that portion of my countrymen who think that the best interests of the nation are to be subserved by the support of the present administration.　I do not pretend to say that you, who think so, embrace all the patriotism and loyalty of the country ; but I do believe, and I trust without personal interest, that the welfare of the country does require that such support and indorsement be given.　I earnestly believe that the consequences of this day's work, if it be as you assume, and as now seems probable, will be to the lasting advantage if not to the very salvation of the country　I cannot, at this hour, say what has been the result of the election, but whatever it may be, I have no desire to modify this opinion : that all who have labored to-day in behalf of the Union organization, have wrought for the best interest of their country and the world, not only for the present, but for all future ages. I am thankful to God for this approval of the people ; but while deeply grateful for this mark of their confidence in me, if I know my heart, my gratitude is free from any taint of personal triumph. I do not impugn the motives of any one opposed to me. It is no pleasure to me to triumph over any one, but I give thanks to the Almighty for this evidence of the people's resolution to stand by free government and the rights of humanity."

When the result was definitely known, at a serenade given in his honor on the night of November 10th, by the various Lincoln and Johnson Clubs of the District, he said :

" It has long been a grave question whether any Government, not too strong for the liberties of its people, can be strong enough to maintain its existence in great emergencies. On this point the present rebellion brought our Government to a severe test, and a Presidential election occurring in a regular course during the rebellion, added not a little to the strain.

" If the loyal people united were put to the utmost of their strength by the rebellion, must they not fail when divided and partially paralyzed by a political war among themselves ? But the election was a necessity—we can not have free government without elections ; and if the rebellion could force us to forego or postpone a national election, it must fairly claim to have already conquered and ruined us. The strife of the election is but human nature practically applied to the facts of the case. What has occurred in this case must ever recur in similar cases. Human nature will not change. In any future great national trial, compared with the men of this, we shall have as weak and as strong, as silly and as wise, as bad and as good.   Let us, therefore, study the incidents of this, as philosophy to learn wisdom from, and none of them as wrongs to be revenged.

"But the election, along with its incidental and undesirable strife, has done good too.   It has demonstrated that a people's government can sustain a national election in the midst of a great civil war.   Until now it has not been known to the world that this was a possibility.   It shows also how sound and how strong we still are.   It shows that, even among the candidates of the same party, he who is most devoted to the Union, and most opposed to treason, can receive most of the people's votes.   It shows also, to the extent yet known, that we have more men now than we had when the war began.   Gold is good in its place; but living, brave, and patriotic men are better than gold.

"But the rebellion continues; and now that the election is over, may not all having a common interest reunite in a common effort to save our common country?   For my own part, I have striven and shall strive to avoid placing any obstacle in the way.   So long as I have been here I have not willingly planted a thorn in any man's bosom.   While I am duly sensible to the high compliment of a reëlection, and duly grateful, as I trust, to Almighty God for having directed my countrymen to a right conclusion, as I think, for their good, it adds nothing to my satisfaction that any other man may be disappointed by the result.

"May I ask those who have not differed with me to join with me in this same spirit toward those who have?   And now let me close by asking three hearty cheers for our brave soldiers and seamen and their gallant and skilful commanders."

As indicative of Mr. Lincoln's warmth and tenderness of heart the following letter will be read with interest.   It was addressed to a poor widow, in Boston, whose sixth son, then recently wounded, was lying in a hospital, and bears date November 21st, 1864.

" DEAR MADAM :—I have been shown in the files of the War Department a statement of the Adjutant-General of Massachusetts, that you are the mother of five sons who have died gloriously on the field of battle. I feel how weak and fruitless must be any word of mine, which should attempt to beguile you from the grief of a loss so overwhelming ; but I cannot refrain from tendering to you the consolation that may be found in the thanks of the Republic they died to save. I pray that our Heavenly Father may assuage the anguish of your bereavement, and leave you only the cherished memory of the loved and lost, and the solemn pride that must be yours, to have laid so costly a sacrifice upon the altar of Freedom.

" Yours very sincerely and respectfully,
"ABRAHAM LINCOLN."

The Thirty-eighth Congress commenced its second session on the 5th of December, 1864. On the following day Mr. Lincoln transmitted what was to be his last annual message :

" FELLOW-CITIZENS OF THE SENATE AND HOUSE OF REPRESENTATIVES :—Again the blessings of health and abundant harvests claim our profoundest gratitude to Almighty God.

" The condition of our foreign affairs is reasonably satisfactory.

" Mexico continues to be a theatre of civil war. While our political relations with that country have undergone no change, we have at the same time strictly maintained neutrality between the belligerents.

"At the request of the States of Costa Rica and Nicaragua, a competent engineer has been authorized to make a survey of the river San Juan and the port of San Juan. It is a source of much satisfaction that the difficulties, which for a moment excited some political apprehension, and caused a closing of the inter-oceanic transit route, have been amicably adjusted, and that there is a good prospect that the route will soon be re-opened with an increase of capacity and adaptation.

"We could not exaggerate either the commercial or the political importance of that great improvement. It would be doing injustice to an important South American State not to acknowledge the directness, frankness, and cordiality with which the United States of Columbia has entered into intimate relation with this Government. A Claim Convention has been constituted to complete the unfinished work of the one which closed its session in 1861.

"The new liberal Constitution of Venezuela having gone into effect with the universal acquiescence of the people, the Government under it has been recognized, and diplomatic intercourse with it has been opened in a cordial and friendly spirit.

"The long-deferred Avis Island claim has been satisfactorily paid and discharged. Mutual payments have been made of the claims awarded by the late Joint Commission for the settlement of claims between the United States and Peru. An earnest and candid friendship continues to exist between the two countries; and such efforts as were in my power have been used to prevent misunderstanding, and avert a threatened war between Peru and Spain.

"Our relations are of the most friendly nature with Chili, the Argentine Republic, Bolivia, Costa Rica, Paraguay, San Salvador, and Hayti. During the past year, no differences of any kind have arisen with any of these Republics. And, on the other hand, their sympathies with the United States are constantly expressed with cordiality and earnestness.

"The claims arising from the seizure of the cargo of the brig Macedonian, in 1821, have been paid in full by the Government of Chili.

" Civil war continues in the Spanish port of San Domingo, apparently without prospect of an early close.

" Official correspondence has been freely opened with Liberia, and it gives us a pleasing view of social and political progress in that Republic. It may be expected to derive new vigor from American influence, improved by the rapid disappearance of slavery in the United States.

" I solicit your authority to promise to the Republic a gunboat, at a moderate cost, to be reimbursed to the United States by instalments. Such a vessel is needed for the safety of that State against the native African races, and in Liberian hands it would be more effective in arresting the African slave-trade than a squadron in our own hands.

" The possession of the least authorized naval force would stimulate a generous ambition in the Republic, and the confidence which we should manifest by furnishing it would win forbearance and favor toward the colony from all civilized nations. The proposed overland telegraph between America and Europe by the way of Behring Strait and Asiatic Russia, which was sanctioned by Congress at the last session, has been undertaken under very favorable circumstances by an association of American citizens, with the cordial good will and support as well of this Government as of those of Great Britain and Russia.

"Assurances have been received from most of the South American States of their high appreciation of the enterprise and their readiness to coöperate in constructing lines tributary to that world-encircling communication.

" I learn with much satisfaction that the noble design of a telegraphic communication between the eastern coast of America and Great Britain has been renewed with full expectation of its early accomplishment.

" Thus it is hoped that with the return of domestic peace the country will be able to resume with energy and advantage her former high career of commerce and civilization.

Our very popular and able representative in Egypt died in April last.

"An unpleasant altercation which arose between the temporary incumbent and the Government of the Pacha, resulted in a suspension of intercourse. The evil was promptly corrected on the arrival of the successor in the consulate, and our relations with Egypt as well as our relations with the Barbary Powers, are entirely satisfactory.

" The rebellion which has so long been flagrant in China, has at last been suppressed with the coöperating good offices of this Government and of the other Western Commercial States. The judicial consular establishment has become very difficult and onerous, and it will need legislative requisition to adapt it to the extension of our commerce, and to the more intimate intercourse which has been instituted with the Government and people of that vast empire.

" China seems to be accepting with hearty good-will the conventional laws which regulate commerce and social intercourse among the Western nations.

" Owing to the peculiar situation of Japan, and the anomalous form of its Government, the action of that Empire in performing treaty stipulations is inconsistent and capricious Nevertheless good progress has been effected by the Western Powers, moving with enlightened concert. Our own pecuniary claims have been allowed, or put in course of settlement, and the Inland Sea has been reopened to Commerce.

" There is reason also to believe that these proceedings have increased rather than diminished the friendship of Japan toward the United States.

" The ports of Norfolk, Fernandino, and Pensacola have been opened by proclamation.

" It is hoped that foreign merchants will now consider whether it is not safer and more profitable to themselves as well as just to the United States, to resort to these and other open ports, than it is to pursue, through many hazards and at vast cost, a contraband trade with other ports which are closed, if not by actual military operations, at least by a lawful and effective blockade.

"For myself, I have no doubt of the power and duty of the Executive, under the laws of nations, to exclude enemies of the human race from an asylum in the United States. If Congress should think that proceedings in such cases lack the authority of law, or ought to be further regulated by it, I recommend that provision be made for effectually preventing foreign slave-traders from acquiring domicil and facilities for their criminal occupation in our country.

"It is possible that if this were a new and open question, the maritime powers, with the light they now enjoy, would not concede the privileges of a naval belligerent to the insurgents of the United States, destitute as they are and always have been, equally of ships, and of ports and harbors.

"Disloyal enemies have been neither less assiduous nor more successful during the last year than they were before that time, in their efforts, under favor of that privilege, to embroil our country in foreign wars. The desire and determination of the maritime States to defeat that design are believed to be as sincere as, and cannot be more earnest than our own.

"Nevertheless, unforseen political difficulties have arisen, especially in Brazilian and British ports, and on the Northern boundary of the United States, which have required and are likely to continue to require the practice of constant vigilance, and a just and conciliatory spirit on the part of the United States, as well as of the nations concerned and their Governments. Commissioners have been appointed under the treaty with Great Britain, in the adjustment of the claims of the Hudson's Bay and Puget Sound Agricultural Companies in Oregon, and are now proceeding to tne execution of the trust assigned to them.

"In view of the insecurity of life in the region adjacent to the Canadian border by recent assaults and depredations committed by inimical and desperate persons who are harbored there, it has been thought proper to give notice that after the expiration of six months, the period conditionally stipulated in the existing arrangements with Great Britain, the United States must hold themselves at liberty to increase their naval armament upon the lakes, if they shall find that proceeding necessary.

"The condition of the Border will necessarily come into consideration in connection with the continuing or modifying the rights of transit from Canada through the United States, as well as the regulation of imposts, which were temporarily established by the Reciprocity Treaty of the 5th of June, 1864. I desire, however, to be understood while making this statement that the Colonial authorities are not deemed to be intentionally unjust or unfriendly toward the United States; but, on the contrary, there is every reason to expect that, with the approval of the Imperial Government, they will take the necessary measures to prevent new incursions across the border.

" The act passed at the last session for the encouragement of immigration has, as far as was possible, been put into operation.

" It seems to need an amendment which will enable the officers of the Government to prevent the practice of frauds against the immigrants while on their way and on their arrival in the ports, so as to secure them here a free choice of avocations and place of settlement.

"A liberal disposition toward this great National policy is manifested by most of the European States, and ought to be reciprocated on our part by giving the immigrants effective National protection. I regard our immigrants as one of the principal replenishing streams which are appointed by Providence to repair the ravages of internal war, and its wastes of National strength and health.

"All that is necessary is, to secure the flow of that stream in its present fullness, and to that end, the Government must, in every way, make it manifest that it neither needs nor designs to impose involuntary military service upon those who come from other lands to cast their lot in our country.

"The financial affairs of the Government have been successfully administered. During the last year the legislation of the last session of Congress has beneficially affected the revenue, although sufficient time has not yet elapsed to experience the full effect of several of the provisions of the act of Congress imposing increased taxation. The receipts during the year, from all sources, upon the basis of warrants signed by the Secretary of the Treasury, including loans and the balance in the Treasury on the first day of July, 1863, were $1,394,796,007 62, and the aggregate disbursements, upon the same basis, were $1,298,056,101 89, leaving a balance in the Treasury, as shown by warrants, of $96,739,905 73. Deduct from these amounts the amount of the principal of the public debt redeemed, and the amount of issues in substitution therefor, and the actual cash operations of the Treasury were: Receipts, $3,075,646 77; disbursements, $865,734,087 76; which leaves a cash balance in the Treasury of $18,842,558 71. Of the receipts, there were derived from customs, $102,316,152 99; from lands, $588,330 29; from direct taxes, $475,648 96; from internal revenues, $109,741,134 10; from miscellaneous sources, $47,511,448; and from loans applied to actual expenditures, including former balance, $623,443,929 13. There were disbursed for the civil service, $27,505,599 46; for pensions and Indians, $7,517,930 97; for the War Department, $60,791,842 97; for the Navy Department, $85,733,292 79; for interest of the public debts, $53,685,421 69; making an aggregate of $865,234,081 86, and leaving a balance in the Treasury of $18,842,558 71, as before stated

"For the actual receipts and disbursements for the first quarter, and the estimated receipts and disbursements for the

22

three remaining quarters of the current fiscal year, and the general operations of the Treasury in detail, I refer you to the report of the Secretary of the Treasury.

"I concur with him in the opinion, that the proportion of the moneys required to meet the expenses consequent upon the war derived from taxation, should be still further increased; and I earnestly invite your attention to this subject, to the end that there may be such additional legislation as shall be required to meet the just expectations of the Secretary.

"The public debt, on the first day of May last, as appears by the books of the Treasury, amounted to $1,740,690,489 49. Probably, should the war continue for another year, that amount may be increased by not far from five hundred millions. Held, as it is for the most part, by our own people, it has become a substantial branch of national, though private property.

"For obvious reasons, the more nearly this property can be distributed among all the people, the better. To forward general distribution, greater inducements to become owners, might, perhaps, with good effect and without injury, be presented to persons of limited means. With this view, I suggest whether it might not be both expedient and competent for Congress to provide that a limited amount of some future issue of public securities might be held, by any *bond fide* purchaser, exempt from taxation and from seizure for debt, under such restrictions and limitations as might be necessary to guard against abuse of so important a privilege. This would enable prudent persons to set aside a small annuity against a possible day of want.

"Privileges like these would render the possession of such securities, to the amount limited, most desirable to every person of small means who might be able to save enough for the purpose. The great advantage of citizens being creditors as well as debtors, is obvious. Men readily perceive that they cannot be much oppressed by a debt which they owe to themselves.

"The public debt on the first day of July last, although somewhat exceeding the estimate of the Secretary of the Treasury made to Congress at the commencement of last session, falls short of the estimate of that office made in the succeeding December as to its probable amount at the beginning of this year, by the sum of $3,995,079 33. This fact exhibits a satisfactory condition and conduct of the operations of the Treasury.

"The National banking system is proving to be acceptable to capitalists and the people. On the 25th day of November, five hundred and eighty-four National Banks had been organized, a considerable number of which were conversions from State banks. Changes from the State system to the National system are rapidly taking place, and it is hoped that very soon there will be in the United States no banks of issue not authorized by Congress, and no bank-note circulation not secured by the government. That the government and the people will derive general benefit from this change in the banking system of the country can hardly be questioned.

"The National system will create a reliable and permanent influence in support of the national credit, and protect the people against losses in the use of paper money. Whether or not any further legislation is advisable for the suppression of State bank issues, it will be for Congress to determine. It seems quite clear that the Treasury cannot be satisfactorily conducted unless the government can exercise restraining power over the bank-note circulation of the country.

"The Report of the Secretary of War, and the accompanying documents, will detail the campaigns of the armies in the field since the date of the last annual Message, and also the operations of the several administrative bureaus of the War Department during the last year.

"It will also specify the measures deemed essential for the

national defence, and to keep up and supply the requisite
military force.

" The Report of the Secretary of the Navy presents a
comprehensive and satisfactory exhibit of the affairs of that
department and of the naval service.   It is a subject of congratulation and laudable pride to our countrymen, that a
navy of such vast proportions has been organized in so brief
a period and conducted with so much efficiency and success.

" The general exhibits of the Navy, including vessels under
construction, on the first of December, 1864, shows a total
of 671 vessels, carrying 4,610 guns, and 510,396 tons—being
an actual increase during the year over and above all losses
by shipwreck or in battle, of 83 vessels, 167 guns, and 42,427
tons.   The total number at this time in the naval service,
including officers, is about 51,000.   There have been captured
by the Navy during the year, 324 vessels, and the whole number of naval captures since hostilities commenced is 1,379,
of which 267 are steamers.   The gross proceeds arising from
the sale of condemned prize property, thus far reported,
amount to $14,396,250 51.

" A large amount of such proceeds is still under adjudication and yet to be reported.   The total expenditures of the
Navy Department, of every description, including the cost of
the immense squadrons that have been called into existence,
from the 4th of March, 1861, to the 1st of November, 1864,
are $238,647,262 35.   Your favorable consideration is in-
vited to the various recommendations of the Secretary of the
Navy, especially in regard to a navy yard and suitable establishment for the construction and repair of iron vessels, and
the machinery and armature for our ships, to which reference
was made in my last annual message.

" Your attention is also invited to the views expressed in
the report in relation to the legislation of Congress at its last
session in respect to prizes on our inland waters.

" I cordially concur in the recommendation of the Secretary

RE-ELECTED. 341

Last Annual Message.   Post-Office Department.   The Territories.

as to the propriety of creating the new rank of Vice-admiral in our naval service.

" Your attention is invited to the report of the Postmaster-General, for a detailed account of the operations and financial condition of the Post-Office Department. The postal revenues for the year ending June 30, 1864, amounted to $12,438,253 78. and the expenditures to $12,644,786 20; the excess of expenditures over receipts being $206,532 42.

" The views presented by the Postmaster-General on the subject of special grants by the Government in aid of the establishment of new lines of ocean mail steamships, and the policy he recommends for the development of increased commercial intercourse with adjacent and neighboring countries, should receive the careful consideration of Congress.

" It is of noteworthy interest that the steady expansion of population, improvement and governmental institutions over the new and unoccupied portions of our country have scarcely been checked, much less impeded or destroyed by our great civil war, which, at first glance, would seem to have absorbed almost the entire energies of the Nation.

" The organization and admission of the State of Nevada has been completed in conformity with law, and thus our excellent system is firmly established in the mountains which once seemed a barren and uninhabitable waste between the Atlantic States and those which have grown up on the coast of the Pacific Ocean.

" The Territories of the Union are generally in a condition of prosperity and growth. Idaho and Montana, by reason of their great distance and the interruption of communication with them by Indian hostilities, have been only partially organized ; but it is understood that those difficulties are about to disappear, which will permit their governments, like those of the others, to go into speedy and full operation.

"As intimately connected with and promotive of this material growth of the Nation, I ask the attention of Congress to

342   LIFE OF ABRAHAM LINCOLN.

Annual Message.   Public Lands.   Pacific Railways and Telegraph.

the valuable information and important recommendation relating to the public lands, Indian affairs, the Pacific Railroad, and mineral discoveries contained in the report of the Secretary of the Interior, which is herewith transmitted, and which report also embraces the subjects of the patents, pensions, and other topics of public interest pertaining to his Department.

"The quantity of public land disposed of during the five quarters ending on the 30th of September last, was 4,221,342 acres, of which 1,538,614 acres were entered under the Homestead law. The remainder was located with military land warrants, agricultural script certified to States for railroads, and sold for cash. The cash received from sales and location fees was $1,019,446. The income from sales during the fiscal year ending June 30, 1864, was $678,007 21, against $136,077 95, received during the preceding year. The aggregate number of acres surveyed during the year has been equal to the quantity disposed of, and there are open to settlement about 133,000,000 acres of surveyed land.

"The great enterprise of connecting the Atlantic with the Pacific States by railways and telegraph lines has been entered upon with a vigor that gives assurance of success, notwithstanding the embarrassments arising from the prevailing high prices of materials and labor. The route of the main line of the road has been definitely located for one hundred miles westward from the initial point at Omaha City, Nebraska, and a preliminary location of the Pacific Railroad of California has been made from Sacramento eastward to the great bend of Mucker river, in Nevada. Numerous discoveries of gold, silver and cinnabar mines have been added to the many heretofore known, and the country occupied by the Sierra Nevada and Rocky Mountains and the subordinate ranges now teems with enterprising labor which is richly remunerative. It is believed that the products of the mines of precious metals in that region have, during the year reached, if not exceeded, $100,000,000 in value.

" It was recommended in my last annual message, that our Indian system be remoddled.   Congress, at its last session, acting upon the recommendation, did provide for reorganizing the system in California, and it is believed that under the present organization the management of the Indians there will be attended with reasonable success.   Much yet remains to be done to provide for the proper government of the Indians in other parts of the country, to render it secure for the advancing settler and to provide for the welfare of the Indian. The Secretary reiterates his recommendations, and to them the attention of Congress is invited.

" The liberal provisions made by Congress for paying pensions to invalid soldiers and sailors of the Republic, and to the widows, orphans and dependent mothers of those who have fallen in battle, or died of disease contracted, or of wounds received in the service of their country, have been diligently administered.

" There have been added to the pension rolls during the year ending the thirtieth day of June last, the names of 16,770 invalid soldiers, and of 271 disabled seamen, making the present number of army invalid pensioners 22,767, and of navy invalid pensioners 712.   Of widows, orphans and mothers, 22,198 have been placed on the army pension rolls, and 248 on the navy rolls.

" The present number of Army pensioners of this class is 25,433, and of Navy pensioners 793.   At the beginning of the year, the number of revolutionary pensioners was 1,430. Only twelve of them were soldiers, of whom seven have since died.   The remainder are those who, under the law, receive pensions because of relationship to revolutionary soldiers.

" During the year ending the thirtieth of June, 1864, $4,504,616 92 have been paid to pensioners of all classes.

" I cheerfully commend to your continued patronage the

benevolent institutions of the District of Columbia, which have hitherto been established or fostered by Congress, and respectfully refer for information concerning them, and in relation to the Washington Aqueduct, the Capitol, and other matters of local interest to the report of the Secretary.

"The Agricultural Department, under the supervision of its present energetic and faithful head, is rapidly commending itself to the great and vital interest it was intended to advance. It is peculiarly the People's Department, in which they feel more directly concerned than in any other, I commend it to the continued attention and fostering care of Congress.

"The war continues. Since the last annual message, all the important lines and positions then occupied by our forces have been maintained, and our armies have steadily advanced, thus liberating the regions left in the rear, so that Missouri, Kentucky, Tennessee, and parts of other States have again produced reasonably fair crops.

"The most remarkable feature in the military operations of the year, is General Sherman's attempted march of three hundred miles directly through insurgent regions. It tends to show a great increase of our relative strength, that our General-in-chief should feel able to confront and hold in check every active force of the enemy, and yet to detach a well-appointed, large army to move on such an expedition. The result not being yet known, conjecture in regard to it is not here indulged.

"Important movements have also occurred during the year to the effect of moulding society for ductility in the Union. Although short of complete success, it is much in the right direction that twelve thousand citizens in each of the States of Arkansas and Louisiana, have organized loyal State governments with free Constitutions, and are earnestly struggling to maintain and administer them.

"The movement in the same direction, more extensive,

though less definite, in Missouri, Kentucky, and Tennessee, should not be overlooked.

"But Maryland presents the example of complete success. Maryland is secure to liberty and union for all the future. The genius of rebellion will no more claim Maryland. Like another foul spirit, being driven out, it may seek to tear her but it will rule her no more.

"At the last Session of Congress, a proposed amendment of the Constitution abolishing slavery throughout the United States, passed the Senate, but failed, for lack of the requisite two-thirds vote in the House of Representatives. Although the present is the same Congress, and nearly the same members, and without question on the patriotism of those who stood in opposition, I venture to recommend the consideration and passage of the measure at the present session.

"Of course the abstract question is not changed, but an intervening election shows almost certainly that the next Congress will pass the measure, if this does not. Hence there is only a question of time as to when the proposed amendment will go to the States for their action ; and as it is to go at all events, may we not agree that the sooner the better? It is not claimed that the election has imposed a duty on members to change their views or their votes any further than as an additional element to be considered. Their judgment may be affected by it.

"It is the voice of the people, now for the first time heard upon the question. In a great national crisis like ours, unanimity of action among those seeking a common end is very desirable, almost indispensable, and yet an approach to such unanimity is attainable, only as some deference shall be paid to the will of the majority, simply because it is the will of the majority.

"In this case, the common end is the maintenance of the Union, and among the means to secure that end, such will, through the election, is most clearly declared in favor of such

Constitutional Amendment. The most reliable indication of public purpose in this country is derived through our popular election. Judging by the recent canvass and its result, the purpose of the people within the loyal States to maintain the integrity of the Union was never more firm nor more nearly unanimous than now.

" The extraordinary calmness and good order with which the millions of voters met and mingled at the polls, give strong assurance of this. Not only those who supported the ' Union Ticket,' so called, but a great majority of the opposing party also, may be fairly claimed to entertain and to be actuated by the same purpose. It is an unanswerable argument to this effect that no candidate to any office whatever, high or low, has ventured to seek votes on the avowal that he was for giving up the Union.

" There has been much impugning of motives, and heated controversy as to the proper means and best mode of advancing the Union cause, but in the distinct issue of Union or no Union, the politicians have shown their distinctive knowledge that there is no diversity among the people. In affording the people a fair opportunity of showing one to another and to the world this firmness and unanimity of purpose, the election has been of vast value to the National cause.

" The election has exhibited another fact not less valuable to be known in the fact that we do not approach exhaustion in the most important branch of the national resources, that of living men. While it is melancholy to reflect that the war has filled so many graves, and carried mourning to so many hearts, it is some relief to know that, compared with the surviving, the fallen have been so few. While corps, and divisions, and brigades, and regiments have formed, and fought and dwindled, and gone out of existence, a great majority of the men who composed them are still living. The same is true of the naval service. The election returns prove this. So many votes could not else be found. The States regularly holding elections, both now and four years ago, to wit: California, Connecticut, Delaware, Illinois, Indiana, Iowa, Kentucky, Maine, Maryland, Massachusetts, Michigan, Minnesota, Missouri, New Hampshire, New Jersey, New York, Ohio, Oregon, Pennsylvania, Rhode Island, Vermont, West Virginia, and Wisconsin, cast 3,982,011 votes now, against 3,870,222 then, to which are to be added 33,762 cast now in the new States of Kansas and Nevada, which States did not vote in 1860; thus swelling the aggregate to 4,075,773, and the net increase during the three years and a half of war to 145,751.

"To this, again, should be added the number of all soldiers in the field from Massachusetts, Rhode Island, New Jersey, Delaware, Indiana, Illinois, and California, who, by the laws of those States, could not vote away from their homes, and which number cannot be less than ninety thousand. Nor yet is this all. The number in organized territories is triple now what it was four years ago, while thousands, white and black, join us as the National army forces back the insurgent lines. So much is shown, affirmatively and negatively, by the election.

"It is not natural to inquire how the increase has been produced, or to show that it would have been greater but for the war, which is partially true; the important fact remaining demonstrated, that we have more men now than we had when the war began; that we are not exhausted, nor in process of exhaustion; that we are gaining strength, and may, if need be, maintain the contest indefinitely. This as to men.

"National resources are now more complete and abundant than ever; the National resources, then, are unexhausted, and, as we believe, inexhaustible. The public purpose to reëstablish and maintain the National authority is unchanged, and, as we believe, unchangeable. The manner of continuing the effort remains to choose. On careful consideration of all the evidence accessible, it seems to me that no attempts at negotiation with the insurgent leader could result in any good.

" He would accept of nothing short of the severance of the Union. His declarations to this effect are explicit and oft-repeated. He does not attempt to deceive us. He affords us no excuse to deceive ourselves. We cannot voluntarily yield it. Between him and us the issue is distinct, simple, and inflexible. It is an issue which can only be tried by war, and decided by victory.

" If we yield, we are beaten; if the Southern people fail him, he is beaten—either way, it would be the victory and defeat following war What is true, however, of him who heads the insurgent cause, is not necessarily true of those who follow. Although he cannot reaccept the Union, they can. Some of them, we know, already desire peace and reunion. The number of such may increase.

" They can at any moment have peace simply by laying down their arms and submitting to the National authority under the Constitution. After so much, the Government could not, if it would, maintain war against them. The loyal people would not sustain, or allow it, If questions should remain, we would adjust them by the peaceful means of legislation, conference, courts, and votes.

" Operating only in constitutional and lawful channels, some certain and other possible questions are and would be beyond the Executive power to adjust; for instance, the admission of members into Congress, and whatever might require the appropriation of money.

" The Executive power itself would be really diminished by the cessation of actual war. Pardons and remissions of forfeiture, however, would still be within Executive control. In what spirit and temper this control would be exercised, can be fairly judged of by the past. A year ago general pardon and amnesty upon specified terms were offered to all except certain designated classes, and it was at this same time made known that the excepted classes were still within contemplation of special clemency.

"During the year many availed themselves of the general provision, and many more would, only that the sign of bad faith in some led to such precautionary measures as rendered the practical power less easy and certain. During the same time, also, special pardons have been granted to individuals of excepted classes, and no voluntary individual application has been denied.

"Thus, practically, the door has been for a full year open to all, except such as were not in condition to make free choice; that is, such as were in custody or under constraint. It is still so open to all; but the time may come, probably will come, when public duty shall demand that it be closed, and that, in lieu, more vigorous measures than heretofore shall be adopted.

"In presenting the abandonment of armed resistance to the National authority, on the part of the insurgents, as the only indispensable condition to ending the war on the part of the Government, I retract nothing heretofore said as to slavery. I repeat the declaration made a year ago, that while I remain in my present position I shall not attempt to retract or modify the Emancipation Proclamation, nor shall I return to slavery any person who is free by the terms of that proclamation or by any of the acts of Congress.

"If the people should, by whatever mode, or means, make it an Executive duty to re-enslave such persons, another, and not I, must be their instrument to perform it.

"In stating a single condition of peace, I mean simply to say that the war will cease on the part of the Government whenever it shall have ceased on the part of those who began it.

"ABRAHAM LINCOLN."

850   LIFE OF ABRAHAM LINCOLN.

Speech at a Serenade.   Reply to a Presentation Address.

CHAPTER XXIII.

TIGHTENING THE LINES.

Speech at a Serenade—Reply to a Presentation Address—Peace Rumors—Rebel Commissioners—Instructions to Secretary Seward—The Conference in Hampton Roads—Result—Extra Session of the Senate—Military Situation—Sherman—Charleston—Columbia—Wilmington—Fort Fisher—Sheridan—Grant—Rebel Congress—Second Inauguration—Inaugural—English Comment—Proclamation to Deserters.

As illustrative of the genial, pleasant manner of the President, take the following, in response to a serenade, December 6th, 1864:

"FRIENDS AND FELLOW-CITIZENS:—I believe I shall never be old enough to speak without embarrassment when I have nothing to talk about. I have no good news to tell you, and yet I have no bad news to tell. We have talked of elections until there is nothing more to say about them. The most interesting news we now have is from Sherman. We all know where he went in at, but I can't tell where he will come out at. I will now close by proposing three cheers for General Sherman and his army."

On the 24th of January, 1865, having been made the recipient of a beautiful vase of skeleton leaves, gathered from the battle-field of Gettysburg, which had been subscribed for at the great Sanitary Fair, held in Philadelphia during the previous summer, in reply to the warmly sympathetic and appreciative address of the Chairman of the Committee entrusted with the presentation, he said:

"REVEREND SIR, AND LADIES AND GENTLEMEN:—I accept, with emotions of profoundest gratitude, the beautiful gift you have been pleased to present to me. You will, of course, expect that I acknowledge it. So much has been said about Gettysburg, and so well said, that for me to attempt to say more may, perhaps, only serve to weaken the force of that which has already been said.

"A most graceful and eloquent tribute was paid to the patriotism and self-denying labors of the American ladies, on the occasion of the consecration of the National Cemetery at Gettysburg, by our illustrious friend, Edward Everett, now, alas! departed from earth. His life was a truly great one, and, I think, the greatest part of it was that which crowned its closing years.

"I wish you to read, if you have not already done so, the glowing, and eloquent, and truthful words which he then spoke of the women of America. Truly the services they have rendered to the defenders of our country in this perilous time, and are yet rendering, can never be estimated as they ought to be.

"For your kind wishes to me, personally, I beg leave to render you, likewise, my sincerest thanks. I assure you they are reciprocated. And now, gentlemen and ladies, may God bless you all."

With the opening of the new year, the air—as often before—was filled with rumors that the insurgents were anxious to negotiate for peace.

Some there were, even among Mr. Lincoln's friends and supporters, who were apprehensive that his " To whom it may concern" announcement of the previous year, was somewhat too curt and blunt. Without claiming to have as good an opportunity as the President for judging in the premises, they could not yet divest themselves of the idea that something definite and tangible might result from an interview with representatives from rebeldom; if nothing more, at least a distinct understanding that no peace could be attained, without separation, unless it were conquered.

Thoroughly familiar with the designs and purposes of the leading rebels as Mr. Lincoln was, and well aware that any such attempt must prove futile, he was nevertheless determined that no valid ground for censure should be afforded by himself, in case a favorable opening presented itself.

Accordingly, when he learned—as he did during the last week of January, from his friend, Francis P. Blair, who had visited Richmond, with the President's permission—that the managers there were desirous of sending certain persons as commissioners to learn from the United States Government upon what terms an adjustment of difficulties could be made, and that A. H. Stephens, of Georgia, R. M. T. Hunter, of Virginia, and J. A. Campbell, of Alabama, had been sent through the enemy's lines by Davis for the purpose of a conference upon the subject, Mr. Lincoln, not choosing that the commissioners should visit Washington, entrusted the matter to Secretary Seward, furnishing him with the following letter of instructions, dated Executive Mansion, Washington, January 31st, 1865 :

"HON. WILLIAM H. SEWARD, Secretary of State :—You will proceed to Fortress Monroe, Virginia, there to meet and informally confer with Messrs. Stephens, Hunter, and Campbell, on the basis of my letter to F. P. Blair, Esq., of January 18, 1865, a copy of which you have.

"You will make known to them that three things are indispensable, to wit :

"1. The restoration of national authority throughout all the States.

"2. No receding by the Executive of the United States, on the slavery question, from the position assumed thereon in the late annual message to Congress, and in preceding documents.

"3. No cessation of hostilities short of an end of the war and the disbanding of all forces hostile to the Government.

" You will inform them that all propositions of theirs not inconsistent with the above, will be considered and passed upon in a spirit of sincere liberality.

" You will hear all they may choose to say, and report it to me.

" You will not assume to definitely consummate any thing
" Yours truly,   A. LINCOLN."

On the 2d of February, the President himself left for the point designated, and on the morning of the 3d, attended by Mr. Seward, received Messrs. Stephens, Hunter, and Campbell, on board a United States steamer anchored in Hampton Roads.

The conference that ensued was altogether informal. There was no attendance of Secretaries, clerks, or witnesses. Nothing was written or read. The conversation, although earnest and free, was calm and courteous and kind, on both sides. The Richmond party approached the discussion rather indirectly, and at no time did they make categorical demands or tender formal stipulations or absolute refusals; nevertheless, during the conference, which lasted four hours, the several points at issue between the Government and the insurgents were distinctly raised and discussed fully, intelligently, and in an amicable spirit. What the insurgent party seemed chiefly to favor was a postponement of the question of separation, upon which the war was waged, and a mutual direction of the efforts of the Government as well as those of the insurgents, to some extraneous policy or scheme for a season, during which passions might be expected to subside, and the armies be reduced, and trade and intercourse between the people of both sections be resumed.

It was suggested by them that through such postponement we might have immediate peace, with some, not very certain, prospect of an ultimate satisfactory adjustment of politica. relations between the Government and the States, section or

23

854   LIFE OF ABRAHAM LINCOLN.

Conference in Hampton Roads.   The Anti-Slavery Policy.   Result.

people engaged in conflict with it. The suggestion, though deliberately considered, was nevertheless regarded by the President as one of armistice or truce, and he announced that we could agree to no cessation or suspension of hostilities except on the basis of the disbandonment of the insurgent forces, and the restoration of the national authority throughout all the States in the Union collaterally, and in subordination to the proposition which was thus announced.

The anti-slavery policy of the United States was reviewed in all its bearings, and the President announced that he must not be expected to depart from the positions he had heretofore assumed in his proclamation of emancipation and other documents, as these positions were reiterated in his annual message.

It was further declared by the President that the complete restoration of the national authority everywhere was an indispensable condition of any assent on our part to whatever form of peace might be proposed. The President assured the other party that while he must adhere to these positions he would be prepared, so far as power was lodged with the Executive, to exercise liberality. Its power, however, is limited by the Constitution, and when peace should be made Congress must necessarily act in regard to appropriations of money and to the admission of representatives from the insurrectionary States.

The Richmond party were then informed that Congress had, on the 31st of January, adopted, by a constitutional majority, a joint resolution submitting to the several States the proposition to abolish slavery throughout the Union, and that there was every reason to expect that it would soon be accepted by three-fourths of the States, so as to become a part of the national organic law.

The conference came to an end by mutual acquiescence, without producing an agreement of views upon the several matters discussed, or any of them.

On the following morning the President and Secretary returned to Washington, and shortly afterward, in compliance with a resolution to that effect, Congress was informed in detail of all that had led to the interview and its issue.

Thus was spiked the last gun bearing upon the terms on which the rebels would consent to peace. Whatever might have been the impression previously it was then well understood that to the armies in the field then converging toward Richmond, and not to the Executive of the nation, resort was to be had for peace upon any basis which loyal men would indorse.

On the 17th of February, in accordance with the general custom at the expiration of a Presidential term, the Senate was convened in active session by the following proclamation:

" WHEREAS, objects of interest to the United States require that the Senate should be convened at twelve o'clock on the fourth of March next, to receive and act upon such communications as may be made to it on the part of the Executive—

" Now, therefore, I, Abraham Lincoln, President of the United States, have considered it to be my duty to issue this my proclamation, declaring that an extraordinary occasion requires the Senate of the United States to convene for the transaction of business, at the Capitol, in the city of Washington, on the fourth day of March next, at twelve o'clock at noon on that day, of which all who shall at that time be entitled to act as members of that body are hereby required to take notice.

" Given under my hand and the seal of the United States, at Washington, the 17th day of February, in the year of our Lord one thousand eight hundred and sixty-five, and of the Independence of the United States of America, the eighty ninth.

" By the President: ABRAHAM LINCOLN.
" WILLIAM H. SEWARD, Secretary of State."

At this time, the military situation was very interesting to every friend of the Union, whatever might have been the feelings it created among those who had so long been in arms against the Government.

Sherman had "come out" at Savannah, capturing it and presenting it as a Christmas gift to the nation, after an extraordinary march from Atlanta—which he had deprived of all power for harm—directly through the heart of Georgia ; a march as to which the rebel journalists made ludicrous efforts to be oracular in advance, predicting all manner of mishaps from the Georgia militia and the various "lions" in his way.

Thomas had fallen back leisurely to Nashville, forcing Hood, his antagonist, who had supplanted Johnston on account of his fighting qualities, to the loss of almost his entire army in a sanguinary battle which occurred near that city, Thomas being the attacking party. With the remnants of his discomfited force, the fighting general had fallen back, where was not definitely known, but evidently to some secure support.

Sherman having recuperated his army, had left Savannah and marched into South Carolina, where, according to the beforenamed veracious chroniclers, he was to flounder in bogs and quagmires, at the mercy of his valorous foes. He floundered on, truly—floundered, so as to flank Charleston, that nursery and hot-bed of treason, which had so long insulted the land—and compel its hurried evacuation ; floundered, so as to capture and occupy Columbia, the capital of the Palmetto State ; floundered, so as to threaten Raleigh, the capital of North Carolina ; and at the time of which we write, had at last floundered to Goldsborough, where he had effected a connection with another column, which had pierced to that point after the capture of Wilmington, North Carolina, the pet port of disinterested blockade-runners—a capture rendered certain by the storming of Fort Fisher, commanding the entrance to its harbor, in connection with which one Major-General was made and another unmade—whether the latter result was brought about with or without the coöperation of the commander of the naval part of the expedition, it boots not here to inquire.

Whither Sherman would flounder next became to all rebeldom a question of the very deepest interest. Davis having been compelled by his Congress to assign the discarded Johnston to a command, and Lee to the command of all the rebel armies, Johnston was dispatched to head Sherman off, should he be insane enough to attempt to move any nearer Richmond—a species of insanity to which, it must be confessed, he had shown a marked tendency.

Sheridan, too, having chased Early up and out of the Shenandoah Valley—that Early the one of whom his troops were wont to remark, that his principal business seemed to be "to trade Confederate cannon for Yankee whiskey"—had been raiding around Richmond in whatsoever direction he listed, severing communications, gobbling up supplies, and creating a general consternation.

And still the bull-dog's teeth were firmly fastened in his victim. Not twistings, nor squirmings, nor strugglings, nor counterbites could do more than to defer—and that but for a short time—the inevitable.

The rebel congress, at the very last moment of its last session, had squeezed through a bill for arming the slaves, and Davis had grimly wished them a safe and pleasant journey to their respective homes. It was too late, both for the slaves and the homes.

Meantime, on Saturday, March 4th—a day which opened unpropitiously, so far as the elements were concerned, but which redeemed itself before noontide, becoming bright and cheerful—at the hour appointed, the oath of office was for the second time administered to Mr. Lincoln—not, however, by the same Chief Justice, for Roger B. Taney slept with his fathers, and in his place stood Salmon P. Chase—after which, on a staging erected at the eastern portico of the Capitol, he read in a clear, distinct voice, his second inaugural, occupying not more than ten minutes in the act:

" FELLOW-COUNTRYMEN :—At this second appearing to take the oath of the Presidential office, there is less occasion for an extended address than there was at the first. Then a statement somewhat in detail of a course to be pursued seemed very fitting and proper. Now, at the expiration of four years, during which public declarations have constantly been called forth on every point and phase of the great contest which still absorbs the attention and engrosses the energies of the nation, little that is new could be presented.

" The progress of our arms, upon which all else chiefly depends, is as well known to the public as to myself, and it is, I trust, reasonably satisfactory and encouraging to all. With high hope for the future, no prediction in regard to it is ventured. On the occasion corresponding to this four years ago, all thoughts were anxiously directed to an impending civil war. All dreaded it, all sought to avoid it. While the inaugural address was being delivered from this place, devoted altogether to saving the Union without war, insurgent agents were in the city seeking to destroy it, without war; seeking to dissolve the Union and divide the effects by negotiation.

" Both parties deprecated war, but one of them would make war rather than let the nation survive, and the other would accept war rather than let it perish, and the war came.

" One-eighth of the whole population were colored slaves, not distributed generally over the Union, but located in the southern part of it. These slaves constituted a peculiar and powerful interest. All knew that this interest was somehow the cause of the war. To strengthen, perpetuate and extend this interest was the object for which the insurgents would rend the Union by war, while the Government claimed no right to do more than to restrict the territorial enlargement of it. Neither party expected the magnitude or the duration which it has already attained. Neither anticipated that the cause of the conflict might cease, even before the conflict itself should cease. Each looked for an easier triumph and a result less fundamental and astounding. Both read the same Bible and pray to the same God, and each invokes his aid against the other. It may seem strange that any man should dare to ask a just God's assistance in wringing his bread from the sweat of other men's faces. But let us judge not, that we be not judged.

"The prayer of both should not be answered. That of neither has been answered fully. The Almighty has his own purposes. 'Woe unto the world because of offences, for it must needs be that offences come, but woe to that man by whom the offence cometh.' If we shall suppose that American slavery is one of these offences which, in the providence of God, must needs come, but which, having continued through his appointed time, he now wills to remove, and that he gives to both North and South this terrible war as the woe due to those by whom the offence came, shall we discern therein any departure from those Divine attributes which the believers in a living God always ascribe to him?

"Fondly do we hope, fervently do we pray that this mighty scourge of war may speedily pass away. Yet, if God wills that it continue until all the wealth piled by the bondman's two hundred and fifty years of unrequited toil shall be sunk and until every drop of blood drawn by the lash shall be paid by another drawn with the sword, as was said three thousand years ago, so still it must be said, that the judgments of the Lord are true and righteous altogether.

"With malice towards none, with charity for all, with firmness in the right, as God gives us to see the right, let us strive on to finish the work we are in, to bind up the nation's wounds, to care for him who shall have borne the battle, and for his widow and his orphans, to do all which may achieve and cherish a just and lasting peace among ourselves and with all nations."

Of this address—which was of course made the subject for the coarsest comments of those who enjoyed nought so much as aiding the pack that bounded Mr. Lincoln while living— an English journal, second to none in ability and judgment, and leader of the better class of thinkers in that country, thus spoke :

" It is the most remarkable thing of the sort, ever pro- nounced by any President of the United States from the first day until now.   Its Alpha and its Omega is *Almighty God*, the God of justice and the Father of mercies, who is working out the purposes of his love.   It is invested with a dignity and pathos, which lift it high above every thing of the kind, whether in the Old World or the New.   The whole thing puts us in mind of the best men of the English Common- wealth ; there is, in fact, much of the old prophet about it."

On the 16th of March, in accordance with an Act of Con- gress, grace was extended to deserters by the following pro- clamation :

" WHEREAS, The twenty-first section of the act of Congress, approved on the 3d instant, entitled ' an act to amend the several acts heretofore passed to provide for the enrolling and calling out of the National forces, and for other purposes,' re- quires that, in addition to the other lawful penalties of the crime of desertion from the military or naval service, ' all persons who have deserted the military or naval service of the United States, who shall not return to the said service or report themselves to a provost-marshal within sixty days after the proclamation hereinafter mentioned, shall be deemed and taken to have voluntarily relinquished and forfeited their rights to become citizens; and such deserters shall be forever incapable of holding any office of trust or profit under the United States, or of exercising any rights of citizens thereof; and all persons who shall hereafter desert the military or naval service, and all persons who, being duly enrolled, shall depart the jurisdiction of the district in which he is enrolled, or go beyond the limits of the United States, with the intent to avoid any draft into the military or naval service duly ordered, shall be liable to the penalties of this section. And the President is hereby authorized and required forthwith, on the passage of this act, to issue his proclamation setting forth the provisions of this section, in which proclamation the President is requested to notify all deserters returning within sixty days, as aforesaid, that they shall be pardoned on condition of returning to their regiments and companies, or to such other organizations as they may be assigned to, unless they shall have served for a period of time, equal to their original term of enlistment'—

"Now, therefore, I, Abraham Lincoln, President of the United States, do issue this my proclamation, as required by said act, ordering and requiring all deserters to return to their proper posts, and I do hereby notify them that all deserters who shall within sixty days from the date of this proclamation, viz.: on or before the tenth day of May, 1865, return to service, or report themselves to a provost-marshal, shall be pardoned, on condition that they return to their regiments and companies or such other organizations as they may be assigned to, and serve the remainder of their original terms of enlistment, and, in addition thereto, a period equal to the time lost by desertion.

"In testimony whereof, I have hereunto set my hand and caused the seal of the United States to be affixed.

"Done at the city of Washington, this eleventh day of March, in the year of our Lord one thousand eight hundred and sixty-five, and of the Independence of the United States the eighty-ninth.

"By the President: ABRAHAM LINCOLN.

"W. H. SEWARD, Secretary of State."

CHAPTER XXIV.

IN RICHMOND

President Visits City Point—Lee's Failure—Grant's Movement—Abraham Lincoln in Richmond—Lee's Surrender—President's Impromptu Speech—Speech on Reconstruction—Proclamation Closing Certain Ports—Proclamation Relative to Maritime Rights—Supplementary Proclamation—Orders from the War Department—The Traitor President.

ON the afternoon of the 23d of March, 1865, the President, accompanied by Mrs. Lincoln, his youngest son, and a few invited guests, left Washington for an excursion to City Point. The trip was taken under advice of his medical attendant, his health having become somewhat impaired by his unremitting attention to the pressing duties of his office.

A desperate attempt had been made by Lee to break through the lines surrounding him. Assaulting our right centre, he had been repulsed with a severe loss.

Shortly after, Grant determined that the moment had arrived for his advance. A movement was ordered along the entire line—Petersburg fell—Richmond was abandoned in hot haste—and Lee's routed army "driven to the wall."

During the progress of the movement, the President forwarded, from time to time, the particulars—pressed on to the evacuated Capital—entered it, conspicuous amid the sweeping mass of men, women, and children, black, white, and yellow, running, shouting, dancing, swinging their caps, bonnets, and handkerchiefs—passed on to the deserted mansion of the rebel chief, cheer upon cheer going up from the excited multitude—there held a levee—left the same evening for City Point—and soon afterward returned to Washington.

Lee, hemmed in on every side, soon after surrendered; the terms of capitulation, which were dictated by the magnanimous President, and dated Appomattox Court House, April ninth, 1865, being as follows:

"GENERAL ROBERT E. LEE, ARMY C. S. :—In accordance with the substance of my letter to you of the 8th inst., I propose to receive the surrender of the army of Northern Virginia on the following terms, to wit: Rolls of all the officers and men to be made in duplicate, one copy to be given to an officer designated by me, the other to be retained by such officer or officers as you may designate, the officers to give their individual paroles not to take up arms against the Government of the United States until properly exchanged, and each company or regimental commander to sign a like parole for the men of their commands. The arms, artillery, and public property to be parked and stacked, and turned over to the officers appointed by me to receive them. This will not embrace the side arms of the officers, nor their private horses or baggage. This done, each officer and man will be allowed to return to their homes, not to be disturbed by United States authority so long as they observe their parole and the laws in force where they may reside.

"Very respectfully,

"U. S. GRANT, Lieutenant-General."

Johnston was next in order; and toward him Sherman was in motion.

The night following the President's arrival in Washington, the workmen of the Navy-yard formed in procession, marched to the White House, in front of which thousands were assembled, bands playing, and the entire throng alive with excitement.

Repeated calls having been made for him, he appeared at

the window, on the entrance door, calm amid the tumult, and was greeted with cheers and waving of hats.

Comparative silence having been secured, he said:

" MY FRIENDS :—I am very greatly rejoiced that an occasion has occurred so pleasurable that the people can't restrain themselves. I suppose that arrangements are being made for some sort of formal demonstration—perhaps this evening or to-morrow night. If there should be such a demonstration, I, of course, will have to respond to it; and I will have nothing to say if you dribble it out of me.

" I see you have a band. I propose now closing up by requesting you to play a certain piece of music, or a tune— I thought 'Dixie' one of the best tunes I ever heard.

" I had heard that our adversaries over the way had attempted to appropriate it. I insisted yesterday we had fairly captured it ! I presented the question to the Attorney General, and he gave it as his opinion that it is our lawful prize. I ask the band to give us a good turn upon it."

The band accordingly played " Dixie," with extraordinary vigor, when " three cheers and a tiger" were given, followed by the tune of " Yankee Doodle." The President then proposed three rousing cheers for Grant and all under his command—and next, three cheers for the Navy and all its forces.

The President then retired, amid cheers, the tune of " Hail Columbia," and the firing of cannon.

On the night of the eleventh of April, the Executive Departments, including the President's House, as also many places of business and private residences, were illuminated, and adorned with transparencies and national flags ; bon-fires blazed in various parts of the city ; and rockets were fired.

In response to the unanimous call of the thousands of both sexes who surrounded the Executive Mansion, Mr. Lincoln appeared at an upper window, and when the cheering with which he was greeted had subsided, spoke as follows in his last public speech :

"FELLOW-CITIZENS :—We meet this evening, not in sorrow, but in gladness of heart. The evacuation of Petersburg and Richmond, and the surrender of the principal insurgent army, give hope of a righteous and speedy peace, whose joyous expression cannot be restrained.

"In the midst of this, however, He, from whom all blessings flow, must not be forgotten. A call for a National Thanksgiving is being prepared, and will be duly promulgated.

"Nor must those, whose harder part gives us the cause of rejoicing, be overlooked—and their honors must not be parcelled out. With others I myself was near the front, and had the high pleasure of transmitting much of the good news to you, but no part of the honor, or praise, or execution, is mine. To General Grant, his skilful officers and brave men, all belongs. The gallant Navy stood ready, but was not in reach to take an active part. By these recent successes the reinauguration of the national authority, and the reconstruction, which has had a large share of thought from the first, is pressed much more closely upon our attention.

"It is fraught with great difficulty. Unlike the case of a war between independent nations, there is no authorized organ for us to treat with. No one man has authority to give up the rebellion for any other man. We simply must begin with and mould from disorganized and discordant elements. Nor is it a small additional embarrassment, that we, the loyal people, differ amongst ourselves as to the mode, manner, and measure of reconstruction.

"As a general rule, I abstain from reading the reports of attacks upon myself, wishing not to be provoked by that to which I cannot properly offer an answer; for, spite of this precaution, however, it comes to my knowledge that I am much censured from some supposed agency in setting up and seeking to sustain the new State Government of Louisiana. In this I have done just so much and no more than the public knows. In the annual Message of December, 1863, and the accompanying Proclamation, I presented a plan of reconstruction, as the phrase goes, which I promised, if adopted by any State, should be acceptable to and sustained by the Executive Government of the nation.

"I distinctly stated that this was not the only plan which might possibly be acceptable; and I also distinctly protested that the Executive claimed no right to say when or whether members should be admitted to seats in Congress from such States. This plan was in advance submitted to the then Cabinet, and as distinctly approved by every member of it.

"One of them suggested that I should then, and in that connection, apply the Emancipation Proclamation to the theretofore excepted parts of Virginia and Louisiana; that I should drop the suggestion about apprenticeship for freed people; and that I should omit the protest against my own power in regard to the admission of members of Congress; but even he approved every part and parcel of the plan which has since been employed or touched by the action of Louisiana. The new Constitution of Louisiana, declaring emancipation for the whole State, particularly applies the proclamation to the part previously excepted. It does not adopt apprenticeship for freed people, and it is silent—as it could not well be otherwise—about the admission of members to Congress; so that, as it applies to Louisiana, every member of the Cabinet fully approved the plan.

"The message went to Congress, and I received many commendations of the plan, written and verbal, and not a single objection to it by any professed emancipationist came to my knowledge until after the news reached Washington that the people of Louisiana had begun to move in accordance with it From about July, 1862, I had corresponded with different persons supposed to be interested in seeking a reconstruction of a State Government for Louisiana. When the message of 1863, with the plan before mentioned, reached New Orleans, and General Banks wrote me that he was confident the people, with his military coöperation, would reconstruct substantially on that plan, I wrote him and some of them to try it. They tried it, and the result is known.

" Such only has been my agency in getting up the Louisiana Government. As to sustaining it, my promise is out, as before stated; but, as bad promises are better broken than kept, I shall treat this as a bad promise, and break it whenever I shall be convinced that keeping it is adverse to the public interest. But I have not yet been so convinced.

" I have been shown a letter on this subject, supposed to be an able one, in which the writer expresses regret that my mind has not seemed to be definitely fixed on the question whether the seceded States, so called, are in the Union or out of it. It would, perhaps, add astonishment to his regret were he to learn that since I have found professed Union men endeavoring to make that a question, I have purposely forborne any public expression upon it, as it appears to me that question has not been, nor yet is, a practically material one, and that any discussion of it while it thus remains practically material could have no effect other than the mischievous one of dividing our friends.

"As yet, whatever it may become hereafter, that question is bad, as the basis of a controversy, and good for nothing at all, a merely pernicious abstraction. We all agree that the seceded States, so-called, are out of their proper practical relation with the Union, and that the sole object of the Government, civil and military, in regard to those States, is to again get them into that proper practical relation. I believe it is not only possible, but in fact easier to do this without deciding or even considering whether these States have ever been out of the Union, than with it; finding themselves safely

368   LIFE OF ABRAHAM LINCOLN.

Last Public Speech.   The Louisiana Government.   Difficulties of Reconstruction.

at home, it would be utterly immaterial whether they had ever been abroad.

" Let us all join in doing the acts necessary to restoring the proper practical relations between these States and the Union, and each forever after, innocently indulge his own opinion whether in doing the acts he brought the States from without into the Union, or only gave them proper assistance, they never having been out of it.

" The amount of constituency, so to speak, on which the new Louisiana Government rests, would be more satisfactory to all if it contained 50,000, 30,000, or even 20,000, instead of only about 12,000, as it does.

" It is also unsatisfactory to some that the elective franchise is not given to the colored men. I would myself prefer that it were conferred on the very intelligent, and on those who serve our cause as soldiers. Still the question is not whether the Louisiana Government, as it stands, is quite all that is desirable. The question is, will it be wiser to take it as it is, and help to improve it, or to reject and disperse it ? Can Louisiana be brought into proper practical relation with the Union sooner by sustaining or by discarding her new State Government ?

" Some twelve thousand voters in the heretofore slave State of Louisiana have sworn allegiance to the Union, assumed to be the rightful political power of the State, held elections, organized a State government, adopted a free State constitution, giving the benefit of public schools equally to black and white, and empowering the Legislature to confer the elective franchise upon the colored man. Their Legislature has already voted to ratify the Constitutional amendment recently passed by Congress, abolishing slavery throughout the Nation. These twelve thousand persons are thus fully committed to the Union, and to perpetual freedom in the State— committed to the very beings and nearly all the things the Nation wants—and they ask the Nation's recognition and its assistance to make good their committal.   Now, if we reject and spurn them, we do our utmost to disorganize and disperse them.   We, in fact, say to the white man, 'You are worthless, or worse; we will neither help you nor be helped by you.'   To the blacks we say, 'This cup of liberty which your old masters there hold to your lips we will dash from you, and leave you to the chances of gathering the spilled and scattered contents in some vague and undefined way when, where, and how.'   If this course, by discouraging and paralyzing both white and black, has any tendency to bring Louisiana into proper practical relations with the Union, I have so far been unable to perceive it.   If, on the contrary, we recognize and sustain the new Government of Louisiana, the converse of all this is made true.

"We encourage the hearts and nerve the arms of the twelve thousand to adhere to their work, and argue for it, and proselyte for it, and fight for it, and feed it, and grow it, and ripen it, to a complete success.   The colored man, too, in seeing all united for him, is inspired with vigilance, and energy, and daring to the same end.   Grant that he desires the elective franchise, will he not attain it sooner by saving the already advanced steps toward it than by running backward over them?   Concede that the new Government of Louisiana is only what it should be, as the egg is to the fowl, we shall sooner have the fowl by hatching the egg, than by smashing it.   [Laughter.]

"Again, if we reject Louisiana, we also reject our vote in favor of the proposed amendment to the National Constitution.   To meet this proposition, it has been argued that no more than three-fourths of those States which have not attempted secession are necessary to validly ratify the amendment   I do not commit myself against this, further than to say that such a ratification would be questionable, and sure to be persistently questioned, while a ratification by three-

24

fourths of all the States would be unquestioned and unquestionable.

" I repeat the question. Can Louisiana be brought into proper practical relation with the Union sooner by sustaining or by discarding her new State Government? What has been said of Louisiana will apply severally to other States; yet so great peculiarities pertain to each State, and such important and sudden changes occur in the same State, and withal so new and unprecedented is the whole case, that no exclusive and inflexible plan can safely be prescribed. As to details and collaterals, such an exclusive and inflexible plan would surely become a new entanglement. Important principles may and must be inflexible.

" In the present situation, as the phrase goes, it may be my duty to make some new announcement to the people of the South. I am considering, and shall not fail to act when satisfied that action will be proper."

On the 11th of April, also, appeared the following proclamation :

" Whereas, By my proclamation of the 19th and 27th days of April, 1861, the ports of the United States of Virginia, North Carolina, South Carolina, Georgia, Florida, Alabama, Mississippi, Louisiana, and Texas were declared to be subject to blockade, but whereas the said blockade has, in consequence of actual military occupation by this Government, since then been conditionally set aside or released in respect to the ports of Norfolk and Alexandria, in the State of Virginia, Beaufort, in the State of North Carolina, Port Royal, in the State of South Carolina, Pensacola and Fernandina, in the State of Florida, and New Orleans, in the State of Louisiana ; and whereas, by the 4th section of the act of Congress approved on the 13th of July, 1861, entitled ' an act further to provide for the collection of duties on imports, and for other purposes,' the President, for the reasons therein set forth, is authorized to close certain ports of entry.

"Now, therefore, be it known that I, ABRAHAM LINCOLN, President of the United States, do hereby proclaim that the ports of Richmond, Tappahannock, Cherry Stone, Yorktown, and Petersburg, in Virginia; of Camden, Elizabeth City, Edenton, Plymouth, Washington, Newbern, Ocracoke, and Wilmington, in North Carolina; of Charleston, Georgetown, and Beaufort, in South Carolina; of Savannah, St. Marys, Brunswick, and Darien, in Georgia; of Mobile, in Alabama; of Pearl river, Shieldsboro', Natchez, and Vicksburg, in Mississippi; of St. Augustine, Key West, St. Marks, Port Leon, St. Johns, Jacksonville, and Apalachicola, in Florida; of Teche and Franklin, in Louisiana; of Galveston, La Salle, Brazos de Santiago, Point Isabel, and Brownsville, in Texas, are hereby closed, and all rights of importation, warehousing, and other privileges shall, in respect to the ports aforesaid, cease until they shall again have been opened by order of the President; and if, while said ports are so closed, any ship or vessel from beyond the United States, or having on board any articles subject to duties, shall attempt to enter any such port, the same, together with its tackle, apparel, furniture, and cargo, shall be forfeited to the United States.

"In witness whereof I have hereunto set my hand and caused the seal of the United States to be affixed.

"Done at the City of Washington this eleventh day of April, in the year of our Lord one thousand eight hundred and sixty-five, and of the Independence of the United States of America the eighty-ninth.

"ABRAHAM LINCOLN.

"WILLIAM H. SEWARD, Secretary of State."

And on the same day the following:

"WHEREAS, for some time past vessels-of-war of the United

States have been refused in certain foreign ports privileges and immunities to which they were entitled by treaty, public law, or the comity of nations, at the same time that vessels-of-war of the country wherein the said privileges and immunities have been withheld have enjoyed them fully and uninterruptedly in ports of the United States, which condition of things has not always been forcibly resisted by the United States, although, on the other hand, they have not at any time failed to protest against and declare their dissatisfaction with the same. In the view of the United States no condition any longer exists which can be claimed to justify the denial to them by any one of said nations of customary naval rights, such as has heretofore been so unnecessarily persisted in—

"Now, therefore, I, ABRAHAM LINCOLN, President of the United States, do hereby make known that if after a reasonable time shall have elapsed for intelligence of this proclamation to have reached any foreign country in whose ports the said privileges and immunities shall have been refused as aforesaid, they shall continue to be so refused, then and thenceforth the same privileges and immunities shall be refused to the vessels-of-war of that country in the ports of the United States; and this refusal shall continue until war-vessels of the United States shall have been placed upon an entire equality in the foreign ports aforesaid with vessels of other countries. *The United States, whatever claim or pretence may have existed heretofore, are now at least entitled to claim and concede an entire and friendly equality of rights and hospitalities with all maritime nations.*

"In witness whereof I have hereunto set my hand and caused the seal of the United States to be affixed.

"Done at the city of Washington this eleventh day of April, in the year of our Lord, one thousand eight hundred and sixty-five, and of the Independence of the United States the eighty-ninth.

"By the President: ABRAHAM LINCOLN.
"WILLIAM H. SEWARD, Secretary of State."

And, on the twelfth April, the following supplementary proclamation :

"WHEREAS, By my proclamation of this date the port of Key West, in the State of Florida, was inadvertently included among those which are not open to commerce :

"Now, therefore, be it known that I, ABRAHAM LINCOLN, President of the United States, do hereby declare and make known that the said port of Key West is and shall remain open to foreign and domestic commerce, upon the same conditions by which that commerce has hitherto been governed.

"In witness whereof I have hereunto set my hand and caused the seal of the United States to be affixed.

"Done at the City of Washington this eleventh day of April, in the year of our Lord, one thousand eight hundred and sixty-five, and of the Independence of the United States of America, the eighty-ninth.

"By the President: ABRAHAM LINCOLN.
"WM. H. SEWARD, Secretary of State."

The light in which the administration regarded the position of affairs can best be judged from the following official bulletin from the War Department, bearing date April thirteenth, 1865 :

"This Department, after mature consideration and consultation with the Lieutenant-General upon the results of the recent campaigns, has come to the following determination, which will be carried into effect by appropriate orders, to be immediately issued :

"*First.* To stop all drafting and recruiting in the loyal States.

"*Second.* To curtail purchases for arms, ammunition, quartermaster's and commissary supplies, and reduce the expenses of the military establishment and its several branches.

"*Third.* To reduce the number of general and staff officers to the actual necessities of the service.

"*Fourth.* To remove all military restrictions upon trade and commerce, so far as may be consistent with the public safety.

"As soon as these measures can be put in operation, it will be made known by public orders.

"EDWIN M. STANTON, Secretary of War."

The Traitor President, who, on the fifth of April, had issued a proclamation to the effect that he should hold on to Virginia—where was he at this time?

CHAPTER XXV.

THE LAST ACT.

Interview with Mr. Colfax—Cabinet Meeting—Incident—Evening Conversation—Possibility of Assassination—Leaves for the Theatre—In the Theatre—Precautions for the Murder—The Pistol Shot—Escape of the Assassin—Death of the President—Pledges Redeemed—Situation of the Country—Effect of the Murder—Obsequies at Washington—Borne Home—Grief of the People—At Rest.

ON the morning of Friday, April fourteenth, 1865, after an interesting conversation with his eldest son, Robert, a captain on General Grant's staff, relative to the surrender of Lee, with the details of which the son was familiar, the President, hearing that Schuyler Colfax, Speaker of the House of Representatives, was in the Executive Mansion, invited the latter to a chat in the reception-room, and during the following hour the talk turned upon his future policy toward the rebellion—a matter which he was about to submit to his Cabinet.

After an interview with John P. Hale, then recently appointed Minister to Spain, as well as with several Senators and Representatives, a Cabinet meeting was held, at eleven o'clock, General Grant being present, which proved to be one of the most satisfactory and important consultations held since his first inauguration. The future policy of the Administration was harmoniously and unanimously agreed upon, and upon the adjournment of the meeting the Secretary of War remarked that the Government was then stronger than at any period since the commencement of the rebellion.

It was afterwards remembered that at this meeting the President turned to General Grant and asked him if he had heard from General Sherman. General Grant replied that he had not, but was in hourly expectation of receiving dispatches from him, announcing the surrender of Johnston.

"Well," said the President, "you will hear very soon now, and the news will be important."

"Why do you think so?" said the General.

"Because," said Mr. Lincoln, "I had a dream last night, and ever since the war began I have invariably had the same dream before any very important military event has occurred." He then instanced Bull Run, Antietam, Gettysburg, etc., and said that before each of these events he had had the same dream, and turning to Secretary Welles, said:

"It is in your line, too, Mr. Welles. The dream is that I saw a ship sailing very rapidly, and I am sure that it portends some important national event."

In the afternoon, a long and pleasant conversation was held with eminent citizens from Illinois.

In the evening, during a talk with Messrs. Colfax and Ashman—the latter of whom presided at the Chicago Convention, in 1860—speaking about his trip to Richmond, when the suggestion was made that there was much uneasiness at the North while he was at what had been the rebel capital, for fear that some traitor might shoot him, Mr. Lincoln portively replied, that he would have been alarmed himself, if any other person had been President and gone there, but that, as for himself, he did not feel in any danger whatever.

This possibility of an assassination had been presented before to the President's mind, but it had not occasioned him a moment's uneasiness. A member of his Cabinet one day said to him, "Mr. Lincoln, you are not sufficiently careful of yourself. There are bad men in Washington. Did it never occur to you that there are rebels among us who are bad enough to attempt your life?" The President stepped to a desk and drew from a pigeon-hole a package of letters. "There," said he, "every one of these contains a threat to assassinate me. I might be nervous, if I were to dwell upon the subject, but I have come to this conclusion : there are opportunities to kill me every day of my life, if there are persons disposed to do it. It is not possible to avoid exposure to such a fate, and I shall not trouble myself about it."

Upon the evening alluded to, while conversing upon a matter of business with Mr. Ashman, he saw that the latter was surprised at a remark which he had made, when, prompted by his well-known desire to avoid any thing offensive, he immediately said, "You did not understand me, Ashman : I did not mean what you inferred, and I will take it all back, and apologize for it." He afterward gave Mr. A. a card, admitting himself and friend for a further conversation early in the morning.

Turning to Mr. Colfax, he said, "You are going with Mrs. Lincoln and me to the theatre, I hope." The President and General Grant had previously accepted an invitation to be present that evening at Ford's Theatre, but the General had been obliged to leave for the North. Mr. Lincoln did not like to entirely disappoint the audience, as the announcement had been publicly made, and had determined to fulfil his acceptance.

Mr. Colfax, however, declining on account of other engagements, Mr. Lincoln said to him, " Mr. Sumner has the gavel of the Confederate Congress, which he got at Richmond to hand to the Secretary of War. But I insisted then that he must give it to you ; and you tell him for me to hand it over." Mr. Ashman alluded to the gavel, still in his possession, which he had used at Chicago ; and about half an hour after the time they had intended to leave for the theatre, the President and Mrs. Lincoln rose to depart, the former reluctant and speaking about remaining at home a half hour longer.

At the door he stopped and said, " Colfax, do not forget to tell the people in the mining regions, as you pass through them, what I told you this morning about the development when peace comes, and I will telegraph you at San Francisco." Having shaken hands with both gentlemen and bidden them a pleasant good-bye, the President with his party left for the theatre.

The box occupied by them was on the second tier above the stage, at the right of the audience, the entrance to it being by a door from the adjoining gallery. One, who had planned Mr. Lincoln's assassination with extraordinary precautions against any failure, having effected an entrance by deceiving the guard, found himself in a dark corridor, of which the wall made an acute angle with the door. The assassin had previously gouged a channel from the plaster and placed near by a stout piece of board, which he next inserted between the wall and the panel of the door.

Ingress then being rendered impossible, he next turned toward the entrances to the President's box, two in number, as the box by a sliding partition could, at pleasure, be converted into two. The door at the bottom of the passage was

378   LIFE OF ABRAHAM LINCOLN.

The Assassin's Precautions.   The Pistol Shot.   The Flight.

open ; that nearer the assassin was closed.   Both had spring-
locks, but their screws had been carefully loosened so as to
yield to a slight pressure, if necessary.

Resort was had to the hither door, in which a small hole
had been bored, for the purpose of securing a view of the
interior of the box, the door first described having first been
fastened, and the discovery made that the occupants had
taken seats as follows: the President in the arm-chair
nearest the audience, Mrs. Lincoln next, then, after a considerable space, a Miss Clara Harris in the corner nearest
the stage, and a Major H. R. Rathbone on a lounge along
the further wall.

The play was, "Our American Cousin."   While all were
intent upon its representation, the report of a pistol first announced the presence of the assassin, who uttered the word
" Freedom !" and advanced toward the front.   The Major
having discerned the murderer through the smoke, and grap-
pled with him, the latter dropped his pistol and aimed with
a knife at the breast of his antagonist, who caught the blow
in the upper part of his left arm, but was unable to detain the
desperado, though he immediately seized him again.   The
villain, however, leaped some twelve feet down upon the
open stage, tangling his spur in the draped flag below the
box and stumbling in his fall.

Recovering himself immediately, he flourished his dagger,
shouted *"Sic semper tyrannis"* and *"The South is avenged,"*
retreated successfully through the labyrinth of the theatre—
perfectly familiar to him—to his horse in waiting below.
Between the deed of blood and the escape there was not the
lapse of a minute.   The hour was about half-past ten.   There
was but one pursuer, and he from the audience, but he was
outstripped.

The meaning of the pistol-shot was soon ascertained.
Mr. Lincoln had been shot in the back of the head, behind
the left ear, the ball traversing an oblique line to the right

THE LAST ACT. 379

Death of the President.   Grief of his Family.   Reflections.

ear. He was rendered instantly unconscious, and never knew friends or pain again. Having been conveyed as soon as possible to a house opposite the theatre, he expired there the next morning, April fifteenth, 1865, at twenty-two minutes past seven o'clock, attended by the principal members of his Cabinet and other friends, from all of whom the heart-rending spectacle drew copious tears of sorrow. Mrs. Lincoln and her son Robert were in an adjoining apartment— the former bowed down with anguish, the latter strong enough to sustain and console her. A disconsolate widow and two sons now constituted the entire family. Soon after nine o'clock, the body was removed to the White House under military escort.

Thus ended the earthly career of Abraham Lincoln, sixteenth President of the United States, on the threshold of his fifty-seventh year and second Presidential term.

"Sic semper tyrannis !" And this the justification for the murder of a ruler who had

> "——borne his faculties so meek, had been
> So clear in his great office, that his virtues
> Will plead like angels, trumpet-tongued, against
> The deep damnation of his taking-off."

"The South avenged !" And by the cold-blooded murder of the best friend that repentant rebels ever had—of one who had long withstood the pressing appeals of his warmest personal and political friends for less lenity and more rigor in dealing with traitors.

It was written in the decrees of the Immutable that he should fall by the bullet—not, indeed, on the battle-field, whose sad suggestings he had so often, and so tenderly, lovingly heeded—but in the midst of his family, while seeking relief from the cares of state—and by a murderer's hand ! —the first President to meet such a fate—thenceforth our martyr-chief !

But sorrow was tempered with mercy. He did not fall

until a benignant Providence had permitted him to enjoy a foretaste, at least, of the blessings which he had been instrumental in conferring upon the land he loved so well.

The pledges of his first Inaugural Address had been amply redeemed—those pledges which so many declared impossible of fulfilment, which not a few mocked as beyond human power to accomplish. The power confided to him had been successfully used "to hold, occupy, and possess the property and places belonging to the Government." No United States fort at the time of his fall flaunted treason in the eyes of the land. The day of his murder the old flag had been flung to the breeze from Sumter with ceremonies befitting the joyous occasion, by the very hands that four years before had been compelled to lower it to arrogant traitors ; and friends of freedom for man, irrespective of color or race, walked the streets of Charleston—a city of desolation, a skeleton of its former self —jubilant that, since God so willed it, in His own good time, Freedom was National and Slavery but a thing of the past.

When he fell, the Nation, brought by the stern necessities of direful war to the discharge of duties befitting a better manhood, passing by all projects for an emancipation of slaves, which should be merely gradual, not content even that such emancipation had been proclaimed as a measure of military necessity, had spoken in favor of such an amendment of the Constitution as should forever prohibit any claim of property in man. Though the final consummation of that great measure had not been reached when our President was removed, it was given him to feel assured that the end was not distant, was even then close at hand.

When he fell, that body of traitors which had assumed to be a Government had fled, one scarcely knew whither, with whatever of ill-gotten gains their greedy hands could grasp—their main army captive, the residue of their military force on the point of surrendering. From what had been their capital, in the mansion appropriated to the special use of the chiefest among the conspirators, he had been permitted to send words of greeting to the nation.

When he fell, treason throughout the land lay gasping, dying.

It needed not that dismal, dreary, mid-April day to in tensify the sorrow. As on the wings of lightning the news sped through the land — "the President is Shot" — "is dying"—"is dead"—men knew scarcely how to credit the tale. When the fearful certainty came home to each, strong men bowed themselves and wept—maid and matron joined in the plaint. With no extraneous prompting, with no impulse save that of the heart alone, the common grief took on a common garb. Houses were draped—the flag of our country hung pensive at half-mast—portraitures of the loved dead were found on all.

And dreary as was the day when first the tidings swept through the country, patriot hearts were drearier still. It was past analysis. It was as if chaos and dread night had come again.

Meanwhile the honored dead lay in state in the country's capitol.

On that dreamy, hazy nineteenth of April—suggesting, were it not for the early green leaves, the fresh springing grass, the glad spring caroling of birds, "that sweet autumnal summer which the Indian loved so well"—on that day when sleep wooed one even in the early morn, his obsequies were celebrated in the country's metropolis.

And throughout the land, minute guns were fired, bells tolled, business suspended, and the thoughtful betook themselves to prayer, if so be that what verily seemed a curse might pass from us.

Thence the funeral *cortege* moved to the final resting-place —the remains of a darling son, earlier called, accompanying those of the father—by the route the President had taken when first he had been summoned to the chair of State. Before half of the mournful task was done, came tidings that the assassin had been sent to his final account by the avenger's hand, gurgling out, as his worthless life ebbed away, " useless ! useless !"

As the sad procession wended its way, where hundreds had gathered in '61, impelled by mere curiosity or by partisan sympathy, thousands gathered, four years later, through affection, through reverence, through deep, abiding sorrow.

Flowers beautified the lifeless remains—dirges were sung—the people's great heart broke out into sobs and sighing.

And so, home to the prairie they bore him whom, when first he was called, the Nation knew not—whom, mid the storms and ragings of those years of civil war, they had learned, had loved, to call father and friend.

In the Oak Ridge Cemetery, in his own Springfield, on the fourth of May, 1865, they laid him to rest, at the foot of a knoll, in the most beautiful part of the ground, over which forest trees—rare denizens of the prairie—look lovingly.

There all that is mortal of ABRAHAM LINCOLN reposes.

" The immortal ?" Hail, and farewell !

CHAPTER XXVI.

THE MAN.

Reasons for His Re-election—What was Accomplished—Leaning on the People—State Paper—His Tenacity of Purpose—Washington and Lincoln—As a Man—Favorite Poem —Autobiography—His Modesty—A Christian—Conclusion.

WHAT shall be said, in summing up, of Abraham Lincoln as a statesman and a man ? That from such humble beginnings, in circumstances so adverse, he rose to be the Chief Magistrate of one of the leading countries of the world, would

were it in any other country, be evidence of ability of the
very highest order.

Here, however, so many from similar surroundings have
achieved similar results that this fact of itself does not necessarily unfold the man clearly and fully to us.   He might have
been put forward for that high station as a skillful and accomplished politician, from whose elevation hosts of partisans
counted upon their own personal advancement and profit.
Or he might have been a successful general; or one possessing merely negative qualities, with no salient points, all
objectionable angularities rounded off till that desirable availability, which has at times been laid hold of for the Presidency
had been reached ; or, yet again, one who had for a long time
been in the front ranks of an old and triumphant party, and,
therefore, as such matters have been managed with us, admitted to have strong claims upon such party ; or, lastly, one
who; having for many years schemed and plotted and labored,
in season and out of season, for the nomination, at last
achieved it.

For such Presidents have been furnished us.   But he was
neither.   And yet the highest point to which an American
may aspire he reached.   Clearly, then, there must have been
something of strength and of worth in the man.

He was reëlected, the first President since Jackson to
whom that honor had been accorded.   And thirty-two years
had passed—eight Presidential terms—since Jackson's reëlection.   He was, moreover, reëlected by a largely increased
vote.

The years covered by his administration were the stormiest
in American history, "piled high," as he himself said, "with
difficulties."   No President was ever more severely attacked,
more unsparingly denounced than he.   None more belittled
than he.   And yet he was triumphantly reëlected.   Why?
For the same reason that first brought him before the country.

Primarily and mainly because the mass of the people had

unbounded confidence in his honesty and devotion to principle. Though these qualities, it is pleasant to say, have been by no means rare in our Presidents, yet Abraham Lincoln seemed so to speak, so steeped and saturated in them that a hold was thereby obtained upon the common mind, the like of which no other President since Washington had secured. The bitterest opponent of his policy was constrained, if candid, to admit, if not the existence of these qualities, at least the prevailing popular belief in their existence.

What shall be said of him as a statesman?

That he found the fabric of our National Government rocking from turret to foundation stone—that he left it, after four years of strife such as, happily, the world rarely witnesses, firmly fixed, and sure; this should serve in some sort, as an answer.

But might not this be owing, or principally so, to the ability of the counsellors whom he gathered about him? Beyond a doubt the meed of praise is to be shared. Yet we should remember that few Presidents have so uniformly acted of and for themselves in matters of state policy, as did Mr. Lincoln. Upon many questions the opinions of his Cabinet were sought—a Cabinet representing the various shades of thought, the various stages of progress, through which the people, of whom they were the exponents, were passing from year to year—after obtaining which, he would act. But, in most instances, perhaps, he struck out for himself, after careful, conscientious reflection, launching his policy upon unknown seas, quietly assured that truth was with him and that he could not be mistaken. Nor was he often.

Having to feel his way along, for the most part—groping in the dark—he could not push on so fast and far as to leave the people out of breath or staring far in his rear. Still, it must not be understood that he never acted against what was plainly the popular will. The man was not of that mould. Unquestionably in his dealings with the two leading Euro pean powers he often acted in direct opposition to the popular wish. Nothing would have been easier than for him to have brought a foreign war upon the country ; and in such action, for a time at least, he would have been sustained by the mass of the people. So, too, as to vindictive measures towards the rebels. By adopting these he would, oftentimes, have been in harmony with the general wish for vengeance and retaliation. In both these instances—to name no others —he chose to act counter to the current sentiment. More politic, with a more piercing outlook than the mass, he saw the end from the beginning, and in the one case chose to overlook what was, to his mind, grossly wrong, and in the other, to stand up for the general interests of humanity through all time rather than to cater to the desire of the hour, natural and, perhaps, pardonable though it was.

What is meant is this—that, in the complications in which the country was involved, he invariably acted, where expediency simply and not principle was concerned, so as to feel sure that the body of the people were with him. If failure were to result, he would have them feel that the responsibility for it rested as much upon them as upon him. He earnestly endeavored to point out what he judged the better way and to bring the people to his conviction ; but, if they relucted, he waited till they should have advanced where, or nearly where, he was. This was generally felt, and it added largely to the confidence reposed in him. By means of it, a general acquiescence was procured in many measures earlier than could have been gained by any other course. We Americans are peculiar people in some respects. We dislike to be led by any man. Nay, we stoutly deny that we are. We are not— when we see the leading strings.

Mr. Lincoln's state papers in their structure and composition were not always what a critical scholar would have desired. Some would say they were presented quite too often in undress. The people are not profound critics. They

25

could comprehend every word. They felt that they were addressed as fellow-citizens. The ordinarily formal and stilted official documents came from his plain pen a talk to them by the fireside. He said, moreover, exactly what he meant and as he meant, in his own clear cogent way, void of verbiage, omely often but always the outgrowth of a profound intelligent conviction. And, generally, he struck home. His were the words to which "the common pulse of man keeps time." How studded are his papers with lucid illustration; how transparently honest and candid, like the man, their author!

His tenacity of purpose was marked. Signing that immortal proclamation, which made him the Liberator of America, on the afternoon of January 1st, 1863, after hours of New Year's hand-shaking, he said to friends that night—"The signature looks a little tremulous, for my hand was tired, but my resolution was firm. I told them in September, if they did not return to their allegiance and cease murdering our soldiers, I would strike at this pillar of their strength. And now the promise shall be kept; and not one word of it will I ever recall." In all the varying scenes through which as our leader he passed, avoiding the extremes of sudden exultation or deep depression, calm and quiet, and resolute and determined, he kept on his course, with duty as his guiding star, an unwarped conscience his prompter. Feeling always that he bore his life in his hands, in the perilous position in which he was placed, as well as he who went forth to do duty in the battle-field, he faltered not, swerved not, compromised not, retracted not, apologized not, but pursued his way with an inflexibility as rare as it is grand and inspiring. Others might doubt—not he. He saw the end toward which the nation and himself must strive. That was ever present to him, and toward that he ever worked. His mission as President was, as he so often and so pointedly stated, to save the Union. And he saved it. There may be those who will contend that such a result might have been reached by other means than those he was impelled to employ. That is theory. He reduced his to practice. For himself, he could work only in his own harness; and patiently, persistently, painfully he worked on till the goal was reached.

Well has Washington been styled the Father of his Country. Yet this arose from veneration rather than from love; for the most felt such an impassable gulf between themselves and the patriot-hero, that to them he appeared of quite another order of beings than themselves.

Abraham Lincoln was both Saviour and Father; for he preserved whatever was most valuable in the old and created a new order of things possessing an inherent dignity and importance which the old never had. And such titles the people bestow upon him through love.

The characteristics of the man stood prominently out in the statesman. He had not one garb as an official and another as a citizen. No change marked his transit from the chat of the drawing-room to the consultation of cabinet. What he was in the one situation he was in the other. His peculiar humor was not, as those who least knew him judged, his habitual disposition. More of melancholy and sadness centred in him than most were aware. His favorite poem— given below for the sufficient reason that it was his favorite —attests the vein of pensiveness which was in him. "There is one poem," he remarked in conversation, "that is almost continually present with me : it comes in my mind whenever I have relief from thought and care."

> Oh, why should the spirit of mortal be proud?
> Like a swift, fleeting meteor, a fast-flying cloud,
> A flash of the lightning, a break of the wave,
> Man passeth from life to his rest in the grave.
>
> The leaves of the oak and the willow shall fade,
> Be scattered around and together be laid ;
> And the young and the old, and the low and the high,
> Shall moulder to dust and together shall lie.

The infant a mother attended and loved;
The mother that infant's affection who proved;
The husband that mother and infant who blessed,
Each, all, are away to their dwellings of Rest.

The maid on whose cheek, on whose brow, in whose eye,
Shone beauty and pleasure—her triumphs are by;
And the memory of those who loved her and praised,
Are alike from the minds of the living erased.

The hand of the king that the sceptre hath borne;
The brow of the priest that the mitre hath worn;
The eye of the sage and the heart of the brave,
Are hidden and lost in the depth of the grave.

The peasant whose lot was to sow and to reap;
The herdsman, who climbed with his goats up the steep;
The beggar, who wandered in search of his bread,
Have faded away like the grass that we tread.

The saint who enjoyed the communion of heaven,
The sinner who dared to remain unforgiven,
The wise and the foolish, the guilty and just,
Have quietly mingled their bones in the dust.

So the multitude goes, like the flowers or the weed
That withers away to let others succeed;
So the multitude comes, even those we behold,
To repeat every tale that has often been told.

For we are the same our fathers have been;
We see the same sights our fathers have seen—
We drink the same stream and view the same sun—
And run the same course our fathers have run.

The thoughts we are thinking our fathers would think;
From the death we are shrinking our fathers would shrink,
To the life we are clinging they also would cling;
But it speeds for us all, like a bird on the wing.

They loved, but the story we cannot unfold;
They scorned, but the heart of the haughty is cold;
They grieved, but no wail from their slumber will come;
They joyed, but the tongue of their gladness is dumb.

THE MAN. 389

His Favorite Poem. | Record of his Life. | Always a Learner.

> They died, aye! they died; and we things that are now,
> Who walk on the turf that lies over their brow,
> Who make in their dwelling a transient abode,
> Meet the things that they met on their pilgrimage road.
>
> Yea! hope and despondency, pleasure and pain,
> We mingle together in sunshine and rain;
> And the smile and the tear, the song and the dirge,
> Still follow each other, like surge upon surge.
>
> 'Tis the wink of an eye, 'tis the draught of a breath;
> From the blossom of health to the paleness of death,
> From the gilded saloon to the bier and the shroud—
> Oh why should the spirit of mortal be proud?

No one was more modest than he. Look at the record of his life as furnished by himself, in 1858, for Lanman's Dictionary of Congress:

"Born February 12, 1809, in Hardin county, Kentucky.

"Education Defective.

"Profession a lawyer.

"Have been a captain of volunteers in the Black Hawk war.

"Postmaster at a very small office.

"Four times a member of the Illinois Legislature.

"And was a member of the lower House of Congress.

"Yours, etc.,   A. LINCOLN."

With no self-conceit, a pupil in the school of events, he was never ashamed to confess himself a learner, and as such he grew and ripened. Equable in his temperament, never wrathful or passionate, none need have been his enemy, unless such an one were intended for an enemy of the human race. Mild and forgiving, he never allowed the unmerited abuse which was heaped upon him to affect in the least his intercourse or dealings with its authors. His very failings leaned to mercy's side. There is scarcely a hamlet in the loyal States that does not contain some witness of his clemency and lenity. One of the most touching incidents connected with his obsequies at Washington was the placing on his coffin of a wreath of flowers, sent from Boston by the sister of a young man whom he had pardoned when sentenced to death for some military offence.

Honored as a private citizen, happy in his domestic relations, successful as a statesman, he was, moreover, an avowed Christian. He often said that his reliance in the gloomiest hours was on his God, to whom he appealed in prayer, although he had never become a professor of religion. To a clergyman who asked him if he loved his Saviour, he replied:

"When I was first inaugurated I did not love him; when God took my son I was greatly impressed, but still I did not love him; but when I stood upon the battle-field of Gettysburg I gave my heart to Christ, and I can now say I do love the Saviour."

Attention has already been called to the reverential spirit which pervades his official papers; and this was the index of the man. Leaving home, he invoked the prayers of his townsmen and friends; during the excitements of his Washington life, he leaned upon a more than human arm; against his pure moral character not even his bitterest enemy could truthfully utter a word.

Such--imperfectly sketched, and at best but in rude outline—was Abraham Lincoln. The manner of his death invests his name with a tragic interest. This will be but temporary. But the more the man as he was is known, the more completely an insight is obtained into his true character, the more his private and public life is studied, the more carefully his acts are weighed, the higher will he rise in the estimation of all whose esteem is desirable. Coming years will detract nought from him. He has passed into history. There no lover of honesty and integrity, no admirer of firmness and resolution, no sympathizer with conscientious conviction, no friend of man need fear to leave—

ABRAHAM LINCOLN.

APPENDIX.

—————•◦◦◦•—————

MR. LINCOLN'S SPEECHES IN CONGRESS AND ELSEWHERE, PROCLAMATIONS, LETTERS, ETC., NOT INCLUDED IN THE BODY OF THE WORK.

SPEECH ON THE MEXICAN WAR.

(In Committee of the Whole House, January 12, 1848.)

Mr. Lincoln addressed the Committee as follows :

" MR. CHAIRMAN :—Some, if not all, of the gentlemen on the other side of the House, who have addressed the Committee within the last two days, have spoken rather complainingly, if I have rightly understood them, of the vote given a week or ten days ago, declaring that the war with Mexico was unnecessarily and unconstitutionally commenced by the President. I admit that such a vote should not be given in mere party wantonness, and that the one given is justly censurable, if it have no other or better foundation. I am one of those who joined in that vote ; and did so under my best impression of the *truth* of the case. How I got this impression, and how it may possibly be removed, I will now try to show. When the war began, it was my opinion that all those who, because of knowing too *little*, or because of knowing too *much*, could not conscientiously approve the conduct of the President (in the beginning of it), should, nevertheless, as good citizens and patriots, remain silent on that point, at least till the war should be ended. Some leading Democrats, including ex-President Van Buren, have taken this same view, as I understand them ; and I adhered to it, and acted upon it, until since I took my seat here ; and I think I should still adhere to it, were it not that the President and his friends will not allow it to be so. Besides, the continual effort of the President to argue every silent vote given for supplies into an indorsement of the justice and wisdom of his conduct ; besides that singularly candid paragraph in his late message, in which he tells us that Congress, with great unanimity (only two in the Senate and fourteen in the House dissenting) had declared that ' by the act of the Republic of Mexico a state of war exists between that Government and the United States ;' when the same journals that informed him of this, also informed him that, when that declaration stood disconnected from the question of supplies, sixty-seven in the House, and not fourteen, merely, voted against it ; besides this open attempt to prove by telling the *truth*, what he could not prove by telling the *whole truth*, demanding of all who will not submit to be misrepresented, in justice to themselves, to speak out ; besides all this, one of my colleagues [Mr. Richardson], at a very early day in the session, brought in a set of resolutions, expressly indorsing the original justice of the war on the part of the President. Upon these resolutions, when they shall be put on their passage, I shall be *compelled* to vote ; so that I can not be silent if I would. Seeing this, I went about preparing myself to give the vote understandingly, when it should come. I carefully examined the President's messages, to ascertain what he himself had said and proved upon the point. The result of his examination was to make the impression, that, taking for t ue all the President states as facts, be falls far short of proving his justification ; and that the President would have gone further with his proof, if it had not been for the small matter that the *truth* would not permit him. Under the impression thus made I gave the vote before mentioned. I propose now to give, concisely, the process of the examination I made, and how I reached the conclusion I did.

" The President, in his first message of May, 1846, declares that the soil was *ours* on which hostilities were commenced by Mexico; and he repeats that declaration, almost in the same language, in each successive annual message—thus showing that he esteems that point a highly essential one. In the importance of that point I entirely agree with the President. To my judgment, it is the *very point* upon which he should be justified or condemned. In his message of December, 1846, it seems to have occurred to him, as is certainly true, that title, ownership to soil, or any thing else, is not a simple fact, but is a conclusion following one or more simple facts; and that it was incumbent upon him to present the facts from which he concluded the soil was ours on which the first blood of the war was shed.

"Accordingly, a little below the middle of page twelve, in the message last referred to, he enters upon that task; forming an issue and introducing testimony, extending the whole to a little below the middle of page fourteen. Now, I propose to try to show that the whole of this—issue and evidence —is, from beginning to end, the sheerest deception. The issue, as he presents it, is in these words: 'But there are those who, conceding all this to be true, assume the ground that the true western boundary of Texas is the Nueces, instead of the Rio Grande; and that, therefore, in marching our army to the east bank of the latter river, we passed the Texan line, and invaded the territory of Mexico.' Now, this issue is made up of two affirmatives and no negative. The main deception of it is, that it assumes as true that *one* river or the *other* is necessarily the boundary, and cheats the superficial thinker entirely out of the idea that *possibly* the boundary is somewhere *between* the two, and not actually at either. A further deception is, that it will let in *evidence* which a true issue would exclude. A true issue made by the President would be about as follows: 'I say the soil *was ours* on which the first blood was shed; there are those who say it was not.'

"I now proceed to examine the President's evidence, as applicable to such an issue. When that evidence is analyzed it is all included in the following propositions:

"1. That the Rio Grande was the western boundary of Louisiana, as we purchased it of France in 1803.

"2. That the Republic of Texas always *claimed* the Rio Grande as her western boundary.

"3. That, by various acts, she had claimed it *on paper*.

"4. That Santa Anna, in his treaty with Texas, recognized the Rio Grande as her boundary.

"5. That Texas *before*, and the United States *after* annexation, had *exercised* jurisdiction *beyond* the Nueces, *between* the two rivers.

"6. That our Congress *understood* the boundary of Texas to extend beyond the Nueces.

"Now for each of these in its turn:

"His first item is, that the Rio Grande was the western boundary of Louisiana, as we purchased it of France in 1803; and, seeming to expect this to be disputed, he argues over the amount of nearly a page to prove it true; at the end of which he lets us know that, by the treaty of 1819, we sold to Spain the whole country, from the Rio Grande eastward to the Sabine. Now, admitting for the present, that the Rio Grande was the boundary of Louisiana, what, under heaven, had that to do with the *present* boundary between us and Mexico? How, Mr. Chairman, the line that once divided your land from mine can *still* be the boundary between us *after* I have sold my land to you, is, to me, beyond all comprehension. And how any man, with an honest purpose only of proving the truth, could ever have *thought* of introducing such a fact to prove such an issue, is equally incomprehensible. The outrage upon common *right*, of seizing as our own what we have once sold, merely because it *was* ours *before* we sold it, is only equaled by the outrage on common *sense* of any attempt to justify it.

"The President's next piece of evidence is, that 'The Republic of Texas always *claimed* this river (Rio Grande) as her western boundary.' That is not true, in fact. Texas *has* claimed it, but she has not *always* claimed it. There is, at least, one distinguished exception. Her State Constitution—the public's most solemn and well-considered act; that which may, without impropriety, be called her last will and testament, revoking all others—makes no such claim. But suppose she had always claimed it. Has not Mexico always claimed the contrary? So that there is but *claim* against *claim*, leaving nothing proved until we get back of the claims, and find which has the better *foundation*.

"Though not in the order in which the President presents his evidence, I now consider that class of his statements, which are, in substance, nothing more than that Texas has by various acts of her Convention and Congress, claimed the Rio Grande as her boundary—*on paper*. I mean here what he says about the fixing of the Rio Grande as her boundary, in her old Constitution (not her State Constitution), about forming congressional districts, counties, etc. Now, all this is but naked *claim;* and what I have already said about claims is strictly applicable to this. If I should claim your land by word of mouth, that certainly would not make it mine; and if I were to claim it by a deed which I had made myself, and with which you had nothing to do, the claim would be quite the same in substance, or rather in utter nothingness.

"I next consider the President's statement that Santa Anna, in his *treaty* with Texas, recognized the Rio Grande as the western boundary of Texas. Besides the position so often taken that Santa Anna, while a prisoner of war—a captive—*could* not bind Mexico by a treaty, which I deem conclusive; besides this, I wish to say something in relation to this treaty so called by the President, with Santa Anna. If any man would like to be amused by a sight at that *little* thing, which the President calls by that *big* name, he can have it by turning to Niles' Register, volume 50, page 386. And if any one should suppose that Niles' Register is a curious repository of so mighty a document as a solemn treaty between nations, I can only say that I learned, to a tolerable degree of certainty, by inquiry at the State Department, that the President himself never saw it anywhere else. By the way, I believe I should not err if I were to declare, that during the first ten years of the existence of that document, it was never by anybody *called* a treaty; that it was never so called till the President, in his extremity, attempted, by so calling it, to wring something from it in justification of himself in connection with the Mexican war. It has none of the distinguishing features of a treaty. It does not call itself a treaty. Santa Anna does not therein assume to bind Mexico; he assumes only to act as President, Commander-in-chief of the Mexican army and navy; stipulates that the then present hostilities should cease, and that he would not *himself* take up arms, nor *influence* the Mexican people to take up arms, against Texas, during the existence of the war of independence. He did not recognize the independence of Texas; he did not assume to put an end to the war, but clearly indicated his expectation of its continuance; he did not say one word about boundary, and most probably never thought of it. It *is* stipulated therein that the Mexican forces should evacuate the territory of Texas, *passing to the other side of the Rio Grande;* and in another article it is stipulated, that to prevent collisions between the armies, the Texan army should not approach nearer than five leagues—of *what* is not said—but clearly, from the object stated, it is of the Rio Grande. Now, if this is a treaty recognizing the Rio Grande as a boundary of Texas, it contains the singular feature of stipulating that Texas shall not go within five leagues of *her own* boundary.

" Next comes the evidence that Texas before annexation, and the United States afterward, exercising jurisdiction beyond the Nueces, and *between* the two rivers. This actual *exercise* of jurisdiction is the very class or quality of evidence we want. It is excellent so far as it goes ; but does it go far enough ? He tells us it went *beyond* the Nueces, but he does not tell us it went *to* the Rio Grande. He tells us jurisdiction was exercised *between* the two rivers, but he does not tell us it was exercised over *all* the territory between them. Some simple-minded people think it possible to cross one river and go beyond it, without going all the way to the next; that jurisdiction may be exercised *between* two rivers without covering *all* the country between them. I know a man, not very unlike myself, who exercises jurisdiction over a piece of land between the Wabash and the Mississippi ; and yet so far is this from being *all* there is between those rivers, that it is just one hundred and fifty-two feet long by fifty wide, and no part of it much within a hundred miles of either. He has a neighbor between him and the Mississippi—that is, just across the street, in that direction—whom, I am sure, he could neither *persuade* nor *force* to give up his habitation ; but which, nevertheless he could certainly annex, if it were to be done, by merely standing on his own side of the street and claiming it, or even sitting down and writing a deed for it.

" But next, the President tells us, the Congress of the United States *understood* the State of Texas they admitted into the Union to extend *beyond* the Neuces. Well, I suppose they did—I certainly so understand it—but how *far* beyond ? That Congress did *not* understand it to extend clear to the Rio Grande, is quite certain by the fact of their joint resolutions for admission expressly leaving all questions of boundary to future adjustment. And, it may be added, that Texas herself is proved to have had the same understanding of it that our Congress had, by the fact of the exact conformity of her new Constitution to those resolutions

" I am now through the whole of the President's evidence; and it is a singular fact, that if any one should declare the President sent the army into the midst of a settlement of Mexican people, who had never submitted, by consent or by force to the authority of Texas or of the United States, and that *there*, and *thereby*, the first blood of the war was shed, there is not one word in all the President has said which would either admit or deny the declaration. In this strange omission chiefly consists the deception of the President's evidence—an omission which, it does seem to me, could scarcely have occurred but by design. My way of living leads me to be about the courts of justice; and there I have sometimes seen a good lawyer, struggling for his client's neck, in a desperate case, employing every artifice to work round, befog, and cover up with many words some position pressed upon him by the prosecution, which he *dared* not admit, and yet *could* not deny. Party bias may help to make it appear so; but, with all the allowance I can make for such bias, it still does appear to me that just such and from just such necessity, are the President's struggles in this case.

" Some time after my colleague (Mr. Richardson) introduced the resolutions I have mentioned, I introduced a preamble, resolution, and interrogatories, intended to draw the President out, if possible, on this hitherto untrodden ground. To show their relevancy, I propose to state my understanding of the true rule for ascertaining the boundary betwen Texas and Mexico. It is, that *wherever* Texas was *exercising* jurisdiction was hers; and wherever Mexico was exercising jurisdiction was hers: and that whatever separated the actual exercise of jurisdiction of the one from that of the other, was the true boundary between them. If, as is probably true, Texas was exercising jurisdiction along the western bank of the Neuces, and Mexico was exercising it along the eastern bank of the Rio Grande, then *neither* river was the boundary, but the uninhabited country between the two was. The extent of our territory in that region depended not on any *treaty-fixed* boundary (for no treaty had attempted it), but on revolution.   Any people anywhere, being inclined and having the power, have the *right* to rise up and shake off the existing government, and form a new one that suits them better. This is a most valuable, a most sacred right—a right which, we hope and believe, is to liberate the world.   Nor is this right confined to cases in which the whole people of an existing government may choose to exercise it.   Any portion of such people that *can* may revolutionize, and make their *own* of so much of their territory as they inhabit.   More than this, a *majority* of any portion of such people may revolutionize, putting down a *minority*, intermingled with, or near about them, who may oppose their movements.   Such minority was precisely the case of the Tories of our own Revolution. It is a quality of revolutions not to go by old lines, or old laws; but to break up both and make new ones.   As to the country now in question, we bought it of France in 1803, and sold it to Spain in 1819, according to the President's statement.   After this, all Mexico, including Texas, revolutionized against Spain; and still later, Texas revolutionized against Mexico.   In my view, just so far as she carried her revolution, by obtaining the *actual*, willing or unwilling submission of the people, so *far* the country was hers, and no further.

" Now, sir, for the purpose of obtaining the very best evidence as to whether Texas had actually carried her revolution to the place where the hostilities of the present war commenced, let the President 'answer the interrogatories I proposed, as before mentioned, or some other similar ones.   Let him answer fully, fairly and candidly.   Let him answer with *facts*, and not with arguments.   Let him remember he sits where Washington sat; and, so remembering, let him answer as Washington would answer.   As a nation *should* not, and the Almighty *will* not, be evaded, so let him attempt no evasion, no equivocation. And if, so answering, he can show that the soil was ours where the first blood of the war was shed—that it was not within an inhabited country, or, if within such, that the inhabitants had submitted themselves to the civil authority of Texas, or of the United States, and that the same is true of the site of Fort Brown—then I am with him for his justification. In that case, I shall be most happy to reverse the vote I gave the other day. I have a selfish motive for desiring that the President may do this; I expect to give some votes, in connection with the war, which, without his so doing, will be of doubtful propriety, in my own judgment, but which will be free from the doubt if he does so. But if he *can not or will not* do this,—if, on any pretence, or no pretence, he shall refuse or omit it,—then I shall be fully convinced, of what I more than suspect already, that he is deeply conscious of being in the wrong; that he feels the blood of this war, like the blood of Abel, is crying to heaven against him; that he ordered General Taylor into the midst of a peaceful Mexican settlement, purposely to bring on a war; that originally having some strong motive— what I will not stop now to give my opinion concerning—to involve the two countries in a war, and trusting to escape scrutiny by fixing the public gaze upon the exceeding brightness of military glory—that attractive rainbow that rises in showers of blood—that serpent's eye that charms to destroy— he plunged into it, and has swept *on* and *on*, till, disappointed in his calculation of the ease with which Mexico might be subdued, he now finds himself he knows not where. How like the half insane mumbling of a fever dream is the whole war part of the late message! At one time telling us that Mexico has nothing whatever that we can get but territory; at another, showing us how we can support the war by levying contributions on Mexico. At one time urging the national honor, the security of the future, the prevention of foreign interference, and even the good of Mexico herself, as among the objects of the war; at another, telling us that, 'to reject indemnity by refusing to accept a cession of territory, would be to abandon all our just demands, and to wage the war, bearing all its expenses, *without a purpose or definite object.*' So, then, the national honor, security of the future, and everything but territorial indemnity, may be considered the *no purposes* and *indefinite* objects of the war! But having it now settled that territorial indemnity is the only object, we are urged to seize, by legislation here, all that he was content to take a few months ago, and the whole province of Lowei California to boot, and to still carry on the war—to take *all* we are fighting for, and *still* fight on. Again, the President is resolved, under all circumstances, to have full territorial indemnity for the expenses of the war; but he forgets to tell us how we are to get the *excess* after those expenses shall have surpassed the value of the *whole* of the Mexican territory. So, again, he insists that the separate national existence of Mexico shall be maintained; but he does not tell us *how* this can be done after we shall have taken *all* her territory. Lest the question I here suggest be considered speculative merely, let me be indulged a moment in trying to show they are not.

"The war has gone on some twenty months; for the expenses of which, together with an inconsiderable old score, the President now claims about one-half of the Mexican territory, and that by far the better half, so far as concerns our ability to make any thing out of it. It is comparatively uninhabited; so that we could establish land offices in it, and raise some money in that way. But the other half is already inhabited, as I understand it, tolerably densely for the nature of the country; and all its lands, or all that are valuable, already appropriated as private property. How, then, are we to make any thing out of these lands with this incumbrance on them, or how remove the incumbrance? I suppose no one will say that we shall kill the people, or drive them out.

26

or make slaves of them, or even confiscate their property ?
How, then, can we make much out of this part of the territory ? If the prosecution of the war has, in expenses, already
equalled the *better* half of the country, how long its future
prosecution will be in equalling the less valuable half is not
a *speculative* but a *practical* question, pressing closely upon
us ; and yet it is a question which the President seems never
to have thought of.

"As to the mode of terminating the war and securing
peace, the President is equally wandering and indefinite.
First, it is to be done by a more vigorous prosecution of the
war in the vital parts of the enemy's country ; and, after
apparently talking himself tired on this point, the President
drops down into a half despairing tone, and tells us, that
'with a people distracted and divided by contending factions,
and a government subject to constant changes, by successive
revolutions, *the continued success of our arms may fail to
obtain a satisfactory peace.*' Then he suggests the propriety
of wheedling the Mexican people to desert the counsels of
their own leaders, and, trusting in our protection, to set up a
government from which we can secure a satisfactory peace,
telling us that '*this may become the only mode of obtaining
such a peace.*' But soon he falls into doubt of this too, and
then drops back on to the already half abandoned ground of
'more vigorous prosecution.' All this shows that the President is in no wise satisfied with his own positions. First, he
takes up one, and, in attempting to argue us into it, he argues
himself *out* of it ; then seizes another, and goes through the
same process ; and then, confused at being able to think of
nothing new, he snatches up the old one again, which he has
some time before cast off. His mind, tasked beyond its power,
is running hither and thither, like some tortured creature on
a burning surface, finding no such position on which it can
settle down and be at ease.

"Again, it is a singular omission in this message, that it

nowhere intimates *when* the President expects the war to terminate. At its beginning, General Scott was, by this same President driven into disfavor, if not disgrace, for intimating that peace could not be conquered in less than three or four months. But now at the end of about twenty months, during which time our arms have given us the most splendid successes—every department, and every part, land and water, officers and privates, regulars and volunteers, doing all that men could do, and hundreds of things which it had ever before been thought that men could *not* do ; after all this, this same President gives us a long message without showing us that *as to the end*, he has himself even an imaginary conception. As I have before said, he knows not where he is. He is a bewildered, confounded, and miserably-perplexed man. God grant he may be able to show that there is not something about his conscience more painful than all his mental perplexity.

SPEECH ON INTERNAL IMPROVEMENTS.

(*In Committee of the Whole House, June* 20, 1848.)

Mr. Lincoln said :

" MR. CHAIRMAN :—I wish at all times in no way to practice any fraud upon the House or the Committee, and I also desire to do nothing which may be very disagreeable to any of the members. I therefore state, in advance, that my object in taking the floor is to make a speech on the general subject of internal improvements ; and if I am out of order in doing so, I give the Chair an opportunity of so deciding, and I will take my seat."

The Chair.—" I will not undertake to anticipate what the gentleman may say on the subject of internal improvements. He will, therefore, proceed in his remarks, and if any question of order shall be made, the Chair will then decide it "

Mr. Lincoln.—"At an early day of this session the President sent to us what may properly be termed an internal improvement veto message. The late Democratic Convention which sat at Baltimore, and which nominated General Cass' for the Presidency, adopted a set of resolutions, now called the Democratic platform, among which is one in these words :

" ' That the Constitution does not confer upon the General Government the power to commence and carry on a general system of internal improvements.'

" General Cass, in his letter accepting the nomination, holds this language :

" ' I have carefully read the resolutions of the Democratic National Convention, laying down the platform of our political faith, and I adhere to them as firmly as I approve them cordially.'

" These things, taken together, show that the question of internal improvements is now more distinctly made—has become more intense, than at any former period. It can no longer be avoided. The veto message and the Baltimore resolution I understand to be, in substance, the same thing ; the latter being the more general statement, of which the former is the amplification—the bill of particulars. While I know there are many Democrats, on this floor and elsewhere, who disapprove that message, I understand that all who shall vote for General Cass will thereafter be considered as having approved it, as having indorsed all its doctrines. I suppose all, or nearly all, the Democrats will vote for him. Many of them will do so, not because they like his position on this question, but because they prefer him, being wrong in this, to another, whom they consider further wrong on other questions. In this way the internal improvement Democrats are to be, by a sort of forced consent, carried over, and arrayed against themselves on this measure of policy. General Cass, once elected, will not trouble himself to make a

APPENDIX. 405

Speech in Congress.　　Internal Improvements.　　President's Position Repudiated.

Constitutional argument, or, perhaps, any argument at all, when he shall veto a river or harbor bill. He will consider it a sufficient answer to all Democratic murmurs, to point to Mr. Polk's message, and to the "Democratic platform." This being the case, the question of improvements is verging to a final crisis; and the friends of the policy must now battle, and battle manfully, or surrender all. In this view, humble as I am, I wish to review, and contest as well as I may, the general positions of this veto message. When I say *general* positions, I mean to exclude from consideration so much as relates to the present embarrassed state of the Treasury, in consequence of the Mexican war.

"Those general positions are: That internal improvements ought not to be made by the General Government:

"1. Because they would overwhelm the treasury

"2. Because, while their *burdens* would be general, their *benefits* would be *local* and *partial*, involving an obnoxious inequality;

"3. Because they would be unconstitutional;

"4. Because the States may do enough by the levy and collection of tonnage duties; or, if not,

"5. That the Constitution may be amended.

"'Do nothing at all, lest you do something wrong,' is the sum of these positions—is the sum of this message; and this, with the exception of what is said about Constitutionality, applying as forcibly to making improvements by State authority as by the national authority. So that we must abandon the improvements of the country altogether, by any and every authority, or we must resist and repudiate the doctrines of this message. Let us attempt the latter.

"The first position is, that a system of internal improvement would overwhelm the treasury.

"That, in such a system, there is a *tendency* to undue expansion, is not to be denied. Such tendency is founded in the nature of the subject. A member of Congress will prefer voting for a bill which contains an appropriation for his district, to voting for one which does not; and when a bill shall be expanded till every district shall be provided for, that it will be too greatly expanded is obvious. But is this any more true in Congress than in a State Legislature? If a member of Congress must have an appropriation for his district, so a member of a Legislature must have one for his county; and if one will overwhelm the national treasury, so the other will overwhelm the State treasury. Go where we will, the difficulty is the same. Allow it to drive us from the halls of Congress, and it will just as easily drive us from the State Legislatures. Let us, then, grapple with it, and test its strength. Let us, judging of the future by the past, ascertain whether there may not be, in the discretion of Congress, a sufficient power to limit and restrain this expansive tendency within reasonable and proper bounds. The President himself values the evidence of the past. He tells us that at a certain point of our history, more than two hundred millions of dollars had been *applied for*, to make improvements, and this he does to prove that the treasury would be overwhelmed by such a system. Why did he not tell us how much was *granted?* Would not that have been better evidence? Let us turn to it, and see what it proves. In the message, the President tells us that 'during the four succeeding years, embraced by the administration of President Adams, the power not only to appropriate money, but to apply it, under the direction and authority of the General Government, as well to the construction of roads as to the improvement of harbors and rivers, was fully asserted and exercised.'

"This, then, was the period of greatest enormity. These, if any, must have been the days of the two hundred millions. And how much do you suppose was really expended for improvements during those four years? Two hundred millions? One hundred? Fifty? Ten? Five? No, sir, less than two millions.   As shown by authentic documents, the expenditures on improvements during 1825, 1826, 1827 and 1828, amounted to $1,879,627 01.   These four years were the period of Mr. Adams' administration, nearly, and substantially   This fact shows that when the power to make improvements was 'fully asserted and exercised,' the Congress *did* keep within reasonable limits ; and what *has* been done it seems to me, *can* be done again.

"Now for the second position of the message, namely, that the burdens of improvements would be *general*, while their *benefits* would be *local* and *partial*, involving an obnoxious inequality.   That there is some degree of truth in this position I shall not deny.   No commercial object of Government patronage can be so exclusively *general*, as not to be of some peculiar *local* advantage ; but on the other hand, nothing is so *local* as not to be of some general advantage.   The navy, as I understand it, was established, and is maintained, at a great annual expense, partly to be ready for war, when war shall come, but partly also, and perhaps chiefly, for the protection of our commerce on the high seas.   This latter object is, for all I can see, in principle, the same as internal improvements.   The driving a pirate from the track of commerce on the broad ocean, and the removing a snag from its more narrow path in the Mississippi river, can not, I think, be distinguished in principle.   Each is done to save life and property, and for nothing else.   The navy, then, is the most general in its benefits of all this class of objects ; and yet even the navy is of some peculiar advantage to Charleston, Baltimore, Philadelphia, New York and Boston, beyond what it is to the interior towns of Illinois.   The next most general object I can think of, would be improvements on the Mississippi river and its tributaries.   They touch thirteen of our States—Pennsylvania, Virginia, Kentucky, Tennessee, Mississippi, Louisiana, Arkansas, Missouri, Illinois, Indiana, Ohio, Wisconsin, and Iowa.   Now, I suppose it will not be denied, that these thirteen States are a little more interested in improvements on that great river than are the remaining seventeen. These instances of the navy, and the Mississippi river show clearly that there is something of local advantage in the most general objects. But the converse is also true. Nothing is so *local* as not to be of some *general* benefit. Take, for instance, the Illinois and Michigan canal. Considered apart from its effects, it is perfectly local. Every inch of it is within the State of Illinois. That canal was first opened for business last April. In a very few days we were all gratified to learn, among other things, that sugar had been carried from New Orleans, through the canal, to Buffalo, in New York. This sugar took this route, doubtless, because it was cheaper than the old route. Supposing the benefit in the reduction of the cost of carriage to be shared between seller and buyer, the result is, that the New Orleans merchant sold his sugar a little *dearer*, and the people of Buffalo sweetened their coffee a little *cheaper* than before; a benefit resulting *from* the canal, not to Illinois, where the canal *is*, but to Louisiana and New York, where the canal is *not*. In other transactions Illinois will, of course, have her share, and perhaps the larger share too, in the benefits of the canal; but the instance of the sugar clearly shows that the *benefits* of an improvement are by no means confined to the particular locality of the improvement itself.

" The just conclusion from all this is, that if the nation refuse to make improvements of the more general kind, because their benefits may be somewhat local, a State may, for the same reason, refuse to make an improvement of a local kind, because its benefits may be somewhat general. A State may well say to the Nation : ' If you will do nothing for me, I will do nothing for you.' Thus it is seen, that if this argument of ' inequality ' is sufficient anywhere, it is sufficient everywhere, and puts an end to improvements altogether. I hope and believe, that if both the Nation and the States would, in faith, in their respective spheres, do what they could in the way of improvements, what of inequality might be produced in one place might be compensated in another, and that the sum of the whole might not be very unequal. But suppose, after all, there should be some degree of inequality : inequality is certainly never to be embraced for its own sake ; but is every good thing to be discarded which may be inseparably connected with some degree of it ? If so, we must discard all government. This Capitol is built at the public expense, for the public benefit ; but does any one doubt that it is of some peculiar local advantage to the property holders and business people of Washington ? Shall we remove it for this reason ? And if so, where shall we set it down, and be free from the difficulty ? To make sure of our object shall we locate it nowhere, and leave Congress hereafter to hold its sessions as the loafer lodged, 'in spots about ?' I make no special allusion to the present President when I say, there are few stronger cases in this world of 'burden to the many, and benefit to the few'—of 'inequality' —than the Presidency itself is by some thought to be. An honest laborer digs coal at about seventy cents a day, while the President digs abstractions at about seventy dollars a day. The *coal* is clearly worth more than the *abstractions*, and yet what a monstrous inequality in the prices ! Does the President, for this reason, propose to abolish the Presidency ? He *does* not, and he *ought* not. The true rule, in determining to embrace or reject any thing, is not whether it have *any* evil in it, but whether it have more of evil than of good. There are few things *wholly* evil or *wholly* good. almost every thing, especially of government policy, is an inseparable compound of the two ; so that our best judgment of the preponderance between them is continually demanded. On this principle, the President, his friends, and the world generally, act on most subjects. Why not apply it, then,

upon this question?   Why, as to improvements, magnify the
evil, and stoutly refuse to see any good in them?

"Mr. Chairman, on the third position of the message (the
Constitutional question) I have not much to say.   Being the
man I am, and speaking when I do, I feel that in any attempt
at an original, Constitutional argument, I should not be, and
ought not to be, listened to patiently.   The ablest and the
best of men have gone over the whole ground long ago.   I
shall attempt but little more than a brief notice of what some
of them have said.   In relation to Mr. Jefferson's views, I
read from Mr. Polk's veto message:

" 'President Jefferson, in his message to Congress in 1806,
recommended an amendment of the Constitution, with a view
to apply an anticipated surplus in the treasury 'to the great
purposes of the public education, roads, rivers, canals, and
such other objects of public improvements as it may be
thought proper to add to the Constitutional enumeration of
the Federal powers.'   And he adds: 'I suppose an amendment to the Constitution, by consent of the States, necessary,
because the objects now recommended are not among those
enumerated in the Constitution, and to which it permits the
public moneys to be applied.'   In 1825, he repeated, in his
published letters, the opinion that no such power had been
conferred upon Congress.'

"I introduce this, not to controvert, just now, the Consti
tutional opinion, but to show, that on the question of *expediency*, Mr. Jefferson's opinion was against the present President—that this opinion of Mr. Jefferson, in one branch at
least, is, in the hands of Mr. Polk, like McFingal's gun:

" 'Bears wide and kicks the owner over.'

"But, to the Constitutional question.   In 1826, Chancellor
Kent first published his Commentaries on American Law.
He devoted a portion of one of the lectures to the question
of the authority of Congress to appropriate public moneys for

internal improvements. He mentions that the question had never been brought under judicial consideration, and proceeds to give a brief summary of the discussions it had undergone between the legislative and executive branches of the Government. He shows that the legislative branch had usually been *for*, and the executive *against*, the power, till the period of Mr. J. Q. Adams' administration; at which point he considers the executive influence as withdrawn from opposition, and added to the support of the power. In 1844, the Chancelor published a new edition of his Commentaries, in which he adds some notes of what had transpired on the question since 1826. I have not time to read the original text, or the notes, but the whole may be found on page 267, and the two or three following pages of the first volume of the edition of 1844. As what Chancellor Kent seems to consider the sum of the whole, I read from one of the notes:

" ' Mr. Justice Story, in his Commentaries on the Constitution of the United States, vol. 2, page 429–440, and again, page 519–538, has stated at large the arguments for and against the proposition that Congress have a Constitutional authority to lay taxes, and to apply the power to regulate commerce, as a means directly to encourage and protect domestic manufactures; and, without giving any opinion of his own on the contested doctrine, he has left the reader to draw his own conclusion. I should think, however, from the arguments as stated, that every mind which has taken no part in the discussions, and felt no prejudice or territorial bias on either side of the question, would deem the arguments in favor of the Congressional power vastly superior.'

" It will be seen, that in this extract, the power to make improvements is not directly mentioned; but by examining the context, both of Kent and of Story, it will appear that the power mentioned in the extract and the power to make improvements, are regarded as identical. It is not to be denied that many great and good men have been *against* the power; but it is insisted that quite as many, as great, and as good, have been *for* it; and it is shown that, on a full survey of the whole, Chancelor Kent was of opinion that the arguments of the latter were *vastly* superior. This is but the opinion of a man; but who was that man? He was one of the ablest and most learned lawyers of his age, or of any other age. It is no disparagement to Mr. Polk, nor, indeed, to any one who devotes much time to politics, to be placed far behind Chancelor Kent as a lawyer. His attitude was most favorable to correct conclusions. He wrote coolly and in retirement. He was struggling to rear a durable monument of fame; and he well knew that *truth* and thoroughly sound reasoning were the only sure foundations. Can the party opinion of a party President, on a law question, as this purely is, be at all compared or set in opposition to that of such a man, in such an attitude as Chancelor Kent?

"This Constitutional question will probably never be better settled than it is, until it shall pass under judicial consideration; but I do think that no man who is clear on this question of expediency need feel his conscience much pricked upon this.

"Mr. Chairman, the President seems to think that enough may be done in the way of improvements, by means of tonnage duties, under State authority, with the consent of the General Government. Now, I suppose this matter of tonnage duties is well enough in its own sphere. I suppose it may be efficient, and perhaps *sufficient*, to make slight improvements and repairs in harbors already in use, and not much out of repair. But if I have any correct general idea of it, it must be wholly inefficient for any generally beneficent purposes of improvement. I know very little, or rather nothing at all, of the practical matter of levying and collecting tonnage duties; but I suppose one of its principles must be, to lay a duty, for the improvement of any particular harbor, *upon the tonnag · coming into that harbor.* To do otherwise

—to collect money in *one* harbor to be expended in improvements in *another*—would be an extremely aggravated form of that inequality which the President so much deprecates. If I be right in this, how could we make any entirely new improvements by means of tonnage duties? How make road, a canal, or clear a greatly obstructed river? The ide that we could, involves the same absurdity of the Irish bul about the new boots: 'I shall never git 'em on,' says Patrick, 'till I wear 'em a day or two, and stretch 'em a little.' We shall never make a canal by tonnage duties, until it shall already have been made awhile, so the tonnage can get into it.

"After all, the President concludes that possibly there may be some great objects of improvements which can not be effected by tonnage duties, and which, therefore, may be expedient for the General Government to take in hand. Accordingly, he suggests, in case any such be discovered, the propriety of amending the Constitution. Amend it for what? If, like Mr. Jefferson, the President thought improvements *expedient* but not Constitutional, it would be natural enough for him to recommend such an amendment; but hear what he says in this very message:

"'In view of these portentous consequences, I can not but think that this course of legislation should be arrested, even were there nothing to forbid it in the fundamental laws of our Union.'

"For what, then, would *he* have the Constitution amended? With *him* it is a proposition to remove *one* impediment merely to be met by *others*, which, in his opinion, can not be removed—to enable Congress to do what, in his opinion, they ought not to do if they could."

[Here Mr. Meade, of Virginia, inquired if Mr. L. under stood the President to be opposed, on grounds of expeaiency to any and every improvement?

To which Mr. Lincoln answered: "In the very part of his

message of which I am now speaking, I understand him as giving some vague expressions in favor of some possible objects of improvement; but, in doing so, I understand him to be directly in the teeth of his own arguments in other parts of it. Neither the President, nor any one, can possibly pecify an improvement, which shall not be clearly liable to one or another of the objections he has urged on the score of expediency; I have shown, and might show again, that no work—no object—can be so general, as to dispense its benefits with precise equality; and this inequality is chief among the 'portentous consequences' for which he declares that improvments should be arrested. No, sir; when the President intimates that something in the way of improvements may properly be done by the General Government, he is shrinking from the conclusions to which his own arguments would force him. He feels that the improvements of this broad and goodly land are a mighty interest; and he is unwilling to confess to the people, or perhaps to himself, that he has built an argument which, when pressed to its conclusion, entirely annihilates this interest.

"I have already said that no one who is satisfied of the expediency of making improvements need be much uneasy in his conscience about its Constitutionality. I wish now to submit a few remarks on the general proposition of amending the Constitution. As a General rule, I think we would do much better to let it alone. No slight occasion should tempt us to touch it. Better not take the first step, which may lead to a habit of altering it. Better rather habituate ourselves to think of it as unalterable. It can scarcely be made better than it is. New provisions would introduce new difficulties, and thus create and increase appetite for further change. No, sir; let it stand as it is. New hands have never touched it. The men who made it have done their work, and have passed away. Who shall improve on what *they* did?

"Mr. Chairman, for the purpose of reviewing this message in the least possible time, as well as for the sake of distinctness, I have analyzed its arguments as well as I could, and reduced them to the propositions I have stated. I have now examined them in detail. I wish to detain the committee only a little while longer, with some general remarks on the subject of improvements. That the subject is a difficult one, can not be denied. Still, it is no more difficult in Congress than in the State legislatures, in the counties or in the smallest municipal districts which everywhere exist. All can recur to instances of this difficulty in the case of county roads, bridges, and the like. One man is offended because a road passes over his land; and another is offended because it does *not* pass over his; one is dissatisfied because the bridge, for which he is taxed, crosses the river on a different road from that which leads from his house to town; another can not bear that the county should get in debt for these same roads and bridges; while not a few struggle hard to have roads located over their lands, and then stoutly refuse to let them be opened, until they are first paid the damages. Even between the different wards and streets of towns and cities, we find this same wrangling and difficulty. Now, these are no other than the very difficulties against which, and out of which, the President constructs his objections of 'inequalty,' 'speculation,' and 'crushing the Treasury.' There is but a single alternative about them—they are *sufficient*, or they are *not*. If sufficient, they are sufficient *out* of Congress as well as *in* it, and there is the end. We must reject them as insufficient, or lie down and do nothing by any authority. Then, difficulty though there be, let us meet and overcome it.

'Attempt the end, and never stand to doubt;
Nothing so hard, but search will find it out.'

"Determine that the thing can and shall be done, and then we shall find the way. The tendency to undue expansion is unquestionably the chief difficulty.   How to do *something*, and still not to do *too much*, is the desideratum.   Let each contribute his mite in the way of suggestion.   The late Silas Wright, in a letter to the Chicago Convention, contributed his, which was worth something ; and I now contribute mine, which may be worth nothing.   At all events, it will mislead nobody, and therefore will do no harm.   I would not borrow money.   I am against an overwhelming, crushing system.   Suppose that at each session, Congress shall first determine *how much* money can, for that year, be spared for improvements ; then apportion that sum to the most *important* objects.   So far all is easy ; but how shall we determine which *are* the most important ?   On this question comes the collision of interests.   *I* shall be slow to acknowledge that *your* harbor or *your* river is more important than *mine*, and *vice versa*.   To clear this difficulty, let us have that same statistical information which the gentleman from Ohio [Mr. Vinton] suggested at the beginning of this session.   In that information we shall have a stern, unbending basis of *facts*— a basis in nowise subject to whim, caprice, or local interest. The pre-limited amount of means will save us from doing *too much*, and the statistics will save us from doing what we do in *wrong places*.   Adopt and adhere to this course, and, it seems to me, the difficulty is cleared.

" One of the gentlemen from South Carolina (Mr. Rhett) very much deprecates these statistics.   He particularly objects, as I understand him, to counting all the pigs and chickens in the land.   I do not perceive much force in the objection.   It is true, that if every thing be enumerated, a portion of such statistics may not be very useful to this object.   Such products of the country as are to be *consumed* where they are *produced*, need no roads and rivers, no means of transportation, and have no very proper connection with this subject.   The *surplus*, that which is produced in *one* place to be consumed in *another ;* the capacity of each locality for producing a *greater* surplus; the natural means of transportation, and their susceptibility of improvement; the hindrances, delays, and losses of life and property during transportation, and the causes of each, would be among the most valuable statistics in this connection. From these it would readily appear where a given amount of expenditure would do the most good. These statistics might be equally accessible, as they would be equally useful, to both the Nation and the States. In this way, and by these means, let the nation take hold of the larger works, and the States the smaller ones; and thus, working in a meeting direction, discreetly, but steadily and firmly, what is made unequal in one place may be equalized in another, extravagance avoided, and the whole country put on that career of prosperity, which shall correspond with its extent of territory, its natural resources, and the intelligence and enterprise of its people."

SPEECH ON THE PRESIDENCY AND GENERAL POLITICS.

(Delivered in the House, July 27, 1848.)

GENERAL TAYLOR AND THE VETO POWER.

"Mr. SPEAKER:—Our Democratic friends seem to be in great distress because they think our candidate for the Presidency don't suit *us.* Most of them can not find out that General Taylor has any principles at all; some, however, have discovered that he has *one,* but that that one is entirely wrong. This one principle is his position on the veto power. The gentleman from Tennessee (Mr. Stanton) who has just taken his seat, indeed, has said there is very little if any difference on this question between General Taylor and all the Presidents; and he seems to think it sufficient detraction from General Taylor's position on it, that it has nothing new in it. But all others whom I have heard speak assail it furiously A new member from Kentucky (Mr. Clarke) of very consid-

27

erable ability, was in particular concern about it.   He thought
it altogether novel and unprecedented for a President, or a
Presidential candidate, to think of approving bills whose
Constitutionality may not be entirely clear to his own mind.
He thinks the ark of our safety is gone, unless Presidents shall
always veto such bills as, in their judgment, may be of *doubtful* Constitutionality.   However clear Congress may be of
their authority to pass any particular act, the gentleman
from Kentucky thinks the President must veto it if *he* has
doubts about it.   Now I have neither time nor inclination to
argue with the gentleman on the veto power as an original
question ; but I wish to show that General Taylor, and not
he, agrees with the earliest statesmen on this question.   When
the bill chartering the first Bank of the United States passed
Congress, its Constitutionality was questioned ; Mr. Madison,
then in the House of Representatives, as well as others, had
opposed it on that ground.   General Washington, as President, was called on to approve or reject it.   He sought and
obtained, on the Constitutional question, the separate written
opinions of Jefferson, Hamilton, and Edmund Randolph, they
then being respectively Secretary of State, Secretary of the
Treasury, and Attorney General.   Hamilton's opinion was
for the power ; while Randolph's and Jefferson's were both
against it.   Mr. Jefferson, in his letter dated February 15th,
1791, after giving his opinion decidedly against the Constitutionality of that bill, closed with the paragraph which I now
read :

" ' It must be admitted, however, that unless the President's mind, on a view of every thing which is urged for and
against this bill, is tolerably clear that it is unauthorized by
the Constitution ; if the pro and the con hang so even as to
balance his judgment, a just respect for the wisdom of the
Legislature would naturally decide the balance in favor of
their opinion ; it is chiefly for cases where they are clearly

misled by error, ambition, or interest, that the Constitution has placed a check in the negative of the President.'

"General Taylor's opinion, as expressed in his Allison letter, is as I now read:

"'The power given by the veto is a high conservative power; but, in my opinion, should never be exercised, except in cases of clear violation of the Constitution, or manifest haste and want of consideration by Congress.

"It is here seen that, in Mr. Jefferson's opinion, if, on the Constitutionality of any given bill, the President *doubts*, he is not to veto it, as the gentleman from Kentucky would have him to do, but is to defer to Congress and approve it. And if we compare the opinions of Jefferson and Taylor, as expressed in these paragraphs, we shall find them more exactly alike than we can often find any two expressions having any literal difference. None but interested fault-finders, can discover any substantial variation.

"But gentlemen on the other side are unanimously agreed that Gen. Taylor has no other principle. They are in utter darkness as to his opinions on any of the questions of policy which occupy the public attention. But is there any doubt as to what he will *do* on the prominent question, if elected? Not the least. It is not possible to know what he will or would do in every imaginable case; because many questions have passed away, and others doubtless will arise which none of us have yet thought of; but on the prominent questions of currency, tariff, internal improvements, and Wilmot proviso, General Taylor's course is at least as well defined as is General Cass's. Why, in their eagerness to get at General Taylor, several Democratic members here have desired to know whether, in case of his election, a bankrupt law is to be established. Can they tell us General Cass's opinion on this question? (Some member answered, 'He is against it.') Aye, how do you know he is? There is nothing about it in the platform, nor elsewhere, that I have seen. If the gentleman knows any thing which I do not, he can show it. But to return : General Taylor, in his Allison letter says :

" 'Upon the subject of the tariff, the currency, the improvement of our great highways, rivers, lakes, and harbors, the will of the people, as expressed through their Representatives in Congress, ought to be respected and carried out by the Executive.'

" Now, this is the whole matter—in substance, it is this : The people say to General Taylor, 'If you are elected shall we have a National bank ?' He answers, '*Your* will, gentlemen, not *mine*.' 'What about the tariff ?' 'Say yourselves.' 'Shall our rivers and harbors be improved ?' 'Just as you please.' 'If you desire a bank, an alteration of the tariff, internal improvements, any or all, I will not hinder you ; if you do not desire them, I will not attempt to force them on you. Send up your members of Congress from the various districts, with opinions according to your own, and if they are for these measures, or any of them, I shall have nothing to oppose ; if they are not for them, I shall not, by any appliances whatever, attempt to dragoon them into their adoption.' Now, can there be any difficulty in understanding this ? To you, Democrats, it may not seem like principle ; but surely you can not fail to perceive the position plain enough. The distinction between it and the position of your candidate is broad and obvious, and I admit you have a clear right to show it is wrong, if you can ; but you have no right to pretend you can not see it at all. We see it, and to us it appears like principle, and the best sort of principle at that—the principle of allowing the people to do as they please with their own business. My friend from Indiana (Mr. C. B. Smith) has aptly asked, 'Are you willing to trust the people ?' Some of you answered, substantially, 'We are willing to trust the people ; but the President is as much the representative of the people as Congress.' In a certain sense, and to a certain extent, he is the representative of the people. He is elected

by them, as well as Congress is.   But can he, in the nature
of things, know the wants of the people as well as three hundred other men coming from all the various localities of the
Nation ?   If so, where is the propriety of having a Congress ?
That the Constitution gives the President a negative on
legislation, all know ; but that this negative should be so
combined with platforms and other appliances as to enable
him, and, in fact, almost compel him, to take the whole of legislation into his own hands, is what we object to—is what General Taylor objects to—and is what constitutes the broad distinction between you and us.   To thus transfer legislation is
clearly to take it from those who understand with minuteness
the interests of the people, and give it to one who does not
and can not so well understand it.   I understand your idea,
that if a Presidential candidate avow his opinion upon a
given question, or rather upon all questions, and the people,
with full knowledge of this, elect him, they thereby distinctly
approve all those opinions.   This, though plausible, is a most
pernicious deception.   By means of it measures are adopted
or rejected, contrary to the wishes of the whole of one party,
and often nearly half of the other.   The process is this :
Three, four, or half a dozen questions are prominent at a
given time ; the party selects its candidate, and he takes his
position on each of these questions.   On all but one his positions have already been indorsed at former elections, and his
party fully committed to them ; but that one is new, and a
large portion of them are against it.   But what are they to do ?
The whole are strung together, and they must take all or
reject all.   They can not take what they like and leave the
rest.   What they are already committed to, being the majority, they shut their eyes and gulp the whole.   Next election, still another is introduced in the same way.   If we run
our eyes along the line of the past, we shall see that almost,
if not quite, all the articles of the present Democratic creed
have been at first forced upon the party in this very way.

And just now, and just so, opposition to internal improvements is to be established if Gen. Cass shall be elected. Almost half the Democrats here are for improvements, but they will vote for Cass, and if he succeeds, their votes will have aided in closing the doors against improvements. Now, this is a process which we think is wrong. We prefer a candidate who, like Gen. Taylor, will allow the people to have their own way regardless of his private opinion ; and I should think the internal-improvement Democrats at least, ought to prefer such a candidate. He would force nothing on them which they don't want, and he would allow them to have improvements, which their own candidate, if elected, will not.

"Mr. Speaker, I have said Gen. Taylor's position is as well defined as is that of Gen. Cass. In saying this, I admit I do not certainly know what he would do on the Wilmot proviso. I am a Northern man, or, rather, a Western free State man, with a constituency I believe to be, and with personal feelings I know to be, against the extension of slavery. As such, and with what information I have, I hope, and *believe*, Gen. Taylor, if elected, would not veto the proviso ; but I do not *know* it. Yet, if I knew he would, I still would vote for him. I should do so, because, in my judgment, his election alone can defeat Gen. Cass ; and because, *should* slavery thereby go into the territory we now have, just so much will certainly happen by the election of Cass ; and, in addition, a course of policy leading to new wars, new acquisitions of territory, and still further extensions of slavery. One of the two is to be President ; which is preferable ?

"But there is as much doubt of Cass on improvements as there is of Taylor on the proviso. I have no doubt myself of Gen. Cass on this question, but I know the Democrats differ among themselves as to his position. My internal improvement colleague (Mr. Wentworth) stated on this floor the other day, that he was satisfied Cass was for improvements, because he had voted for all the bills that he (Mr. W.) had. So far so good. But Mr. Polk vetoed some of these very bills; the Baltimore Convention passed a set of resolutions, among other things, approving these vetoes, and Cass declares, in his letter accepting the nomination, that he has carefully read these resolutions, and that he adheres to them as firmly as he approves them cordially. In other words, Gen. Cass voted for the bills, and thinks the President did right to veto them; and his friends here are amiable enough to consider him as being on one side or the other, just as one or the other may correspond with their own respective inclinations. My colleague admits that the platform declares against the Constitutionality of a general system of improvement, and that Gen. Cass indorses the platform; but he still thinks Gen. Cass is in favor of some sort of improvements. Well, what are they? As he is against *general* objects, those he is *for*, must be *particular* and *local*. Now, this is taking the subject precisely by the wrong end. *Particularity*—expending the money of the *whole* people for an object which will benefit only a *portion* of them, is the greatest real objection to improvements, and has been so held by Gen. Jackson, Mr. Polk, and all others, I believe, till now. But now, behold, the objects most general, nearest free from this objection, are to be rejected, while those most liable to it are to be embraced. To return : I can not help believing that Gen. Cass, when he wrote his letter of acceptance, well understood he was to be claimed by the advocates of both sides of this question, and that he then closed the door against all further expressions of opinion, purposely to retain the benefits of that double position. His subsequent equivocation at Cleveland, to my mind, proves such to have been the case.

"One word more, and I shall have done with this branch of the subject. You Democrats, and your candidate, in the main are in favor of laying down, in advance, a platform—a set of party positions, as a unit; and then of enforcing the people, by every sort of appliance, to ratify them, however unpalatable some of them may be.   We, and our candidate, are in favor of making Presidential elections and the legislation of the country distinct matters; so that the people can elect whom they please, and afterward legislate just *as* they please, without any hindrance, save only so much as may guard against infractions of the Constitution, undue haste, and want of consideration.   The difference between us is clear as noonday.   That we are right we can not doubt. We hold the true Republican position.   In leaving the people's business in their hands we can not be wrong.   We are willing, and even anxious, to go to the people on this issue.

"But I suppose I can not reasonably hope to convince you that we have any principles.   The most I can expect is, to assure you that we think we have, and are quite contented with them.   The other day, one of the gentlemen from Georgia (Mr. Iverson), an eloquent man, and a man of learning, so far as I can judge, not being learned myself, came down upon us astonishingly.   He spoke in what the Baltimore *American* calls the 'scathing and withering style.' At the end of his second severe flash I was struck blind, and found myself feeling with my fingers for an assurance of my continued physical existence.   A little of the bone was left, and I gradually revived.   He eulogized Mr. Clay in high and beautiful terms, and then declared that we had deserted all our principles, and had turned Henry Clay out, like an old horse, to root.   This is terribly severe.   It can not be answered by argument; at least, I can not so answer it.   I merely wish to ask the gentleman if the Whigs are the only party he can think of, who sometimes turn old horses out to root?   Is not a certain Martin Van Buren an old horse which your own party have turned out to root? and is he not rooting a little to your discomfort about now?   But in not nominating Mr. Clay, we deserted our principles, you say. Ah! in what? Tell us, ye men of principles what principle we violated? We say you did violate principle in discarding Van Buren, and we can tell you how. You violated the primary, the cardinal, the one great living principle of all Democratic representative government—the principle that the representative is bound to carry out the known will of his constituents. A large majority of the Baltimore Convention of 1844 were, by their constituents, instructed to procure Van Buren's nomination if they could. In violation, in utter, glaring contempt of this, you rejected him—rejected him, as the gentlemen from New York (Mr. Birdsall), the other day expressly admitted, for *availability*—that same 'general availability' which you charge upon us, and daily chew over here, as something exceedingly odious and unprincipled. But the gentleman from Georgia (Mr. Iverson), gave us a second speech yesterday, all well considered and put down in writing, in which Van Buren was scathed and withered a 'few' for his present position and movements. I can not remember the gentlemen's precise language, but I do remember he put Van Buren down, down, till he got him where he was finally to 'stink' and ' rot.'

"Mr. Speaker, it is no business or inclination of mine to defend Martin Van Buren. In the war of extermination now waging between him and his old admirers, I say, devil take the hindmost—and the foremost. But there is no mistaking the origin of the breach; and if the curse of 'stinking' and ' rotting' is to fall on the first and greatest violaters of principle in the matter, I disinterestedly suggest, that the gentleman from Georgia and his present co-workers are bound to take it upon themselves."

Mr. Lincoln then proceeded to speak of the objections against Gen. Taylor as a mere military hero; retorting with effect, by citing the attempt to make out a military record for Gen. Cass; and referring, in a bantering way, to his own services in the Black Hawk war, as already quoted.　He then said :

"While I have Gen. Cass in hand, I wish to say a word about his political principles.　As a specimen, I take the record of his progress on the Wilmot Proviso.　In the Washington Union, of March 2, 1847, there is a report of the speech of Gen. Cass, made the day before in the Senate, on the Wilmot Proviso, during the delivery of which, Mr. Miller, of New Jersey, is reported to have interrupted him as follows, to wit :

"'Mr. Miller expressed his great surprise at the change in the sentiments of the Senator from Michigan, who had been regarded as the great champion of freedom in the North-west of which he was a distinguished ornament.　Last year the Senator from Michigan was understood to be decidedly in favor of the Wilmot Proviso ; and, as no reason had been stated for the change, he (Mr. Miller) could not refrain from the expression of his extreme surprise.'

"To this Gen. Cass is reported to have replied as follows, to wit :

"Mr. Cass said, that the course of the Senator from New Jersey was most extraordinary.　Last year he (Mr. Cass) should have voted for the proposition had it come up.　But circumstances had altogether changed.　The honorable Senator then read several passages from the remarks as given above, which he had committed to writing, in order to refute such a charge as that of the Senator from New Jersey.'

"In the 'remarks above committed to writing,' is one numbered 4, as follows, to wit :

"'4th. Legislation would now be wholly imperative, because no territory hereafter to be acquired can be governed without an act of Congress providing for its government. And such an act, on its passage, would open the whole subject, and leave the Congress, called on to pass it, free to exercise its own discretion, entirely uncontrolled by any declaration found in the statute book.'

"In Niles' Register, vol. 73, page 293, there is a letter of General Cass to A. O. P. Nicholson, of Nashville, Tennessee dated December 24, 1847, from which the following are cor rect extracts:

"'The Wilmot Proviso has been before the country some time. It has been repeatedly discussed in Congress, and by the public press. I am strongly impressed with the opinion that a great change has been going on in the public mind upon this subject—in my own as well as others; and that doubts are resolving themselves into convictions, that the principle it involves should be kept out of the National Legislature, and left to the people of the Confederacy in their respective local Governments.

"'Briefly, then, I am opposed to the exercise of any jurisdiction by Congress over this matter; and I am in favor of leaving the people of any territory which may be hereafter acquired, the right to regulate it themselves, under the general principles of the Constitution. Because,

"'1. I do not see in the Constitution any grant of the requisite power to Congress; and I am not disposed to extend a doubtful precedent beyond its necessity—the establishment of territorial governments when needed—leaving to the inhabitants all the rights compatible with the relations they bear to the Confederation.'

"These extracts show that, in 1846, General Cass was for the Proviso *at once;* that, in March, 1847, he was still for it, *but not just then;* and that in December, 1847, he was *against* it altogether. This is a true index to the whole man. When the question was raised in 1846, he was in a blustering hurry to take ground for it. He sought to be in advance, and to avoid the uninteresting position of a mere follower; but soon he began to see glimpses of the great Democratic ox-gad waving in his face, and to hear indistinctly, a voice saying, 'back,'

' back, sir,' ' back a little.' He shakes his head and bats his eyes, and blunders back to his position of March, 1847 ; but still the gad waves, and the voice grows more distinct, and sharper still—' back, sir !' ' back, I say !' ' further back !' and back he goes to the position of December, 1847 ; at which the gad is still, and the voice soothingly says—' So !' ' Stand still at that.'

" Have no fears, gentlemen, of your candidate ; he exactly suits you, and we congratulate you upon it. However much you may be distressed about *our* candidate, you have all cause to be contented and happy with your own. If elected, he may not maintain all, or even any of his positions previously taken ; but he will be sure to do whatever the party exigency, for the time being, may require ; and that is precisely what you want. He and Van Buren are the same ' manner of men ;' and like Van Buren, he will never desert *you* till you first desert *him*."

After referring at some length to extra " charges" of General Cass upon the Treasury, Mr. Lincoln continued :—

" But I have introduced General Cass's accounts here, chiefly to show the wonderful physical capacities of the man. They show that he not only did the labor of several men at the same *time*, but that he often did it, at several *places* many hundred miles apart, *at the same time*. And at eating, too, his capacities are shown to be quite as wonderful. From October, 1821, to May, 1822, he ate ten rations a day in Michigan, ten rations a day here, in Washington, and nearly five dollar's worth a day besides, partly on the road between the two places. And then there is an important discovery in his example—the art of being paid for what one eats, instead of having to pay for it. Hereafter, if any nice young man shall owe a bill which he can not pay in any other way, he can just board it out. Mr. Speaker, we have all heard of the animal standing in doubt between two stacks of hay, and starving to death; the like of that would never happen to General Cass. Place the stacks a thousand miles apart, he would stand stock-still, midway between them, and eat them both at once; and the green grass along the line would be apt to suffer some too, at the same time. By all means, make him President, gentlemen. He will feed you bounteously—if if—there is any left after he shall have helped himself.

"But as General Taylor, is, par excellence, the hero of the Mexican war; and, as you Democrats say we Whigs have always opposed the war, you think it must be very awkward and embarrassing for us to go for General Taylor. The declaration that we have always opposed the war, is true or false accordingly as one may understand the term 'opposing the war.' If to say 'the war was unnecessarily and unconstitutionally commenced by the President,' be opposing the war, then the Whigs have very generally opposed it. Whenever they have spoken at all, they have said this; and they have said it on what has appeared good reason to them: The marching an army into the midst of a peaceful Mexican settlement, frightening the inhabitants away, leaving their growing crops and other property to destruction, to *you* may appear a perfectly amiable, peaceful, unprovoking procedure; but it does not appear so to *us*. So to call such an act, to us appears no other than a naked, impudent absurdity, and we speak of it accordingly. But if, when the war had begun, and had become the cause of the country, the giving of our money and our blood, in common with yours, was support of the war, then it is not true that we have always opposed the war. With few individual exceptions, you have constantly had our votes here for all the necessary supplies. And, more than this, you have had the services, the blood, and the lives of our political brethren in every trial, and on every field The beardless boy and the mature man—the humble and the distinguished, you have had them. Through suffering and death, by disease and in battle, they have endured, and fought, and fallen with you. Clay and Webster each gave a son, never to be returned. From the State of my own residence, besides other worthy but less known Whig names, we sent Marshall, Morrison, Baker, and Hardin; they all fought, and one fell, and in the fall of that one, we lost our best Whig man. Nor were the Whigs few in number, or laggard in the day of danger. In that fearful, bloody, breathless struggle at Buena Vista, where each man's hard task was to beat back five foes, or die himself, of the five high officers who perished, four were Whigs.

"In speaking of this, I mean no odious comparison between the lion-hearted Whigs and Democrats who fought there. On other occasions, and among the lower officers and privates on *that* occasion, I doubt not the proportion was different. I wish to do justice to all. I think of all those brave men as Americans, in whose proud fame, as an American, I too have a share. Many of them, Whigs and Democrats, are my constituents and personal friends; and I thank them—more than thank them—one and all, for the high, imperishable honor they have conferred on our common State.

"But the distinction between the cause of the *President* in beginning the war, and the cause of the *country* after it was begun, is a distinction which you can not perceive. To *you*, the President and the country seem to be all one. You are interested to see no distinction between them; and I venture to suggest that *possibly* your interest blinds you a little. We see the distinction, as we think, clearly enough; and our friends, who have fought in the war, have no difficulty in seeing it also. What those who have fallen would say, were they alive and here, of course we can never know; but with those who have returned there is no difficulty. Colonel Haskell and Major Gaines, members here, both fought in the war; and one of them underwent extraordinary perils and hardships ; still they, like all other Whigs here, vote on the record that the war was unnecessarily and unconstitutionally commenced by the President. And even General Taylor himself, the noblest Roman of them all, has declared that, as a citizen, and particularly as a soldier, it is sufficient for him to know that his country is at war with a foreign nation, to do all in his power to bring it to a speedy and honorable termination, by the most vigorous and energetic operations, without inquiring about its justice, or any thing else connected with it.

" Mr. Speaker, let our Democratic friends be comforted with the assurance that we are content with our position, content with our company, and content with our candidate ; and that although they, in their generous sympathy, think we ought to be miserable, we really are not, and that they may dismiss the great anxiety they have on *our* account."

SPEECH IN REPLY TO MR. DOUGLAS, ON KANSAS, THE DRED SCOTT DECISION, AND THE UTAH QUESTION.

(Delivered at Springfield, Ill., June 26, 1857.)

" FELLOW-CITIZENS :—I am here, to-night, partly by the invitation of some of you, and partly by my own inclination. Two weeks ago Judge Douglas spoke here, on the several subjects of Kansas, the Dred Scott decision, and Utah. I listened to the speech at the time, and have read the report of it since. It was intended to controvert opinions which I think just, and to assail (politically, not personally) those men who, in common with me, entertain those opinions. For this reason I wished then, and still wish to make some answer to it, which I now take the opportunity of doing.

" I begin with Utah. If it prove to be true, as is probable, that the people of Utah are in open rebellion against the United States, then Judge Douglas is in favor of repealing their territorial organization, and attaching them to the adjoining States for judicial purposes. I say, too, if they are in rebellion, they ought to be somehow coerced to obedience; and I am not now prepared to admit or deny, that the Judge's mode of coercing them is not as good as any. The Republicans can fall in with it, without taking back any thing they have ever said. To be sure, it would be a considerable backing down by Judge Douglas, from his much vaunted doctrine of self-government for the territories; but this is only additional proof of what was very plain from the beginning, that that doctrine was a mere deceitful pretence for the benefit of slavery. Those who could not see that much in the Nebraska act itself, which forced Governors, and Secretaries, and Judges on the people of the territories, without their choice or consent, could not be made to see, though one should rise from the dead.

" But in all this, it is very plain the Judge evades the only question the Republicans have ever pressed upon the Democracy in regard to Utah. That question the Judge well knew to be this: 'If the people of Utah shall peacefully form a State Constitution tolerating polygamy, will the Democracy admit them into the Union?' There is nothing in the United States Constitution or law against polygamy; and why is it not a part of the Judge's 'sacred right of self-government' for the people to have it, or rather to keep it, if they choose? These questions, so far as I know, the Judge never answers. It might involve the Democracy to answer them either way, and they go unanswered.

"As to Kansas. The substance of the Judge's speech on Kansas, is an effort to put the Free State men in the wrong for not voting at the election of delegates to the Constitutional Convention. He says: 'There is every reason to hope and believe that the law will be fairly interpreted and impartially executed, so as to insure to every bona fide inhabitant the free and quiet exercise of the elective franchise.'

" It appears extraordinary that Judge Douglas should make such a statement. He knows that, by the law, no one can vote who has not been registered ; and he knows that the Free State men place their refusal to vote on the ground that but few of them have been registered. It is possible this is not true, but Judge Douglas knows it is asserted to be true in letters, newspapers, and public speeches, and borne by every mail, and blown by every breeze to the eyes and ears of the world. He knows it is boldly declared, that the people of many whole counties, and many whole neighborhoods in others, are left unregistered ; yet he does not venture to contradict the declaration, or to point out how they can vote without being registered ; but he just slips along, not seeming to know there is any such question of fact, and complacently declares, ' There is every reason to hope and believe that the law will be fairly and impartially executed, so as to insure to every bona fide inhabitant the free and quiet exercise of the elective franchise.'

" I readily agree that if all had a chance to vote, they ought to have voted. If, on the contrary, as they allege, and Judge Douglas ventures not particularly to contradict, few only of the Free State men had a chance to vote, they were perfectly right in staying from the polls in a body.

" By the way, since the Judge spoke, the Kansas election has come off. The Judge expressed his confidence that all the Democrats in Kansas would do their duty—including ' Free State Democrats' of course. The returns received here, as yet, are very incomplete ; but, so far as they go, they indicate that only about one-sixth of the registered voters, have really voted ; and this, too, when not more, perhaps, than one-half of the rightful voters have been registered, thus showing the thing to have been altogether the most exquisite farce ever enacted. I am watching with considerable interest, to ascertain what figure ' the Free State Democrats' cut in the concern. Of course they voted—all Democrats do their

28

duty—and of course they did not vote for Slave State candidates. We soon shall know how many delegates they elected, how many candidates they have pledged to a free State, and how many votes were cast for them.

"Allow me to barely whisper my suspicion, that there were no such things in Kansas as 'Free State Democrats'— that they were altogether mythical, good only to figure in newspapers and speeches in the free States. If there should prove to be one real, living free State Democrat in Kansas, I suggest that it might be well to catch him, and stuff and preserve his skin, as an interesting specimen of that soon to be extinct variety of the genus Democrat.

"And now, as to the Dred Scott decision. That decision declares two propositions—first, that a negro cannot sue in the United States Courts; and secondly, that Congress can not prohibit slavery in the Territories. It was made by a divided court—dividing differently on the different points. Judge Douglas does not discuss the merits of the decision, and in that respect, I shall follow his example, believing I could no more improve upon McLean and Curtis, than he could on Taney.

" He denounces all who question the correctness of that decision, as offering violent resistance to it. But who resists it ? Who has, in spite of the decision, declared Dred Scott free, and resisted the authority of his master over him ?

" Judicial decisions have two uses—first, to absolutely determine the case decided; and secondly to indicate to the public how other similar cases will be decided when they arise. For the latter use, they are called ' precedents' and ' authorities.'

" We believe as much as Judge Douglas (perhaps more) in obedience to, and respect for the judicial department of Government. We think its decisions on Constitutional ques tions, when fully settled, should control, not only the partic ular cases decided, but the general policy of the country subject to be disturbed only by amendments of the Constitution, as provided in that instrument itself. More than this would be revolution. But we think the Dred Scott decision is erroneous. We know the court that made it has often overruled its own decisions, and we shall do what we can to have it overrule this. We offer no resistance to it.

"Judicial decisions are of greater or less authority as precedents, according to circumstances. That this should be so, accords both with common sense, and the customary understanding of the legal profession.

"If this important decision had been made by the unanimous concurrence of the judges, and without any apparent partisan bias, and in accordance with legal public expectation, and with the steady practice of the departments, throughout our history, and had been in no part based on assumed historical facts which are not really true; or, if wanting in some of these, it had been before the court more than once, and had there been affirmed and re-affirmed through a course of years, it then might be, perhaps would be, factious, nay, even revolutionary, not to acquiesce in it as a precedent.

"But when, as is true, we find it wanting in all these claims to the public confidence, it is not resistance, it is not factious, it is not even disrespectful, to treat it as not having yet quite established a settled doctrine for the country. But Judge Douglas considers this view awful. Hear him:

"'The courts are the tribunals prescribed by the Constitution and created by the authority of the people to determine expound, and enforce the law. Hence, whoever resists the final decision of the highest judicial tribunal, aims a deadly blow to our whole Republican system of government—a blow which, if successful, would place all our rights and liberties at the mercy of passion, anarchy and violence. I repeat, therefore, that if resistance to the decisions of the Supreme Court of the United States, in a matter like the points decided in the Dred Scott case, clearly within their jurisdiction as de fined by the Constitution, shall be forced upon the country as a political issue, it will become a distinct and naked issue between the friends and enemies of the Constitution—the friends and enemies of the supremacy of the laws.'

" Why, this same Supreme Court once decided a national bank to be Constitutional; but General Jackson, as President of the United States, disregarded the decision, and vetoed a bill for a re-charter, partly on Constitutional ground, declaring that each public functionary must support the Constitution, 'as he understands it.' But hear the General's own words. Here they are, taken from his veto message:

" ' It is maintained by the advocates of the bank, that its Constitutionality, in all its features, ought to be considered as settled by precedent, and by the decision of the Supreme Court. To this conclusion I can not assent. Mere precedent is a dangerous source of authority, and should not be regarded as deciding questions of Constitutional power, except where the acquiescence of the people and the States can be considered as well settled. So far from this being the case on this subject, an argument against the bank might be based on precedent. One Congress, in 1791, decided in favor of a bank; another, in 1811, decided against it. One Congress, in 1815, decided against a bank; another, in 1816, decided in its favor. Prior to the present Congress, therefore, the precedents drawn from that source were equal. If we resort to the States, the expression of legislative, judicial, and executive opinions against the bank have been probably to those in its favor as four to one. There is nothing in precedent, therefore, which, if its authority were admitted, ought to weigh in favor of the act before me.'

" I drop the quotations merely to remark, that all there ever was, in the way of precedent up to the Dred Scott decision, on the points therein decided, had been against that decision. But hear General Jackson further:

" ' If the opinion of the Supreme Court covered the whole

APPENDIX. **437**

Speech at Springfield. Reply to Judge Douglas. The Dred Scott Decision.

ground of this act, it ought not to control the co-ordinate authorities of this Government. The Congress, the Executive and the Court, must each for itself be guided by its own opinion of the Constitution. Each public officer, who takes an oath to support the Constitution, swears that he will support it as he understands it, and not as it is understood by others.'

"Again and again have I heard Judge Douglas denounce that bank decision, and applaud General Jackson for disregarding it. It would be interesting for him to look over his recent speech, and see how exactly his fierce philippics against us for resisting Supreme Court decisions, fall upon his own head. It will call to mind a long and fierce political war in this country, upon an issue which, in his own language, and, of course, in his own changeless estimation, was 'a distinct issue between the friends and the enemies of the Constitution,' and in which war he fought in the ranks of the enemies of the Constitution.

" I have said, in substance, that the Dred Scott decision was, in part, based on assumed historical facts which were not really true, and I ought not to leave the subject without giving some reasons for saying this; I, therefore, give an instance or two, which I think fully sustain me. Chief Justice Taney, in delivering the opinion of the majority of the Court, insists at great length, that negroes were no part of the people who made, or for whom was made, the Declaration of Independence, or the Constitution of the United States.

" On the contrary, Judge Curtis, in his dissenting opinion, shows that in five of the then thirteen States, to wit: New Hampshire, Massachusetts, New York, New Jersey, and North Carolina, free negroes were voters, and, in proportion to their numbers, had the same part in making the Constitution that the white people had. He shows this with so much particularity as to leave no doubt of its truth ; and as a sort of conclusion on that point, holds the following language :

" 'The constitution was ordained and established by the people of the United States, through the action, in each State, of those persons who were qualified by its laws to act thereon in behalf of themselves and all other citizens of the State. In some of the States, as we have seen, colored persons were among those qualified by law to act on the subject. These colored persons were not only included in the body of 'the people of the United States,' by whom the Constitution was ordained and established ; but in at least five of the States they had the power to act, and, doubtless, did act, by their suffrages, upon the question of its adoption.'

"Again, Chief Justice Taney says : 'It is difficult, at this day to realize the state of public opinion in relation to that unfortunate race, which prevailed in the civilized and enlightened portions of the world at the time of the Declaration of Independence, and when the Constitution of the United States was framed and adopted.' And again, after quoting from the Declaration, he says : 'The general words above quoted would seem to include the whole human family, and if they were used in a similar instrument at this day, would be so understood.'

"In these the Chief Justice does not directly assert, but plainly assumes, as a fact, that the public estimate of the black man is more favorable now than it was in the days of the Revolution. This assumption is a mistake. In some trifling particulars, the condition of that race has been ameliorated ; but as a whole, in this country, the change between then and now is decidedly the other way ; and their ultimate destiny has never appeared so hopeless as in the last three or four years. In two of the five States—New Jersey and North Carolina—that then gave the free negro the right of voting, the right has since been taken away ; and in the third —New York—it has been greatly abridged ; while it has not been extended, so far as I know, to a single additional State, though the number of the States has more than doubled. In those days, as I understand, masters could, at their own pleasure, emancipate their slaves; but since then such legal restraints have been made upon emancipation as to amount almost to prohibition. In those days 'Legislatures held the unquestioned power to abolish slavery in their respective States; but now it is becoming quite fashionable for State Constitutions to withold that power from the Legislatures. In those days by common consent, the spread of the black man's bondage to the new countries was prohibited; but now, Congress decides that it will not continue the prohibition— and the Supreme Court decides that it could not if it would. In those days our Declaration of Independence was held sacred by all, and thought to include all; but now, to aid in making the bondage of the negro universal and eternal, it is assailed, sneered at, construed, hawked at, and torn, till, if its framers could rise from their graves, they could not at all recognize it. All the powers of earth seem rapidly combining against him. Mammon is after him; ambition follows, philosophy follows, and the theology of the day is fast joining the cry. They have him in his prison-house; they have searched his person, and left no prying instrument with him. One after another they have closed the heavy iron doors upon him; and now they have him, as it were, bolted in with a lock of a hundred keys, which can never be unlocked without the concurrence of every key; the keys in the hands of a hundred different men, and they scattered to a hundred different and distant places; and they stand musing as to what invention, in all the dominions of mind and matter, can be produced to make the impossibility of his escape more complete than it is.

"It is grossly incorrect to say or assume, that the public estimate of the negro is more favorable now than it was at the origin of the Government

" Three years and a half ago, Judge Douglas brought forward his famous Nebraska bill. The country was at once in a blaze. He scorned all opposition, and carried it through Congress. Since then he has seen himself superseded in a Presidential nomination, by one indorsing the general doctrine of his measure, but at the same time standing clear of the odium of its untimely agitation, and its gross breach of national faith ; and he has seen that successful rival Constitutionally elected, not by the strength of friends, but by the division of his adversaries, being in a popular minority of nearly four hundred thousand votes. He has seen his chief aids in his own State, Shields and Richardson, politely speaking, successively tried, convicted, and executed, for an offence not their own, but his. And now he sees his own case, standing next on the docket for trial.

" There is a natural disgust, in the minds of nearly all white people, to the idea of an indiscriminate amalgamation of the white and black races ; and Judge Douglas evidently is basing his chief hope upon the chances of his being able to appropriate the benefit of this disgust to himself. If he can, by much drumming and repeating, fasten the odium of that idea upon his adversaries, he thinks he can struggle through the storm. He, therefore, clings to this hope, as a drowning man to the last plank. He makes an occasion for lugging it in from the opposition to the Dred Scott decision. He finds the Republicans insisting that the Declaration of Independence includes ALL men, black as well as white, and forthwith he boldly denies that it includes negroes at all, and proceeds to argue gravely that all who contend it does do so only because they want to vote, eat and sleep, and marry with negroes He will have it that they can not be consistent else. Now, I protest against the counterfeit logic which concludes that because I do not want a black woman for a slave I mus' necessarily want her for a wife. I need not have her fo' either I can just leave her alone. In some respects sh certainly is not my equal ; but in her natural right to eat the bread she earns with her own hands, without asking leave of any one else, she is my equal, and the equal of all others.

" Chief Justice Taney, in his opinion in the Dred Scott case, admits that the language of the Declaration is broad enough to include the whole human family ; but he and Judge Douglas argue that the authors of that instrument did not intend to include negroes, by the fact that they did not at once actually place them on an equality with the whites. Now, this grave argument comes to just nothing at all, by the other fact, that they did not at once, or ever afterward, actually place all white people on an equality with one another. And this is the staple argument of both the Chief Justice and the Senator for doing this obvious violence to the plain, unmistakable language of the Declaration.

" I think the authors of that notable instrument intended to include *all* men, but they did not intend to declare all men equal *in all respects*. They did not mean to say all were equal in color, size, intellect, moral developments, or social capacity. They defined with tolerable distinctness in what respects they did consider all men created equal—equal with ' certain inalienable rights, among which are life, liberty, and the pursuit of happiness.' This they said, and this meant. They did not mean to assert the obvious untruth, that all were then actually enjoying that equality, nor yet that they were about to confer it immediately upon them. In fact, they had no power to confer such a boon. They meant simply to declare the *right*, so that the *enforcement* of it might follow as fast as circumstances should permit.

SPEECH IN REPLY TO SENATOR DOUGLAS.

(At Chicago, on the evening of July 10, 1858.)

" MY FELLOW-CITIZENS : On yesterday evening, upon the occasion of the reception given to Senator Douglas, I was furnished with a seat very convenient for hearing him, and was otherwise very courteously treated by him and his friends, for which I thank him and them.   During the course of his remarks my name was mentioned in such a way as, I suppose, renders it at least not improper that I should make some sort of reply to him.   I shall not attempt to follow him in the precise order in which he addressed the assembled multitude upon that occasion, though I shall perhaps do so in the main.

" There was one question to which he asked the attention of the crowd, which I deem of somewhat less importance—at least of propriety for me to dwell upon—than the others, which he brought in near the close of his speech, and which I think it would not be entirely proper for me to omit attending to, and yet if I were not to give some attention to it now, I should probably forget it altogether.   While I am upon this subject, allow me to say that I do not intend to indulge in that inconvenient mode sometimes adopted in public speaking, of reading from documents ; but I shall depart from that rule so far as to read a little scrap from his speech, which notices this first topic of which I shall speak—that is, provided I can find it in the paper. [Examines the morning's paper.]

" 'I have made up my mind to appeal to the people against the combination that has been made against me ! the Republican leaders having formed an alliance, an unholy and unnatural alliance, with a portion of unscrupulous federal office-holders.   I intend to fight that allied army wherever I meet them.   I know they deny the alliance, but yet these men who are trying to divide the Democratic party for the purpose of electing a Republican Senator in my place, are just as much the agents and tools of the supporters of Mr. Lincoln. Hence I shall deal with this allied army just as the Russians dealt with the allies at Sebastopol—that is, the Russians did not stop to inquire, when they fired a broadside, whether it hit an Englishman, a Frenchman, or a Turk. Nor will I stop to inquire, nor shall I hesitate, whether my blows shall hit these Republican leaders or their allies, who are holding the federal offices and yet acting in concert with them.'

"Well, now, gentlemen, is not that very alarming? Just to think of it! right at the outset of his canvass, I, a poor, kind, amiable, intelligent gentleman, I am to be slain in this way. Why, my friends, the Judge, is not only, as it turns out, not a dead lion, nor even a living one—he is the rugged Russian Bear!

"But if they will have it—for he says that we deny it— that there is any such alliance as he says there is—and I don't propose hanging very much upon this question of veracity—but if he will have it that there is such an alliance—that the Administration men and we are allied, and we stand in the attitude of English, French and Turk, he occupying the position of the Russian, in that case, I beg that he will indulge us while we barely suggest to him that these allies took Sebastopol.

"Gentlemen, only a few more words as to this alliance. For my part, I have to say, that whether there be such an alliance, depends, so far as I know, upon what may be a right defini tion of the term *alliance*. If for the Republican party to see the other great party to which they are opposed divided among themselves, and not try to stop the division and rather be glad of it—if that is an alliance, I confess I am in ; but if it is meant to be said that the Republicans had formed an alliance going beyond that, by which there is contribution of money or sacrifice of principle on the one side or the other, so far as the Republican party is concerned, if there be any such thing, I protest that I neither know any thing of it, nor do I believe it   I will, however, say—as I think this branch of the argument is lugged in—I would, before I leave it, state, for the benefit of those concerned, that one of those same Buchanan men did once tell me of an argument that he made for his opposition to Judge Douglas.   He said that a friend of our Senator Douglas had been talking to him, and had among other things said to him : ' Why, you don't want to beat Douglas ?'   ' Yes,' said he, ' I do want to beat him, and I will tell you why.   I believe his original Nebraska Bill was right in the abstract, but it was wrong in the time that it was brought forward.   It was wrong in the application to a Territory in regard to which the question had been settled ; it was brought forward in a time when nobody asked him ; it was tendered to the South when the South had not asked for it, but when they could not well refuse it ; and for this same reason he forced that question upon our party ; it has sunk the best men all over the nation, everywhere ; and now when our President, struggling with the difficulties of this man's getting up, has reached the very hardest point to turn in the case, he deserts him, and I *am* for putting him where he will trouble us no more.'

" Now, gentlemen, that is not my argument—that is not my argument at all.   I have only been stating to you the argument of a Buchanan man.   You will judge if there is any force in it.

" Popular sovereignty ! everlasting popular sovereignty ! Let us for a moment inquire into this vast matter of popular sovereignty.   What is popular sovereignty ?   We recollect that in an early period in the history of this struggle, there was another name for the same thing—*Squatter Sovereignty.* It was not exactly Popular Sovereignty, but Squatter Sovereignty.   What do those terms mean ?   What do those terms mean when used now ?   And vast credit is taken by our friend, the Judge, in regard to his support of it, when he declares the last years of his life have been, and all the future years of his life shall be, devoted to this matter of popular sovereignty. What is it? Why it is the sovereignty of the people! What was Squatter Sovereignty? I suppose if it had any significance at all it was the right of the people to govern themselves, to be sovereign in their own affairs while they were squatted down in a country not their own, while they had squatted on a Territory that did not belong to them, in the sense that a State belongs to the people who inhabit it—when it belonged to the nation—such right to govern themselves was called 'Squatter Sovereignty.'

"Now I wish you to mark. What has become of that Squatter Sovereignty? What has become of it? Can you get any body to tell you now that the people of a Territory have any authority to govern themselves, in regard to this mooted question of slavery, before they form a State Constitution? No such thing at all, although there is a general running fire, and although there has been a hurrah made in every speech on that side, assuming that policy had given the people of a Territory the right to govern themselves upon this question; yet the point is dodged. To-day it has been decided—no more than a year ago it was decided by the Supreme Court of the United States, as is insisted upon to-day, that the people of a Territory have no right to exclude slavery from a Territory, that if any one man chooses to take slaves into a Territory, all of the rest of the people have no right to keep them out. This being so, and this decision being made one of the points that the Judge approved, and one in the approval of which he says he means to keep me down—*put* me down I should not say, for I have never been up. He says he is in favor of it, and sticks to it, and expects to win his battle on that decision, which says that there is no such thing as Squatter Sovereignty; but that any one man may take slaves into a Territory, and all the other men in the

446   LIFE OF ABRAHAM LINCOLN.

Speech at Chicago.   Reply to Senator Douglas.   Negro Slavery.

Territory may be opposed to it, and yet by reason of the Constitution they can not prohibit it. When that is so, how much is left of this vast matter of Squatter Sovereignty I should like to know? [A voice—'It is all gone.']

"When we get back, we get to the point of the right of the people to make a Constitution. Kansas was settled, for example, in 1854. It was a Territory yet, without having formed a Constitution, in a very regular way, for three years. All this time negro slavery could be taken in by any few individuals, and by that decision of the Supreme Court, which the Judge approves, all the rest of the people can not keep it out; but when they come to make a Constitution they may say they will not have slavery. But it is there; they are obliged to tolerate it some way, and all experience shows it will be so—for they will not take negro slaves and absolutely deprive the owners of them. All experience shows this to be so. All that space of time that runs from the beginning of the settlement of the Territory until there is sufficiency of people to make a State Constitution—all that portion of time popular sovereignty is given up. The seal is absolutely put down upon it by the Court decision, and Judge Douglas puts his on the top of that, yet he is appealing to the people to give him vast credit for his devotion to popular sovereignty.

"Again, when we get to the question of the right of the people to form a State Constitution as they please, to form it with slavery or without slavery—if that is any thing new, I confess I don't know it. Has there ever been a time when any body said that any other than the people of a Territory itself should form a Constitution? What is now in it that Judge Douglas should have fought several years of his life, and pledge himself to fight all the remaining years of his life for? Can Judge Douglas find any body on earth that said that any body else should form a Constitution for a people? [A voice, 'Yes.'] Well, I should like you to name him; I should like to know who he was. [Same voice, 'John Calhoun.']

"No, Sir, I never heard of even John Calhoun saying such a thing. He insisted on the same principle as Judge Douglas; but his mode of applying it in fact, was wrong. It is enough for my purpose to ask this crowd, when ever a Republican said any thing against it? They never said any thing against it, but they have constantly spoken for it; and whosoever will undertake to examine the platform, and the speeches of responsible men of the party, and of irresponsible men, too, if you please, will be unable to find one word from anybody in the Republican ranks, opposed to that Popular Sovereignty which Judge Douglas thinks that he has invented. I suppose that Judge Douglas will claim in a little while, that he is the inventor of the idea that the people should govern themselves; that nobody ever thought of such a thing until he brought it forward. We do remember, that in that old Declaration of Independence, it is said that 'We hold these truths to be self-evident, that all men are created equal; that they are endowed by their Creator with certain inalienable rights; that among these are life, liberty, and the pursuit of happiness; that to secure these rights, governments are instituted among men, deriving their just powers from the consent of the governed.' There is the origin of the Popular Sovereignty Who, then, shall come in at this day and claim that he invented it"?

After referring, in appropriate terms, to the credit claimed by Douglas for defeating the Lecompton policy, Mr. Lincoln proceeds:

"I defy you to show a printed resolution passed in a Democratic meeting—I take it upon myself to defy any man to show a printed resolution of a Democratic meeting, large or small, in favor of Judge Trumbull, or any of the five to one Republican who beat the bill. Every thing must be for the

Democrats! They did every thing, and the five to the one that really did the thing, they snub over, and they do not seem to remember that they have an existence upon the face of the earth.

"Gentlemen, I fear that I shall become tedious. I leave this branch of the subject to take hold of another. I take up that part of Judge Douglas's speech in which he respectfully attended to me.

"Judge Douglas made two points upon my recent speech at Springfield. He says they are to be the issues of this campaign. The first one of these points he bases upon the language in a speech which I delivered at Springfield, which I believe I can quote correctly from memory. I said there that 'we are now far on in the fifth year since a policy was instituted for the avowed object, and with the confident promise of putting an end to slavery agitation; under the operation of that policy, that agitation had not only not ceased, but had constantly augmented. I believe it will not cease until a crisis shall have been reached and passed. A house divided against itself can not stand. I believe this Government can not endure permanently half slave and half free. I do not expect the Union to be dissolved'—I am quoting from my speech—'I do not expect the house to fall, but I do expect it will cease to be divided. It will come all one thing or the other. Either the opponents of slavery will arrest the spread of it, and place it where the public mind shall rest in the belief that it is in the course of ultimate extin. tion, or its advocates will push it forward until it shall have become alike lawful in all the States, North as well as South.'

"In this paragraph which I have quoted in your hearing, and to which I ask the attention of all, Judge Douglas thinks he discovers great political heresy. I want your attention particularly to what he has inferred from it. He says I am in favor of making all the States of this Union uniform in all their internal regulations; that in all their domestic concerns

I am in favor of making them entirely uniform. He draws this inference from the language I have quoted to you. He says that I am in favor of making war by the North upon the South for the extinction of slavery; that I am also in favor of inviting, as he expresses it, the South to a war upon the North, for the purpose of nationalizing slavery. Now, it is singular enough, if you will carefully read that passage over, that I did not say that I was in favor of any thing in it. I only said what I expected would take place. I made a prediction only—it may have been a foolish one perhaps. I did not even say that I desired that slavery should be put in course of ultimate extinction. I do say so now, however, so there need be no longer any difficulty about that. It may be written down in the next speech.

"Gentlemen, Judge Douglas informed you that this speech of mine was probably carefully prepared. I admit that it was. I am not master of language; I have not a fine education; I am not capable of entering into a disquisition upon dialects, as I believe you call it; but I do not believe the language I employed bears any such construction as Judge Douglas puts upon it. But I don't care about a quibble in regard to words. I know what I meant, and I will not leave this crowd in doubt, if I can explain it to them, what I really meant in the use of that paragraph.

"I am not, in the first place, unaware that this Government has endured eighty-two years, half slave and half free. I know that. I am tolerably well acquainted with the history of the country, and I know that it has endured eighty-two years, half slave and half free. I *believe*—and that is what I meant to allude to there—I *believe* it has endured, because during all that time, until the introduction of the Nebraska bill, the public mind did rest all the time in the belief that slavery was in course of ultimate extinction. That was what gave us the rest that we had through that period of eighty-two years; at least, so I believe. I have always hated

29

450   LIFE OF ABRAHAM LINCOLN.

Speech at Chicago.   Reply to Senator Douglas.   The Nation's Belief.

slavery, I think, as much as any Abolitionist. I have been an Old Line Whig. I have always hated it, but I have always been quiet about it until this new era of the introduction of the Nebraska Bill began. I always believed that everybody was against it, and that it was in course of ultimate xtinction. [Pointing to Mr. Browning, who stood near by :] Browning thought so ; the great mass of the Nation have rested in the belief that slavery was in the course of ultimate extinction. They had reason so to believe.

"The adoption of the Constitution and its attendant history led the people to believe so ; and that such was the belief of the framers of the Constitution itself. Why did those old men, about the time of the adoption of the Constitution, decree that slavery should not go into the new territory, where it had not already gone ? Why declare that within twenty years the African slave-trade, by which slaves are supplied, might be cut off by Congress ? Why were all these acts ? I might enumerate more of such acts—but enough. What were they but a clear indication that the framers of the Constitution intended and expected the ultimate extinction of that institution ? And now, when I say, as I said in this speech that Judge Douglas has quoted from, when I say that I think the opponents of slavery will resist the further spread of it, and place it where the public mind shall rest with the belief that it is in course of ultimate extinction, I only mean to say, that they will place it where the founders of this Government originally placed it.

" I have said a hundred times, and I have no inclination to take it back, that I believe there is no right, and ought to be no inclination in the people of the free States to enter into the slave States, and to interfere with the question of slavery at all. I have said that always. Judge Douglas has heard me say it—if not quite a hundred times, at least as good as a hundred times ; and when it is said that I am in favor of interfering with slavery where it exists, I know that it is unwarranted by any thing I have ever intended, and, as I believe, by any thing I have ever said. If, by any means, I have ever used language which could fairly be so construed (as, however, I believe I never have), I now correct it.

"So much, then, for the inference that Judge Douglas draws, that I am in favor of setting the sections at war with one another. I know that I never meant any such thing, and I believe that no fair mind can infer any such thing from any thing I have ever said.

"Now in relation to his inference that I am in favor of a general consolidation of all the local institutions of the various States. I will attend to that for a little while, and try to inquire, if I can, how on earth it could be that any man could draw such an inference from any thing I said. I have said, very many times, in Judge Douglas's hearing, that no man believed more than I in the principle of self-government; that it lies at the bottom of all my ideas of just government, from beginning to end. I have denied that his use of that term applies properly. But for the thing itself, I deny that any man has ever gone ahead of me in his devotion to the principle, whatever he may have done in efficiency in advocating it. I think that I have said it in your hearing—that I believe each individual is naturally entitled to do as he pleases with himself and with the fruit of his labor, so far as it in no wise interferes with any other man's rights—that each community, as a State, has a right to do 'exactly as it pleases with all the concerns within that State that interfere with the right of no other State, and that the General Government, upon principle, has no right to interfere with any thing other than that general class of things that does concern the whole. I have said that at all times. I have said as illustrations, that I do not believe in the right of Illinois to interfere with the cranberry laws of Indiana, the oyster laws of Virginia, or the liquor laws of Maine. I have said these things over and over again, and I repeat them here as my sentiments. . . . .

" So much then as to my disposition—my wish—to have all the State Legislatures blotted out, and to have one consolidated government, and a uniformity of domestic regulations in all the States ; by which I suppose it is meant, if we raise corn here, we must make sugar-cane grow here too, and we must make those which grow North grow in the South. All this I suppose he understands I am in favor of doing. Now, so much for all this nonsense—for I must call it so. The Judge can have no issue with me on a question of established uniformity in the domestic regulations of the States.

" A little now on the other point—the Dred Scott decision. Another of the issues he says that is to be made with me, is upon his devotion to the Dred Scott decision, and my opposition to it.

" I have expressed heretofore, and I now repeat my opposition to the Dred Scott decision, but I should be allowed to state the nature of that opposition, and I ask your indulgence while I do so. What is fairly implied by the term Judge Douglas has used, ' resistance to the decision ?' I do not resist it. If I wanted to take Dred Scott from his master, I would be interfering with property, and that terrible difficulty that Judge Douglas speaks of, of interfering with property would arise. But I am doing no such thing as that, but all that I am doing is refusing to obey it as a political rule. If I were in Congress, and a vote should come up on a question whether slavery should be prohibited in a new Territory, in spite of the Dred Scott decision, I would vote that it should.

" That is what I would do. Judge Douglas said last night, that before the decision he might advance his opinion, and it might be contrary to the decision when it was made ; but *after* it was made he would abide by it until it was reversed. Just so ! We let this property abide by the decision, but we will try to reverse that decision. [Loud applause] We will try to put it where Judge Douglas will not object, for he says he will obey it until it is reversed. Somebody has to reverse that decision, since it was made, and we mean to reverse it, and we mean to do it peaceably.

"What are the uses of decisions of courts? They have two uses. As rules of property they have two uses. First— they decide upon the question before the court. They decide in this case that Dred Scott is a slave. Nobody resists that. Not only that, but they say to everybody else, that persons standing just as Dred Scott stands, is as he is. That is, they say that when a question comes up upon another person, it will be so decided again unless the court decides in another way, unless the court overrules its decision. Well, we mean to do what we can to have the court decide the other way. That is one thing we mean to try to do.

"The sacredness that Judge Douglas throws around this decision, is a degree of sacredness that has never been before thrown around any other decision. I have never heard of such a thing. Why, decisions apparently contrary to that decision, or that good lawyers thought were contrary to that decision, have been made by that very court before. It is the first of the kind; it is an *astonisher* in legal history. It is a new wonder of the world. It is based upon falsehoods in the main as to the facts—allegation of facts upon which it stands are not facts at all in many instances, and no decision made on any question—the first instance of a decision made under so many unfavorable circumstances—thus placed, has ever been held by the profession as law, and it has always needed confirmation before the lawyers regarded it as settled law. But Judge Douglas will have it that all hands must take this extraordinary decision, made under these extraordinary circumstances, and give their vote in Congress in accordance with it, yield to it and obey it in every possible sense. Circumstances alter cases. Do not gentlemen here remember the case of that same Supreme Court, twenty-five or thirty years ago, deciding that a National Bank was Constitutional? I ask, if somebody does not remember that a National Bank was declared to be Constitutional? Such is the truth, whether it be remembered or not. The Bank charter ran out, and a re-charter was granted by Congress. That re-charter was laid before General Jackson. It was urged upon him, when he denied the Constitutionality of the Bank, that the Supreme Court had decided that it was Constitutional; and that General Jackson then said that the Supreme Court had no right to lay down a rule to govern a co-ordinate branch of the Government, the members of which had sworn to support the Constitution—that each member had sworn to support that Constitution as he understood it. I will venture here to say, that I have heard Judge Douglas say that he approved of General Jackson for that act. What has now become of all his tirade about ' resistance to the Supreme Court?'   *   *

"We were often—more than once, at least—in the course of Judge Douglas's speech last night, reminded that this Government was made for white men—that he believed it was made for white men. Well, that is putting it into a shape in which no one wants to deny it; but the Judge then goes into his passion for drawing inferences that are not warranted. I protest, now, and forever, against that counterfeit logic which presumes that because I did not want a negro woman for a slave, I do necessarily want her for a wife. My understanding is that I need not have her for either; but, as God made us separate, we can leave one another alone, and do one another much good thereby. There are white men enough to marry all the white women, and enough black men to marry all the black women, and in God's name let them be so married. The Judge regales us with the terrible enormities that take place by the mixture of races; that is the inferior race bears the superior down. Why, Judge, if you do not let them get together in the Territories they won't mix there

"Now, it happens that we meet together once every year, some time about the Fourth of July, for some reason or other. These Fourth of July gatherings I suppose have their uses. If you will indulge me, I will state what I suppose to be some of them.

We are now a mighty nation; we are thirty, or about thirty millions of people, and we own and inhabit about one-fifteenth part of the dry land of the whole earth. We run our memory back over the pages of history for about eighty-two years, and we discover that we were then a very small people in point of numbers, vastly inferior to what we are now, with a vastly less extent of country, with vastly less of every thing we deem desirable among men—we look upon the change as exceedingly advantageous to us and to our posterity, and we fix upon something that happened away back, as in some way or other being connected with this rise of posterity. We find a race of men living in that day whom we claim as our fathers and grandfathers; they were iron men; they fought for the principle that they were contending for; and we understood that by what they then did it has followed that the degree of prosperity which we now enjoy has come to us. We hold this annual celebration to remind ourselves of all the good done in this process of time, of how it was done and who did it, and how we are historically connected with it; and we go from these meetings in better humor with ourselves—we feel more attached the one to the other, and more firmly bound to the country we inhabit. In every way we are better men in the age, and race, and country in which we live, for these celebrations. But after we have done all this, we have not yet reached the whole. There is something else connected with it. We have, besides these— men descended by blood from our ancestors—those among us perhaps, half our people, who are not descendants at all of these men; they are men who have come from Europe— German, Irish, French, and Scandinavian—men that have come from Europe themselves, or whose ancestors have come hither and settled here, finding themselves our equals in all things.   If they look back through this history to trace their connection with those days by blood, they find they have none ; they cannot carry themselves back into that glorious epoch and make themselves feel that they are part of us ; but when they look through that old Declaration of Independence, they find that those old men say that 'we hold these truths to be self-evident, that all men are created equal,' and then they feel that that moral sentiment, taught on that day, evidences their relation to those men, that it is the father of all moral principle in them, and that they have a right to claim it as though they were blood of the blood and flesh of the flesh of the men who wrote that Declaration, and so they are. That is the electric cord in that Declaration that links the hearts of patriotic and liberty-loving men together, that will link those patriotic hearts as long as the love of freedom exists in the minds of men throughout the world.

"Now, sirs, for the purpose of squaring things with this idea of 'don't care if slavery is voted up or voted down,' for sustaining the Dred Scott decision, for holding that the Declaration of Independence did not mean any thing at all, we have Judge Douglas giving his exposition of what the Declaration of Independence means, and we have him saying that the people of America are equal to the people of England.   According to his construction, you Germans are not connected with it.   Now I ask you in all soberness, if all these things, if indulged in, if ratified, if confirmed and indorsed, if taught to our children and repeated to them, do not tend to rub out the sentiment of liberty in the country, and to transform this Government into a government of some other form.   These arguments that are made, that the inferior race are to be treated with as much allowance as they are capable of enjoying ; that as much is to be done for them as their condition will allow—what are these arguments ?   They are the arguments that Kings have made for enslaving the people in all ages of the world. You will find that all the arguments in favor of King-craft were of this class; they always bestrode the necks of the people, not that they wanted to do it, but because the people were better off for being ridden. That is their argument, and this argument of the Judge is the same old serpent that says: You work, and I eat, you toil and I will enjoy the fruits of it. Turn it whatever way you will—whether it come from the mouth of a King, an excuse for enslaving the people of his country, or from the mouth of men of one race as a reason for enslaving the men of another race, it is all the same old serpent, and I hold if that course of argumentation that is made for the purpose of convincing the public mind that we should not care about this, should be granted, it does not stop with the negro. I should like to know if, taking this old Declaration of Independence, which declares that all men are equal upon principle, you begin making exceptions to it, where you will stop? If one man says it does not mean a negro, why not another say it does not mean some other man? If that declaration is not the truth, let us get the statute book, in which we find it, and tear it out! Who is so bold as to do it? If it is not true, let us tear it out! [cries of 'no, no,']; let us stick to it then; let us stand firmly by it then.

"It may be argued that there are certain conditions that make necessities and impose them upon us, and to the extent that a necessity is imposed upon a man, he must submit to it I think that was the condition in which we found ourselves when we established this Government. We had slaves among us; we could not get our Constitution unless we permitted them to remain in slavery; we could not secure the good we did secure if we grasped for more; and having, by necessity, submitted to that much, it does not destroy the principle that is the charter of our liberties. Let that charter stand as our standard.

"My friend has said to me that I am a poor hand to quote Scripture. I will try it again, however. It is said in one of the admonitions of our Lord : 'As your Father in heaven is perfect, be ye also perfect.' The Saviour, I suppose, did not expect that any human creature could be perfect as the Father in Heaven ; but He said : 'As your Father in Heaven is perfect, be ye also perfect.' He set that up as a standard, and he who did most toward reaching that standard, attained the highest degree of moral perfection. So I say in relation to the principle that all men are created equal, let it be as nearly reached as we can. If we cannot give freedom to every creature, let us do nothing that will impose slavery upon any other creature. Let us then turn this Government back into the channel in which the framers of the Constitution originally placed it. Let us stand firmly by each other. If we do not do so we are turning in the contrary direction, that our friend Judge Douglas proposes—not intentionally—as working in the traces tends to make this one universal slave nation. He is one that runs in that direction, and as such I resist him.

"My friends, I have detained you about as long as I desired to do, and I have only to say, let us discard all this quibbling about this man and the other man—this race and that race and the other race being inferior, and therefore they must be placed in an inferior position—discarding our standard that we have left us. Let us discard all these things, and unite as one people throughout this land, until we shall once more stand up declaring that all men are created equal.

"My friends, I could not, without launching off upon some new topic, which would detain you too long, continue to-night. I thank you for this most extensive audience that you have furnished me to-night. I leave you, hoping that the lamp of liberty will burn in your bosoms until there shall no longer be a doubt that all men are created free and equal."

OPENING PASSAGES OF HIS SPEECH AT FREEPORT.

"LADIES AND GENTLEMEN:—On Saturday last, Judge Douglas and myself first met in public discussion. He spoke one hour, I an hour and a half, and he replied for half an hour. The order is now reversed. I am to speak an hour, he an hour and a half, and then I am to reply for half an hour. I propose to devote myself during the first hour to the scope of what was brought within the range of his half-hour speech at Ottawa. Of course there was brought within the scope of that half-hour's speech something of his own opening speech. In the course of that opening argument Judge Douglas proposed to me seven distinct interrogatories. In my speech of an hour and a half, I attended to some other parts of his speech, and incidentally, as I thought, answered one of the interrogatories then. I then distinctly intimated to him that I would answer the rest of his interrogatories on condition only that he should agree to answer as many for me. He made no intimation at the time of the proposition, nor did he in his reply allude at all to that suggestion of mine. I do him no injustice in saying that he occupied at least half of his reply in dealing with me as though I had *refused* to answer his interrogatories. I now propose that I will answer any of the interrogatories, upon condition that he will answer questions from me not exceeding the same number. I give him an opportunity to respond. The judge remains silent. I now say that I will answer his interrogatories, whether he answers mine or not; and that after I have done so, I shall propound mine to him.

"I have supposed myself, since the organization of the Republican party at Bloomington, in May, 1856, bound as a party man by the platforms of the party, then and since. If in any interrogatories which I shall answer, I go beyond the scope of what is within these platforms, it will be perceived that no one is responsible but myself.

" Having said thus much, I will take up the judge's inter-rogatories as I find them printed in the Chicago *Times*, and answer them *seriatim*. In order that there may be no mis-take about it, I have copied the interrogatories in writing, and also my answers to them. The first one of these inter-rogatories is in these words :

Question 1. " 'I desire to know whether Lincoln to-day stands, as he did in 1854, in favor of the unconditional repeal of the Fugitive Slave law ?'

Answer. "I do not now, nor ever did, stand in favor of the unconditional repeal of the Fugitive Slave law.

Q. 2. " 'I desire him to answer whether he stands pledged to-day, as he did in 1854, against the admission of any more slave States into the Union, even if the people want them ?'

A. "I do not now, nor ever did, stand pledged against the admission of any more slave States into the Union.

Q. 3. " 'I want to know whether he stands pledged against the admission of a new State into the Union with such a Con-stitution as the people of that State may see fit to make ?'

A. " I do not stand pledged against the admission of a new State into the Union, with such a Constitution as the people of that State may see fit to make.

Q. 4. " 'I want to know whether he stands to-day pledged to the abolition of slavery in the District of Columbia ?'

A. "I do not stand to-day pledged to the abolition of slavery in the District of Columbia.

Q. 5. " 'I desire him to answer whether he stands pledged to the prohibition of the slave-trade between the different States ?'

A. " I do not stand pledged to the prohibition of the slave-trade between the different States.

Q. 6. " 'I desire to know whether he stands pledged to prohibit slavery in all the Territories of the United States, North as well as South of the Missouri Compromise line ?'

A. " I am impliedly, if not expressly, pledged to a belief

in the *right* and *duty* of Congress to prohibit slavery in all the United States Territories.

Q. 7. "'I desire him to answer whether he is opposed to the acquisition of any new territory unless slavery is first prohibited therein ?'

A. "I am not generally opposed to honest acquisition of territory ; and, in any given case, I would or would not oppose such acquisition, accordingly as I might think such acquisition would or would not agitate the slavery question among ourselves.

" Now, my friends, it will be perceived upon an examination of these questions and answers, that so far I have only answered that I was not *pledged* to this, that or the other. The judge has not framed his interrogatories to ask me any thing more than this, and I have answered in strict accordance with the interrogatories, and have answered truly that I am not *pledged* at all upon any of the points to which I have answered. But I am not disposed to hang upon the exact form of his interrogatory. I am rather disposed to take up at least some of these questions, and state what I really think upon them.

"As to the first one, in regard to the Fugitive Slave law, I have never hesitated to say, and I do not now hesitate to say, that I think, under the Constitution of the United States, the people of the Southern States are entitled to a Congressional Slave law. Having said that, I have had nothing to say in regard to the existing Fugitive Slave law, further than that I think it should have been framed so as to be free from some of the objections that pertain to it, without lessening its efficiency. And inasmuch as we are not now in an agitation in regard to an alteration or modification of that law, I would not be the man to introduce it as a new subject of agitation upon the general question of slavery.

" In regard to the other question, of whether I am pledged to the admission of any more Slave States into the Union, I state to you very frankly that I would be exceedingly sorry ever to be put in a position of having to pass upon that question. I should be exceedingly glad to know that there would never be another slave State admitted into the Union; but I must add, that if slavery shall be kept out of the Territories during the Territorial existence of any one given Territory, and then the people shall, having a fair chance and a clear field, when they come to adopt the Constitution, do such an extraordinary thing as to adopt a slave Constitution, uninfluenced by the actual presence of the institution among them, I see no alternative if we own the country, but to admit them into the Union.

"The third interrogatory is answered by the answer to the second, it being, as I conceive, the same as the second.

"The fourth one is in regard to the abolition of slavery in the District of Columbia. In relation to that, I have my mind very distinctly made up. I should be exceedingly glad to see slavery abolished in the District of Columbia. I believe that Congress possesses the constitutional power to abolish it. Yet as a member of Congress, I should not with my present views, be in favor of *endeavoring* to abolish slavery in the District of Columbia, unless it would be upon these conditions : *First*, that the abolition should be gradual ; *second*, that it should be on a vote of the majority of qualified voters in the District ; and *third*, that compensation should be made to unwilling owners. With these three conditions, I confess I would be exceedingly glad to see Congress abolish slavery in the District of Columbia, and, in the language of Henry Clay, 'sweep from our Capital that foul blot upon our nation.'

"In regard to the fifth interrogatory, I must say here, that as to the question of the abolition of the slave-trade between the different States, I can truly answer, as I have, that I am *pledged* to nothing about it. It is a subject to which I have not given that mature consideration that would make me feel authorized to state a position so as to hold myself entirely bound by it. In other words, that question has never been prominently enough before me to induce me to investigate whether we really have the Constitutional power to do it. I could investigate it if I had sufficient time to bring myself to a conclusion upon that subject; but I have not done so, and I say so frankly to you here, and to Judge Douglas. I must say, however, that if I should be of opinion that Congress does possess the Constitutional power to abolish slave-trading among the different States, I should still not be in favor of the exercise of that power unless upon some conservative principle as I conceive it, akin to what I have said in relation to the abolition of slavery in the District of Columbia.

"My answer as to whether I desire that slavery should be prohibited in all Territories of the United States, is full and explicit within itself, and can not be made clearer by any comments of mine. So I suppose in regard to the question whether I am opposed to the acquisition of any more territory unless slavery is first prohibited therein, my answer is such that I could add nothing by way of illustration, or making myself better understood, than the answer which I have placed in writing.

"Now in all this, the judge has me, and he has me on the record. I suppose he had flattered himself that I was really entertaining one set of opinions for one place and another set for another place—that I was afraid to say at one place what I uttered at another. What I am saying here I suppose I say to a vast audience as strongly tending to Abolitionism as any audience in the State of Illinois, and I believe I am saying that which, if it would be offensive to any persons and render them enemies to myself, would be offensive to persons in this audience."

LETTER TO GENERAL McCLELLAN.

"WASHINGTON, April 9, 1862.

"MY DEAR SIR : Your dispatches, complaining that you ar
not properly sustained, while they do not offend me, do pai
me very much.

"Blenker's division was withdrawn from you before you left
here, and you know the pressure under which I did it, and, as
I thought, acquiesced in it—certainly not without reluc-
tance.

"After you left, I ascertained that less than twenty thousand unorganized men, without a single field battery, were
all you designed to be left for the defence of Washington and
Manassas Junction, and part of this even was to go to Gen.
Hooker's old position.   General Banks' corps, once designated
for Manassas Junction, was diverted and tied up on the line
of Winchester and Strasburgh, and could not leave it without
again exposing the Upper Potomac and the Baltimore and
Ohio Railroad.   This presented, or would present, when
McDowell and Sumner should be gone, a great temptation to
the enemy to turn back from the Rappahannock and sack
Washington.   My explicit order that Washington should, by
the judgment of all the commanders of army corps, be
left entirely secure, had been neglected.   It was precisely
this that drove me to detain McDowell.

"I do not forget that I was satisfied with your arrangement
to leave Banks at Manassas Junction : but when that arrangement was broken up, and nothing was substituted for it, of
course I was constrained to substitute something for it myself.
And allow me to ask, do you really think I should permit
the line from Richmond, *via* Manassas Junction, to this city,
to be entirely open, except what resistance could be presented
by less than twenty thousand unorganized troops ?   This is
a question which the country will not allow me to evade.

" There is a curious mystery about the number of troops now with you. When I telegraphed you on the 6th, saying you had over a hundred thousand with you, I had just obtained from the Secretary of War a statement taken, as he said, from your own returns, making one hundred and eight thousand then with you and *en route* to you. You say you will have but eighty-five thousand when all *en route* to you shall have reached you. How can the discrepancy of twenty-three thousand be accounted for ?

"As to General Wool's command, I understand it is doing for you precisely what a like number of your own would have to do if that command was away.

" I suppose the whole force which has gone forward for you is with you by this time. And if so, I think it is the precise time for you to strike a blow. By delay, the enemy will relatively gain upon you—that is, he will gain faster by fortifications and reinforcement than you can by reinforcements alone. And once more let me tell you, it is indispensable to you that you strike a blow. I am powerless to help this. You will do me the justice to remember I always insisted that going down the bay in search of a field, instead of fighting at or near Manassas, was only shifting, and not surmounting a difficulty ; that we would find the same enemy, and the same or equal intrenchments, at either place. The country will not fail to note, is now noting, that the present hesitation to move upon an intrenched enemy is but the story of Manassas repeated.

"I beg to assure you that I have never written you or spoken to you in greater kindness of feeling than now, nor with a fuller purpose to sustain you, so far as, in my most anxious judgment, I consistently can. But you must act.

" Yours, very truly,

" Maj.-Gen. McCLELLAN."   A. LINCOLN.

30

466   LIFE OF ABRAHAM LINCOLN.

Letter to Gen. Schofield.   Gen. Curtis and Gov. Bramble.   Proclamation.

LETTER TO GEN. SCHOFIELD RELATIVE TO THE REMOVAL OF GEN. CURTIS.

"*Executive Mansion*, Washington, May 27, 1863.

" Gen. J. M. Schofield—*Dear Sir:* Having removed Gen. Curtis and assigned you to the command of the Department of the Missouri, I think it may be of some advantage to me to state to you why I did it. I did not remove Gen. Curtis because of my full conviction that he had done wrong by commission or omission. I did it because of a conviction in my mind that the Union men of Missouri, constituting, when united, a vast majority of the people, have entered into a pestilent, factious quarrel among themselves, Gen. Curtis, perhaps not of choice, being the head of one faction, and Gov. Gamble that of the other. After months of labor to reconcile the difficulty, it seemed to grow worse and worse, until I felt it my duty to break it up somehow, and as I could not remove Gov. Gamble, I had to remove Gen. Curtis. Now that you are in the position, I wish you to undo nothing merely because Gen. Curtis or Gov. Gamble did it, but to exercise your own judgment, and do right for the public interest. Let your military measures be strong enough to repel the invaders and keep the peace, and not so strong as to unnecessarily harass and persecute the people. It is a difficult *role*, and so much more will be the honor if you perform it well. If both factions, or neither, shall abuse you, you will probably be about right. Beware of being assailed by one and praised by the other.

" Yours, truly,   A. Lincoln."

THREE HUNDRED THOUSAND MEN CALLED FOR.

" Whereas, The term of service of part of the volunteer forces of the United States will expire during the coming year; and *whereas*, in addition to the men raised by the present draft, it is deemed expedient to call out three hundred thousand volunteers, to serve for three years or the war—not, however, exceeding three years.

"Now, therefore, I, Abraham Lincoln, President of the United States and Commander-in-Chief of the Army and Navy thereof, and of the militia of the several States when called into actual service, do issue this my proclamation, calling upon the Governors of the different States to raise and have enlisted into the United States service, for the various companies and regiments in the field from their respective States, their quotas of three hundred thousand men.

"I further proclaim that all the volunteers thus called out and duly enlisted shall receive advance pay, premium and bounty, as heretofore communicated to the Governors of States by the War Department, through the Provost-Marshal General's office, by special letters.

"I further proclaim that all volunteers received under this call, as well as all others not heretofore credited, shall be duly credited and deducted from the quotas established for the next draft.

"I further proclaim that, if any State shall fail to raise the quota assigned to it by the War Department under this call; then a draft for the deficiency in said quota shall be made in said State, or on the districts of said State, for their due proportion of said quota, and the said draft shall commence on the fifth day of January, 1864.

"And I further proclaim that nothing in this proclamation shall interfere with existing orders, or with those which may be issued for the present draft in the States where it is now in progress or where it has not yet been commenced.

"The qoutas of the States and districts will be assigned by the War Department, through the Provost-Marshal General's office, due regard being had for the men heretofore furnished, whether by volunteering or drafting, and the recruiting will be conducted in accordance with such instructions as have been or may be issued by that department.

"In issuing this proclamation I address myself not only to the Governors of the several States, but also to the good and loyal people thereof, invoking them to lend their cheerful, willing and effective aid to the measures thus adopted, with a view to reinforce our victorious armies now in the field and bring our needful military operations to a prosperous end, thus closing forever the fountains of sedition and civil war.

"In witness whereof I have hereunto set my hand and caused the seal of the United States to be affixed.

"Done at the city of Washington, this seventeenth day of October, in the year of our Lord one thousand eight hundred and sixty-three, and of the independence of the United States the eighty-eighth.

"By the President :   "ABRAHAM LINCOLN.

"WM. H. SEWARD, Secretary of State."

REV. DR. M'PHEETERS—THE PRESIDENT'S REPLY TO AN APPEAL FOR INTERFERENCE.

"*Executive Mansion*, Washington, December 23, 1863.

"I have just looked over a petition signed by some three dozen citizens of St. Louis, and their accompanying letters, one by yourself, one by a Mr. Nathan Ranney, and one by a Mr. John D. Coalter, the whole relating to the Rev. Dr. McPheeters. The petition prays, in the name of justice and mercy, that I will restore Dr. McPheeters to all his ecclesiastical rights.

"This gives no intimation as to what ecclesiastical rights are withdrawn. Your letter states that Provost Marshal Dick, about a year ago, ordered the arrest of Dr. McPheeters, pastor of the Vine-street Church, prohibited him from officiating, and placed the management of affairs of the church out of the control of the chosen trustees; and near the close you state that a certain course 'would insure his release.' Mr. Ranney's letter says: 'Dr. Samuel McPheeters is enjoying all the rights of a civilian, but can not preach the gospel!' Mr. Coalter, in his letter, asks: 'Is it not a strange illustration of the condition of things, that the question who shall be allowed to preach in a church in St. Louis shall be decided by the President of the United States?'

"Now, all this sounds very strangely; and, withal, a little as if you gentlemen making the application do not understand the case alike—one affirming that this doctor is enjoying all the rights of a civilian, and another pointing out to me what will secure his *release!* On the second of January last, I wrote to Gen. Curtis in relation to Mr. Dick's order upon Dr. McPheeters; and, as I suppose the Doctor is enjoying all the rights of a civilian, I only quote that part of the letter which relates to the church. It was as follows: 'But I must add that the United States Government must not, as by this order, undertake to run the churches. When an individual, in a church or out of it, becomes dangerous to the public interest, he must be checked; but the churches, as such, must take care of themselves. It will not do for the United States to appoint trustees, supervisors, or other agents for the churches.'

"This letter going to Gen. Curtis, then in command, I supposed, of course, it was obeyed, especially as I heard no further complaint from Dr. Mc. or his friends for nearly an entire year. I have never interfered, nor thought of interfering, as to who shall or shall not preach in any church; nor have I knowingly or believingly tolerated any one else to interfere by my authority. If any one is so interfering by color of my authority, I would like to have it specifically made known to me.

"If, after all, what is now sought is to have me put Dr Mc. back over the heads of a majority of his own congrega-

470　　　　LIFE OF ABRAHAM LINCOLN.

Election Ordered in Arkansas.　　　　　　　　　　Gen. Steele's Instructions.

tion, that, too, will be declined.　I will not have control of any church on any side.　　　　　　　　　　A. LINCOLN."

AN ELECTION ORDERED IN THE STATE OF ARKANSAS.

"*Executive Mansion*, Washington, January 20, 1864.

. " MAJ. GEN. STEELE : Sundry citizens of the State of Arkansas petition me that an election may be held in that State, at which to elect a Governor; that it be assumed at that election, and henceforward, that the Constitution and laws of the State, as before the rebellion, are in full force, except that the Constitution is so modified as to declare that there shall be neither slavery nor involuntary servitude, except in the punishment of crimes whereof the party shall have been duly convicted; that the General assembly may make such provisions for the freed people as shall recognize and declare their permanent freedom, and provide for their education, and which may yet be construed as a temporary arrangement, suitable to their condition as a laboring, landless, and homeless class ; that said election shall be held on the 28th of March, 1864, at all the usual places of the State, or all such as voters may attend for that purpose; that the voters attending at 8 o'clock in the morning of said day may choose judges and clerks of election for such purpose; that all persons qualified by said Constitution and laws, and taking the oath presented in the President's proclamation of December 8, 1863, either before or at the election, and none others, may be voters; that each set of judges and clerks may make returns directly to you on or before the — th day of —— next; that in all other respects said election may be conducted according to said Constitution and laws; that on receipt of said returns, when five thousand four hundred and six votes shall have been cast, you can receive said votes and ascertain all who shall thereby appear to have been elected; that on the — day of —— next, all persons so appearing to have been elected, who shall appear before you at Little Rock, and take the oath, to be by you severally administered, to support the Constitution of the United States, and said modified Constitution of the State of Arkansas, may be declared by you qualified and empowered to immediately enter upon the duties of the offices to which they shall have been respectively elected.

"You will please order an election to take place on the 28th of March, 1864, and returns to be made in fifteen days thereafter.   A. LINCOLN."

Later, the President wrote the following letter:

"WILLIAM FISHBACK, ESQ.: When I fixed a plan for an election in Arkansas, I did it in ignorance that your Convention was at the same work.   Since I learned the latter fact, I have been constantly trying to yield my plan to theirs.   I have sent two letters to Gen. Steele, and three or four dispatches to you and others, saying that he (Gen. Steele) must be master, but that it will probably be best for him to keep the Convention on its own plan.   Some single mind must be master, else there will be no agreement on any thing; and Gen. Steele, commanding the military, and being on the ground, is the best man to be that master.   Even now citizens are telegraphing me to postpone the election to a later day than either fixed by the Convention or me.   This discord must be silenced.   A. LINCOLN."

CALL FOR FIVE HUNDRED THOUSAND MEN.

"WHEREAS, By the Act approved July 4, 1864, entitled 'An Act further to regulate and provide for the enrolling and calling out the National Forces, and for other purposes,' it is provided that the President of the United States may, at his discretion, at any time hereafter, call for any number of men as volunteers, for the respective terms of one, two, or three years, for military service, and ' that in case the quota, or any part thereof, of any town, township, ward of a city, precinct, or election district, or of a county not so subdivided, shall not be filled within the space of fifty days after such call, then the President shall immediately order a draft for one year to fill such quota, or any part thereof, which may be unfilled.'

"AND WHEREAS, The new enrollment heretofore ordered is so far completed as that the aforementioned Act of Congress may now be put in operation for recruiting and keeping up the strength of the armies in the field, for garrisons, and such military operations as may be required for the purpose of suppressing the rebellion and restoring the authority of the United States Government in the insurgent States :

" Now, therefore, I, Abraham Lincoln, President of the United States, do issue this, my call, for five hundred thousand volunteers for the military service ; provided, nevertheless, that all credits which may be established under Section Eight of the aforesaid Act, on account of persons who have entered the naval service during the present Rebellion, and by credits for men furnished to the military service in excess of calls heretofore made for volunteers, will be accepted under this call for one, two, or three years, as they may elect, and will be entitled to the bounty provided by the law for the period of service for which they enlist.

"And I hereby proclaim, order, and direct, that immediately after the fifth day of September, 1864, being fifty days from the date of this call, a draft for troops to serve for one year, shall be held in every town, township, ward of a city, precinct, election district, or a county not so subdivided, to fill the quota which shall be assigned to it under this call, or any part thereof which may be unfilled by volunteers on the said fifth day of September, 1864.

" In testimony whereof, I have hereunto set my hand and

APPENDIX. 473

Letter to Mrs. Gurney.   The Friends and the War.

caused the seal of the United States to be affixed. Done at the city of Washington, this eighteenth day of July, in the year of our Lord, one thousand eight hundred and sixty-four, and of the independence of the United States the eighty-ninth.

"By the President: ABRAHAM LINCOLN.

"WILLIAM H. SEWARD, Secretary of State."

LETTER TO MRS. GURNEY.

This letter was written by the President prior to his re-election to Mrs. Eliza P. Gurney, an American lady, the widow of the late well-known Friend and philanthropist, Joseph John Gurney, one of the wealthiest bankers of London.

"MY ESTEEMED FRIEND: I have not forgotten, probably never shall forget, the very impressive occasion when yourself and friends visited me on a Sabbath forenoon two years ago. Nor had your kind letter, written nearly a year later, ever been forgotten. In all it has been your purpose to strengthen my reliance in God. I am much indebted to the good Christian people of the country for their constant prayers and consolations, and to no one of them more than to yourself. The purposes of the Almighty are perfect and must prevail, though we erring mortals may fail to accurately perceive them in advance. We hoped for a happy termination of this terrible war, long before this, but God knows best, and has ruled otherwise. We shall yet acknowledge His wisdom and our own errors therein; meanwhile we must work earnestly in the best lights He gives us, trusting that so working still conduces to the great ends He ordains. Surely, He intends some great good to follow this mighty convulsion which no mortal could make, and no mortal could stay.

"Your people—the Friends—have had, and are having very great trials, on principles and faith opposed to both war and oppression. They can only practically oppose oppression by war. In this hard dilemma, some have chosen one horn and some the other.

For those appealing to me on conscientious grounds I have done and shall do the best I could, and can, in my own conscience under my oath to the law. That you believe this, I doubt not, and believing it, I shall still receive for our country and myself your earnest prayers to our father in Heaven.

" Your sincere friend,

"A. LINCOLN."

THE TENNESSEE TEST OATH.

"*Executive Mansion*, Washington, D. C.,
Saturday, October 22, 1864

"MESSRS. WM B. CAMPBELL, THOMAS A. R. NELSON, JAMES T. P. CARTER, JOHN WILLIAMS, A. BLIZZARD, HENRY COOPER, BAILIE PEYTON, JOHN LILLYETT, EMERSON ETHERIDGE, AND JOHN D. PERRYMAN.

"GENTLEMEN: On the fifteenth day of this month, as I remember, a printed paper manuscript, with a few manuscript interlineations, called a protest, with your names appended thereto, and accompanied by another printed paper, purporting to be a proclamation by ANDREW JOHNSON, Military Governor of Tennessee, and also a manuscript paper purporting to be extracts from the code of Tennessee, were laid before me."

[The protest is here recited, and also the proclamation of Gov. JOHNSON, dated September 30, to which it refers, together with a list of the counties in East, Middle, and West Tennessee; also extracts from the code of Tennessee in relation to electors of President and Vice President, qualifications of voters for members of the General Assembly, and places of holding elections and officers of popular elections.]

"At the time these papers were presented as before stated, I had never seen either of them, nor heard of the subject to which they relate, except in a general way, only one day previously.

"Up to the present moment, nothing whatever upon the subject has passed between Gov. JOHNSON, or any one else connected with the proclamation and myself.

"Since receiving the papers, as stated, I have given the subject such brief consideration as I have been able to do, in the midst of so many pressing duties.

"My conclusion is, that I can have nothing to do with the matter, either to sustain the plan as the Convention and Gov. JOHNSON have initiated it, or to modify it as you demand. By the Constitution and laws the President is charged with no duty in the Presidential election in any State. Nor do I, in this case, perceive any military reason for his interference in the matter.

"The movement set a-foot by the Convention and Gov. JOHNSON does not, as seems to be assumed by you, emanate from the National Executive.

"In no proper sense can it be considered other than as an independent movement of at least a portion of the loyal people of Tennessee.

"I do not perceive in the plan any menace, or violence, or coercion toward any one.

"Gov. JOHNSON, like any other loyal citizen of Tennessee has the right to form any political plan he chooses, and as Military Governor it is his duty to keep the peace among and for the loyal people of the State.

"I cannot discern that by his plan he purposes any more— but you object to the plan.

" Leaving it alone will be your perfect security against it. It is not proposed to force you into it.

" Do as you please on your own account peaceably and loyally, and Gov. Johnson will not molest you, but will protect you against violence so far as in his power.

" I presume that the conducting of a Presidential election in Tennessee, in strict accordance with the old code of the State, is not now a possibility.

" It is scarcely necessary to add, that if any election shall be had, and any votes shall be cast in the State of Tennessee for President and Vice-President of the United States, it will belong not to the military agents nor yet to the Executive Department, but exclusively to another department of the Government, to determine whether they are entitled to be counted in conformity with the Constitution and laws of the United States.

" Except it be to give protection against violence, I decline to interfere in any way with any Presidential election.

"ABRAHAM LINCOLN."

THE END.

LIST OF NEW BOOKS

PUBLISHED BY

JOHN E. POTTER.

MAILING NOTICE.—Any of these Books will be sent to any address, free of postage, on receipt of price. Address JOHN E. POTTER, PUBLISHER, *No. 617 Sansom Street, Philadelphia.*

OUR CAMPAIGNS; or, the Marches, Bivouacs, Battles, Incidents of Camp Life and History of our Regiment during its three years term of service; together with a Sketch of the Army of the Potomac under Generals McClellan, Burnside, Hooker, Meade and Grant. By E. M. WOODWARD, Adjutant Second Pennsylvania Reserves. 12mo., cloth. Price $2.00.

OUR BOYS. The Personal Experiences of a Soldier in the Army of the Potomac; the rich and racy scenes of Army and Camp Life; the lively, piquant, and well-told story of the Battle, the Bivouac, the Picket, and the March, as seen and participated in by one of the rank and file, and who has himself lost a leg in the service of his country. By A. F. HILL, of the Eighth Pennsylvania Reserves. 12mo., paper. Price $1.50; cloth, $2.00.

THRILLING STORIES OF THE GREAT REBELLION: comprising Heroic Adventures and Hair-breadth Escapes of Soldiers, Scouts, Spies, and Refugees; Daring Exploits of Smugglers, Guerrillas, Desperadoes, and others; Tales of Loyal and Disloyal Women; Stories of the Negro, etc., etc. With Incidents of Fun and Merriment in Camp and Field. By a DISABLED OFFICER. With colored illustrations. 12mo., paper. Price $1.50; cloth, $2.00.

THE LIFE AND ADVENTURES OF MISS MAJOR PAULINE CUSHMAN, the celebrated Union Spy and Scout: comprising her Early History, her entry into the Secret Service of the Army of the Cumberland, and Dashing Adventures with the Rebel Chieftains and others while within the enemy's lines, together with her capture and sentence to death by General Bragg, and rescue at Shelbyville, Tenn., by the Union Army under General Rosecrans. The whole carefully prepared from her notes and memoranda. By F. L. SARMIENTO, Esq., of the Philadelphia Bar. With a portrait on steel, and illustrations on wood. 12mo., paper. Price $1.50; cloth, $2.00.

THRILLING ADVENTURES AMONG THE EARLY SETTLERS: embracing Desperate Encounters with the Indians, Tories, and Refugees; Daring Exploits of Texan Rangers and others, and Incidents of Guerrilla Warfare; Fearful Deeds of the Gamblers and Desperadoes, Rangers and Regulators of the West and Southwest; Hunting Stories, Trapping Adventures, etc., etc. By WARREN WILDWOOD, Esq. Illustrated by 200 engravings. 12mo., paper. Price $1.50; cloth, $2.00.

LIFE OF KIT CARSON, the great Western Hunter and Guide: comprising Wild and Romantic Exploits as a Hunter and Trapper in the Rocky Mountains; Thrilling Adventures and Hair-breadth Escapes among the Indians and Mexicans; his Daring and Invaluable Services as a Guide to Scouting and other Parties, etc., etc. With an account of various Government Expeditions to the Far West. By CHAS. BURDETT. 12mo., illustrated, cloth. Price $2.00.

LIFE OF DANIEL BOONE, the Great Western Hunter and Pioneer: comprising an account of his Early History; his Daring and Remarkable Career as the First Settler of Kentucky; his Thrilling Adventures with the Indians; and his wonderful skill, coolness and sagacity under all the hazardous and trying circumstances of Western Border Life. By CECIL B. HARTLEY. To which is added his Autobiography complete, as dictated by himself, and showing his own belief that he was an instrument ordained to settle the Wilderness. With illustrations. 12mo., cloth. Price $2.00.

LIFE OF DAVID CROCKETT, the Original Humorist and Irrepressible Backwoodsman: comprising his Early History; his Bear Hunting and other Adventures; his Services in the Creek War; his Electioneering Speeches and Career in Congress; with his triumphal tour through the Northern States and Services in the Texan War. To which is added an account of his glorious death at the Alamo, while fighting in defence of Texan Independence. With illustrations. 12mo., cloth. Price $2.00.

THE LIFE OF STEPHEN A. DOUGLAS: to which are added his Speeches and Reports. By H. M. FLINT. With a portrait on steel. 12mo., cloth. Price $2.00; plain sheep, $2.50.

THE HORSE AND HIS DISEASES: embracing his History and Varieties, Breeding and Management and Vices: with the Diseases to which he is subject, and the Remedies best adapted to their Cure. By ROBERT JENNINGS, V. S., Professor of Pathology and Operative Surgery in the Veterinary College of Philadelphia; Professor of Veterinary Medicine in the late Agricultural College of Ohio; Secretary of the American Veterinary Association of Philadelphia, etc., etc. To which are added Rarey's Method of Taming Horses, and the Law of Warranty, as applicable to the purchase and sale of the animal. Illustrated by nearly 100 engravings. 12mo., cloth. Price $2.00.

CATTLE AND THEIR DISEASES: embracing their History and Breeds, Crossing and Breeding, and Feeding and Management; with the Diseases to which they are subject, and the Remedies best adapted to their Cure. To which are added a List of the Medicines used in treating Cattle, and the Doses of the various remedies requisite. By ROBERT JENNINGS, V. S., Author of "The Horse and his Diseases," etc., etc. With numerous Illustrations. 12mo., cloth. Price $2.00.

SHEEP, SWINE, AND POULTRY: embracing the History and Varieties of each; the best modes of Breeding; their Feeding and Management; together with the Diseases to which they are respectively subject, and the appropriate Remedies for each. By ROBERT JENNINGS, V. S., Author of "The Horse and his Diseases," "Cattle and their Diseases," etc., etc. With numerous illustrations. 12mo., cloth. Price $2.00.

EVERYBODY'S LAWYER AND COUNSELLOR IN BUSINESS: containing plain and simple instructions to everybody for transacting their business according to law, with legal forms for drawing the various necessary papers connected therewith; together with the laws of all the States, for Collection of Debts, Property Exempt from Execution, Mechanics' Liens, Execution of Deeds and Mortgages, Rights of Married Women, Dower, Usury, Wills, etc. By FRANK CROSBY, Esq., of the Philadelphia Bar. 12mo., law half sheep. Price $2.00.

MODERN COOKERY, in all its branches: embracing a series of plain and simple instructions to private families and others, for the careful and judicious preparation of every variety of food, as drawn from practical observation and experience. Embracing upwards of Twelve Hundred recipes, appropriately illustrated. By Miss ELIZA ACTON. The whole carefully revised by Mrs. S. J. HALE. 12mo., cloth. Price $2.00.

THE LADIES' MEDICAL GUIDE AND MARRIAGE FRIEND: a plain and instructive treatise on the structure and functions of the reproductive organs in both sexes; the Diseases peculiar to Females, and the Diseases of Children, with the appropriate Remedies for each, and valuable Directions and Recipes for the Toilet, Beautifying the Skin, Cultivating and Arranging the Hair, etc., etc. By S. PANCOAST, M.D., Professor of Microscopic Anatomy, Physiology, and the Institute of Medicine in Penn Medical University, Philadelphia. With upwards of 100 illustrations. 12mo., cloth. Price $2.00.

THE FAMILY DOCTOR: a Counsellor in Sickness, Pain and Distress, for Childhood, Manhood, and Old Age; containing in plain language, free from medical terms, the Causes, Symptoms, and Cure of Diseases in every form, with important Rules for Preserving the Health, and Directions for the Sick Chamber, and the Proper Treatment of the Sick; the whole drawn from extensive observation and practice. By Professor HENRY S. TAYLOR, M.D. Illustrated with numerous engravings of Medicinal Plants and Herbs. 12mo., cloth. Price $1.50; plain sheep $2.00.

THE BEAUTIFUL SPY: an Exciting Story of Army and High Life in New York in 1776. By CHARLES BURDETT, Author of "Three Per Cent A Month," "Second Marriage," "Marion Desmond," etc., etc. 12mo., paper. Price $1.50; cloth $2.00.

THE ROYALIST'S DAUGHTER AND THE REBELS; or, the Dutch Dominie of the Catskills. A Tale of the Revolution of unusual power and interest. By Rev. DAVID MURDOCH, D.D. 12mo., paper. Price $1.50; cloth $2.00.

THE HERO GIRL and how she became a Captain in the Army. A Tale of the Revolution. By THRACE TALMON. With illustrations. 12mo., paper. Price $1.50; cloth $2.00.

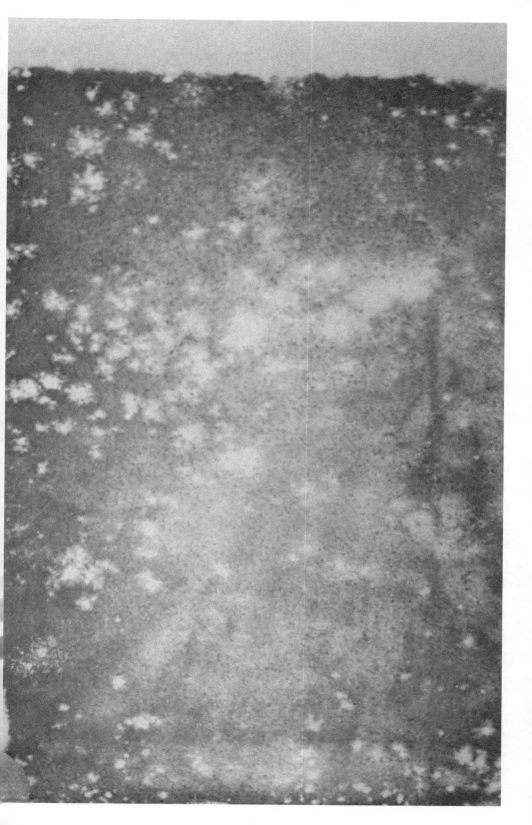

Check Out More Titles From HardPress Classics Series In this collection we are offering thousands of classic and hard to find books. This series spans a vast array of subjects — so you are bound to find something of interest to enjoy reading and learning about.

Subjects:
Architecture
Art
Biography & Autobiography
Body, Mind &Spirit
Children & Young Adult
Dramas
Education
Fiction
History
Language Arts & Disciplines
Law
Literary Collections
Music
Poetry
Psychology
Science
…and many more.

Visit us at www.hardpress.net